THE LIVING TRUST KIT

*Save Taxes, Avoid Probate,
and Ensure Financial Security
for Your Loved Ones*

By Karen Ann Rolcik
Attorney at Law

SPHINX® PUBLISHING
AN IMPRINT OF SOURCEBOOKS, INC.®
NAPERVILLE, ILLINOIS
www.SphinxLegal.com

First Edition, 2004

Published by: Sphinx® Publishing, A Division of Sourcebooks, Inc.®

Naperville Office
P.O. Box 4410
Naperville, Illinois 60567-4410
630-961-3900
Fax: 630-961-2168
www.sourcebooks.com
www.SphinxLegal.com

This publication is designed to provide accurate and authoritative information in regard to the subject matter covered. It is sold with the understanding that the publisher is not engaged in rendering legal, accounting, or other professional service. If legal advice or other expert assistance is required, the services of a competent professional person should be sought.

From a Declaration of Principles Jointly Adopted by a Committee of the American Bar Association and a Committee of Publishers and Associations

This product is not a substitute for legal advice.

Disclaimer required by Texas statutes.

Library of Congress Cataloging-in-Publication Data
Rolcik, Karen Ann.
  The living trust kit : save taxes, avoid probate, and ensure financial security for your loved ones/ by Karen Ann Rolcik.-- 1st ed.
      p. cm.
    ISBN 1-57248-449-7 (pbk. : alk. paper)
    1. Living trusts--United States--Popular works. I. Title.
  KF734.Z9R64 2004
  346.7305'2--dc22
                                                    2004019172

Printed and bound in the United States of America.
VHG — 10 9 8 7 6 5 4 3 2 1

DEDICATION

This book is dedicated to my two greatest sources of inspiration—my mother and my father. They have been stalwarts—always giving encouragement, support, insight, and love. From them I learned the importance of family, giving of myself, and sharing with others.

Now that Dad has gone to be with the saints, Mom has given of herself—twofold. Dad, I miss you everyday. Mom, I love you more everyday.

Contents

Using Self-Help Law Books

Before using a self-help law book, you should realize the advantages and disadvantages of doing your own legal work. You should also understand the challenges and diligence that doing your own legal work requires.

The Growing Trend

Many people have decided that they want to handle their own legal matters. This may range from writing their own will, incorporating a business, managing their divorce, handling landlord/tenant issues, or representing themselves in small claims court. In some states, more than seventy-five percent (75%) of divorces and other cases have at least one party representing him- or herself. The reason for this growing trend is the rising costs of legal services. Courts struggle to make it easier for people to represent themselves. There are, however, judges that frown upon people who do not use an attorney. Judges and courthouse staff cannot give legal advice and therefore must be very careful as to what information they give to individuals who are handling their own legal matters. There are some judges that have established their own rules about parties representing themselves. In some courts, the judges simply do not allow it— They require that all parties use attorneys. This is unfair and, in the opinion of many people, violates not only state law but also the United States Constitution.

At Sphinx, self-help books are written to give people an alternative to the often complicated and confusing legal books found in most law libraries. Our authors strive to make the explanations of the law as simple and easy to understand as possible. Of course, it is impossible for every situation to be addressed.

Circumstances are different for every person. An attorney who is experienced in a particular matter can identify and discuss planning options that are not readily apparent to a nonattorney.

Cost/Benefit Analysis

No matter what service or product you are shopping for, the levels of quality and price vary. When you decide what product or service to buy, you make a cost/benefit analysis on the basis of your willingness to pay and the quality you desire.

When you purchase a car, there are several factors that influence your decision. Every car serves the purpose of providing transportation. The question is what kind of transportation do you want? Comfort, status, power, and versatility may bear on your decision and determine whether you drive off the lot with a Neon, Lincoln, SUV, Mercedes, or Porsche. Your decision is not made before you weigh the merits of each option against the cost.

The same cost/benefit analysis must be made when deciding to do your own legal work. Many legal situations are straightforward, requiring a simple form and no complicated analysis. Anyone with a little intelligence and a book of instructions can handle the matter without the assistance of an attorney.

There are situations, however, that are more complicated and involve issues that only an attorney would recognize. To simplify the law into a book like this, several legal cases often must be condensed into a single sentence or paragraph. This simplification—by its very nature—leaves out many details and nuances that would apply to special or unusual situations. Also, there are many ways to interpret most legal questions. For example, your case may come before a judge who disagrees with the analysis of the authors of self-help books.

Therefore, in making a decision to use a self-help law book and do your own legal work, you must realize that you are making a cost/benefit analysis. You have decided that the money you will save by doing your legal work yourself without the guidance of an attorney outweighs the chance that your case will not turn out to your satisfaction. Most people handling their own simple legal matters never have a problem. Occasionally, a problem arises and people find that it ends up costing them more to have an attorney straighten out the situation than it would have if they had hired an attorney in the beginning. You should keep this in mind if you decide to handle your own legal matters. Be sure to consult an attorney if you have specific questions or feel you need additional guidance.

Local Rules

It is important to understand that a book that covers the law for the entire nation, or even for an entire state, cannot possibly include every procedural nuance of every state or county court. Whenever possible, the exact form needed for a certain situation is provided. However, in some areas, each county or judge may require unique forms and procedures. In a *national* book such as this, the forms are sometimes even more general than state-specific forms. The forms are designed to give a good idea of the type of form that will be acceptable in most states. Nevertheless, a particular state, court, or judge may have a requirement, or use a form, that is not included in this book.

Legal Guidance

This book is not intended to be the only resource from which information can be obtained regarding your legal issue. This book is intended to serve as a guide to give you specific information whenever possible and to help you find out what else you will need to know.

The primary advantage to creating your own living trust is that you can save money and be certain that your living trust is completed when you are ready. Many attorneys have workloads that can often result in matters being delayed for extended periods of time. If you are creating your own living trust, you can do it at your own pace.

Should you decide that you need to use the services of an attorney, the information in this book can serve as a good background when you meet with the attorney. Going back to the car buying example, many consumers do some homework before they go to a car dealership. This accounts for the popularity of *Consumer Reports,* car buying guides, and similar publications. It has often been said that an informed consumer is a smart consumer. This is true when choosing an attorney.

One of the first questions you should consider and the most likely reason you are reading this book is how much it will cost to hire an attorney. Attorneys who are experienced in the legal area in which you need help can charge anywhere from $75 to $300 per hour. Many attorneys, however, have a fixed fee schedule for certain legal matters such as estate planning, bankruptcy, divorce, real estate closings, etc. It has been my experience that fixed fees for a living trust range from $1,500 to $4,500.

If you decide to hire an attorney, find one who has experience in the specific legal matter. An experienced attorney can make the legal matter less stressful and costly for you. You can find out whether an attorney is certified in that area of law or is a member of bar associations or other professional associations related to that area of law.

If you decide to use an attorney to help you with a living trust, it is important to find one who is familiar not only with state law regarding trusts, wills, and probate, but also with state and federal tax law. Almost all attorneys claim that they can prepare wills and living trusts. However, such type of legal work may only be a small percentage of the attorney's overall caseload and he or she may not be current with all of the applicable state and federal laws and planning ideas.

There is a middle ground. You may prepare your own living trust and find an attorney who is willing to answer questions you may have, give you help when you need it, and review the living trust when it is complete. The attorney should be willing to accept an hourly fee for this service. In this manner, you can save legal fees but still get professional assistance if you need it.

No matter how you find an attorney, it is very important that you and the attorney have a clear understanding of his or her role, the amount of the fee, how the fee will be calculated, what exactly will be done for that fee, and what additional expenses may be charged. You should also establish a clear understanding of when the work is expected to be started and concluded. For example, if the attorney charges a fixed fee, what does the fee include? Does it include transferring assets into the living trust? All of these issues should be decided *before* you actually hire the attorney. In addition, the terms of your agreement should be put into writing and signed by you and the attorney. Be wary of an attorney who will not put the fee agreement in writing!

Introduction

During the past twenty years, *how to avoid probate* has become the subject of countless speeches, books, and seminars. The cost and time delays of probate and the court system have caused many people (including attorneys) to look for alternatives to the probate process.

In my own practice, I have seen the emotional and financial stress and uncertainty experienced by families when they are faced with the probate of a loved one's estate. After the death of a loved one, the family should spend time healing and adjusting to the loss of their loved one, not meeting with attorneys and attending court hearings. Unfortunately, the most immediate concern of family is whether money will be available to pay bills and funeral expenses, house and car payments, utility bills, school tuition, and the ordinary living expenses that do not halt upon the death of a loved one. A living trust can ease this concern.

Three years ago, my father was diagnosed with an aggressive form of brain cancer. The doctors advised us that he may only survive for three to six months. The family was in shock. My father had never been sick. At 67 years of age, the only time he had been hospitalized or had anything resembling a serious illness was gallbladder surgery. Within days after the tumor was found, my father was scheduled for surgery to remove the brain tumor. The risks associated with the surgery included death, paralysis, or brain damage. We were faced with two immediate scenarios. First, my father could survive the surgery but be incapacitated—unable to make medical or financial decisions for himself. Second, my father could die during surgery.

Fortunately, we were prepared for either scenario. My parents previously had signed financial and medical powers of attorney, living wills, pour-over wills, and living trusts. If my father had become incapacitated as a result of surgery, the powers of attorney and living trust would make sure that the usual bills could be paid and funds could be accessed to pay for medical care.

My father survived surgery with no adverse affects. However, he died five months later. While the family was not emotionally prepared to lose him, we were financially prepared. All his property was either in his living trust, a joint survivorship bank account, or retirement plans that passed to my mother by virtue of the beneficiary designation. My mother was able to grieve without worrying about accessing money to pay bills or going to court to probate a will. No money was lost to probate costs and attorney fees.

Today there are a variety of probate alternatives available. These include life insurance contracts, pay on death accounts, joint tenancy accounts, retirement accounts, annuities, and various types of trusts. For many people, these methods may be used to avoid probate completely without any complications.

The most popular probate alternative is the *living trust.* The living trust is a very effective method to avoid the probate process, not only after a person's death, but also during a person's life (in the event the person becomes incapacitated).

The purpose of this book is to acquaint you with the various probate alternatives and to show you which ones will work best for your estate. A special emphasis is placed on the living trust because it has always been popular and on the whole is the most effective method by which to avoid the evils and agony of probate. If you decide a living trust is best suited to your situation, several basic forms are included to help you create your own. However, you may learn from this book that simpler methods are better suited for your particular situation.

Keep in mind that each of the probate alternatives discussed can be used in conjunction with one or more of the others. For example, you can use the beneficiary designation in your *Individual Retirement Account* (IRA) to transfer any assets remaining in your IRA at your death directly to your beneficiaries without making them pass through the probate process. The living trust can be used similarly to transfer your other assets to your beneficiaries without making them pass through the probate process.

As the value of your estate increases, planning considerations change. Under current federal estate (death) tax law, there is no tax payable to the Internal Revenue Service on the first $1,500,000 of property owned by the decedent on the date of his or her death. This includes life insurance and retirement plans. This amount is called the *unified credit exclusion*. This amount increases in steps until 2010, when the federal estate tax ceases to exist (at least for one year). A discussion of federal and state estate and inheritance taxes is included in Chapter 3. Your estate may not exceed this threshold this year, but may do so at a future date. Your living trust should be amended to respond to this situation.

If the value of your estate or the combined value of your estate and your spouse's estate exceeds the applicable credit amount, and you wish to avoid estate taxes, there are forms in this book that can help you achieve this goal. However, it is recommended that you consult a professional with estate tax planning experience, generally a CPA or tax/estate planning attorney. Many times, an initial consultation can be inexpensive and you can get some valuable insights into your estate planning situation. Armed with this insight, you can return home to create your own living trust.

Additionally, if you own assets of an unusual character, such as oil or gas royalty interests, partnership interests, closely held business stock, annuities, leasehold interests, or if there are complicated beneficiary distributions or conditions you wish to include in your living trust, you should consult an experienced estate planning professional. In many communities, living trusts are available at reasonable prices. No book of this type can address every contingency in every case, but knowledge of the basics will help you to make the right decisions regarding your property.

> **Author's Advice:** There are many mass marketing and commercialized packages of living trusts. Many of these packages are attempts by the promoters to get involved with your financial planning. The living trust can be a loss leader. The promoters may view the real money as the commissions earned by selling the client alternate investments like annuities, mutual funds, etc.

There are reputable seminars and planners whose primary concern is your estate plan and saving the costs and delays of probate. I have been associated with such planners in the past because I have been convinced of their integrity.

If you are invited to or attend one of these seminars, do your homework. Make it clear that you are interested only in the living trust and make certain that the planner is willing to proceed on that basis.

I have read numerous books about using living trusts. Many of these books are very comprehensive and are designed to inform you about living trusts, the probate process, and other estate planning topics. I am dismayed when the books portray attorneys as having only one goal—charging extraordinary fees for basic estate planning and basic probate administration. It seems that the legal profession is defined by highlighting those attorneys who abuse the legal system and take economic advantage of the public. Interestingly, many of the authors of living trust books who have created companies to prepare estate planning documents charge fees that are similar to those charged by attorneys.

My purpose in writing this book is to empower you. I have endeavored to give you enough information to prepare your own living trust. The reality is that many people do not have the funds to pay the fees charged by attorneys or estate planning marketers. I do not believe that money should dictate whether or not you can take advantage of a living trust and other probate alternatives.

My hope is that those of you who read this book—and who feel comfortable with what you have read and with the documents included in this book—will take advantage of an estate planning tool that should not be reserved for the rich.

Chapter 1:
Probate

The Good, The Bad, and The Ugly

The *agony of probate* and the *evils of probate* are catch phrases used by many financial planners, accountants, insurance agents, and some attorneys in an effort to convince a client to create a living trust. The term *probate* has gotten such a bad reputation that its mere mention can send shivers down the spine. It is true that the probate process can be unduly burdensome, time-consuming, and costly.

However, for every war story that is told to emphasize the agony or evils of probate, there is a story that demonstrates the effectiveness and efficiency of probate. An attorney who is well-acquainted with the probate process and who is sensitive to the emotional and financial needs of the client can make the probate process less stressful, costly, and time consuming for the client. For some, the probate process is better suited to meet their needs than using trusts or drafting complicated wills.

To help make a decision on what estate planning steps you need to make, it is important that you understand the probate process. Doing so will also give you a better understanding of the benefits that can be obtained by *avoiding probate*.

Understanding the Probate Process

Probate is the legal process by which property in an estate is transferred to the heirs and beneficiaries of a deceased person (the *decedent*). *Heirs* are persons who are entitled to receive a decedent's property if the decedent died *without* a will. *Beneficiaries* are persons who are named in a decedent's will to receive property.

The *probate process* (also referred to as estate administration) begins by presenting to the judge the will of the decedent or, if there is no will, by presenting to the judge a list of the decedent's property and a list of the people to whom it is proposed that the property be given.

The person who will represent the estate and handle the probate process is given certain powers by the court to complete the estate administration. Traditionally, a person you name in your will to administer your estate was called your *executor* and if you died without a will, an *administrator* was appointed by the court. In most states, the duties of the administrator and executor are very similar. Today, more and more states are using the term *personal representative* to describe the person handling the estate—whether there is a will or not. (That term will be used in this text but can be interchanged with executor or administrator.)

Although each state will differ in the specific steps involved in the probation of a will, the following is a fairly representative outline of the process.

◆ A *petition* or *application* is filed with the probate court either asking that a will be admitted to probate or stating that a person died without leaving a will.

◆ A hearing is held in which the testimony of a family member, executor, or witness to the will is presented to the court to establish proof of death, proof of the will, or, if the person died without a will, proof of the heirs of the decedent.

◆ If there is a will, an order is signed acknowledging the will, and some type of document is issued by the court giving the personal representative named in the will power to act for the estate. This may be called *Letters of Administration, Letters Testamentary, Letters of Authority,* or something similar.

◆ If there is no will, the court will issue some type of document identifying the heirs of the decedent according to the state statutes of descent and distribution.

◆ Whether named in a will or appointed by the court, a person to act as personal representative for the estate will be *appointed.*

◆ The personal representative must meet the qualifications of the state statutes, which set forth who the state believes is competent to serve as personal representative.

◆ Unless the court grants special permission, the personal representative must post a surety bond.

◆ Notice of death is published or sent to the heirs and beneficiaries.

◆ A notice is sent to creditors or published in a newspaper to permit them to file claims against the estate.

◆ Actual written notice is given to banks, financial institutions, brokerage firms, and creditors with whom the decedent had dealings.

◆ The personal representative must collect all of the assets of the decedent. This may include transferring title of the assets into the name of the estate until the assets are ready to be distributed to the beneficiaries and collecting life insurance policies, annuities, retirement plans, and the like made payable to the estate. When such assets are collected, the personal representative must manage the assets during the estate administration.

◆ The personal representative inventories the personal property, such as household goods, personal effects, vehicles, etc., and must arrange for the safekeeping of such assets until distribution to the beneficiaries.

◆ The personal representative collects income from the assets, such as interest, dividends, etc., during the administration of the estate.

◆ Assets are appraised to obtain a current fair market value.

◆ An inventory of assets and debts owed by the decedent is prepared and filed with the court.

◆ The personal representative must pay the debts of the decedent and the expenses of the estate administration, including attorney, accountant, and appraiser fees, probate costs, and the like.

◆ If claims are filed against the estate, the personal representative must review and analyze the claims to determine whether or not such claims are valid. The personal representative reports to the creditor and to the court whether or not he or she has determined the claims are valid.

◆ Assets are sold to raise cash to pay debts and expenses, if necessary.

◆ A final income tax return for the decedent is filed. The personal representative must make certain that all prior income tax returns have been filed and income tax liabilities have been paid.

◆ If there is more than $600 of income during administration of the estate, the *estate* must file an income tax return. If the administration of the estate continues for more than twelve months, the personal representative may have to file more than one income tax return for the estate. The personal representative will be responsible for paying any income tax liability of the estate during the administration as part of the debts and expenses of the estate.

- ◆ If the value of the estate is in excess of the applicable credit amount ($1,500,000 for years 2004 and 2005), the personal representative must prepare and file a federal estate tax return within nine (9) months of the decedent's death. If federal estate tax is due, the tax must be paid when the estate tax return is filed.
- ◆ The personal representative must determine whether an inheritance or estate tax return must be filed under state law. Generally, inheritance or estate tax returns must be filed and any inheritance and estate tax paid within nine (9) months of the decedent's death.
- ◆ During the administration of the estate, the personal representative must file periodic accountings with the court detailing the receipts and disbursements of the estate.
- ◆ To *close* the estate, a detailed final accounting of the assets of, expenses of, and income received by the estate during administration and distributions to beneficiaries made by the estate is filed with the probate court. Persons who have an interest in the estate (*i.e.,* the heirs and beneficiaries) are notified of the accounting and a hearing is held by the court. Once the account is approved by the court, the personal representative may distribute the remaining assets to the beneficiaries.
- ◆ The personal representative's and attorney's fees are paid.
- ◆ The personal representative obtains a final discharge from the court to be relieved of his or her duties.

Understanding when Probate is Necessary

Probate may be necessary whether or not a decedent had a will. While the will is the primary document used in the probate process, it does not eliminate the need for probate. Probate is required if the decedent *owned property in his or her individual name* at the time of his or her death.

If a decedent died without having signed a will, then the decedent died *intestate* the property will pass to his or her *heirs at law.* The probate code of each state lists the heirs of a decedent, the order in which they will inherit from the decedent, and the amount of that inheritance. In effect, the state has written a will for the decedent and dictates who will receive the property without regard to the wishes of the decedent or the true needs of the decedent's family situation. If no living relative of the decedent can be located, all of the decedent's property *escheats* to the state. That is, the state is the beneficiary of the decedent's entire estate.

In general, if a person dies without a will, state law provides for distribution of the assets *down the family tree.* If the person dies and leaves a surviving spouse, a significant portion—if not all of the assets—will go to the surviving spouse. If there are minor children, assets may be set aside to be distributed to them upon them attaining age 18. If there is no surviving spouse, the assets go to children or grandchildren. If there are no surviving spouse, children, or grandchildren, the assets are distributed to the parents, and then to any brothers and sisters, of the decedent.

If a decedent died with a signed will, then the decedent died *testate* and his or her property passes to the individuals named in his or her will—the beneficiaries. If a person challenges the validity of the decedent's will, often called *contesting the will,* the probate court will get involved in determining whether the beneficiaries named in the decedent's will are legally entitled to receive the property or whether the will should be followed at all.

Each state has a statute setting forth a value that provides a threshold for an estate administration. If the value of the estate is less than the amount set forth in your state's statutes, procedures are available for an informal or expedited administration of the estate.

In addition to whether a decedent owned property in his or her individual name at the time of death, the value of all the property making up the estate may impact whether or what type of an estate administration must take place. There may be other qualifications or requirements that must be met to invoke an informal or expedited administration.

NOTE: *Each state statute should be reviewed to determine other qualifications or requirements to invoke informal or expedited administration.*

Property Subject to Probate

Not all property owned by a decedent at the time of his or her death has to go through the probate process. Only *probate property* is subject to the probate process. Probate property includes property owned in the individual name of the decedent alone or in the individual name of the decedent and another person without survivorship rights. Common examples of probate property are bank accounts, securities, tangible personal property (*e.g.,* jewelry, stamp collections, furniture, car, etc.), and real estate.

If a husband and wife owned property jointly as *tenants by the entireties* or if two people owned property as *joint tenants with rights of survivorship,* the property passes automatically to the survivor and does not go through the probate process. A certified copy of the decedent's death certificate is generally all that is required to show that the entire property interest in such accounts is held by the survivor.

(Chapter 7 explains various methods (other than the living trust) by which assets can be titled so that such property will not be subject to the probate process and will instead pass to the joint owner or beneficiary automatically upon death.)

The Role of Your Will in the Probate Process

A will serves a number of different purposes. The most obvious role of the will is to direct the disposition of your property after your death. You can give specific gifts of personal items to individuals, make specific bequests or gifts of money to individuals, and allocate the balance of your assets among individuals in varying percentages. You can also leave gifts to churches, schools, and charities.

Without a will, you have no control over who will receive your property and how much they will receive. The identity of your heirs and the share to which they are entitled is established by state law.

A will also allows you to decide who will be the personal representative of your estate. A personal representative is the person who gathers all of your assets and distributes them to the beneficiaries. The personal representative is responsible for reporting to the court about the status of the estate, which includes the payment of debts, taxes, and expenses and the distribution of assets to the beneficiaries. If you do not name a personal representative in your will, or if you do not have a will, the personal representative of your estate will be appointed by the court. Each state has a statute that establishes an order of priority as to who can be appointed as a personal representative. While family members are generally favored under statutes, it is possible that an unrelated person, a bank or trust company, or even a creditor of your estate can be appointed personal representative of your estate.

With a will, you can provide that your personal representative does not have to post a *surety bond* with the court in order to serve. This can save the estate a sizeable amount of money. The personal representative can also be granted broad powers in addition to the powers given to personal representatives by law to handle estate matters. If you own a business, you can designate that the personal representative has full authority to operate the business without posting a bond or employing a professional business advisor.

Perhaps one of the most overlooked purposes of a will is the designation of a *guardian* for minor children. In a will, you can designate who will be entrusted with the care and upbringing of your children. This way, you can avoid fights among relatives and make sure that the person who is most familiar with you and your children will raise your children. If you do not appoint a guardian for your minor children, state law designates who will be eligible to be appointed guardian. Often, to assist the court with this determination, a social study will be conducted by the child services department to evaluate who is best suited to raise your children.

Many people have definite ideas about who they want to raise their minor children, but are not confident in the guardian's ability to manage the children's inheritance. In your will, you can also designate a separate person to act as guardian of your children's financial inheritance.

Finally, in those states that have simplified probate procedures available, your will can direct that your estate be administered in accordance with such procedures.

Disadvantages of Probate

There are many disadvantages to the probate process. Each disadvantage is a good reason for taking steps to avoid the probate process. When the disadvantages are evaluated as a whole, the importance of reducing exposure to probate is unquestioned.

Costs of Probate

The costs of probate can be very significant. Because of these costs, the size of your estate can be reduced and large amounts of property you worked a lifetime to collect can be lost. The costs of probate include court filing fees, appraiser's fees, personal representative's fees, and attorney's fees. Each state has its own method by which probate attorneys can determine their fees for probate matters. Probate attorneys' fees may be calculated on an hourly basis, on a percentage of the value of the probate assets, or a combination of the two. Under any method, attorney's fees for probate can be very significant.

Common practice calculates attorney's fees by a percentage of the assets that are probated. However, there may be complicated issues to be addressed during the administration of the estate, and attorneys will charge fees *in addition* to their normal fees.

Example: *An estate may be worth $500,000 and the normal fee may be 5% of the value of the estate. The fee will be $25,000 regardless of the amount of time and effort spent by the attorney on this matter. If the estate involves complicated issues, such as joint property rights, creditor claims, unique assets such as antiques, artwork, or oil, gas, or mineral rights, the attorney may charge a premium fee. The final fee for the estate administration could run as high as $50,000 or $75,000.*

In addition to attorney fees, the personal representative is entitled to receive a fee for his or her services as personal representative. Once again, some states have established a fee schedule for personal representatives that is based on the total value of the estate. In addition, an executor may be entitled to receive compensation if estate assets had to be sold or income generated by estate assets had to be collected.

> **Author's Advice:** I have seen estates where an asset such as a $100,000 CD has to be transferred. The time spent by an attorney to write a simple letter to the financial institution enclosing appropriate probate documents and instructing distribution of the CD to a beneficiary is minimal—perhaps less than one hour. Yet the attorney can receive a fee of as much as 5–8% of the value of the CD!

Finally, creditors, attorney fees, personal representative commissions, and probate costs must be paid before an estate can be fully distributed to the beneficiaries. This may require the liquidation of estate assets to raise enough cash to pay the fees. Assets sold at a gain would result in an income tax liability to the estate, further decreasing the amount of assets for beneficiaries. The opposite situation could also occur—the assets may have to be sold at less than fair market value or at a loss to raise the necessary cash. The only winners are the creditors and the attorney!

Time-Consuming

The probate process is very time-consuming and can cause long delays in transferring assets to your beneficiaries. Generally, the *minimum* period required to complete the probate process is six months. It is not unusual for the typical probate process to take as many as two years. (Many probates can take as long as three or even five years.) During this time, money is tied up and household expenses (other than the most basic expenses such as mortgage or rent payments, property taxes, and utilities) can be interrupted until the probate is completed. College and school tuition can also be interrupted. It may be possible to get some of the estate's assets released prior to the completion of the probate by asking special permission from the probate court. However, this may cost additional money for attorney fees and will generally require a showing of need. This all becomes part of the public record and can at times be embarrassing for the surviving family members. All of this applies whether or not you have a will.

Further, if you die without a will, your *heirs* must be located. This does not just mean your spouse or children. Each state has statutory procedures in place to locate heirs. These procedures are exhaustive and take a substantial amount of time and can be quite costly. This significantly increases the delay in settling the affairs of the decedent.

Lack of Privacy

Once your will is offered to probate, it becomes a matter of public record. Anyone who has an interest in such matters can go to the courthouse and look at your will. When your will is brought to the courthouse, a notice is published in the newspaper or posted at the courthouse stating the fact of death, the identity of the proposed personal representative, and that a will has been offered for probate.

Although some states seal the inventory of the estate, the identity of your beneficiaries and the inventory of your assets, including their value, are generally available for inspection by anyone who asks. It is not uncommon for financial advisors, insurance agents, estate liquidators, and the like to look up estate values in the courthouse and contact the family offering services to *assist* the family in their time of need.

Should your family need to file requests with the court for distribution of estate assets for payment of expenses other than basic household and living expenses, the court will often require a showing of financial need. This personal financial information will be made part of the court record and, therefore, be available for public inspection.

> **Author's Advice:** In certain counties in which I have probated estates, with every will offered to probate, I receive no less than five letters from estate liquidators, real estate appraisers and brokers, and financial advisors. Often the executor will receive the same mailings. Such mailings are intrusive and unwarranted and serve only to reinforce the "evils" of probate.

While you are alive, you do not publish articles in the newspaper that tell the world what assets you own or to whom you want to give your assets. Why should you allow this same information to be published after your death? You value your privacy during your life, and this privacy should be maintained for your spouse, children, and beneficiaries.

Lack of Control

Personal representatives are required to act in accordance with the statutes governing them. There may be little or no discretion given to a personal representative as to how certain assets or debts must be handled. Personal representatives are subject to reporting requirements to the court and to the state. In certain circumstances, a personal representative must obtain court approval prior to taking action. For instance, the stock market may rise and the personal representative may determine that the best interests of the estate would be to sell stocks to maximize profits. If the personal representative must obtain the court's permission to sell the stock, the stock price may fall before the court enters an order permitting the sale of stock.

If disgruntled heirs challenge a will, the administration of the estate may be delayed for a significant period of time. Often, disgruntled heirs will also challenge the appointment of the personal representative named in the will. The court may appoint a temporary administrator or temporary executor with limited powers to administer the estate until the court determines who will serve as personal representative. The temporary administrator or executor may make decisions without consulting the heirs or beneficiaries and the fees and expenses associated with the temporary administrator or executor must be borne by the estate.

Warning: I was brought into a situation by a surviving spouse that was frustrated with the delay and lack of resolution in his wife's estate. He was married for twenty-seven years. His wife had three sons from a prior marriage. She died without a will. The sons, although raised by my client as his own sons, immediately disputed my client's rights in the estate. The sons' attitudes were to wait out my client who was 78 years old. Their hope was that my client would pass away before a trial could be held on the merits of the case.

After two years and more than $7,500 in attorney fees, the case still has not been resolved. As a result of having no control over the process, my client has not been able to make any improvements to the residence and one particular stock has lost more than 40% of its value since the decedent's death!

Advantages of Probate

Despite the problems of probate, there are several reasons why in some cases probate should not be avoided *entirely*. While many people will not view these reasons as *advantages* to probate, there are benefits that can be gained from probate.

Recognizes Guardianship for Minor Children

A will can name *guardians* to take care of your minor children. A guardianship provision in a trust is not effective. The probate court will almost always honor a designation of guardian in a will. Only in those rare circumstances that the court finds evidence that the person named in the will is not suitable to take care of and raise your children will the court appoint someone else whom it believes is better qualified. If you have minor children, you should have a will that names a guardian and the will should be admitted to probate. This does not mean, however, that your *assets* must go through probate.

Limits Creditor Claims

After the will is admitted to probate, the personal representative will be required to give notice to any creditor you may have at the time of your death. Often, this notice is published in a newspaper. As soon as the notice is given, the clock starts ticking and the creditors only have a limited period of time during which to contact the personal representative and formally file a claim for payment against the estate.

If the creditor does not file the claim within the prescribed time period, its claim is cut off in the future. This time period is called the *statute of limitations*—a statute that limits the amount of time during which the creditor may file its claim against the estate. If you have only limited known debts, this may not be a problem, but if there are any potential claims against your estate, such as from a business venture, heirs you left out of your will, or unpaid taxes, you may wish to have a probate filed at your death to cut off those claims. Even if only $100 is subject to probate, your will can invoke the protections of the probate system, such as starting the statute of limitations.

Transfers Assets

If probate alternatives are used, including the living trust, there may be some assets that do not get transferred to the trust or that are not covered by a beneficiary designation. Such assets may include last minute inheritances, lawsuit awards, etc. In addition, it is possible that some assets may be mistakenly overlooked and not be transferred to your living trust or a proper beneficiary designation may not have been made. Your will makes certain that such property goes to the beneficiaries you designate and does not pass pursuant to the *will* that the state writes for you if you die intestate.

It is not necessary to write a will that names the beneficiaries of the probate assets. Instead, a *pourover will* can be used. The pourover will states that any assets subject to the probate process are given to the trustee of the living trust to be administered and distributed according to the terms of the trust. Once again, this ensures the privacy of the distribution of your assets. Forms 3, 4, 5, and 6 (pp.175–181) are examples of pour over wills. Because each state has different rules regarding the appointment of personal representatives, guardians, and the like, it is important to consult an attorney or a self-help law book that specifically deals with the requirement for wills in your state.

Provides Duly Appointed Personal Representative

A will provides a duly appointed personal representative to sign the tax returns and request a discharge of personal liability for payment of federal estate tax. A personal representative must be discharged before a trustee can be discharged from personal liability. In addition, it appears that only a personal representative designated by the court can be discharged from personal liability for a decedent's federal income and gift taxes.

Conclusion

For these reasons, not everyone would be advised to avoid probate completely. Instead, you should take advantage of every alternative available to minimize the contact your estate will have with the probate process, but have a will that can be probated in the event one or more of the discussed situations occur. The laws authorize the probate alternatives discussed in the following chapter. Take advantage of them to the greatest extent possible.

Chapter 2:
Probate Alternatives and Beneficiary Designations

Side Stepping the Probate Process

Title to an asset can be written in a variety of ways. While all of the forms of title discussed in this chapter provide an alternative method for owning property instead of in your name alone, not all of these forms of title keep your assets from going through probate after your death. The probate alternatives include various forms of joint tenancy, contractual dispositions of property, and lifetime gifts. These alternatives are not mutually exclusive. You can use more than one alternative at a time. In fact, it is often advisable to use several probate alternatives. It is very important, however, that you coordinate the use of the probate alternatives to make certain that your wishes are carried out.

For example, you may wish to make provisions in your living trust to ensure financial security not only for your spouse and children, but also for your parents. However, if your life insurance and retirement plan beneficiary designations and joint bank accounts name your spouse as the sole beneficiary, your parents and perhaps your children will not receive the financial benefits of those assets. In such a case, it would be important to change those beneficiary designations to name your living trust as the primary beneficiary. The property will then be subject to the terms of the living trust and your intentions will not be thwarted. (Funding your living trust is discussed in detail in Chapter 7.)

Benefits of Probate Alternatives

There are many benefits associated with probate alternatives:

- ◆ saved time;
- ◆ privacy;
- ◆ flexibility; and,
- ◆ lower costs.

Perhaps the most attractive aspect of probate alternatives is the ability to bypass the probate process and its costs and delays. Title to the asset passes to the co-owner of the property automatically upon death. Generally, the only document that must be presented to the bank or financial institution to formalize the passage of title is a copy of the decedent's death certificate. The identity of the co-owner or beneficiary of assets is not published at the courthouse as part of the probate proceedings. The value of the asset and identity of the new owner remain private.

Probate alternatives are also very flexible. For example, bank accounts can be opened and closed easily, and generally without cost to the account owner. If you want to change the joint tenant on an account, you can simply go to the bank and change the account name and signature card.

Probate alternatives are generally very inexpensive to establish. It does not cost to add another person as owner or beneficiary of an asset. Ownership of bank accounts, stock certificates, and other investments can easily be changed by completing new account or title information forms. Beneficiary designations for life insurance policies, retirement plans, and annuities are established by completing the appropriate forms.

Dangers of Probate Alternatives

While there are many benefits to using probate alternatives, there are also several dangers to be aware of:

- ◆ surviving owner takes it all;
- ◆ probate may only be delayed; and,
- ◆ equal ownership results in possible creditor claims.

When one owner of a jointly owned asset dies, the entire asset is owned by the survivor. This may not be consistent with the decedent's desires as to the distribution of his or her estate assets.

When the first owner of an asset dies, the time and expense of probate can be avoided. However, upon the death of the second owner, the asset must go through the probate process. This is a problem that commonly occurs with married couples. Husbands and wives often own property jointly. When the first spouse dies, the property avoids probate until the death of the second spouse. Therefore, probate is not entirely avoided—just delayed.

Many probate alternatives establish title in the names of both individuals. Each individual has rights of ownership in the asset. Not only can the individual exercise his or her rights of ownership in the asset, but the asset is then susceptible to the claims of his or her creditors. Therefore, the original owner of the asset may lose the asset to the claims of the joint owner's creditors.

Methods of Holding Title to Assets

There are three common methods of holding title to an asset:

- ◆ joint tenancy with rights of survivorship;
- ◆ tenancy by the entirety; and,
- ◆ tenancy in common.

Under these forms of asset ownership, each individual has some form of ownership interest in the asset. With joint tenancy with rights of survivorship, one owner can dispose of the asset without the other owner's knowledge or consent. This can be very dangerous. With tenancy by the entirety and tenancy in common, each person has a specific ownership interest in the asset. An owner cannot dispose of the asset without the other owner's knowledge and consent.

Joint Tenancy

Joint tenancy is the easiest and most inexpensive way to avoid probate. A joint tenancy is created by the instrument giving title to the asset. Common examples of this type of instrument are deeds, stock certificates, and bank or brokerage accounts. Generally, three types of joint tenancy can be created, but only two avoid probate.

Joint Tenants with Rights of Survivorship

The most popular form of joint tenancy is *joint tenants with rights of survivorship* (JTWROS). This form of joint tenancy can exist between any two or more individuals—it is not limited to husband and wife. Common JTWROS assets are real estate, bank or brokerage accounts, stocks, bonds, and the like. The most common uses of JTWROS are bank accounts and real estate.

During a lifetime, each joint tenant has full rights of ownership with respect to only the portion of the property that he or she contributed to the account. However, each owner has full access to all of the property. He or she can withdraw all of the funds even though he or she may have only contributed a minimal amount to the account. The financial institution is not required to determine whether he or she is withdrawing more than his or her contribution.

At death, a joint tenant's share automatically passes to the surviving tenant and is not subject to the probate process. However, when the surviving tenant later dies, the property is included in his or her probate estate and must go through the probate process prior to being distributed to the beneficiaries.

Typically, a JTWROS designation is made by using the words *as joint tenants with rights of survivorship*. For example, *Thomas or Roberta as joint tenants with rights of survivorship.*

Example: *Angie put $10,000 into a bank account and named her son Dave as joint tenant with rights of survivorship. When Angie became sick and could not handle her financial affairs, Dave could pay her bills because he was one of the owners of the account. There was no need to go through the lengthy process of having David appointed guardian for Angie to handle her financial affairs. Upon Angie's death, the bank account passed to Dave automatically, without going through the probate process. However, at Dave's later death, the assets will pass through the probate process unless he adds another joint tenant to the account.*

You must be aware that a JTWROS account is risky. While it provides convenience by giving another person access to the funds, that same convenience can cause problems. If you put your real estate into joint ownership with someone, you cannot sell it or mortgage it without that person's signature. If you put your bank account in joint ownership with someone, he or she can take some or all of the money in the account without your consent or knowledge.

Also, if you put property in joint ownership with someone:

- ◆ if he or she is married, the spouse may claim a portion of the property in a divorce;
- ◆ if he or she gets sued, the person getting a judgment may try to take the property to satisfy the judgment; and,
- ◆ if he or she files for bankruptcy, the bankruptcy trustee may try to bring the property into the bankruptcy proceedings.

Example 1: *Alex put his bank accounts into joint ownership with his daughter Mary. Mary fell in love with Doug, who was in trouble with the law. Doug convinced Mary to borrow $30,000 from the account for a business deal that went sour. Later, she borrowed $25,000 more to pay Doug's bail bond. When Alex found out that his money was gone, it was too late.*

Example 2: *Jane put her bank account into joint ownership with her son Joe, who is married to Lisa. Two years later, Lisa filed for divorce and claimed the bank account as part of her marital property. Now Jane has to hire a lawyer to fight Lisa's claim.*

If JTWROS is used, it overrides a will and a living trust. Therefore, if you use JTWROS, it is very important to make certain that the ownership of the account is consistent with your overall intentions. If you want all of your estate to go to your sister and make her the sole beneficiary of your will or living trust, do not put your assets into a joint account with your brother. If you do, they will automatically go to him without even going into your estate.

Example: *Bill's will leaves all of his property to his wife Mary. Bill dies owning the house jointly with his sister, Ann, and a bank account jointly with his son, Don. Upon Bill's death, Ann gets the house, Don gets the bank account, and Mary gets nothing.*

Personal property and joint tenancy. While the issue of who owns personal property does not come up often, when the property is valuable, you should take the necessary steps to be sure that it is titled as you wish. Property that is represented by a physical title, such as shares of stock, bank accounts, and real estate, is easy to set up in joint tenancy, but personal property, such as furniture, coins, antiques, collectibles, etc. is a little trickier. To make it clear what type of ownership governs such property, you need some sort of paper for your records. This can be the receipt you received from the store or a bill of sale. You can also prepare a document that says you own the property and are transferring it to yourself and your spouse or your children as joint tenants with rights of survivorship.

Example: *John owns antique furniture that is quite valuable. He wants the property to pass to his daughter, Sally, after his death, without having to go through the probate process. He prepares a letter describing the antiques and includes a statement that he is transferring the antiques from himself individually to himself and his daughter, Sally, as joint tenants with rights of survivorship.*

NOTE: *While all States recognize JTWROS, not every state treats it the same. In Alaska, only a husband and wife may hold real estate in joint tenancy. In Pennsylvania it is not clear whether real estate can be held in joint tenancy. In Tennessee no property may be held in joint tenancy except by a husband and wife.*

Two cautionary statements with regard to the creation of JTWROS for personal property. First, there is no guarantee that JTWROS will be recognized in your state for personal property. Second, such transfers may be considered a gift, which may have tax consequences if the value of the property is great enough. Therefore, you may want to consult your tax advisor before making a transfer. (For more information, see the section on *Outright Gifts* on page 30.)

Tenancy by the Entireties

A second type of joint tenancy is *tenancy by the entireties*. This form of joint tenancy is similar to JTWROS, but can only exist between a husband and wife and is not recognized in all states.

Tenancy by the entireties historically served as a form of protection for the interests of spouses in real estate acquired during the marriage. It prevented a husband from selling or otherwise transferring real estate without his wife's knowledge or permission.

Today, each spouse owns an equal share of the asset. Tenancy by the entireties can be dissolved by divorce, death, or sale of the asset. At the death of a spouse, his share passes automatically to the surviving spouse and is not subject to the probate process. Like with JTWROS, if you use tenancy by the entireties, you must make certain that the ownership is consistent with your overall intentions. If you have children from a previous marriage that you want an account to go to at your death, but you use tenancy by the entireties, your spouse—not your children—will get the account.

Example: *Mike and Jan are married. During their marriage, they purchase a home and title the property as tenants by the entireties. While they are alive, both have the right to use the property. Neither can sell or give away his or her interest in the property without the other's permission. When Mike dies, his interest in the home automatically passes to Jan. His will does not control the property, and therefore, the property is not subject to probate.*

The following states recognize tenancy by the entireties for *real estate*.

Alabama	Michigan	Oregon
Arkansas	Mississippi	Pennsylvania
Delaware	Missouri	Rhode Island
District of Columbia	New Jersey	Tennessee
Florida	New York	Utah
Hawaii	North Carolina	Vermont
Indiana	Ohio	Virginia
Maryland	Oklahoma	Wyoming
Massachusetts		

(If tenancy by the entireties is not available in your state, review the previous section on joint tenancy with rights of survivorship.)

Personal property and tenancy by the entireties. Tenancy by the entireties for *personal property* is not recognized in all states. The following states recognize tenancy by the entireties for personal property.

Alaska	Massachusetts	Rhode Island
Arkansas	Mississippi	Tennessee
Delaware	Missouri	Utah
District of Columbia	Ohio	Vermont
Florida	Oklahoma	Virginia
Hawaii	Oregon	Wyoming
Maryland	Pennsylvania	

If the personal property is purchased, a receipt or bill of sale should be used. You must make sure that your receipt or bill of sale lists you and your spouse as follows:

John Smith and Mary Smith, husband and wife, in an estate by the entireties.

-or-

John Smith and Mary Smith, husband and wife, as tenants by the entireties.

Tenancy in Common

The third form of joint tenancy is *tenancy in common*. A tenancy in common requires no less than two people to own the asset. Each person owns a share of the property (often an equal 50-50 share, but it does not have to be), and while alive, each person can use the property. At the death of an owner, his or her share of the property passes pursuant to his or her will, or if there is no will, to his or her heirs by law. It does not automatically pass to the other tenant in common. Property held in tenancy in common does not avoid the probate process.

Example: *John and Mary aren't married, but own a house as tenants in common. While they are alive, both are entitled to use the property. John can sell or give away his interest in the property without Mary's permission. Consequently, Mary can become a tenant in common with a complete stranger. When John dies, his ownership interest in the house passes to the beneficiaries named in his will. Those beneficiaries now are tenants in common with Mary. Mary still owns her share.*

Community Property

Community property is a special type of ownership that exists only between a husband and wife. Special state laws govern and protect the rights of a spouse in property that is acquired during the marriage. Only eight states recognize *community property* as a method of asset ownership. Those states are:

Arizona	Nevada
California	New Mexico
Idaho	Texas
Louisiana	Washington

(In addition, Wisconsin has a method of asset ownership between husbands and wives that is nearly identical to community property.)

Similar to a tenancy by the entireties, a spouse owns only one-half of the property and cannot sell, transfer, or encumber the property without the other spouse's permission. Community property status attaches to most property acquired during the marriage. If a spouse inherits property or receives property as a gift during the marriage, such property is generally considered the *separate property* of that spouse. The other spouse does not have ownership rights to inherited or gifted property.

Just as with property owned as a tenant in common, a spouse that owns community property can transfer his or her interest in that property to another person either during his or her lifetime or at death. However, a spouse can only give away his or her one-half of the property. Therefore, whoever receives the property will become a tenant in common with the other spouse. The deceased spouse's share of the community property, whether given to the surviving spouse or to another person, must pass through the probate process.

Transfers of Property by Contract

Some types of property avoid the probate process through the *contract* that establishes the ownership rights of the property. A contract is a written agreement that exists between two or more parties that sets forth the rules governing the relationship between the parties and the property that is the subject matter of the contract. The contract describes how the property may be used during your lifetime and how it will be distributed at your death. You designate the *beneficiary* of the property (*i.e.,* the person who will receive it at your death). The other party to the contract must comply with the terms of the contract and distribute the property to that person after your death. Because the property is governed by the terms of a private contract, it is not subject to the probate process.

Two common examples of property held under a contract agreement are annuities and stock option contracts.

Example: *Heather purchases an annuity that provides annual payments to her during her life. The annuity contract states that upon Heather's death, the money that has not been distributed to Heather during her life, will be distributed to her daughter.*

The most common instances when property can be transferred by contract are:

- ◆ pay on death bank accounts;
- ◆ pay on death securities registration;
- ◆ transfer on death automobile registration;
- ◆ land trusts;
- ◆ life insurance; and,
- ◆ retirement plans.

Pay on Death Bank Accounts

Financial institutions will allow you to set up your account so that upon your death it will go to the person or persons you name as beneficiary. This is not a joint account—the beneficiary has no access to the money until you die. You retain complete control of the account during your life. Such an account may be called a *POD (pay on death)* account, a *TOD (transfer on death)* account, or an *I/T/F (in trust for)* account. Lawyers call them *Totten trusts* after the party who first went to court to settle the issue that these accounts are legal.

With a pay on death account, you can change the beneficiary at any time. The person who will receive the money upon your death does not need to know that they are a beneficiary of the account until your death.

Example: *Michael opened a bank account in his name I/T/F Judy. When Michael dies, the account automatically passes to Judy without going through probate. During his life, Michael has complete control over the account and can name someone other than Judy as beneficiary simply by changing the title on the account. Judy cannot withdraw any funds during Michael's life.*

Pay on Death Securities Registration

The drawback of pay on death accounts was that they could only be used for cash in a bank account. Anyone with stocks or bonds had to set up a living trust to keep them out of probate. But beginning in 1990, various states began passing a law allowing securities (stocks, bonds, and mutual fund shares) to be registered in pay on death form. This change in the law has made avoiding probate easier for many more people.

As of the writing of this book, forty-four states have passed this new law. In a few years, it will probably be accepted throughout the country.

The states that currently allow pay on death accounts are listed in the following table, along with the reference to the relevant state statute. If your state is not listed, call your broker or mutual fund agent to see if the law in your state has changed recently.

Alabama	Ala. Code Secs. 8-6-140 to 8-6-151
Alaska	Alaska. Stat. Secs. 13.06.050; 13.33.301 to 13.33.310
Arizona	Ariz. Rev. Stat. Secs. 14-1201;14-6301 to 14-6311
Arkansas	Ark. Code Ann. Secs. 28-14-101 to 28-14-112
California	Cal. Prob. Code Sec 5500 to 5512
Colorado	Colo. Rev. Stat. Secs. 15-10-201; 15-15-301 to 15-15-311
Connecticut	Conn. Gen. Stat. Secs. 45a-468 to 45a-468m
Delaware	Del. Code Ann. tit. 12, Secs. 801 to 812
Florida	Fla. Stat. Secs. 711.50 to 711.512
Georgia	Ga. Code Ann. Secs. 53-5-60 to 71
Hawaii	Haw. Rev. Stat. Secs. 539-1 to 539-12
Idaho	Idaho Code Secs. 15-6-301 to 15-6-312
Illinois	815 ILCS 10/0.01 to 10/12
Indiana	Ind. Code Secs. 32-4-1.6-1 to 32-4-1.6-15
Iowa	Iowa Code Secs. 633.800 to 633.811
Kansas	Kan. Stat. Ann. 17-49a 01 to 17-49a 12
Kentucky	Ky. Rev. Stat. Ann. Secs. 292.6501 to 292.6512
Maine	Me. Rev. Stat. Ann. tit. 18a, Secs. 6-301 to 6-312
Maryland	Md. Estates & Trusts Code Ann., Secs. 16-101 to 16-112
Massachusetts	Mass. Gen. Laws Ch. 201e, Secs. 101 to 402
Michigan	Mich. Comp. Laws Secs. 451.471 to 451.481
Minnesota	Minn. Stat. Secs. 542.1-201; 524.6-301 to 524.6-311
Mississippi	Miss. Code Ann. Secs. 91-21-1 to 91-21-25
Montana	Mont. Code Ann. Secs. 72-1-103; 72-6-301 to 72-6-311
Nebraska	Neb. Rev. Stat. Secs. 30-2209; 30-2734 to 30-2746
Nevada	Nev. Rev. Stat. Secs. 111.480 to 111.650
New Hampshire	N.H. Rev. Stat. Ann. Secs. 563-C: to 563-C:12
New Jersey	N.J. Stat. Ann. Secs. 3b:30-1 to 3b:30-12
New Mexico	N.M. Stat. Ann. 1978, Secs. 45-1-201; 45-6-301 to 45-6-311
North Dakota	N.D. Cent. Code 30.1-01-06; 30.1-31-21 to 30.1-31-30
Ohio	Ohio Rev. Code Ann. Secs. 1709.01 to 1709.11
Oklahoma	Okla. Stat. tit. 71, Secs. 901 to 913
Oregon	Or. Rev. Stat. 59.535 to 59.585
Pennsylvania	20 Pa. Cons. Stat. Secs. 6401 to 6413

Rhode Island	R.I. Gen. Laws Secs. 7-11.1-1 to 7-11.1-12
South Carolina	S.C. Code Ann. Secs. 35-6-10 to 35-6-100
South Dakota	S.D.Codified Laws 29a-6-301 to 29a-6-311
Utah	Utah Code Ann. Secs. 75-6-301 to 75-6-313
Vermont	Vt. Stat. Ann. Secs. 4351 to 4360
Virginia	Va. Code Ann. 1950, Secs. 64-1-206 to 64.1-206.8
Washington	Wash. Rev. Code Secs. 21.35.005 to 21.35.901
West Virginia	W.Va. Code Secs. 36-10-1 to 36-10-12
Wisconsin	Wis. Stat. Secs. 705.21 to 705.30
Wyoming	Wyo. Stat. Ann. Secs. 2-16-101 to 2-16-112

Example: *Michelle owns 100 shares of stock in XYZ Corp. She wants those shares to go to her niece, Brittany, upon her death without going through probate. Michelle titles the shares of stock in her name with a pay on death designation naming Brittany as the beneficiary of the shares.*

Transfer on Death Automobile Registration

Several states, including California, Missouri, and Ohio allow transfer on death automobile registration. However, in the next few years other states may pass similar laws. Check with your motor vehicle registration department to see if this type of registration is allowed in your state.

Land Trusts

Although real estate cannot be registered in transfer on death forms and joint ownership may cause problems, land trusts are becoming popular in many states to accomplish the same objective—passing property to a beneficiary without the property going through the probate process.

A *land trust* is an arrangement in which you put title to your property in the name of a trustee, but you have all the rights and responsibilities for the property as if it were in your name. This type of trust is typically called an *Illinois-type* land trust or a *title-holding trust.* (Illinois was the first state to allow such trusts.) Under this trust, the only thing the trustee does is hold title.

The trustee can be a bank, your attorney, a relative, or even yourself. Some people set up a separate trust for each property they own. The terms of the trust provide that upon your death a named beneficiary becomes the owner of the trust and can immediately take charge of the property. Land trusts offer many benefits other than probate avoidance, such as keeping your name off the public records and keeping the purchase and sales price secret.

Currently, not all states allow land trusts, but the American Bar Association is working on a law that can be passed in all states, so they may become more widely available. States that currently recognize land trusts include:

Arizona	Hawaii	North Dakota
Arkansas	lllinois	Ohio
Florida	Indiana	Virginia

Land trusts may be created in many other states if they are carefully worded. Consult an attorney with experience in land trusts if you wish to use such a trust.

Life Insurance

Another popular probate alternative is *life insurance*. A life insurance policy is a contract between the owner of the policy and the life insurance company. Generally, the person who purchases the policy, the *owner*, is also the person whose life is insured. When the policy is purchased, the life insurance company will ask the owner to designate the beneficiary of the life insurance policy. The beneficiary is the person who will receive the money that the policy pays when the owner dies—the death benefit. The owner will name a beneficiary and this beneficiary designation becomes part of the life insurance contract.

As long as the owner pays the premiums on the policy, the life insurance company agrees to pay the proceeds of the policy to the beneficiary when the owner dies. Typically, when the owner dies, the life insurance company will require proof of death in the form of a death certificate; will require that a claim form be completed; and, will pay the policy proceeds directly to the beneficiary. This happens completely outside of the probate process. The cash is available to the beneficiary quickly, which often will help a surviving spouse make mortgage payments, pay utility bills and pay college tuition bills. Unless the owner has designated his or her estate as beneficiary of the policy, the policy proceeds will not be subject to the probate process.

Example: *Mark buys a life insurance policy from Life Company and designates Rebecca as beneficiary of the policy proceeds upon his death. As long as Mark continues to pay the premiums, at his* *death, Life Company will be required to pay the proceeds to Rebecca. Since the life insurance policy provides that the proceeds are to be paid directly to Rebecca, they are not subject to the probate process.*

However, if Mark had named his estate as beneficiary, upon his death, Life Company would not pay the proceeds to his estate until probate proceedings are started. Life Company would require a copy of the will accepted by the court, a copy of the court's order accepting the will and appointing the personal representative, and a copy of the letters testamentary issued to the personal representative of the estate. Life Company will also require that the personal representative obtain a taxpayer identification number for the estate.

Often, a parent or grandparent will name a minor child as beneficiary of a life insurance policy. Typically, insurance companies will require that a legal *guardianship* be established for the minor before it pays the proceeds of the policy. Such a guardianship requires filing documents with the probate court. This costs money and takes time. Under a guardianship for a minor, the guardian will be required to hold the policy proceeds for the minor and distribute them to the minor when he or she reaches age 18 (or 21 in some states). A living trust can provide that such life insurance proceeds be held for the child's benefit beyond the age of 18 or 21.

A common misconception about life insurance is that the proceeds of the life insurance policy are not subject to taxes of any sort. The beneficiary of the life insurance policy is not required to pay income tax on the proceeds of the policy. However, the value of the proceeds is included in determining the value of the estate for federal estate tax purposes. If the value of the estate, including life insurance proceeds, is over $1,500,000, federal estate tax will need to be paid.

One way to avoid the inclusion of life insurance policy proceeds in the value of the estate is for the policy to be owned by a person other than the decedent. For example, if you wish to purchase a life insurance policy on yourself, you could give money to your son and have him purchase the policy for you. That way he owns the policy, and when you die, the policy proceeds are not included in your estate. Of course, if the money you give to your son to purchase the policy or pay premiums is in excess of $11,000 per year, you may have to pay a *gift tax* on the money.

This type of arrangement can be risky. As the owner of the policy, your son can change the beneficiary of the policy. Therefore, if you intended that the policy be paid to all of your children equally, your son can change the beneficiary designation without your knowledge and make himself the sole beneficiary of the policy. An alternative to such an arrangement is to use an *irrevocable life insurance trust* to own the life insurance policy. A *irrevocable life insurance trust* names the trustee as the owner and beneficiary of the life insurance policy. The potential problem with such a trust is that it is irrevocable and, once created, it cannot be changed or cancelled.

As you can see, this area of the law can get complicated, so if you wish to use all the benefits, you should consult an expert in estate planning.

Retirement Plans

Individual Retirement Accounts (IRAs), company pension plans, profit-sharing plans, and 401(k) plans are very popular retirement plans. Each of these retirement plans are funded with assets such as cash, stocks, bonds, mutual funds, etc. These retirement plans are essentially a specialized form of a savings account subject to very strict tax rules. When a person retires or reaches a certain age (often 62 or 65), he or she can begin to withdraw funds from the retirement plan. If the owner dies before receiving all of the funds in his or her retirement plan, a beneficiary designated by the owner receives the funds remaining in the retirement plan.

Just like an insurance contract, the owner of the retirement plan completes a beneficiary designation that directs the employer, brokerage firm, or bank (if the retirement plan is an IRA bank account) to pay the funds to a specific individual (or individuals) upon his or her death. The employer, brokerage firm, or bank is required to honor the contract and make the payment after the death of the owner.

Example: *Kevin worked for USA Company and made contributions to a 401(k) retirement plan sponsored by the company, naming Glenda as beneficiary. Kevin retires and begins to receive payments each year from the plan. Kevin dies with $50,000 remaining in the plan. USA Company must pay the $50,000 directly to Glenda without going through the probate process.*

There are many, very specialized tax rules governing who may be named beneficiary of a retirement plan. In recent years, laws have changed that make it possible to provide payment of an IRA account to your spouse, children, and grandchildren after your death. This is called *stretching* your IRA and can result in substantial income tax savings to your family over several generations.

Some tax options are *only* available to a surviving spouse. If you are considering naming someone other than your spouse (this includes naming your living trust) as beneficiary of your retirement plans, consult a professional with experience in this specialized tax area.

Gifts

In addition to the transfers of property by joint tenancy or contract, there are two other commonly used methods to transfer property without going through the probate process—outright gifts and trusts.

Property can be transferred to your beneficiaries by means of an *outright gift* during your lifetime. However, the federal government only allows you to give away a certain amount of your property without paying a gift tax. In the past, people gave away a lot of their property in an effort to avoid paying estate tax. The federal government closed this loophole by creating a gift tax.

Gift tax must be paid on any property given to a person other than your spouse. However, there are two exceptions to this general rule. First, under the current federal gift tax law, an individual can give up to $11,000 a year, or a husband and wife can together give up to $22,000 a year, to any number of people, free of gift tax. This $11,000 amount is often called the *gift tax annual exclusion*. Second, The person receiving the property must receive it with *no strings attached*. The property becomes that person's under his or her complete control. The person receiving the property does not have to pay income tax on the property he or she receives.

Federal tax law also permits you to transfer up to $1,500,000, either during your lifetime or at your death, free of federal estate or gift tax. Thus, in addition to the annual exclusion gift, you can make gifts of up to this amount during your lifetime with no gift tax. However, if you give away more than this amount during your lifetime, then at your death every dollar that your beneficiaries receive is taxed—and the rate starts at forty-eight percent!

If you give any gifts in excess of the annual exclusion gift during a year, you are required to file a *federal gift tax return* even if no tax is due because you are using up your $1,500,000 exemption. This gift tax return is due on April 15th of the year following the year in which you make the gifts.

Chapter 3:
Estate and Inheritance Taxes

Is Uncle Sam a Beneficiary of Your Estate?

You work hard throughout your lifetime to save assets for retirement, and perhaps, leave a legacy to your children. You have paid income and employment taxes on your salary and income or capital gains taxes on your investments. When you die, the Internal Revenue Service and your state treasurer want to take yet another bite of the apple in the form of estate or inheritance taxes.

Estate tax is a tax imposed by the federal government and some states on the estate of a decedent. It is imposed on the assets themselves. The estate tax is calculated on the value of the estate as a whole. The estate taxes are paid by the representative of the estate *before* distributions are made to beneficiaries.

Some states that do not impose an estate tax, instead impose an *inheritance tax* on the right to inherit property. The inheritance tax is calculated on the value of property received by each beneficiary. The rate of tax varies depending upon the relationship of the beneficiary to the decedent. For example, the rate of tax on property passing to a spouse or children is different than the rate of tax on property passing to parents, brothers, sisters, and others. The inheritance tax is paid by the representative of the estate *before* distributions are made to beneficiaries.

Without proper planning, your estate can be reduced by as much as 50% because of estate and inheritance taxes. The assets that you thought would provide for the surviving spouse and children can be lost to the tax system. Fortunately, steps can be taken to avoid or reduce the amount of estate tax paid by your estate.

(Appendix A contains charts listing the states that have estate and inheritance taxes.)

Federal Estate Tax

The federal government created an estate tax in an attempt to generate more revenue. When first adopted, the estate tax was aimed at taxing the wealthy, imposing tax rates as high as 60%. An *exemption* amount was included in the estate tax system. A person could own a certain amount of property without having to pay estate tax. During the past twenty years, Congress has enacted a series of laws that increased the exemption amount and decreased the estate tax rates.

The most recent change in the federal estate tax law came in 2001. The *Economic Growth and Tax Relief Reconciliation Act of 2001* reduced the highest federal estate tax rate from 60% and increased the applicable credit amount (the exemption) from $600,000. The amount of the applicable credit has been structured to increase in stages until, in 2010, there is no estate tax. In effect, there will be an unlimited credit amount. The estate tax rate for any amount in excess of the applicable credit amount will be gradually reduced from 48% to 45%. The following table contains the scheduled changes in the federal estate tax law.

Year	Estate Tax Applicable Credit Amount	Highest Estate Tax Rate
2004	$1,500,000	48%
2005	$1,500,000	47%
2006	$2,000,000	46%
2007	$2,000,000	45%
2008	$2,000,000	45%
2009	$3,500,000	45%
2010	Repealed	—
2011	Reinstated at $1,000,000	55%

As you can see from the table, in 2010 the estate tax is repealed. Unless Congress takes action to make the repeal permanent, however, the estate tax will come back into effect in 2011. Most tax experts believe that the estate tax will never be repealed. Speeches promising repeal made by politicians appeal to the voters. But budget deficits will continue and, when the revenue raised by the estate tax is analyzed, it would be unsound fiscal policy to repeal the estate tax.

> **Author's Advice:** I recommend that my clients plan as if the estate tax will remain in effect. If the tax is in fact repealed, estate planning documents can be revised accordingly.

Unlimited Marital Deduction

A long-standing provision of the federal estate tax system is the *unlimited marital deduction*. Spouses are permitted to give an unlimited amount of property to one another without paying federal estate tax. Thus, a surviving spouse is not required to liquidate assets to pay estate tax.

The unlimited marital deduction can be a trap for the unwary. The deduction does not avoid payment of estate tax completely—it simply postpones payment of estate tax until the death of the surviving spouse. Proper planning, however, can make certain that estate tax is not paid unnecessarily. (This will be discussed later in this chapter.)

Stepped-Up Valuation of Estate Assets

When you purchase an asset, the price you pay for the asset is considered the *basis* of the asset. When you sell the asset at a later time, the gain or loss from the asset is computed by subtracting the basis of the asset from the selling price. This is how capital gains and losses are computed for income tax purposes.

Until 1981, when a person died and his or her assets passed to his or her beneficiaries, there existed the opportunity for a double tax. This happened because when the beneficiary received assets from the estate, the beneficiary's basis in the asset was the same as the decedent's basis in the asset. This is referred to as *carryover basis*.

Example: *John buys 100 shares of stock for $5 per share. His basis in the stock is $500. Ten years later John dies. The value of the stock on the date of John's death is $40 per share. The value of John's estate is calculated by using the value of the stock on the date of John's death. However, when the stock is distributed to Sally, Sally's basis in the stock is $500. When she later sells the stock, her gain is calculated using $500 as the basis.*

The problem with carryover basis is that it creates the potential for a hidden form of double taxation. If, in the above example, John's estate exceeds the applicable credit amount, estate tax must be paid on the value of all of the assets included in the estate. Later, when Sally sells the stock at a gain, she must pay capital gains on that gain.

In 1981, Congress made an attempt to eliminate the risk of double taxation and introduced the concept of *stepped-up* basis. Upon a person's death, the basis of his or her assets is adjusted to the value of the assets on the date of his or her death. The original basis is stepped-up (or inflated) to the date of death value. Referring again to the previous example, Sally's basis in the stock will be $4,000. Any gain or loss will be calculated using $4,000 as the basis.

Unfortunately, the 2001 tax law provides for the elimination of *stepped-up* basis in 2010. During 2010, the basis of a decedent's asset will be equal to the *lesser* of the decedent's original basis in the asset and the fair market value of the asset on the date of death. Thus, while there may not be an estate tax imposed on the assets in an estate, when the assets are sold by the beneficiaries, capital gains tax must be paid on the appreciated value of the assets.

Planning to Reduce Your Estate Tax Burden

Each person has the benefit of the applicable credit amount. In 2004, each person can transfer $1.5 million to his or her beneficiaries (in addition to anything transferred to a spouse) at death without paying federal estate tax. Without proper planning, however, the full benefit of the exclusion can be lost.

Estate Stacking

Estate stacking is a concept that applies to all individuals, but is primarily an estate tax trap with spouses. As discussed earlier in this chapter, an individual can leave an unlimited amount of property to a spouse without paying estate tax. This often leads married couples to have an estate plan that involves *I Love You* planning. I Love You wills give all property to the surviving spouse thus avoiding estate tax at the death of the first spouse. However, estate tax is not avoided—it is simply postponed until the death of the surviving spouse.

The problem with estate stacking is that estate tax savings can be lost to the family as a whole.

Example: *Bob and Susan are married. Bob dies and his estate is worth $800,000. He leaves all of his property to his wife. No estate tax is due because of the unlimited marital deduction. When Susan dies, her estate is worth $1.6 million. Because Susan's applicable credit amount is only $1.5 million, estate tax will have to be paid on $100,000 at a rate of 48%.*

Maximizing Use of the Unified Credit

With proper planning, no estate tax would be due at Susan's death. Because each person can transfer $1.5 million free of estate tax, together Bob and Susan could pass as much as $3.0 million without estate tax. This can be accomplished by including an estate tax saving trust in Bob's estate plan.

Example: *Instead of leaving all of his property to his wife, Bob leaves his property in trust for the benefit of Susan. Susan can use the income and principal of the trust as needed. However, upon her death, the value of the assets remaining in the trust is not included in the value of her estate—it is not stacked upon her assets. The assets in the trust are distributed to the beneficiaries automatically upon Susan's death. The value of Susan's estate, $800,000, is below the $1.5 million applicable credit amount and is completely excluded from estate tax. Therefore, $1.6 million of assets passes to the family without paying any estate tax.*

(Estate tax planning is discussed in greater detail in Chapter 8.)

Trusts

In addition to the living trust, there are a variety of trusts that can be used to reduce the overall estate tax burden on a person's estate. These trusts include:

- ◆ Life Insurance Trusts
- ◆ Personal Residence Trusts
- ◆ Grantor Retained Annuity Trusts (GRATs)
- ◆ Grantor Retained Income Trusts (GRITs)
- ◆ Charitable Remainder Trusts
- ◆ Charitable Lead Trusts

Detailed discussion of these types of trusts is beyond the scope of this book. Because such trusts are complex and must comply with very stringent rules under federal tax law, you should consult a professional tax advisor who has experience in these areas.

Chapter 4:
Living Trusts

The Nuts and Bolts

For hundreds of years, trusts have been the most popular way to avoid probate, especially for large estates. Today, with pay on death accounts and the other methods described in earlier chapters, trusts may not be necessary for as many estates, but they can still provide advantages for many situations.

Trusts

A *trust* is a legal *person* that comes into existence when an individual signs a legal document that contains certain provisions. The trust is a contract between the maker of the trust, the trustee, and the beneficiaries. The trust agreement contains the terms of the contract—the rights, duties, and obligations of the parties. A trust is a legally enforceable agreement. A trust is an arrangement for the ownership of property. When property is transferred to a trust, *legal title* to the assets is vested in the trustee. Legal title allows the trustee to manage, administer, and distribute the trust assets. The *beneficial interest* in the property (the right to receive the benefits of the property, such as income, appreciation, and use) is vested in the beneficiaries of the trust.

Each state has comprehensive statutes to govern trusts, which defines things such as:

- ◆ the standard of care trustees must use with regard to managing trust property;
- ◆ the obligations of trustees making distributions to the beneficiaries;
- ◆ the types of property or investments held in a trust; and,
- ◆ the rights of trust beneficiaries.

Trust Types

There are two types of trusts—*testamentary trusts* and *inter vivos trusts*. A *testamentary trust* is written into a person's last will and testament. Because a testamentary trust is part of a will, it does not become effective until the death of the testator (the person who has created the will). A testamentary trust cannot be funded with assets during the testator's lifetime. Once a person dies, the trust is funded with some or all of the assets owned by the person at the time of death. The testamentary trust is irrevocable.

An *inter vivos trust* is a separate document, created apart from a will, that becomes effective during the lifetime of the *grantor* (the person who creates the trust). Because an inter vivos trust is created during a person's life and is effective while the grantor is living, such a trust has commonly been called a *living trust.* For a living trust to be effective, at least a nominal amount of assets must be transferred to the trust. It is possible to create a trust with as little as $10.00. Without assets, a living trust is considered a *dry trust* and is invalid under state law.

Inter vivos trusts can be revocable or irrevocable. An *irrevocable* trust cannot be altered or amended by the grantor. The typical use of an irrevocable trust is for a person to make a gift of some asset either permanently or for a significant period of time. Insurance trusts, charitable lead and remainder trusts, residence trusts, and annuity trusts are typical examples of irrevocable trusts. In order to accomplish the person's gift intention, irrevocable trusts are almost always funded during the lifetime of the grantor.

A *revocable* trust is a trust over which the grantor retains the power to revoke, alter, or amend the trust during his or her lifetime. If the trust is revoked during the grantor's lifetime, the trust assets are returned to the grantor. Upon the death of the grantor, the trust becomes irrevocable.

A revocable trust can be funded or unfunded during the lifetime of the grantor. Should he or she decide to fund the trust, the grantor will typically transfer a substantial part or all of his or her assets to the trust. The assets transferred to the trust will not be part of the decedent's probate estate. Therefore, the costs of probate will be avoided. If the trust is unfunded, the grantor transfers only a nominal amount of assets to the trust during his or her lifetime. Assets will be transferred to the trust upon the death of the grantor.

In most revocable trusts, the grantor of the trust is the primary beneficiary of the trust throughout his or her lifetime and is generally the trustee, responsible for the management and distribution of trust assets.

Parties to a Trust

There are three fundamental parties to a trust: the grantor of the trust, the trustee, and the beneficiaries. The role and rights of each party is discussed in the following sections.

Grantor of the Trust

The person who creates a trust and transfers property to it is generally called the *grantor*. A grantor is sometimes called a *settlor, maker, donor,* or *trustor.* In a living trust, the grantor retains the right to amend, alter, or revoke the trust. In some circumstances, two or more people may decide to create a trust and are collectively referred to as *grantors.* Generally, both people must agree to amend, alter, or revoke the trust.

Trustee and Successor Trustee

The person in charge of managing the trust, who is often the same person who created the trust, is called a *trustee.* In most states, any person or entity (such as banks, trust companies, and some brokerage firms), who is capable of taking legal title to property, can be appointed trustee. Trustees have a legal duty (often called a *fiduciary duty*) to protect the assets of the trust and make certain that the purposes of the trust are followed.

The trustee is responsible for the management of the trust assets. The trustee has legal title of the trust assets and the power to buy, sell, borrow against, or transfer the trust assets. The trust agreement sets forth the rights, duties, and obligations of the trustee. In addition, state law imposes certain duties and obligations on trustees. The trustee need not be a resident of the state in which the trust is formed.

When a living trust is established, the grantor is usually also the trustee of the trust. The reason is simple. The grantor has managed the assets adequately before the assets are transferred to the trust and remains capable of managing the assets now that they are in the trust.

This brings to light a common misconception about living trusts. Many people believe that by transferring assets into the living trust, they lose control over the assets. That is absolutely not true. The grantor keeps full control over his or her property. As trustee of a living trust, the grantor can do everything he or she could do prior to creating the trust.

When the grantor is no longer able to serve as trustee, whether because of death, incapacity, or illness, the *successor trustee* named in the trust agreement takes over management of the living trust. The successor trustee has the same powers, rights, duties, and responsibilities as the original trustee. The successor trustee steps into the shoes of the original trustee. Court approval is not required to permit the successor trustee to begin acting. While the successor trustee has all of the powers, rights, duties, and responsibilities as the original trustee, the successor trustee has no authority to alter, amend, or revoke the living trust. His or her role is limited to managing the assets and distributing the assets to the trust beneficiaries *in accordance with the desires of the grantor as set forth in the living trust agreement.*

In some circumstances, such as illness or age, a grantor may choose not to continue to act as trustee of his or her living trust. Although the grantor may not be considered *incapacitated* as defined in the living trust agreement or under state law, the grantor may relinquish his or her role as trustee by a written statement to that effect. In such a case, the grantor retains the right to resume his or her role as trustee when he or she feels fit and able to do so. In addition, the grantor retains the right to remove the successor trustee and replace the successor trustee, either with the next person named in trust to serve as trustee or with a person not named in the trust.

In the event of the grantor's incapacity (as defined in the living trust agreement), the successor trustee will assume the role of trustee without a court determination of incapacity. This maintains the privacy of the grantor and his or her living trust as a whole and permits the management of the grantor's assets without interruption or court supervision.

When married couples establish living trusts, they name each other as successor trustee of one another's trust. Often, one or more adult children are named as successor trustees in the event neither husband nor wife is serving as trustee. It is not uncommon for parents to name two or more of their children to serve jointly as successor trustees. Generally, both children must agree in order to take action. However, a well-drafted trust agreement will provide that if more than two trustees are serving, the decision of a majority of the trustees controls.

In addition, most trusts contain provisions authorizing trustees to delegate responsibility for certain actions to one trustee. This is common when children live in different parts of the country. One child may be authorized to manage the trust assets on a daily basis, subject to review by the other trustees on a quarterly, semi-annual, or annual basis. Another child may be authorized to make distributions to beneficiaries within certain monetary limitations.

Beneficiaries

The person who benefits from the trust is a *beneficiary*. The beneficiary is entitled to receive the benefits of the income and principal of the trust. There are several categories of beneficiaries—the primary beneficiary, the contingent beneficiary (sometimes referred to as a secondary beneficiary), and the remainder beneficiary.

The *primary beneficiaries* are the persons who are first to receive the benefits of the trust assets. In a living trust, there is typically only one primary beneficiary—the grantor. After all, the assets in the trust are his or her assets. Commonly, the grantor's spouse is also a beneficiary of the living trust. If the grantor has minor children or children who are dependent upon the grantor for support such as children who are disabled or in college, these children can also be named as beneficiaries of the trust.

Contingent beneficiaries are entitled to receive the benefits of the trust assets after the primary beneficiaries. Contingent beneficiaries are designated in the trust agreement to receive trust benefits in the future. In addition, contingent beneficiaries may also receive benefits from the trust in the sole discretion of the trustee. That is, if the trustee believes that the contingent beneficiaries need money, the trustee can pay money to the contingent beneficiaries. The identity of the contingent beneficiaries and the scope of their future beneficial interest in the trust can be changed by the grantor at any time until the living trust becomes irrevocable (*i.e.*, at the death of the grantor).

When the trust becomes irrevocable upon the death of the grantor, the contingent beneficiaries become remainder beneficiaries. Their right to future benefits of the trust cannot be altered, amended, or revoked. This does not mean, however, that they will receive trust assets. In the case of a married couple, after the death of the grantor, the surviving spouse is the primary beneficiary of the living trust. The living trust provides that all of the income and principal of the living trust can be used for the health, education, maintenance, and support of the surviving spouse throughout his or her lifetime. It is possible that the trust assets could be exhausted for the benefit of the surviving spouse, leaving nothing for the children.

Example: *Bill creates a living trust. His is married to Phyllis and has two children. During his lifetime, he is the primary beneficiary of the trust. After his death, Bill's wife, Phyllis, is the primary beneficiary of the trust. She is entitled to receive the income and principal of the trust during her lifetime. After Phyllis' death, the trust assets are divided into two equal shares—one for each child.*

Beneficiaries are not restricted to family members or other individuals. Nonprofit institutions or charities can be named as beneficiaries of a trust. Beneficiaries may be given different rights in the trust property. Some beneficiaries may be *income beneficiaries* and may be entitled to receive only the income from the trust property. This may be interest from a savings account or bond, dividends from stock, rental income from real estate, etc. Other beneficiaries may be *principal beneficiaries* and be entitled to receive the actual trust assets— for example, the money in the savings account, the stock, or rental real estate. Sometimes the beneficiary may be entitled to receive both income and principal.

The identities and rights of beneficiaries are established by the grantor when creating the living trust and can be changed during his or her lifetime.

Living Trust Advantages

A living trust offers many advantages over a will. Some of these advantages include:

- ◆ avoidance of probate;
- ◆ timely distribution of assets to beneficiaries;
- ◆ privacy (the terms of trust are confidential);
- ◆ difficult to contest;
- ◆ control of assets maintained during incapacity or at death;
- ◆ guardianship alternative in the event of incapacity;
- ◆ minimizes emotional stress on family;
- ◆ prevents unintended disinheritance;

◆ inexpensive to create and maintain;

◆ flexibility (the trust is amendable and revocable at any time);

◆ protects financial inheritance of minor children from court-supervised guardianships;

◆ protects family members with special needs;

◆ permits continuation of business;

◆ avoids ancillary probate administration; and,

◆ continuity of asset management and income flow.

Avoidance of Probate

Assets placed in a living trust prior to death do not go through the probate process. This results in significant savings to the estate. Probate costs (including executor's fees and bond), attorney's fees, and appraiser's fees are avoided or significantly reduced. Because the assets in the living trust are not subject to the time-consuming probate process, estate debts, claims, and expenses can be paid on a timely basis. Court approval is not required to make these payments.

Timely Distribution of Assets to Beneficiaries

Because living trusts are not subject to the probate process, trust assets can be distributed to the beneficiaries without delay.

Privacy

A living trust is completely confidential. It is not subject to disclosure to the probate court as is a will. Wills become public documents and can be read by anyone who takes the time and has an interest in doing so. Also, when a will is probated the court requires that an inventory of assets (and sometimes debts) be filed with the court. These inventories are public record and reveal the types of assets that comprise the estate and the value of the assets.

Because the living trust is not recorded with the probate court, the assets in the trust, the terms of the trust, and the identities of the beneficiaries are not made public. The only persons who need be aware of the trust's existence, its assets, and its terms are the grantor, the trustee, and the trust beneficiaries.

There are several states that require a trust be registered with the court where the trustee lives or administers the trust. The trustee must file certain information with the court, including the name of the grantor, the name of the trustee, the date on which the trust was created, and some form of written acceptance of the trust by the trustees. This acceptance is often evidenced by the trustee's signature on the trust document.

This registration requirement impacts and undercuts the privacy advantage of the living trust. The following states have laws governing the registration of living trusts.

Alaska	Idaho	Missouri
Colorado	Maine	Nebraska
Florida	Michigan	North Dakota
Hawaii		

In order to retain the privacy of the living trust, language may be included in the living trust that specifically exempts the registration of the living trust. (All of the forms in this book contain such language that exempts registration of the living trust.)

Difficult to Contest

Trusts are generally more difficult to contest by disgruntled heirs or beneficiaries. Since the trust is often used for a period of time before the death of the grantor, it shows, through actual practice, what the true intention of the grantor is. Since a will only takes effect after the testator's death, that intent is subject to interpretation. Also, while there can be issues with the validity of a trust based on how it is executed, those problems will, at most, always be corrected before a disgruntled heir or beneficiary comes into the picture. If there is a problem with how a will was executed or some other question with the will's validity, there is little change to correct it.

Control of Assets Maintained

While you are alive, you continue to manage and control the assets in the living trust just as you did prior to establishing the trust. You continue to direct how the assets will be invested and how the assets will be used during your lifetime and after your death. As trustee, you can designate someone to assist you with the investment of trust assets or hire an investment advisor—just as you would individually.

In a living trust, you personally select the successor trustee who will control your assets in the event of your incapacity or after your death. The living trust contains your specific instructions regarding how the assets are to be invested and distributed. Property passing through the probate process is subject to many complex state laws imposing rules on executors that often limits the investments and distributions executors can make.

Guardianship Alternative

In the event of your incapacity, the living trust enables the successor trustee to continue the management of your assets without a court-supervised *guardianship*. Typically, if a person is unable to manage his or her financial matters, a court-supervised guardianship will be established and a guardian appointed by the court will collect and manage the assets. A guardianship is costly and time consuming. Because a person's incapacity can extend for a number of years, it is possible that a significant amount of assets will be spent for court costs, attorney fees, and the guardian's fees. In addition, the court-appointed guardian may not be a person who you would normally choose to serve in that role. The successor trustee you have designated in your living trust will step in to manage your assets.

Minimizes Emotional Stress on Family

Your family will not be required to attend probate proceedings or deal with attorneys to probate your estate. Court proceedings are naturally stressful. During a time when family is dealing with the loss of a loved one, stress from outside sources, such as courts and attorneys, is avoided.

Prevents Unintended Disinheritance

A living trust designates who will receive your property upon your death. The beneficiaries of your estate and the amount of their inheritance are set forth in the trust agreement. If you die without a will, state statutes designate who will receive your property and how much they will receive. These statutes may not reflect your wishes. For instance, your children may be financially stable and you may wish to give your property to your grandchildren to pay for college tuition. Without a will, your children are entitled to receive your property. Your grandchildren would not receive any property.

Inexpensive to Establish and Maintain

The cost for establishing a living trust is a small fraction of the cost of a probate administration. The cost to maintain the living trust during your lifetime and after your death is minimal at best.

Flexibility

The living trust is amendable and revocable at any time during your life. If your family circumstances change—if you divorce, have children or grandchildren, if a family member becomes ill, or if a beneficiary dies—a living trust can be amended to reflect these changes. Also, if you move to a different state, your living trust will be valid in that state. By contrast, changes to wills are more time consuming and expensive, because strict state laws governing the creation and amendment of a will impose many burdens on the person making the will.

Protects Financial Inheritance of Minor Children

If a minor child (under the age of 18) inherits property, the courts will order that such property be held in a court-supervised account watched by a custodian until the child attains age 18. While the custodian is often a family member, he or she does not have unsupervised freedom to manage the property or make distributions to the child. A living trust permits the trustee to manage assets set aside for a minor child without court supervision. In addition, a living trust can also extend the age at which the child would receive his or her inheritance. Often, the age of distribution is extended to 21 or 25.

Protects Family Members with Special Needs

A living trust can provide for the management of a disabled family member's inheritance without a court-supervised guardianship. Often, disabled persons receive government assistance in the form of income subsidies and medical care. Most of these assistance programs are based on financial need. If the disabled person has a net worth above a certain amount (typically $5,000 or less), he or she may not qualify for government assistance. However, if assets are held in trust for the benefit of the disabled person, the assets are generally not counted as the assets of the disabled person and government assistance can continue.

Permits Continuation of Business

Living trusts are very useful to business owners. Whether the business is a sole proprietorship, corporation, or partnership, the business owner can transfer business assets into the living trust. If the business owner dies or becomes disabled, the successor trustee can step into the business owner's shoes and handle the day-to-day affairs of the business without interruption. Because the business may be the primary source of income to the owner and his or her family, after the owner's death or disability, it is important that the business continue to operate and generate the income needed to support the owner's family.

Avoids Ancillary Probate Administration

If you own property in more than one state, it is necessary to have a probate proceeding in each state in which your property is located in order to transfer title to the property to your beneficiaries. The probate proceedings in a state other than the state in which the decedent had his or her primary residence is called an *ancillary administration.* For example, if you live in Illinois and own real estate in Florida, upon your death your executor must begin two probate proceedings—one in Illinois to deal with your assets in Illinois and one in Florida to transfer title to your Florida real estate. If the real estate is transferred into your living trust during your lifetime, upon your death, that property will not be subject to probate either in Illinois or Florida.

Continuity of Asset Management and Income Flow

The living trust allows the successor trustee to continue management of the assets in the trust without court involvement. The successor trustee can continue to collect income in the form of interest and dividends, sell and purchase assets, and make distributions to beneficiaries.

Living Trust Disadvantages

Discussion of living trusts would be incomplete if the potential disadvantages of a living trust were not explained. While some of the disadvantages listed, such as no income or estate tax savings, may not be *disadvantages* in the true sense of the word, they are misconceptions about living trusts that need to be addressed.

No Income Tax Savings

The living trust does not avoid or save income taxes while you are alive. You retain control of the assets in your living trust, you receive the benefits of the trust, and you are both the grantor and trustee of the trust. The income earned by the assets in the living trust will be taxed to you. Although Forms 1099, K-1, and other such forms will be titled in the name of the living trust, you will be required to report this income on your individual income tax return, Form 1040. During your lifetime, there is no requirement that a *taxpayer identification number* be obtained for the living trust and no separate income tax return has to be filed for the trust.

After your death, the living trust must obtain a taxpayer identification number by filing Form SS-4, *Application for Employer Identification Number* with the

Internal Revenue Service. The taxpayer identification number is similar to a person's Social Security number. All income earned by the living trust will be reported under the living trust's taxpayer identification number. The living trust will be required to file a separate income tax return, Form 1041 to report all income received by the trust. Form 1041 will show how much of the income received by the trust was paid to the trust beneficiaries. The living trust does not pay income tax on income that is distributed to the trust beneficiaries during the tax year. The beneficiaries pay income tax on the income they receive from the trust. If the living trust does not distribute all of its income, it must pay income tax on the undistributed income. Tax rates for a trust are the same as those for individuals but the tax brackets are much more compressed. That is, trusts pay tax at the highest rate very quickly.

No Estate Tax Savings

The living trust does not eliminate federal or state estate taxes. The assets in your living trust are included in your estate in calculating such tax liability. As discussed in Chapter 3, if your estate does not exceed the applicable credit amount, no federal estate tax will be due. Many states impose their own estate or inheritance tax. While there may be no federal estate tax liability, there may be a state estate tax liability. If you are married, a living trust offers planning opportunities to minimize estate tax on the combined estates of you and your spouse.

No Deadlines for Claims of Creditors

When a will is probated (or an estate without a will is probated), a deadline is imposed on creditors of the decedent. Creditors are required to present their claim to the executor of the estate within a time period, specified by statute. Each state has its own statute establishing this time period which can range from a few months to one year, and the procedures that a creditor must follow to present its claim.

If a creditor does not follow the procedures within the statutory time period, the creditor loses its right to the assets of the estate and is forever prohibited from suing the estate to collect the assets it is due. In most states, however, a living trust is not subject to the same statutory procedures. Therefore, a creditor can sue the trust or its beneficiaries for amounts due long after you have died. Even after the trust has terminated and all of the trust assets are distributed to the beneficiaries, creditors can sue the beneficiaries for claims it has against the decedent.

Does Not Avoid Creditor Claims During Your Life

A living trust does not prevent your creditors from suing you or suing your trust to collect debts during your lifetime. Because you have maintained complete control over the trust assets, the courts treat you as the owner of the assets in the living trust and can force you to pay trust assets to your creditors. If you know that you owe a creditor money and you transfer all of your assets to your living trust in an attempt to keep them away from your creditor, the courts will view the transfer as a *fraudulent conveyance* and may force you not only to pay the creditor, but also pay a fine.

Does Not Eliminate the Need for a Will

Even though you have a living trust that is funded with all of your assets during your lifetime, it is important to have a will. The will can name a guardian for your minor children, appoint a personal representative of your probate estate, and provide that no bond be required of your personal representative. There may be assets that you forgot to transfer to your living trust, such as an unexpected inheritance, or a lawsuit that must be filed on behalf of your estate after your death. A will covers these assets even if the will only provides that such assets *pour over* to your living trust. Without a will, you have died *intestate* and your family must follow the probate procedures for intestacy. Intestacy procedures are complex, time-consuming, and generally very expensive.

The following chart is a comparison of the consequences of incapacity and death if you die intestate (without a will), testate (with a will), or with a living trust in effect. It compares the differences in flexibility, control, and privacy of each situation.

COMPARISON OF INTESTACY, WILLS, AND LIVING TRUSTS

	With No Will	With a Will	With a Living Trust
At Physical/Mental Incapacity	*Probate:* Court appoints conservator/guardian who oversees your care, must keep detailed records, and reports to court. Court controls your finances and assets, approves all expenses.	*Probate:* Same as with no will.	*No probate:* Successor trustee manages your financial affairs according to the instructions you have set forth in your living trust for as long as necessary.
Court Costs	You pay all court costs and legal fees.	Same as with no will.	None.
At Death	*Probate:* Court orders debts paid and possessions distributed according to state law, which may not be what you would have wanted.	*Probate:* After verifying your will, court orders debts paid and possessions distributed according to terms of your will.	*No Probate:* Debts are paid & possessions immediately distributed to beneficiaries by successor trustee according to instructions in living trust.
Court Costs	Estate pays all court costs and legal fees (average between 4%–10% or more of the gross value of the estate).	Same as with no will. Costs can be higher if will is contested.	None.
Time	Often one to two years or more before property is distributed to heirs.	Same as with no will.	Usually four to six weeks for smaller estates, three to six months for larger estates.
Flexibility and Control	*None:* Property is controlled and distributed by the probate court in accordance with state law.	*Limited:* Will can be changed at any time. Wills can be contested by disgruntled heirs. Family has no control over probate costs or time delays.	*Complete:* Living trust can be changed or revoked at any time. Property remains under the control of the trust, even in the event of your incapacity. Living trust is difficult to contest.
Privacy	*None:* Probate proceedings are part of the public record. Family is exposed to unethical solicitors and disgruntled heirs.	*None:* Same as with no will.	*Complete:* Privacy of the parties (grantor, trustees, beneficiaries) is maintained. Living trusts are not recorded at the courthouse and are not public record.

Chapter 5:
Your Assets

*What Do You Have and
How Much Do You Have?*

Whether you are applying for a home loan, saving for a child's education, or planning retirement, you need to know how much you are worth. *Net worth* means the value of the assets you own in comparison to the liabilities or debts that you owe. The formula to determine your net worth is simple:

Assets - Liabilities = Net Worth.

Of course, each of us would like to have a positive net worth, but the amount of your net worth is impossible to know until you calculate it.

Calculating Your Net Worth

Before you establish your living trust, it is important to identify your net worth. This is true for several reasons. First, the primary purpose of your living trust is to own title to your assets so that upon your death or in the event of your incapacity, your assets may be invested and distributed without the involvement of the court. Therefore, you must *fund* your living trust. This requires transferring title of the assets into the name of your living trust.

Second, estate and inheritance taxes affect the manner in which your living trust is structured. If your net worth exceeds certain amounts, your living trust should be structured to take advantage of the estate and inheritance tax exemptions available to you. (Chapter 3 contains a detailed explanation of the impact of estate and inheritance taxes on your estate.)

Third, as you detail your assets, you may discover that your investments may be concentrated more heavily in one form of investment than another. This may prompt you to review your investment portfolio to determine whether you want to change your mix of stocks, bonds, mutual funds, CDs, etc.

Finally, as you go through the process of identifying your assets, you may uncover items that require your attention. This may include updating beneficiary designations on life insurance policies or retirement plans.

During the process of identifying your assets, gather important documents associated with each asset you list. This may include deeds for real estate, life insurance policies, retirement plan summaries, beneficiary designation forms, safe deposit box information, and recent brokerage and bank account statements. Identifying your assets and calculating your net worth is not a daunting task. You should not let the process overwhelm you. You may be surprised at things you find when you start investigating. For example, one client, while going through his papers, discovered a retirement annuity to which he was entitled. This retirement annuity was from a company he had worked for more than 40 years ago!

The Worksheet

Included in this chapter is a WORKSHEET that consists of three sections. The first section is the *Inventory*. On the INVENTORY, list your assets and their values as well as your debts and liabilities in detail. The second section of the WORKSHEET contains a *Summary,* on which you can calculate your net worth. The last section of the WORKSHEET, *Personal Contacts,* allows you to list the names, addresses, and telephone numbers of your important advisors. The WORKSHEET is structured for use by a married couple, husband and wife. If you are not married, use only one column on the worksheet. When filling in values, you do not have to be exact—round your figures to the next highest thousand dollars.

If you own a business or are self-employed, you should calculate a separate net worth for the business. It is not necessary to list the assets or liabilities attributable to the business. Simply include a value of the business as a whole.

Do not allow the WORKSHEET to discourage you and become a stumbling block to creating your living trust. It is comprehensive in nature, and is intended to help you gain a more accurate assessment of your net worth and to assist you when funding your living trust. Unless your estate is very complicated, you should be able to complete the worksheet in half an hour.

The following paragraphs contain detailed descriptions of the various sections of the NET WORTH WORKSHEET contained at the end of this chapter.

Identify Your Assets

Your most recent tax return can be a very valuable resource in identifying your assets and liabilities. Copies of W-2s, Form 1099s, and Schedule K-1s are excellent reminders of assets you may have forgotten about. These documents will, in turn, lead you to such things as brokerage statements, bank statements, royalty statements, and loan interest summaries.

Investments—Marketable Securities

Stocks, bonds (including US savings bonds), mutual funds, United States Treasury bills and notes, and certificates of deposits should be included in the *Investments* section of the *Inventory*. Each investment should be listed individually with a total for each category of investment. Brokerage statements, 1099INT forms, and 1099DIV forms are excellent resources from which detailed information can be obtained. Of course, the value of marketable securities fluctuates daily. You should use the most recent value available. The *Inventory* contains lines where you can list the dates on which you acquired the investment and the initial cost of the investment. This information will be useful in the future to calculate capital gains or losses when the investment is sold.

Cash

Cash and cash equivalents include your checking and savings accounts, money market funds, share accounts at credit unions, and similar accounts.

Retirement/Employment Related Plans

Retirement plans include employer-sponsored pension or profit-sharing plans, 401(k) (company savings) plans, KEOGH or SEP (Simplified Employee Pension) programs, IRAs, deferred compensation plans, and ESOPs (employee stock option plan).

Real Estate

Real estate includes your home, vacation home(s), and any investment real estate, such as rental properties or apartments. If you have not had an appraisal or market analysis of your real estate done within the past two years, you can use property tax statements as a guide. Property tax statements often understate the market value of the real estate. A general rule of thumb is to increase the property tax value by 10% to obtain an estimated market value of your property. However, check with your county tax assessor's office to determine how it calculates property values.

Of course, if you have made significant improvements to your real estate, such as room additions, remodeling, or upgrades, you should take the same into account. Remodeling and improvements do not increase the value of the property on a dollar-for-dollar basis. To avoid overstating the value, increase the market value by 75% of the cost of the remodeling and improvements. For instance, if you spent $3,000 to put ceramic tile in your kitchen, $3,000 to remodel your bathroom, and $5,000 to replace your windows, you should increase the value of your real estate by $7,500, instead of $10,000.

Life Insurance

Many life insurance policies do not have a *cash value*. Individual term and group term life insurance policies only provide a *death benefit*. While the death benefits of these policies do not affect your net worth, the death benefit increases the value of your estate for estate and inheritance tax purposes. Because the WORKSHEET is intended to assist you with determining whether your living trust must be designed to include estate tax savings provisions, it is important that the death benefits from life insurance policies are included.

If you have credit life insurance that will pay off your mortgage upon your death, include a conservative estimate of the death benefit of such a policy. Remember, credit life insurance benefits decrease as the outstanding balance of the loan decreases.

Do not include accidental death or dismemberment policies on the WORKSHEET. The likelihood of receiving such benefits is minimal, and including such benefits in your net worth calculation would unnecessarily overstate your net worth.

Whole, universal, and variable life policies have a cash value. This cash value should be included on the *Inventory*. In addition, if you have taken loans against the policy, the loan should be taken into account in determining the net cash value of the policy.

The WORKSHEET *Summary* section has a separate line in which you can include the death benefits from life insurance policies to determine the net worth of your estate after your death.

Business Interests

If you own interest in a business, include the value of your ownership interest. This may be the value of common stock in a corporation, units in a limited liability company, or general or limited partnership interests in a limited partnership. If you operate an unincorporated business, such as a sole proprietorship, general partnership, or joint venture, include the value of your share of the net worth of the business.

Personal Property

Personal property includes furniture, household goods, automobiles, recreational vehicles (motor homes, boats, ATVs, etc.), clothing, furs, jewelry, tools, artwork, antiques, collectibles, and many other items. If you have items that are separately listed on your homeowners insurance policy, such as jewelry, artwork, antiques, or for which you have a separate insurance policy, use the value for which you have these items insured.

Miscellaneous Assets

Promissory notes, annuities, oil and gas royalties, leasehold interests, and investments in commodities, including gold and silver, should be listed in this section.

Identify Your Liabilities

Many attorneys and financial planners calculate net worth without regard to most debts and liabilities owed by their client. Typically, the only debts that are taken into account are mortgages on real estate. Such an omission can significantly overstate a client's net worth. For example, many people have student loan obligations that exceed $50,000.00. Credit card debt can often exceed the amount of a car loan. In addition, personal loans—whether secured or unsecured—can be significant. To calculate an accurate sum for your net worth, complete the section on the WORKSHEET that details liabilities.

Calculate Your Net Worth

Now that you have identified your assets and liabilities, subtract the amount of your liabilities from the value of your assets to determine your net worth. Keep in mind that your net worth will fluctuate almost daily. This reflects things like the change in the value of your investments and the reduction in loan obligations.

The process of determining your net worth gives you insight as to the type of living trust you should establish. As time passes and your financial situation changes, you will need to revisit your net worth and, if necessary, update your living trust to reflect your new financial position. For example, when you first read this book, you may determine that your net worth does not support a living trust that includes estate tax planning. As time goes by and the value of your estate increases, you may need to revise your living trust to include such planning.

NOTE: *A second* WORKSHEET *is included in Appendix D.*

Net Worth Worksheet

Inventory

Type of Account	# of Shares/ Units	Date(s) Acquired	Cost	Current Market Value*	Husband	Wife
INVESTMENTS						
Stocks						
TOTAL						
Bonds						
TOTAL						
Mutual Funds						
TOTAL						
CDs						
TOTAL						

Net Worth Worksheet
Inventory

Type of Account	# of Shares/ Units	Date(s) Acquired	Cost	Current Market Value*	Husband	Wife
US Bonds						
TOTAL						
US Treasury Notes/Bills						
TOTAL						
CASH						
Checking						
TOTAL						
Savings						
TOTAL						
Money Market						
TOTAL						

Net Worth Worksheet

Inventory

Type of Account	# of Shares/ Units	Date(s) Acquired	Cost	Current Market Value*	Husband	Wife
RETIREMENT PLANS						
Pension/ Profit Shg.						
TOTAL						
401 (k)						
TOTAL						
Keogh/SEP						
TOTAL						
IRAs						
TOTAL						
DEFERRED COMPENSATION						
TOTAL						
ESOP						
TOTAL						
REAL ESTATE						
Home						
Vacation Home						

Net Worth Worksheet
Inventory

Type of Account	# of Shares/ Units	Date(s) Acquired	Cost	Current Market Value*	Husband	Wife
Rental Properties						
TOTAL						
Life Insurance						
Group Term						
Whole Life						
Universal Life						
Variable Life						
TOTAL						
Business Interests						
Corporation						
Sole Prop.						
Ltd. Pshps.						
TOTAL						
Personal Property						
Autos						
Vehicles						
Furnishings						
Jewelry/ Furs						
Artwork						
Antiques						
Collections						
Other						
TOTAL						

Net Worth Worksheet
Inventory

Type of Account	# of Shares/ Units	Date(s) Acquired	Cost	Current Market Value*	Husband	Wife
Misc. Prop.						
Oil & Gas Royalties						
Leases						
Notes Receivable						
Annuities						
Commodity Investments						
TOTAL						

TOTAL ASSETS $_____ $_____ $_____

Liability

Type of Loan	Lender	Balance Due*	Husband	Wife
Home Mortgage				
Home Equity				
Vacation Home Mortgage				
Personal Loans				
Automobile				
Vehicles				
Education Loans				
Life Insurance				
Credit Cards				
Income Taxes				
TOTAL				

TOTAL ASSETS $_____ $_____ $_____

*This column should represent the combined value of the asset/liability. The columns for Husband and Wife reflect the assets that are titled in their individual names. If the investment/account/liability is owned jointly, one-half of the combined value should be included in each column.

Net Worth Summary

ASSETS:

INVESTMENTS:
Stocks _____

Bonds _____

Mutual Funds _____

CDs _____

US Bonds _____

US Treasury Bills/Notes _____

TOTAL $_____

CASH:
Checking _____

Savings _____

Money Market _____

TOTAL $_____

RETIREMENT PLANS:
Pension/Profit Sharing _____

401(k) _____

Keogh/SEP _____

IRA _____

Deferred Compensation _____

ESOP _____

TOTAL $_____

REAL ESTATE:
Primary Residence _____

Vacation Residence _____

Rental Properties _____

TOTAL $_____

LIFE INSURANCE: (Cash Value)
Whole/Universal/Variable Life _____

BUSINESS INTERESTS:
Corporation/Sole Proprietorship/Limited Partnership _____

PERSONAL PROPERTY:

Automobiles _____

Other Vehicles _____

Household Furnishings/Personal Effects _____

Jewelry/Furs _____

Artwork _____

Antiques _____

Collectibles _____

Other _____

TOTAL $_____

MISCELLANEOUS PROPERTY:

Oil & Gas Royalties   _____

Leases _____

Notes Receivable _____

Annuities _____

Commodities _____

TOTAL $_____

TOTAL ASSETS $_____

LIABILITIES:

Mortgage–Primary Residence _____

Mortgage–Vacation Residence _____

Mortgage–Rental Properties _____

Home Equity Loans _____

Personal Loans _____

Automobile _____

Other Vehicles _____

Education _____

Life Insurance _____

Credit Cards _____

Income Taxes _____

TOTAL LIABILITIES $_____

NET WORTH (ASSETS Minus LIABILITIES) $_____

NET WORTH
INCLUDING LIFE INSURANCE DEATH BENEFITS $_____

Personal Contacts

ACCOUNTANT

Name:_____ Address:_____

Company:_____ Telephone: _____

Email:_____

ATTORNEY

Name:_____ Address:_____

Company:_____ Telephone: _____

Email:_____

BANKER

Name:_____ Address:_____

Company:_____ Telephone: _____

Email:_____

CLERGY

Name:_____ Address:_____

Religious Organization: _____ Telephone: _____

Email:_____

FINANCIAL PLANNER

Name:_____ Address:_____

Company:_____ Telephone: _____

Email:_____

INVESTMENT MANAGER

Name:_____ Address:_____

Company:_____ Telephone: _____

Email:_____

PERSONAL REPRESENATIVE OF ESTATE

Name:_____ Address:_____

Company:_____ Telephone: _____

Email:_____

STOCKBROKER

Name:_____ Address:_____

Company:_____ Telephone: _____

Email:_____

SUCCESSOR TRUSTEE(S)

Name:_____   Address:_____

Company:_____   Telephone: _____

                                                         Email:_____

Name:_____   Address:_____

Company:_____   Telephone: _____

                                                         Email:_____

Name:_____   Address:_____

Company:_____   Telephone: _____

                                                         Email:_____

INSURANCE AGENTS

Automobile

Name:_____   Address:_____

Company:_____   Telephone: _____

                                                         Email:_____

Disability

Name:_____   Address:_____

Company:_____   Telephone: _____

                                                         Email:_____

Homeowners

Name:_____   Address:_____

Company:_____   Telephone: _____

                                                         Email:_____

Life

Name:_____   Address:_____

Company:_____   Telephone: _____

                                                         Email:_____

PHYSICIANS

Name:_____   Address:_____

Company:_____   Telephone: _____

                                           Email:_____

Name:_____   Address:_____

Company:_____   Telephone: _____

                                           Email:_____

Name:_____   Address:_____

Company:_____   Telephone: _____

                                           Email:_____

OTHER

Name:_____   Address:_____

Company:_____   Telephone: _____

                                           Email:_____

Name:_____   Address:_____

Company:_____   Telephone: _____

                                           Email:_____

Name:_____   Address:_____

Company:_____   Telephone: _____

                                           Email:_____

Chapter 6:
Creating Your Living Trust
Putting It All into Action

A living trust is created by a written document that is clear and specific. It does not have to contain fancy legal terms. The living trust document will serve as the road map describing how you want your assets to be distributed during your lifetime and after your death. You need to identify the trustees, the beneficiaries, and the trust assets.

When you write your trust, it is important to identify each of the parties to the trust—the grantor, trustee, and beneficiaries—so that it is absolutely clear who they are.

In order to create a valid trust, the trust document must be signed by you and the trustee. Although not required in all states, the trust should be notarized by a notary public, particularly if you plan to transfer real estate to the trust. Because a trust is not legally created until assets are transferred to it, you should plan to transfer property to the trust when you sign the document. Often, grantors attach a $10.00 bill to the trust document to satisfy this requirement. (Chapter 7 contains a detailed discussion of how to fund your trust.)

Before you create your living trust, take a few moments to read Chapter 5 and complete the NET WORTH WORKSHEET. This worksheet will help you collect all of the information you need to create and fund your trust. The worksheet will also be helpful to your family because it should identify all of your assets, which ultimately saves your family the time-consuming process of collecting such information after your death. If you find that your total assets, including life insurance benefits and retirement plan benefits, exceed the amount of the applicable credit amount, and you wish to minimize your estate taxes, read Chapters 6 and 8.

Several basic living trust forms are included in this book. Forms 7, 8, and 9 are designed for an unmarried individual. Forms 11 and 14 are designed for use by married individuals. The provisions contained in these forms are the most popular among persons interested in establishing a living trust. Of course, the distribution provisions within the trust documents can be changed to reflect your individual intentions, and other forms with additional provisions are also included.

The Trustee

When you create your living trust, you will be the initial trustee. This permits you to maintain control over your assets.

It is important to name at least one—and preferably two—successor trustees. One or both of these successors will step into your shoes in the event you cannot serve as trustee. Generally, for married couples, the spouse is named as the successor trustee. Adult children, parents, brothers, sisters, or other trusted family members may also be named as a successor trustee.

Some people prefer to name an institution, such as a bank or trust company, to serve as successor trustee if all of the persons named in the trust are unable to serve as trustee. However, you should check the institution's fee schedule. Some corporate trustees charge fees that are outrageously high and some will not accept a trust if it does not have a minimum value.

A trust is a contract between the grantor and trustee. The trustee agrees to be bound by the terms of the trust and act in accordance with the wishes of the grantor as set forth in the document. This is a tremendous responsibility. It is important that you talk to the successor trustees and get their permission to name them as trustees. If all of the successor trustees you name refuse or fail to serve, the court would have to appoint a successor trustee. The person or institution appointed by the court may not be one you would have chosen. If an institution is appointed to serve, the fee it charges will reduce the amount of trust assets that will pass to your beneficiaries.

The forms included in this book contain language that permits the trust bene-ficiaries to designate a successor trustee if the persons you name fail or cease to serve as trustee. This language is intended to avoid the court's involvement in the selection of a successor trustee.

If you decide to name two or more individuals to serve as trustee together, to be *co-trustees,* generally all individuals must agree before any investments or distributions can be made. Some states require that only the agreement of a majority of the trustees is required. Some grantors give one trustee veto or tie-breaking power.

The forms included in this book contain language permitting action to be taken by the vote of a majority of the trustees serving.

Sometimes a person you want to designate to serve as trustee may have a lot of knowledge about investments and property management, but may not be responsive to the needs to others—namely, the trust beneficiaries. In contrast, you may have in mind a person who is very understanding about the needs of the beneficiaries, but who has no investment management skills. You can name both of these people to serve as trustees and designate the primary role that each will play as trustee. The investment-wise individual may have the final word with regard to transactions involving the investment of trust property, and the other individual may be given the final word with regard to the nature, amount, and timing of distributions to the beneficiaries.

Once you have identified who will serve as trustee and successor trustee, the trust agreement must set forth the duties and responsibilities of the trustees.

Duties of a Trustee

Each state has laws that impose certain duties on trustees. If the trustee does not fulfill these duties, he or she is said to have *breached* his or her duty and can be sued by the grantor, the beneficiaries, or both. If the trustee loses the lawsuit, he or she can be ordered to pay money to the grantor or beneficiaries to recover losses the trust suffered while he or she served as trustee. The trustee can also be ordered to pay the attorney's fees and court costs of the grantor and benefi-ciaries. Finally, he or she can also be removed as trustee.

Possessing and controlling trust assets. A trustee may collect and take pos-session of trust property as quickly as possible after becoming a trustee. This does not mean that the trustee must take actual physical possession of trust assets. He or she must, however, take whatever steps are necessary to take control of the assets. For instance, the trustee does not have to take actual possession of the stock certificates held by a brokerage firm. Instead, the trustee must make certain that legal title to the stock is transferred into the name of the trust and that the trustee is authorized to deal with the stock.

Preserving trust assets. After the trustee has located and taken control of the trust assets, the trustee must preserve and protect the trust assets. The trustee must make certain that the trust assets are not wasting away or in danger of losing value. For instance, if the trust assets include an interest in a family business, the trustee must make certain that the business is being managed appropriately and that there is no interruption in the business. You certainly would not want to lose customers, income, or the reputation that the business has developed.

Investing trust assets. The trustee must invest and maintain the trust assets so that they produce income for the benefit of the beneficiaries. A trust is not established with the idea that the trust assets will be idle and not produce income that can be given to the beneficiaries. Traditionally, almost every state requires that a trustee adhere to the *prudent person rule* with regard to investing trust assets. The prudent person rule requires the trustee to invest, reinvest, supervise, and manage trust property using the judgment and care that persons of ordinary prudence, discretion, and intelligence would use with regard to their own property.

Trustees are generally authorized to acquire and maintain every kind of property (real, personal, and mixed) and every kind of investment (including stocks, bonds, securities, real estate partnerships, and the like).

Under the prudent person rule, a trustee *should*:
   ◆ diversify the trust assets among may types of investments such as stocks and bonds;
   ◆ diversify the trust among various industries;
   ◆ consider current income as well as long-term increase in value of the asset since the beneficiaries of income and those who will eventually receive trust principal may not be the same; and,
   ◆ seek professional advice for initial investment and continuing review of investments.

Under the prudent person rule, a trustee *should not*:

- ◆ invest in risky ventures hoping to make a quick fortune;
- ◆ lend trust property to him- or herself, except at fair value and with the consent of the beneficiary (or all beneficiaries);
- ◆ buy assets from the trust except at appraised value;
- ◆ continue to hold investments that a prudent person would no longer hold;
- ◆ continue to hold investments transferred to the trust without independently investigating their quality; and,
- ◆ delegate investment decisions to others. It is acceptable to seek advice from others, but ultimately, the trustee must make the actual investment decisions.

While most states still use the prudent person rule, some states are adopting the *prudent expert rule*. This rule requires the trustee to use—

the care, skill, prudence, and diligence under the circumstances then prevailing that a prudent person acting in a like capacity and familiar with such matters would use in the conduct of an enterprise of a like character and with like aims.

This may result in a greater likelihood of someone being reluctant to serve as a trustee.

With most of the forms in this book, you or your spouse will be serving as trustee, or alternatively, will be closely supervising the trustee. Given that, there should be few, if any, problems with regard to the trust investments. In all of the forms included in this book, the trustee is given broad discretion with regard to investment authority. The trustee—by state law—will be bound by the prudent person rule or the prudent expert rule.

If you wish to restrict the investment power of the trustee, you may want to add a provision or do a trust amendment that contains specific investment guidelines for the trustee. These guidelines could limit investments to stock in Fortune 500 companies and bonds with a minimum credit rating, or prohibit investment in real estate ventures. However, you must be careful and try to think into the future when you limit a trustee's investment powers. The trustee needs some degree of flexibility to take into account the changing economic circumstances and investment situations.

Example: *David established a trust in the early 1980s when certificates of deposit were earning as much as 15%. David limited the trustee's investment power to certificates of deposit and any other financial instrument backed by the U.S. government with comparable interest rates. Because interest rates on CDs are now yielding less than 5%, they would no longer be a good investment.*

Any restriction on the type of investments a trustee can make must be included in the trust document and must be very specific. If you do not leave clear instructions, the trustee can unknowingly undermine your intentions.

Informing beneficiaries. The trustee must also inform the trust beneficiaries of the existence of the trust and explain its provisions. To do that, the trustee must understand all of the trust's provisions. Because the trust is a private document between the grantor and the trustee (who is usually the grantor also), the beneficiaries will often not be aware of the trust's existence until after the grantor dies or becomes incapacitated.

Accounting. The trustee has a responsibility to report to the beneficiaries and keep them informed of all of the trust transactions. This includes reporting all assets received, sold, or exchanged by the trust, any income earned, any expenses incurred by the trust, and any distributions made to beneficiaries. The date, amount, and a short explanation of each transaction should be included in the reports. These reports can be done on a monthly, quarterly, or annual basis. You may include a specific instruction in the trust as to how frequently these reports must be given or you may give the trustee the discretion to determine the frequency of such reports.

Keeping trust assets separate. Importantly, the trustee must keep the trust assets separate from his or her own assets. The trust assets must be clearly identified. Titles to items such as bank accounts and stocks should have the name of the trustee, *as trustee*, on them. Income earned by the trust assets must be kept separate as well. Failure to do this is called *commingling* and is one of the primary reasons lawsuits are brought against trustees.

Trustees should never borrow assets from the trust, sell assets to the trust, or purchase or lease assets from the trust for his or her own purposes, unless it is at fair market value with full disclosure to the beneficiaries and with their written consent.

Making distributions. The trustee must make distributions to the trust beneficiaries as provided in the trust document. The trustee is not allowed to substitute his or her judgment for the terms of the trust. If the trust permits the trustee to use his or her discretion in making distributions to the beneficiaries, the trustee must be reasonable in his or her decisions. For instance, it would be inappropriate for a trustee to favor one beneficiary over another when making distributions simply because the trustee does not like the beneficiary or does not agree with how the beneficiary behaves.

Payment of Expenses, Claims, and Taxes. The trustee must pay the expenses of administering the trust. This includes investment or brokerage fees if the trustee uses an investment or financial advisor to assist the trustee in evaluating trust investments and selling trust assets. If a creditor of the grantor presents a claim to the trustee for payment, the trustee must investigate the claim to determine its validity. If the claim is valid, the trustee is under an obligation to pay the claim. The trustee must also pay any taxes, whether income or gift, attributable to the trust assets or distributions from the trust.

The forms in this book contain language that authorizes and directs the trustee to pay any expenses, claims, or taxes against the grantor's *probate* estate if the personal representative of the estate makes a request for payment.

Trustee Powers

Each state has specific laws giving trustees powers to administer the trust. As creator of the trust, you can broaden the scope of those powers or you may restrict the powers. For example, you may wish to prohibit the trustee from selling the vacation home you inherited from your parents.

The powers often given to trustees under state law include:
- invest and sell trust assets;
- collect trust income and rents;
- invest in stocks and real estate;
- open bank accounts;
- join in litigation to protect the trust assets;

- hire professionals, such as accountants and attorneys, to assist the trustee in fulfilling his or her duties;
- operate a business that is part of the trust assets;
- borrow money on behalf of the trust or renew any existing mortgage or other indebtedness;
- collect life insurance proceeds from policies made payable to the trust; and,
- make appropriate elections to receive distributions from retirement plans.

You can grant a trustee special powers, such as the power to distribute funds to a beneficiary before the time designated in the trust agreement, if the trustee believes that the beneficiary is in need of the funds.

Often, it is advisable to include a provision in the trust agreement allowing a trustee to terminate the trust and distribute the remaining trust assets to the income beneficiaries if the trust has become economically too small to continue. Additionally, trustees should be empowered to merge the trust with another trust that has the same beneficiaries and the same terms. This often occurs when a husband and wife have living trusts that each provide upon their death that their children will be beneficiaries of the trusts. It would be less expensive and administratively more efficient to combine the husband's and wife's trusts into one trust for the children.

Removing a Trustee

Sometimes it is important to be able to remove a trustee without having to involve a court. Generally, the trust document gives the grantor the right to remove the trustee and name an alternate trustee. You may wish to include a provision in the trust giving your beneficiaries or a third party the power to remove a trustee if the trustee is stealing from the trust, is not fulfilling his or her duties under the law, or is not following the terms of the trust agreement.

A trustee may also voluntarily choose to quit. If your trust does not contain instructions on how a trustee can resign, the trustee must obtain the approval of the court to resign. The beneficiaries cannot simply agree to accept the trustee's resignation.

Incapacity

The trust must contain a clear definition of *incapacity* and the resulting effect on who will serve as . A definition of incapacity in the trust will avoid the need of a formal court determination of a trustee's incapacity. When a trustee is determined to be incapacitated, a successor trustee will automatically step in the trustee's shoes and continue the administration of the trust. If a definition of incapacity is not included in the trust, some of the benefits of probate avoidance are lost. A court declaration of incapacity of a trustee can be costly and time consuming, and the terms of the living trust may become part of the court's public record, shattering the privacy aspect of the trust.

The Beneficiaries

When you establish your living trust, you must decide who will be the beneficiaries of the trust, how much each beneficiary will receive, and when the beneficiaries will receive their gifts from the trust.

While you are alive, you will be the primary beneficiary of your living trust. You may also wish to name your spouse and minor children as beneficiaries while you are alive. Then, if you become incapacitated, the successor trustee can make distributions not only for your care, but also for the care of your spouse and minor children. This is particularly important if you are the primary income earner in the family. Your trust assets will earn income that can assist your family as it adjusts to the loss of your paycheck.

You may name beneficiaries to receive income only, principal only (principal is the property that you transfer to the trust), or both income and principal. After your death, you may wish to give all of the trust property to your spouse with the intention that he or she assume your role and provide for himself or herself and your children. If your spouse has established a living trust of his or her own, the trust assets in your trust can be distributed to your spouse's living trust.

Spouse as Beneficiary

Most married couples name their surviving spouse as the primary beneficiary of their living trust after their death. There are several options available to accomplish this result. Some of the options take into account—and may be driven by—estate tax implications.

Outright Distribution. If the combined value of your estate and the estate of your spouse does not exceed $1.5 million (for 2004 and 2005, see chart on p.32 for years after 2005), there is no estate tax reason to keep the assets in trust after your death. You may wish to distribute the assets in your living trust to your spouse outright or to his or her living trust. This permits your spouse the greatest flexibility in managing and using those assets.

However, even if there is not an estate tax reason to keep your assets in trust, there are a number of non-tax reasons to keep the assets in trust after your death. The primary reason for keeping assets in trust is to retain control of the disposition of the assets after your death. If you keep the assets in trust, you can make certain that the assets remaining after providing for your spouse will be distributed to your intended beneficiaries. These beneficiaries may be your children, parents, siblings, or others. This control can be extremely important if you and your spouse have children from previous marriages. It may be your intention that your assets be available to your surviving spouse, but upon his or her death go to your children and not your spouse's children.

Another reason to keep the assets in trust rather than distributing them outright is to protect the assets from the creditors of the beneficiaries. A basic trust principal is that if assets are held in trust for a beneficiary and the beneficiary does not have uncontrolled access to the trust assets, creditors of a beneficiary cannot force payment of the trust assets to satisfy credit obligations. If a beneficiary has experienced credit difficulties in the past or is in a profession that is subject to litigation (such as attorneys, doctors, engineers, etc.), it may be wise to keep the beneficiary's inheritance sheltered from creditors and litigants.

The forms in this book include a *Spendthrift Provision* that prevents a beneficiary from pledging trust assets to and protects the assets from the claims of the beneficiary's individual creditors.

Family Trust. If the value of your estate exceeds the applicable credit amount ($1.5 million in 2004-2005), at least the amount of the applicable credit amount should be set aside in a *Family Trust* rather than distributed outright to the surviving spouse. (This type of tax planning is discussed in Chapter 8.) Your surviving spouse and/or your children can be beneficiaries of the Family Trust and be entitled to receive income, principal, or both from the Family Trust.

Marital Trust. To the extent the value of your estate exceeds the applicable credit amount, such excess can be kept in a separate trust of which your surviving spouse is the sole beneficiary. The assets placed in this *Marital Trust* will not be subject to estate tax at your death because the Marital Trust is designed to qualify for the unlimited marital deduction. Upon your spouse's death, the value of the assets in the Marital Trust will be included in calculating the value of your spouse's estate.

To qualify for the unlimited marital deduction, the Marital Trust must pay all of the income from the trust to the surviving spouse. The surviving spouse must be the only beneficiary of the Marital Trust. In addition, if the surviving spouse serves as trustee of the Marital Trust, he or she must be limited to making distributions of principal only for his or her health, education, maintenance, or support.

Children as Beneficiaries

If you are unmarried or if your spouse has sufficient assets to provide for him- or herself, you may wish to distribute the remaining trust assets to your children upon your death. Again, there are several options available to accomplish this result.

Outright Distribution. You may wish to distribute the assets remaining in your living trust to your children outright and free of trust. However, as previously discussed with regard to an outright distribution to a spouse, there are important reasons to keep the assets in trust for the benefit of the children. In addition to protecting the trust assets from the claims of your children's creditors, keeping the assets in trust permits you further control of the ultimate distribution of the trust assets.

If your children are minors, there is a very important reason to avoid an outright distribution of your assets to your children. Under the laws of most states, if a minor chid receives an inheritance, the inheritance must be set aside in a custodial account that is subject to court supervision. A custodian of the property who is charged with the duty to manage the assets in the account and make distributions for the benefit of the minor children will be appointed. The list of permissible investments and grounds for distribution to the beneficiary are very restrictive. Once again, the courts are involved in the financial affairs of the beneficiaries that undermines the privacy of the beneficiaries and the efficiency of trust distributions. Additionally, under most state laws, a child's inheritance is distributed to the child upon attaining age 18. Most parents do not feel that their children are mature enough to manage and invest assets of any substantial value at age 18.

Children's Trust. If a trust is established for the benefit of your children, the trustee should be authorized to make distributions of income and principal for the health, education, maintenance, and support of the children. While the assets are held in trust, if medical or tuition bills need to be paid the trustee can make distributions either to the child or to the doctor or college. Generally, such discretionary distributions are limited to food, clothing, shelter, health care, education, special events (such as weddings), and major purchases (such as a car or home).

There are several options as to when final distributions of the trust property can be made to the children. The first option is to keep the assets in trust for the children throughout their lifetimes. This could mean the trust will be in operation for decades.

A second option to is make a single distribution of the assets to the child when the child attains a specified age or a specified event occurs such as graduation from college or marriage. Until the child attains that age or the event occurs, the trustee can make distributions of income and principal to or for the benefit of the child.

The third option is to stagger distributions of the trust principal. The trustee may be authorized to make principal distributions of specified amounts, whether a specific dollar amount or a percentage of the trust assets, at specified intervals. For example, you may provide that when the child attains age 21, one-third of the trust will be distributed to the child; when the child attains age 25, one-half of the balance of the trust assets will be distributed; and, when the child attains age 30, the balance of the trust assets will be distributed to the child. Throughout the term of the trust, the trustee will continue to make distributions of income and/or principal for the benefit of the child. This approach allows the trust to terminate over time while not sacrificing the needs of the child.

As you can see, the planning options are limited only by your creativity.

> **Warning:** I warn clients that care should be taken to avoid making distributions contingent upon the happening of a certain event. For instance, restrictions such as college graduation or the birth of a grandchild may keep a child from ever receiving the trust property. Children are different from each other and even from their parents. You should not put restrictions in your trust that force your child to live up to expectations that cannot be changed after you have died.

The forms in this book provide that a separate trust is established for the benefit of each child. You may wish to consider different distribution options for each of your children. This may be especially important if you have a disabled child who has special needs.

Issues Applicable to All Beneficiaries

There are several issues or rules of law that apply whether the beneficiary of a trust is the surviving spouse, children, family members, or others.

Rule against Perpetuities. If you decide to keep property in trust for the benefit of your children or beneficiaries other than your spouse, you should be aware of a rule governing the length of time that property can be held in trust. This rule is called the *rule against perpetuities*. The rule prohibits a trust grantor from controlling the distribution of trust property for an extended period of time.

To prevent trusts from extending several generations and keeping family wealth tied up for extremely long periods of time, the rule against perpetuities states that a trust cannot keep property for longer than the life of any person living when the trust was created plus twenty-one years. At that time, the full ownership rights in the trust property must be given to the beneficiaries. Most people do not have to concern themselves with this rule because most trust documents (including the forms in this book) contain a clause to make sure that the rule against perpetuities is not violated.

Example: *Tom creates a trust for the benefit of his children. When Tom dies, his children are ages 10 and 15. The trust can remain in existence for the lifetimes of the children. Upon the death of the last child, the trust must terminate after 21 years.*

Death of a Beneficiary before Distribution. What happens if a child dies before you do or dies before his or her share of the trust is completely distributed? Most people would like their grandchildren to be provided for and inherit the property their children would have received. Attorneys commonly use either the phrase *per capita* or *per stirpes* in the clause specifying how the property will be distributed.

Per Capita. *Per capita* distributions are *pro rata* or *share and share alike* distributions. That means that all of the surviving descendants, regardless of generation, get equal shares of the trust property.

Example: *Michael has four adult children: George, Tom, Judy, and Karen. Karen has three children and dies before Michael. At Michael's death, his living trust provides that the trust property is to be distributed to his descendants per capita. The trust property will be distributed in six equal shares—one for each living child of Michael and one for each of Karen's children.*

Per Stirpes. *Per stirpes* distributions are by *representation*, or literally, *by the root*. This means that if one of your children dies before you do, the amount that child would have received is divided equally among that child's direct descendants.

Example: *With the same facts as the previous example, except at Michael's death the trust property is to be distributed per stirpes. The trust property is divided into four equal shares—one for each of his children and one to be subdivided among Karen's three children.*

Specific Gifts

You may chose to leave certain assets to selected beneficiaries. For instance, you may want your oldest child to receive the vacation home that has been in the family for generations. You may want your daughter to receive a specific sum of money or a specific asset, such as all of the shares in ABC Corporation. These specific gifts should be set forth in the living trust with sufficient detail to make certain there will be no confusion when distributions must be made by the trustee.

Gifts of Tangible Personal Property

You may have specific intentions regarding gifts of certain items of tangible personal property. For instance, you may want your oldest daughter to receive your grandmother's wedding ring and your son to receive your antiques. Sometimes the list of specific gifts of tangible personal property may be lengthy. Rather than include all of the specific gifts in the trust agreement, you may leave a signed, written memorandum in addition to your living trust that lists the specific items of your tangible personal property to be distributed. Your living trust must, however, refer to this memorandum.

Forms included in this book refer to the memorandum. If you choose not to leave specific gifts, you need not complete the memorandum. If you wish to change the specific gifts, you can simply change the memorandum and do not have to sign a new living trust document. The memorandum should not be used for real estate, stocks, bonds, or anything other than tangible personal items. Specific gifts like these should be detailed in your living trust agreement.

Charitable Beneficiaries

If you would like to leave a gift to your church or a charitable organization, you can include a provision in your living trust giving that organization a specified dollar amount or a percentage of the assets in the living trust. Remember, your living trust acts as a substitute for a will, so any gifts you would have included in your will can be included in your living trust.

Special Circumstances

There may be special circumstances that require your living trust to contain unique provisions. For instance, you may wish to provide for a disabled or special needs child or you may have a child who is financially irresponsible and needs more restrictions on his or her share. You may have children from two marriages and wish to provide for them differently. Your parents may depend on you for support and would require continued financial assistance after your death. If you have a special circumstance, your living trust can have provisions added to meet your situation's specific needs.

Gifts to Pets

Except in California and Tennessee, you cannot leave property to your pets. This is because a pet is property and property cannot own other property. If you wish to have a pet cared for after your death, you should make arrangements with a person you trust and leave a specific bequest of money to that person for that purpose. Otherwise, you might be able to sign up for a *life care contract* with an animal shelter, refuge, or a veterinarian.

Executing Your Living Trust

Now that you have designed your living trust by choosing your successor trustees, your beneficiaries, the trustee powers and duties, and the distribution pattern of the trust property, you must sign the document as both grantor and trustee. Three witnesses should watch you sign the document and sign the document themselves. (Most states only require two witnesses, but a few states require three.) All of this should be done in the presence of a notary public, who should sign and notarize the living trust. (Notary requirements may vary from state to state, but the notary public you use should know how to modify the forms to meet these requirements.)

To get started, you should fund your trust with $10 by attaching a $10 bill to the last page of the trust document. Now you are ready to fund your trust. After you have established a bank account in the name of your living trust, you can deposit the $10 into the account.

Amending the Living Trust

At various times during your life, events may occur that may impact your estate plan, particularly the terms of your living trust. Significant life events may require that your living trust be amended partially or revised in its entirety.

The following is a list of changes in family personal relationships, financial situations, and changes outside the family that may have an affect on provisions in your estate planning documents.

Review this list at least annually to determine whether any of the events have occurred since the creation of your living trust. If any of the events affect the living trust or any of the ancillary documents discussed in Chapter 9, such documents should be amended or, if necessary, revoked. Form 28 in Appendix D is an **Amendment to the Living Trust** that enables you to delete provisions from your living trust that are no longer applicable and permits replacement provisions, if necessary. Form 29 in the appendix is an **Amendment to the Living Trust** that permits the addition of provisions in the living trust.

Changes in Family/Personal Relationships

Changes in relationships between the grantor and individuals who may be beneficiaries or successor trustees may have a serious impact on the living trust.

Several of the most significant changes in family and personal relationships that may impact the living trust include:

- divorce (dissolution of marriage) of the original grantor of the trust;
- divorce (dissolution of marriage) of the original trustee or successor trustee;
- death of spouse of grantor/trustee/beneficiary;
- marriage of grantor/trustee/beneficiary;
- births of children, grandchildren, or other beneficiaries;
- changes regarding children, grandchildren, or other beneficiaries, such as:
  - disability;
  - substance abuse;
  - marriage;
  - divorce; and,
  - significant increase/decrease in wealth.
- marriage of the grantor's child;
- adoption of a child by the grantor's child;
- second marriages by children or other beneficiaries;
- attitude changes by children, beneficiaries, or successor trustee toward the grantor; and,
- financial irresponsibility of children, beneficiaries, or successor trustee.

Changes in Financial or Personal Condition of Grantor

Events may occur in the life of the grantor of a living trust that impact its terms. Such events include:

- significant increase/decrease in net worth;
- change in employment;
- change in business interests (*e.g.,* ownership in corporations, sole proprietorships, limited liability companies, or limited partnerships);
- move to a new state;
- acquisition of property in a state other than the state of personal residence;
- significant change in health; and,
- retirement from employment or business.

Changes in the Personal or Financial Condition of Trustees or Beneficiaries

Events may occur in the life of the trustees or beneficiaries of a living trust that impact its terms, such as:

- significant increase/decrease in net worth;
- death or disability;
- move to new state/possible residence problem;
- significant change in health; and,
- financial irresponsibility.

External Changes

Changes may occur in state or federal law that may affect provisions of a living trust. These changes include:

- material changes in local, state, and federal tax laws (income, estate, and inheritance taxes);
- material changes in federal gift tax laws; and,
- material changes in will, trust, and probate laws.

Generally, an amendment to the living trust need not be notarized. However, if the specific terms of the amendment affect the distribution of real estate that is owned by the living trust, the amendment should be notarized and witnessed.

Revocation of the Living Trust

On rare occasion, events may occur that make a living trust unnecessary. Such a situation may occur if there is a need to plan for medical assistance. Planning to qualify for medical assistance under programs such as Medicaid requires arranging the financial and personal affairs of a person in a manner that is contrary to many of the provisions of a living trust. (Appendix D includes a form by which a living trust can be revoked.)

It is important to remember that if a living trust is revoked, all of the assets that had been transferred to the living trust must be transferred back to the grantor of the living trust. In addition, any beneficiary designations that had been changed to name the living trust as the primary or contingent beneficiary must be changed to name one or more individuals as primary or contingent beneficiary. This includes life insurance policies, retirement plans, and annuities. If the important step of *unfunding* the living trust is not taken, the assets may be entangled in the probate process upon the death or disability of the grantor of the living trust.

Chapter 7:
Funding Your Living Trust

If You've Got It, Fund It!

The most common mistake committed by attorneys, living trust promoters, and people who create their own living trust is failing to fund the living trust. The primary purpose for creating your living trust is to avoid probate during your lifetime (such as during an incapacity) and after your death. The advantages of a living trust cannot be realized unless and until your assets are transferred to your living trust.

Many clients mistakenly believe that if they list their assets on a schedule and attach it to the living trust, they have funded their trust. Listing assets on a schedule does not transfer title of the assets into the name of the trust. Remember, a trust is an arrangement for the ownership of property. When property is transferred to a trust, legal title to the assets is vested in the trustee. Legal title allows the trustee to manage, administer, and distribute the trust assets. Specific steps must be taken to transfer legal title of the assets to your living trust.

Deciding which Property to Transfer

The first question most people have about funding their living trust is *how much property should I transfer to my trust?* There is no rule of thumb as to how much or what property you should transfer to your living trust. Obviously, the more property transferred to your living trust, the less property that is subject to the expense and delay of probate upon your incapacity or after your death. Ideally, all of your property should be transferred to your living trust to take advantage of all of its benefits.

Because a living trust is a completely new concept to most people, some individuals choose to transfer assets to their living trust over a period of time. This gives them time to adjust to and become comfortable with their living trust. Keep in mind, however, that your living trust is amendable and revocable at any time. You have the power to withdraw assets from your living trust if you choose to do so. For this reason, it is recommended that all assets be transferred to your living trust. Later, if you are not comfortable with the living trust's ownership of some assets, you can withdraw them from the living trust. In the meantime, you have the benefit of probate avoidance in the event of your incapacity or death.

Often, it is advisable to keep some cash in a checking account that is a joint tenancy account with right of survivorship (JTWROS) or pay-on-death (POD) account. Grocery stores, department stores, and the like are not familiar with checks drawn on trust accounts and signed by trustees. Rather than deal with the hassles caused by a store clerk who hesitates or refuses to accept a trust check, it is advisable to keep at least one bank account out of the trust. Since the account is a JTWROS or POD account it will not be subject to probate upon your death.

Title

Assets transferred to your living trust must be retitled in the name of the trust. The basic title that is recommended for use in holding all assets in the trust is as follows.

___[YOUR NAME]___, Trustee of the ___[YOUR NAME]___ Living Trust, dated _____, 20_____.

Brokerage firms may request language similar to:

___[YOUR NAME]___, u/t/a dtd. ___/___/___, FBO _____

This indicates that you are acting under trust agreement (u/t/a) for benefit of (FBO) the named beneficiary. Each institution may require slightly different wording. However, the name of the trust, the name of the trustee, and the date on which the trust was created are normally all that is required.

Whenever you execute documents on behalf of your living trust and transact business on behalf of the Trust, you should sign your name:

[YOUR NAME], TRUSTEE

Taxpayer Identification Number

The institutions with whom you are dealing will ask you for a *federal tax iden-tification number* for your living trust. Because you are the grantor of the living trust as well as a trustee, your living trust is considered a *grantor trust* under the Internal Revenue Code and does not require a separate federal tax identification number. Your Social Security Number should be supplied to the institutions.

After your death, the successor trustee will be required to get a separate tax identification number for your living trust. This is done by completing **Form SS-4, Application for Employer Identification Number**. (see form 31, p.343.) If the terms of your living trust require the creation of a *Marital Trust* and a *Family Trust*, a separate tax identification number should be obtained for each trust. There are several ways to file Form SS-4: by mail, telephone, fax, or on the Internet. The most time-efficient method is the Internet. You can obtain a tax identification number as soon as you complete the online form.

Asset Ownership

As you prepare to transfer assets to your living trust, confirm the exact name in which the asset is titled. If you are married and you choose to equalize the estates to take advantage of the estate tax savings opportunities explained in Chapter 8, as you transfer assets to each spouse's living trust this equalization can be accomplished.

Transferring Assets to Your Living Trust

No matter what type of asset you transfer to your living trust, when you are deal-ing with a third party, such as a bank, brokerage firm, insurance company, or gov-ernment agency, you may be asked to provide a copy of the living trust agreement. It is not necessary to provide a copy of the entire trust agreement to such institu-tions. Instead, you can supply an **Affidavit of Trust**. (see form 27, p.335.)

The **Affidavit of Trust** provides the following information:
- the name and date of the living trust;
- name(s) of the trustee(s); and,
- pages of the trust agreement showing:
  - the name of the living trust;
  - the name of the initial trustee;
  - successor trustee provisions;

- ◆ trustee powers; and,
- ◆ the signature page.

The **Affidavit of Trust** is sworn to and signed by you, as grantor and trustee, in the presence of a notary public. This **Affidavit of Trust** provides third parties with sufficient information for their purposes and maintains the privacy of the personal provisions of the living trust, namely the identity of your beneficiaries and the manner of distribution to them.

It is advisable to have several **Affidavits of Trust** prepared and notarized so that you will have a sufficient number available to provide third parties and not be delayed in completing the transfer of assets into your living trust.

Tangible Personal Property

Tangible personal property includes furniture, household goods, personal effects, jewelry, automobiles, boats, gold, silver, and collectibles. These items can be transferred to your living trust by completing an **Assignment of Personal Property**. (see form 24, p.329.) With regard to automobiles, motor homes, and boats, you should check with the appropriate government agency to obtain and complete the appropriate registration form. When including any major asset such as an automobile, motor home, or boat on the *Assignment of Personal Property*, you should include the VIN for that asset as a clear means of identification.

> **Author's Advice:** Prior to transferring tangible personal property to your living trust, check with the company insuring the property. Confirm that the transfer of the property will not result in an increase in insurance premiums for vehicles, boats, or personal property insured under your homeowners policy.

If there are certain items of jewelry, antiques, collectibles, or precious metals (such as gold or silver) that are of significant value, it is recommended that such items be listed separately on the **Assignment of Personal Property**. They should be described in sufficient detail to identify them and, if possible, an estimated value of the asset should be included. If any item of personal property is separately insured on a homeowners policy or under a separate policy, such item should be separately listed on the **Assignment of Personal Property**.

It is also possible to place items such as jewelry, gold, silver, and collectibles in a safe deposit box registered in the name of your living trust. You can simply go to the bank and have new owner cards for the safe deposit box rewritten in the name of your living trust. Be sure, however, to have a successor trustee or another person designated on the card to have access to the safe deposit box in the event of your death. In some cases, banks have sealed a safe deposit box upon the death of the trustee. By having the successor trustee or another person designated on the card, access to the safe deposit box can be maintained after the death of the trustee.

Cash Accounts

Title-to-cash accounts, such as checking accounts, savings accounts, money market accounts, and certificates of deposit, whether held at a bank or other financial institution, are traditionally represented by the signature card for the account. An officer of the bank or financial institution will be able to provide you with new signature cards for these accounts. Institutional regulations will require appropriate documentation certifying the living trust and those authorized to act on its behalf. The **Affidavit of Trust** is sufficient for this purpose. (see form 27, p.335.) All of the current trustees should sign the signature card.

U.S. Savings Bonds

United States savings bonds, such as Series EE Bonds, should be retitled in the name of your living trust. Your bank will have the appropriate forms to make the transfer. The bonds will be reissued in the name of your living trust. There will be no change in the rate of interest or maturity date.

Real Estate

Whether the real estate is your personal residence, vacation home, or real estate held for investment purposes, it should be transferred to your living trust. Federal law prohibits a financial institution that holds a mortgage on your personal residence or vacation home from triggering the due-on-sale clause in the mortgage when the property is transferred to a revocable trust. This is true so long as the borrower is and remains a beneficiary and the transfer does not relate to a transfer of rights of occupancy in the property.

Real estate other than your principal residence or vacation home that is subject to indebtedness may create some transfer problems. The provisions of the mortgage or deed of trust should be reviewed carefully to determine whether a transfer will accelerate payment of indebtedness.

Transfer of real estate can be accomplished by a simple *quitclaim deed*. Such a deed does not require a determination of the nature and scope of your interest in the real estate. A quitclaim deed avoids the need to have a title opinion or a title insurance update performed.

Most transfers of real estate into your living trust will not result in a transfer tax. However, confirm this with your county property tax assessor. In addition, prior to transferring real estate to your living trust, you should be aware of any deed recording fees that may be assessed. You should also confirm that your title insurance will not be impaired by the transfer. Many insurance companies will require a new endorsement of your title policy.

If you own property in more than one state, the form of quitclaim deed necessary to transfer title may vary. You can obtain a sample form of a quitclaim deed recognized in your state from your local library. You can also contact the board of realtors to obtain a state-approved form of quitclaim deed.

In some states there is a *homestead exemption* for real estate taxes on your home. The exemption can result in significant real estate tax savings over the years. Once your homestead property is transferred to your living trust, you no longer own the property—your living trust has legal title to the property. Trusts generally do not qualify for the homestead exemption. However, most, if not all, states recognize that your living trust is your *alter ego* and the homestead exemption is not affected by the transfer of the property to your living trust. Again, confirm this with your county property tax assessor.

When you acquire additional real estate in the future, you can tell the title company to prepare and record title to the real estate in the name of your living trust. The title company will want to see a copy of the trust agreement to ensure that the trustee has the power to make mortgage payments, pay real estate taxes, make expenditures to maintain real estate, and other such necessities. Once again, the **Affidavit of Trust** is sufficient to satisfy the title company.

If you are having trouble with real estate transfers or if you own real estate outside your state of residence, contact an attorney who can assist you. The charge for this service should be nominal. Often, the fee paid to the attorney is well worth it because it can save you a lot of time and frustration.

Privately Held Securities

Privately held securities, such as stock in private corporations, limited liability companies, and limited partnerships, can be transferred to your living trust simply by having new stock or membership certificates prepared in the name of the living trust and surrendering the existing certificates.

Publicly Traded Stocks, Bonds, Securities, etc.

Many individuals own marketable securities that are held in a *street account* with a stock broker. These securities can be easily transferred into your living trust in two ways:

1. establish a street account in the name of your living trust and transfer the securities to that account or
2. retitle your existing account into the name of your living trust.

If the certificates to your individual marketable securities are in your name, these securities can be transferred to your living trust by registering the certificates to reflect the name of your living trust. There are two methods by which you can transfer such certificates into the name of your living trust. First, you can take the certificates to the stock broker with whom you do business and request that the broker have the certificate re-registered. Normally, the stock broker will want to review your living trust agreement to make certain that the trustee is authorized to own and manage such assets. The **Affidavit of Trust** will provide the stock broker with sufficient information to satisfy this inquiry. The broker will send the certificate to the transfer agent to be cancelled and reissued in the name of the living trust. Second, you can deal with the transfer agent for the stock directly.

No matter which method you use, you must sign the back of the stock certificate or an irrevocable stock power and your signature must be guaranteed by a bank, trust company, or a brokerage firm registered with the New York Stock Exchange. The name of your living trust should be included on the certificate or stock power as the transferee.

If you own an interest in a mutual fund, the stock broker can retitle the account for you. You will likely have to provide the broker with an **Affidavit of Trust**.

Bearer bonds or other bearer securities are not registered. Therefore, they present no title problems. You can transfer bearer securities to your living trust by specifically listing them on an **Assignment of Property**. In addition, you can place such securities in a safe deposit titled in the name of your living trust.

Life Insurance

Ownership of a life insurance policy need not be transferred to your living trust. However, your living trust should be named as the primary beneficiary of the policy. The alternate or contingent beneficiaries should be your spouse, children, or other persons. The beneficiary change can be accomplished by obtaining the appropriate change of beneficiary form from the agent handling the policy or from the insurance company itself.

Retirement Plans

Pension plans, profit-sharing plans, IRAs, Keoghs, SEPs, and other qualified retirement plans present unique planning issues. First, there are a variety of distribution options such as qualified joint and survivor annuity, qualified preretirement survivor annuity, lump-sum distribution, and spousal rollover. These distribution options are not all available to the trustee of a living trust. In addition, there are income tax issues that should be considered when designating the beneficiary of such retirement plans.

For married couples, it is desirable to designate the spouse as the primary beneficiary of the retirement plans. The spouse has the opportunity for continued deferral of income tax or a tax-free rollover to the spouse's IRA. Your living trust should be named as the alternate or contingent beneficiary of the retirement plan if you want to keep each child's share in trust until he or she attains a certain age. If you are not married, your living trust should be designated as primary beneficiary of your retirement plans.

Beneficiary designation forms can be obtained from the benefits department of your employer, the plan administrator, or the account holder.

> **Author's Advice:** Due to the unique income tax issues and distribution options associated with retirement plans, it is wise to consult with a tax professional who is familiar with and has experience in planning for such issues.

Annuities

Most annuities provide for the payment of some or all of the annuity payments to a beneficiary after the death of the annuity owner. In most circumstances, your living trust should be named the primary beneficiary of the annuity contract. The change of beneficiary forms can be obtained from the agent from whom you purchased the annuity or from the company that issued the annuity. An **Affidavit of Trust** will often be required to effect the change of beneficiary.

Oil, Gas, and Mineral Interests

Transferring oil, gas, and mineral interests to your living trust is not as straightforward as it may seem. Depending on where the interest is located, how it was acquired, and how it is treated under state law, the method by which it should be transferred to your living trust varies. If the interests are treated as personal property, a general Assignment of Personal Property would be appropriate. If the interests are treated as real estate, a deed will be required to transfer title to your living trust.

Also, if differing interests exist on the same property, multiple conveyance documents may be required. You should examine the document under which you obtained ownership of the interest. A transfer of this interest to your living trust will be accomplished with the same type of document.

Miscellaneous Property

Other property can be transferred into your living trust by executing an *assignment* for that property. If there is a document of title for such property, then a similar document should be prepared reflecting you as the transferor and your living trust as the transferee.

Living Trust Recordkeeping

Once you have funded your living trust, you must keep separate records for the trust property. As you acquire property in the future, you should title it directly in the name of the living trust. As you sell trust property, you should keep the proceeds in a special bank account titled in the living trust's name. As the trustee of your living trust, you can distribute the trust property to yourself at any time with little or no additional effort, so there is no reason to allow the proceeds to wind up outside the living trust.

There is much to be gained by keeping the property in the living trust. Take the extra time to make certain that the goal of your living trust—probate avoidance—is met.

Appendix D contains two forms that will help with recordkeeping for your living trust. Form 25, **Schedule of Trust Assets**, is intended to maintain a list of the assets initially transferred to your living trust. *This* **Schedule of Trust Assets** *does not transfer title to the assets to the living trust.*

Form 26, **Changes to Schedule of Trust Assets,** is intended to reflect the assets acquired by or disposed by your living trust.

Accurate and organized recordkeeping is important, as it will assist a successor trustee when the time presents itself. As part of this recordkeeping process, you should revise and update your NET WORTH WORKSHEET periodically. Not only will this help your successor trustee, but by going through the process, you may identify assets that have not been transferred to your living trust or that, when acquired, were not properly titled in the name of your living trust.

Many people do not keep copies of their beneficiary designations for retirement plans, life insurance policies, or annuities. To facilitate collection of these payments after your death, keep a copy of the beneficiary designations with other living trust asset information.

Chapter 8:
Estate Tax and Probate Savings of Living Trusts

You Earn It, You Keep It!

Now that you have an understanding of the living trust, the next step is to determine whether your living trust must be designed to minimize estate tax.

As explained in Chapter 3, federal estate tax is imposed on estates in excess of the applicable credit amount, which changes annually through 2011. Many people mistakenly assume that estate tax is imposed on the estates of married couples in excess of their combined applicable credit amount ($3 million for years 2004 and 2005). This is only true if proper planning is done to take advantage of each spouse's applicable credit amount.

An entire chapter of this book is devoted to determining your net worth. If you have not already read Chapter 5 and completed the NET WORTH WORKSHEET, do so at this time.

I Love You Wills

Because federal estate tax law permits a spouse to transfer all of his or her assets to his or her surviving spouse without paying estate tax, many estate planners draft simple wills that leave all assets to the surviving spouse. These *I Love You Wills* are a serious tax trap for the unwary.

Each person only has a set applicable credit amount against estate tax. If the credit is not used when a person dies, it is lost. Unlike the assets, the credit does not pass to the surviving spouse.

Case Studies

The following five case studies should demonstrate the estate tax savings that can be gained through the use of a living trust. The case studies are divided into planning for an unmarried person and planning for a married couple. The case studies are applicable to persons dying in 2004 or 2005. The case studies are based on the following situations.

1. Unmarried person with estate of $1.5 million or less.
2. Unmarried person with estate in excess of $1.5 million.
3. Married couple with combined estates less than $1.5 million. (Each spouse has an estate of $600,000.)
4. Married couple with combined estates more than $1.5 million and less than $3.0 million. (Each spouse has an estate of $900,000.)
5. Married couple with combined estate more than $3.5 million. (Each spouse has an estate of $2.0 million.)

The case studies do not make provision for payment of debts, funeral expenses, expenses of the last illness, or administration expenses. Administration expenses will be minimal with a living trust. If a living trust is not used, administration expenses would be increased greatly as a result of the costs of probate. It is reasonable to assume that if a living trust were not used, no less than 3% and as much as 10% of the value of the estate would be lost to court costs, attorney's fees, and the like.

NOTE: *Often, charts are the most effective method of communicating the estate tax planning options of a living trust. Hopefully the following charts and their explanation will help you understand a subject that is not straightforward. Keep in mind that as the amount of the applicable credit amount increases during the next few years, the numbers used in the charts should be revised.*

1. Unmarried Person— Estate Less than $1.5 Million

The estate of an unmarried person valued at less than $1.5 million will not have an estate tax obligation. Probate costs are calculated at 3% of the total estate.

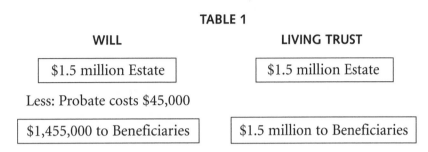

TABLE 1

WILL	LIVING TRUST
$1.5 million Estate	$1.5 million Estate
Less: Probate costs $45,000	
$1,455,000 to Beneficiaries	$1.5 million to Beneficiaries

TOTAL SAVINGS TO BENEFICIARIES: $45,000.

2. Unmarried Person— Estate in Excess of $1.5 million

The estate of an unmarried person valued in excess of $1.5 million must pay estate tax on the amount over $1.5 million. Probate costs are calculated at 3% of the total estate. The marginal tax rate on the amount in excess of $1.5 million is 48%. Therefore, if the estate is worth $2.0 million, the estate tax bill is $211,200. (($2.0 million - probate costs $60,000) x 48%)

TABLE 2

WILL	LIVING TRUST
$2.0 million Estate	$2.0 million Estate
Less: Probate costs $60,000	Less: Probate costs $0
Estate tax $211,200	Estate tax $211,200
$1,728,800 to Beneficiaries	$1,728,800 to Beneficiaries

TOTAL SAVINGS TO BENEFICIARIES: $60,000

3. Married Couple—
Combined Estates Less than $1.5 Million

Each spouse has an estate valued at $600,000. Probate costs are calculated at 3% of each spouse's total estate. Assume that all of the property is given to the surviving spouse.

TABLE 3

Death of First Spouse

WILL	LIVING TRUST
$600,000 Estate	$600,000 Estate

Less: Probate costs $18,000

$582,800 to Surviving Spouse	$600,000 to Surviving Spouse

Death of Second Spouse

WILL	LIVING TRUST
$2.0 million Estate	$2.0 million Estate

Less: Probate costs $35,460

$1,146,540 to Beneficiaries	$1,200,000 to Beneficiaries

TOTAL SAVINGS TO BENEFICIARIES: $ 53,460

4. Married Couple—
Combined Estates More than $1.5 Million

Each spouse has an estate valued at $900,000. Probate costs are calculated at 3% of each spouse's total estate. Assume that all of the property is given to the surviving spouse.

TABLE 4

Death of First Spouse

WILL	LIVING TRUST
$900,000 Estate	$900,000 Estate

Less: Probate costs $27,000

$873,000 to Surviving Spouse	$900,000 to Surviving Spouse

Death of Second Spouse

WILL	LIVING TRUST
$1,443,000 Estate	$1,800,000 Estate

Less: Probate costs $53,190   Less: Estate tax $144,000
    Estate tax $105,509

$1,614,301 to Beneficiaries	$1,656,000 to Beneficiaries

TOTAL SAVINGS TO BENEFICIARIES: $ 41,699

5. Married Couple— Combined Estates More than $3.5 Million

Each spouse has an estate valued at $2.0 million. Probate costs are calculated at 3% of each spouse's total estate. Assume that all of the property is given to the surviving spouse.

TABLE 5

Death of First Spouse

WILL	LIVING TRUST
$2,000,000 Estate	$2,000,000 Estate

Less: Probate costs $60,000

$1,940,000 to Surviving Spouse	$2,000,000 to Surviving Spouse

Death of Second Spouse

WILL	LIVING TRUST
$3,940,000 Estate	$4,000,000 Estate

Less: Probate costs $118,200   Less: Estate tax $1,200,000

    Estate tax $1,114,464

$2,707,336 to Beneficiaries	$2,800,000 to Beneficiaries

TOTAL SAVINGS TO BENEFICIARIES: $ 92,664

Estate Tax Planning with Living Trust

The preceding examples show the savings to estates using one or more living trusts. These savings are a direct result of avoiding probate and the costs associated with the probate process. In every instance, using a living trust increases the amount of assets that are ultimately given to the estate beneficiaries.

Living trusts can also be used to minimize a married couple's combined estate tax liability thereby further increasing the amount of assets given to the estates' beneficiaries. This is accomplished by taking advantage of each spouse's applicable credit amount. Each spouse's living trust is designed to *capture* the applicable credit amount. The living trust provides that upon the death of the trust grantor, an amount equal to the applicable credit amount, rather than being distributed to the surviving spouse, is held in trust. This trust is referred to as the *Credit Shelter Trust*, *Family Trust*, or *Trust B*. The illustrations and forms in this book refer to this trust as the *Family Trust*.

The *Family Trust* is discussed in detail in Chapter 8. The surviving spouse and children are beneficiaries of the Family Trust and thus, using the Family Trust to minimize estate taxes does not do so at their expense.

Look at the examples described in Tables 4 and 5 (pgs.98–99). If, at the death of the first spouse, a Family Trust is established instead of giving the property in the living trust to the surviving spouse, the total savings to the beneficiaries changes significantly. The Family Trust is funded with trust assets up to $1.5 million in value. The balance of the property is distributed to the surviving spouse. (More complicated planning involves keeping any amount in excess of $1.5 million in a separate trust called the *Marital Trust*. This planning is discussed in detail in Chapter 8.) Once the assets are placed in the Family Trust and the applicable credit amount allocated to the Family Trust, the assets will pass to the beneficiaries after the death of the surviving spouse without being subject to estate tax. Once excluded from estate tax, the property passes to the trust beneficiaries without being included in the estate of the surviving spouse.

Before continuing, it is appropriate to discuss a married couple's ownership of their property. In most states, ownership of assets between a married couple is determined by looking at the manner in which the asset is titled or the source of funds from which the asset was purchased. For instance, stock certificates may have been issued in the name of one spouse only, an automobile registered in the name of only one spouse, or real estate titled in the name of one spouse only. In order to accomplish the estate planning discussed here, it may be necessary to retitle some assets. It is important that each spouse own enough property to maximize use of the $1.5 million credit. Often it is desirable to *equalize* the estates to maximize estate tax savings.

Example: *Tom establishes a brokerage account in his name. He and Linda marry and throughout the marriage purchase investments through the account. The name on the account is never changed. In calculating the net worth of each spouse, the value of the account should be included in Tom's name. If, however, Tom and Linda lived in a community property state (Arizona, California, Idaho, Louisiana, Nevada, New Mexico, Texas, Washington, and Wisconsin), one half of the value of the account would be included in each spouse's net worth.*

When completing the NET WORTH WORKSHEET in Chapter 5, be certain to confirm the ownership of your marital assets. If you determine that the net worth of a spouse needs to be adjusted in order to take full advantage of the applicable credit amount, this can be accomplished when each spouse's living trust is funded. Chapter 7 discusses funding your living trust.

> **Warning:** There are non-tax consequences associated with transferring assets to your spouse. In the event of a divorce, it may be difficult to reacquire such assets. In addition, if litigation is brought against the spouse to whom the assets are transferred, those assets are exposed to the risk of litigation.

Because federal gift tax law allows a spouse to transfer an unlimited amount of property to his or her spouse during his or her lifetime, asset transfers to your spouse to achieve equalization do not give rise to federal gift tax.

The following two tables show the savings benefit when both spouses use living trusts and incorporate the use of Family Trusts into them. The two tables follow the factual situations of Tables 4 and 5, but show the dramatic increase of assets going to beneficiaries when Family Trusts are added into estate planning.

Married Couple— Combined Estates More than $1.5 Million

Each spouse has an estate valued at $900,000, which is in his or her living trust. At the death of the first spouse, his or her entire estate is transferred to a *Family Trust.*

TABLE 6

ESTATE OF FIRST SPOUSE	ESTATE OF SURVIVING SPOUSE
Family Trust $900,00 at Death of First Spouse	$900,000 Living Trust

At Death of Second Spouse

$900,000 to Beneficiaries	$900,000 to Beneficiaries

$1,800,000 to Beneficiaries

TOTAL SAVINGS TO BENEFICIARIES (compare to Table 4): $144,000

Married Couple— Combined Estates More than $3.5 Million

Each spouse has an estate valued at $2,000,000, which is in his or her living trust. At the death of the first spouse, $1.5 million is placed into the *Family Trust* with remaining $500,000 outright to surviving spouse. (An amount equal to the applicable credit amount is put into a Family Trust with the remainder outright to the surviving spouse.)

TABLE 7

ESTATE OF FIRST SPOUSE	ESTATE OF SURVIVING SPOUSE
Family Trust $1,500,00 at Death of First Spouse	$2,000,000 Living Trust
	$500,000 from First Spouse

At Death of Second Spouse

$1,500,000 to Beneficiaries	$2,500,000 to Beneficiaries

Less: Estate Tax: $480,000

$3,520,000 to Beneficiaries

TOTAL SAVINGS TO BENEFICIARIES (compare to Table 5): $720,000

Family Trust Appreciation

A commonly overlooked benefit of using the *Family Trust* is that of appreciation of assets without estate tax liability. Once assets are placed in a *Family Trust* and the applicable credit amount applied to the *Family Trust*, the assets and all appreciation on them, is exempt from estate tax at the death of the surviving spouse.

All of the case studies ignore the impact of the appreciation in value of assets from the death of the first spouse until the death of the surviving spouse. However, it is important to keep this principle in mind when evaluating the appropriateness of estate tax planning in your living trust. Reviewing the illustration in Table 3, while the combined value of the married couple's estates is less than $1.5 million, it is possible that by the death of the second spouse, the value of the surviving spouse's estate will exceed $1.5 million. If a *Family Trust* is not used, the result is the same as shown in Table 4. Estate tax must be paid because only the surviving spouse's $1.5 million credit is available.

If you and your spouse have combined estates of $1.0 million or more, utilize a *Family Trust* upon the death of the first spouse. It is common for surviving spouses to live five to ten years beyond the death of their spouse. In many cases, spouses live for as much as fifteen or twenty years beyond the death of their spouse. It is easy to see how the value of an estate can appreciate by as much as 75% or more after death. This appreciation can cause an inadvertent estate tax. Because the assets of the *Family Trust* are available to the surviving spouse with relatively little restriction, it makes sense to play it safe. Use the *Family Trust* and preserve every opportunity to minimize estate taxes and maximize the amount of property that will pass to your heirs.

As our population ages it becomes more likely that a member of your family will be faced with an incapacity of some type, whether temporary or permanent. In addition, statistics indicate that at least one spouse will spend some time in a nursing home. At present, the average stay in a nursing home is eighteen months. As we get older, we must rely on family members to assist us with the management of our finances and making health-care decisions on our behalf.

In earlier chapters, the expense and time delay of probate after a person's death was discussed. The evils and agony of probate after death can also occur during a person's life. If you become mentally or physically incapacitated, you may not be able to handle your financial or personal affairs. You also may not be able to make informed decisions regarding your health care. In such situations, it may be necessary to file a petition with the court to have a *guardian* appointed to make financial and health care decisions for the incapacitated person. Guardianships are often called *living probate,* because they involve the court in very personal decisions affecting the incapacitated person.

Guardianships—the Living Probate

Guardianships are expensive and time consuming. To establish a guardianship, proof of a person's incapacity or incompetence must be provided to the court. Generally, this proof must be provided by the sworn opinion of at least one and sometimes two or three medical professionals who have either treated the person or who have evaluated the person specifically for the guardianship proceeding. These opinions become part of the court's file and, therefore, become part of the public record. The information in such reports is extremely personal and should not be shared with the public. The most private issues in a person's life are no longer private.

Once the court determines the person is incapacitated or incompetent, the court must appoint a person to act as the guardian. The court-appointed guardian may or may not be a family member. The guardian must act within strict guidelines of the court. Each state has enacted very specific laws regarding the duties and role of the guardian. Common to all of these laws is the requirement that the guardian obtain the court's permission to sell certain assets, pay expenses, and make major medical decisions for the incapacitated person (referred to as the *ward*). This causes time delays and unnecessary expenses in the form of attorney fees and court costs.

Chapter 9:
Ancillary Documents to Avoid Living Probate

*Complete Your Planning
with All the Documents You Need*

Most states require that a guardian prepare and file annual accounts with the court. These annual accounts require a detailed itemization of the following:

- ◆ assets owned by the ward and over which the guardian has supervision;
- ◆ funds received by the guardian for the benefit of the ward;
- ◆ funds distributed for the benefit of the ward;
- ◆ if the ward has a spouse or minor children, funds distributed for the benefit of the spouse or minor children; and,
- ◆ funds paid to for attorney fees, court costs and the guardian's fee.

In addition to the financial information a guardian must report to the court, an annual assessment of the guardian's physical and mental condition must be provided to the court. In essence, the court must be convinced of the ongoing need for the guardianship. Again, very private medical records and evaluations must be provided to the court.

> **Author's Advice:** In my experience, living probate is much more emotionally disturbing and stressful to family members than probate after death. The strictures of guardianships are a constant reminder of a loved one's physical or mental illness. Long-term illness is difficult not only for the patient but for family members as well. Imposition of stringent, impersonal laws for guardianships is an invasion of family life that should and can be avoided.

Powers of Attorney— Guardianship Alternatives

Guardianships are required to ensure that a person's financial affairs are handled and appropriate medical decisions are made. Each state has enacted laws creating powers of attorney for financial and health-care matters. If such documents have been signed by a person, the need for a guardianship no longer exists.

Durable powers of attorney are documents signed by a person (often called the *principal*) prior to incompetency or incapacity, appointing one or more agents to act on behalf of that person in financial matters or for health-care matters. The powers of attorney are *durable* in that they are effective when signed and continue to be effective upon the later incapacity or incompetency of the principal. These documents do not have to be filed with any court to be effective. The privacy of the principal is protected and the agent can act without the interference of the court.

Durable Powers of Attorney for Financial Matters

Durable powers of attorney for financial matters authorize the agent to perform a variety of tasks with regard to the principal's financial assets. Typically, the authority given to the agent is very broad and, in essence, allows the agent to step into the shoes of the principal and continue business as usual.

A durable power of attorney for financial matters should be viewed as a backup document as it relates to asset management. Ideally, the successor trustee of the principal's living trust will step into the principal's shoes and manage the principal's financial affairs. That is one of the purposes of a living trust—avoiding probate at death and during periods of incapacity. The durable power of attorney is also important to have in place in the event the principal becomes incapacitated before completely funding his or her living trust.

Another function of a durable power of attorney is designating the agent to represent the principal with government agencies such as the Internal Revenue Service, Social Security Administration, and state and local authorities including those administering Medicaid programs. The trustee of a living trust does not have such authority.

Often, married couples designate each other as the agent under the durable power of attorney. This is consistent with the manner in which most married couples handle their financial affairs. At least one and perhaps two alternate agents should be designated in the event the spouse is not able or willing to serve. It is advisable, although not required, that the successor trustee named in your living trust be named as the alternate agent of your durable power of attorney.

Durable Powers of Attorney for Health Care

A *health care* or *medical power of attorney* designates an agent to make decisions regarding routine health care of the principal. The agent is authorized to consent to, or withhold consent to, medical treatment. Incapacity often makes an individual unable to make informed decisions about his or her medical care. Hospitals and physicians are reluctant to perform routine medical procedures and provide routine medical care without the written consent of the patient or someone authorized to give consent on behalf of the patient.

In the mid 1990s, as part of the *Omnibus Budget Reconciliation Act*, Congress established a law requiring any medical facility that receives federal funding to inform patients of their right to have a health care power of attorney and living will. Indeed, upon admission to a hospital, a patient will be asked if he or she has such documents and will be given a form of each document to sign if he or she does not have already have them. One of the reasons this law was enacted was because hospitals were in a budget crisis. There were individuals who could not make health-care decisions for themselves and no family members could be located. The hospital had an ethical duty to provide a minimum level of health care. In rare instances, individuals required life support and, once started on life support, the hospital could not discontinue it without court authorization. The hospitals had to bear the expense of such care. By making all of these documents available to patients when they come to the hospital, it was hoped that hospitals would avoid such financial obligations.

All states have a statute that establishes who is authorized to make health-care decisions for a person who is unable to make such decisions. The order of preference is generally as follows:

- ◆ spouse;
- ◆ an adult child;
- ◆ parent;
- ◆ brother or sister;
- ◆ other family member; or,
- ◆ court-appointed guardian.

Reliance on the statute is dangerous. If both spouses are involved in a common accident, neither may be able to make decisions for him- or herself, much less their spouse. If there is more than one adult child, medical providers are not required to obtain the input of all children. They can rely on the opinion of one child. This opinion may not be an accurate reflection of the opinions of the other adult children. If there are no adult children, the parents may not be alive or may not be competent to make informed health-care decisions.

A health care power of attorney takes the guesswork out of the decision making process. The principal designates a person whom he or she trusts to make some of the most important decisions any person can be asked to make. The agent could be faced with making life and death decisions. With the health care power of attorney in place, health-care decisions can be made privately, on a timely basis, and without involvement of the court.

More often than not, a health care power of attorney will be needed in an emergency. Give a copy of your health care power of attorney to your family physician to be made part of your medical records. Keep extra copies of your health care power of attorney easily accessible so that they can be given to hospitals and other medical providers when necessary.

Living Will

A *living will* is a document that sets forth a person's intention with regard to the level of medical care that will be given if the person has a terminal illness and death is expected within a short period of time or is in a condition such as a coma or vegetative state from which the person is not expected to recover.

For many years, the states and courts argued about whether a person could authorize medical providers to discontinue or withhold life sustaining treatment. The two most famous legal cases—involving Karen Ann Quinlan and Nancy Cruzan—took years to wind their way through the court system. Finally, on June 25, 1990, the United States Supreme Court ruled on the case of Nancy Cruzan and affirmed the right of individuals to determine their quality of life and express their intention that life sustaining treatment be withheld or terminated if its only purpose is to prolong life and postpone a natural death.

A living will is an expression of the circumstances under which you want to be allowed to die a natural death. While in many states, family members can make this decision and medical providers implement that decision, a living will has several important advantages. First, all members of the family may not agree with your decision. Second, the living will takes the burden of making such a difficult decision off the shoulders of your family.

Give a copy of your living will to your family physician to be made part of your medical records.

Each state has statutes governing durable powers of attorney for financial matters, health care powers of attorney, and living wills. Appendix B contains a comprehensive list of state statutes. Many of the statutes include forms of the durable powers of attorney and living wills that are recognized in that state.

Declaration of Guardian in Advance of Need

Many states authorize the appointment of a guardian in advance of need. A person can designate the person to serve as guardian in the event a guardianship becomes necessary in the future. While such a declaration does not avoid involvement of the courts, it does allow a person to decide who will serve as guardian and not leave this decision to the courts.

Durable powers of attorney, living wills, and declaration of guardian in advance of need respond to the needs of adults in the event of incapacity and illness. These documents help minimize stress not only for the individual but for his or her family as well. They also can avoid the delay and expense of living probate.

Designation of Guardian for Minor Children

There is an additional document that you should consider including in your planning—*designation of guardian for minor children*. If you have minor children, you need to do additional planning. A living trust cannot designate a guardian of your minor children in the event you and your spouse pass away. If you create a pourover will, include a designation of guardian. However, if you have fully funded your living trust and there is no other reason to probate your will, a designation of guardian for minor children can keep your will from the probate process. The designation can be filed with the court and the guardian is vested with the appropriate powers and duties.

Most states recognize a designation of guardian, which can be effective either during life or after death. For example, you may become incapacitated and unable to care for your minor children during your incapacity. The designation of guardian avoids the involvement of child services and the courts in determining who will have custody of and act as guardian of your minor children. You should review your state's laws to find the applicable statute that will often include a form document for this purpose.

Chapter 10:
Administration of Your Living Trust after Your Death
The Final Steps

After the grantor of a living trust passes away, the living trust must be managed and the trust assets distributed in accordance with the wishes of the grantor set forth in the trust agreement. The successor trustee steps into the shoes of the trustee and takes over the management of the trust assets. Distributions to beneficiaries such as a surviving spouse, minor children, and others designated in your living trust should be continued while the affairs of the decedent are finalized. There are a number of steps that must be taken after a person's death. If he or she is not the surviving spouse, the successor trustee should work together with the surviving spouse.

The discussion in this chapter is necessarily brief. Its purpose is to familiarize you with the process of trust and/or estate administration after a person has died. A comprehensive discussion of this subject is beyond the scope of this book.

Obtain Death Certificates

It is important to obtain several death certificates. A separate death certificate will be required for each life insurance policy and retirement plan account. It will also be necessary to have a death certificate for each parcel of real estate held in the living trust. Obtain at least ten death certificates. The death certificates must be *certified copies*. These certified copies bear an official seal and are the only documents accepted by most financial institutions and insurance companies.

A death certificate and a copy of the living trust or an *Affidavit of Trust* will enable the successor trustee to manage the living trust in exactly the same manner as did the decedent.

Funeral directors offer to obtain certified copies of death certificates for you. If this opportunity is not available, you will need to contact the local county clerk or department of vital statistics. It may take as long as two or three weeks to obtain the death certificates.

Gather Personal Information

Make certain that you have the decedent's birth date, date of death, Social Security number, address, name of surviving spouse, maiden name (applies only to women), and place of birth. All of this information can be obtained from the death certificate.

If the decedent was a member of the military, military discharge papers should be located so that appropriate military benefits can be pursued. Dates of military service should be confirmed.

The names, ages, and addresses of the beneficiaries of the living trust should be gathered. If the beneficiaries have not already been notified of the decedent's death, they should be notified.

Contact Social Security Administration

If the decedent was receiving Social Security benefits, the Social Security Administration should be contacted. There is a small death benefit that can be collected.

Safe Deposit Box

If the decedent had a safe deposit box, the contents will need to be inventoried. The safe deposit box may contain important papers and assets such as life insurance policies, bearer securities, collectibles, and the like. If the safe deposit box was registered in the name of the living trust, the successor trustee should be able to obtain access to the box without difficulty. An **Affidavit of Trust** and a death certificate should be all that is required by the bank to gain access to the safe deposit box.

If the box is not registered in the name of the living trust and there is no other owner of the box, there are procedures set forth in your state's probate code detailing how access to a decedent's safe deposit box can be obtained.

Obtain Tax Identification Number for Trust

Throughout the grantor's life, the tax identification number for the living trust was the grantor's Social Security number. After the grantor's death, a separate tax identification number must be obtained for the living trust. If the living trust provides for the creation of a Marital Trust and Family Trust, a separate tax identification number must be obtained for each Trust. A separate **Form SS-4, Application for Employer Identification Number**, must be filed with the Internal Revenue Service either by telephone, fax, or online.

Contact Life Insurance Companies

Each life insurance company should be contacted and informed of the decedent's death. Each company will have its own claim forms. With a death certificate and the completed claim forms, policy proceeds will be paid to the living trust.

Inventory Assets

The decedent's assets should be identified and inventoried. It is important to determine if there are any assets that were not transferred to the living trust. If there are probate assets, you will need to determine what probate proceeding should be used to transfer the assets to the appropriate beneficiary. You need to determine whether or not the decedent had a will. The existence of a will dictates which probate proceedings are available.

If the living trust was funded as previously described, there is no need to change the title to these assets. The successor trustee can continue the management of the trust assets and continue distributions of income and principal to the beneficiaries named in the living trust.

When preparing an inventory of assets, the total value of the decedent's assets must be calculated. If the value of the assets exceeds the applicable credit amount, the successor trustee or a representative of the decedent must prepare and file Form 706 with the Internal Revenue Service. Form 706, **United States**

Estate Tax Return, must be filed within nine months of the decedent's death. Any estate tax that is due must be paid when Form 706 is filed. Because the preparation of Form 706 is quite detailed, you should consider hiring an attorney, accountant, or other tax professional who has experience with the preparation of Form 706.

Regardless of whether or not Form 706 must be filed with the Internal Revenue Service, a state estate or inheritance tax return may have to be filed. The requirements for filing a state estate or inheritance tax return, as well as the appropriate forms, can be obtained from the state treasurer or state tax department.

In calculating the value of the decedent's estate, it is necessary to obtain fair market values for the assets as of the date of death of the decedent. Written valuations of real estate, securities, and other assets should be obtained. In addition determining whether or not an estate tax return must be filed, the written valuations establish the new basis of the asset. When a person dies, his or her cost basis in the assets is *stepped-up* to the value on the date of death. The living trust and beneficiaries will use this new basis to calculate their gain or loss on a future sale of the asset.

Identify Debts of Decedent

The debts of the decedent must be identified and itemized. Debts may include credit cards, automobile loans, mortgages, unsecured personal loans, student loans, and the like. Investigation should made to determine whether credit life insurance policies exist that will pay off the outstanding indebtedness. If credit life policies exist, efforts to collect the policies should be taken immediately.

Provisions should be made by the successor trustee to make certain that there is not an inadvertent default on any debt obligation. This is especially important if there is a surviving spouse or minor children. The successor trustee should make certain that there are sufficient liquid assets in the living trust to make the required payments on debt as they become due.

Final Income Tax Return

A final income tax return, Form 1040, must be filed for the decedent for the calendar year of his or her death. If the decedent is married, the final return can be filed jointly with the surviving spouse. The final income tax return is due on April 15th during the year following death.

Trust Income Tax Returns

After the grantor's death, income earned by the living trust must be reported on a separate income tax return. Having obtained a tax identification number for the trust(s), an income tax return will be filed to report the income or loss recognized by the trust after the death of the grantor. Form 1041, **U.S. Income Tax Return for Estates and Trusts**, will be filed for the trust on an annual basis. (see form 32, p.345.)

In many instances, all of income from the trust will be distributed to one or more beneficiaries. The trust will issue Form K-1 to each beneficiary who received income from the trust. Form K-1 has the same purpose as a 1099 or W-2, it informs the Internal Revenue Service as well as the income recipient of the amount of income received by or distributed to that person. The income must be included on the beneficiary's personal income tax return.

Distribution of Assets to Beneficiaries

After debts, expenses, and taxes are paid or adequately provided for, the successor trustee should distribute the remaining assets in the living trust in accordance with the terms of the trust agreement. More likely than not, the living trust will contain provisions directing the distribution of personal property to beneficiaries. The living trust may also contain specific gifts of trust assets to individuals and/or charities. The successor trustee should make these distributions as soon as practical.

If the living trust requires the creation of a *Family Trust* and a *Marital Trust*, the successor trustee must allocate the remaining trust assets between these trusts. There are a number of issues, both tax and non-tax, that must be taken into consideration when determining which assets should be allocated to each trust. It is advisable to consult a tax and investment professional when making these allocations.

Epilogue

The most personal planning that a professional can do for a client is estate planning. Estate planning is not limited to making provisions for the distribution of assets to designated beneficiaries. Estate planning also includes planning for the management and distribution of assets during life.

The living trust and other documents discussed in this book help you manage your assets during your lifetime, designate persons to make health-care decisions on your behalf, and stand as a statement of your wishes regarding prolonging life. Completion of such planning simplifies your financial affairs and the health-care decision making process. This planning also provides comfort and security to your family in the event of your disability or incapacity.

Of course, the living trust and pourover will work in tandem to make settlement of your financial affairs after your death easier and less stressful for your family and loved ones. Death is difficult. The importance of taking advantage of every tool available to make your passing less emotional and stressful for your family cannot be stressed enough.

If nothing else, these documents can serve as a starting point for further planning. Whether you prepare documents yourself or decide to meet with an estate planning professional, it is my hope that the information and forms in this book will encourage you to complete this important planning not only for yourself, but for you family and loved ones as well.

Good Luck!

Glossary

A

administrator (administratrix, if female). A person appointed by the court to oversee distribution of the property of someone who died (either without a will or if the person designated in the will is unable to serve).

affidavit regarding debts and taxes. A document sworn to by the personal representative of the estate that all of the taxes, expenses, and debts of the decedent have been paid and that the property of the decedent has been distributed to the beneficiaries.

annual account. A sworn, written account prepared by a personal representative and filed with the court within a specified period or periods of time after appointment of the personal representative showing all property received by the personal representative, payments made, income received, distributions to beneficiaries, etc.

annual exclusion. For federal gift tax purposes, the amount of property a person can give to another person per year that is not counted against the lifetime applicable credit amount. Currently, the amount of the annual exclusion is $11,000.00.

annuity trust. Charitable remainder trust that pays the donor a fixed annual income.

applicable credit amount. Formerly the *unified credit*. The credit against federal estate tax that is allowed each person or estate.

assets. Money and real or personal property owned by a person or organization.

attorney *ad litem*. An attorney appointed by the court to represent the interests of heirs whose names or whereabouts are not known or to represent the interests of an heir who is a minor or who is incompetent.

B

beneficial interest. Right to enjoy or profit from property held in trust; the person with the beneficial interest is the beneficiary.

beneficiary. Person who is named to receive some benefit or money from a legal document such as a trust, life insurance policy, or will.

bequest. Gift of personal property left in a will.

bond. Monetary guarantee that, should a trustee steal trust funds, compensation will be awarded up to the bond's limit.

bypass trust. Trust typically created by a married couple to hold title to property that will not be included, for estate tax purposes, in the estate of the surviving spouse. The surviving spouse normally receives income from the trust and some but not all of the principal.

C

charitable lead trust. Trust that donates to a charity income from trust assets while reserving the assets for later distribution to other beneficiaries. Compare with charitable remainder trust.

charitable remainder trust. Trust that pays income from trust assets to the donor or beneficiaries while reserving the assets for later contribution to a charity. Compare with charitable lead trust.

children's trust. A trust set up to hold property given to children. Usually it provides that the children will not receive their property until they reach a higher age than the age of majority.

codicil. A written change or amendment to a will.

community property. Property acquired during marriage that was not a gift to or inheritance of one spouse or property that is specifically kept separate from property acquired during the marriage.

contesting the will. Challenging the will of a decedent to determine whether the will is valid and legally disposes of the decedent's property.

contingent beneficiary. A person who is entitled to receive property from a person who died only if the first beneficiary named is not alive or is not entitled to receive the property. Sometimes referred to as a *alternate beneficiary*.

contingent interest. Interest in property that is dependent on the occurrence of a future event, such as a college graduation, not on the passage of time.

credit estate tax. State tax on the assets of someone who has died. Applies only in some states and only to estates that are required to pay federal estate taxes. The estate does not pay double taxes but instead, by paying a credit estate tax, rebates part of the federal estate tax owed back to the state.

creditor. Person or corporation to whom money is due.

credit shelter trust. Another name for bypass trust.

D

decedent. Person who has died.

declaration of guardian. In the event neither the financial power of attorney nor health care power of attorney are effective, the declaration specifies who is to serve as guardian of the person should a court appointed guardianship be necessary.

descendant. A person related to another individual by blood or adoption (a child, grandchild, great-grandchild, etc.).

domicile. A person's primary residence.

donee. Recipient of a gift, trust, or power left in a trust; beneficiary of a trust.

donor. Person or corporation that gives a gift to or confers a power on another; creator of a trust.

E

estate. All property, real or personal, that a person owns.

estate tax. Type of death tax (state and federal) based on the decedent's right to transfer property; not a tax on the property itself. Federal estate taxes range from eighteen to fifty-five percent.

executor (if female, executrix). A person or corporation appointed in a will or by a court to settle the estate of a deceased person. Duties include collecting assets, discharging the decedent's debts, inventorying the estate, paying estate and inheritance taxes, and distributing assets to the beneficiaries.

F

family allowance. An amount deemed reasonable by the court that is paid to the surviving spouse and minor children of the decedent to defray living expenses during the year following death.

family trust. Another name for a bypass trust.

federal estate tax. Federal tax assessed against the assets of a person who has died if the value of the taxable assets exceeds the applicable credit amount.

fiduciary. Person in a position of trust and confidence; a person who has a duty to act primarily for the benefit of another. A trustee or personal representative acts as a fiduciary.

financial power of attorney. Legal document whereby one person authorizes another to make financial decisions on his or her behalf in the event of illness, incapacity, or disability. The power of attorney is designed to avoid a court supervised and controlled guardianship in the event the person becomes incapacitated.

future interest. Interest in property that cannot be possessed or enjoyed until a specified period of time passes or a future event (*e.g.*, a 21st birthday) occurs.

G

generation-skipping trust. Trust designed to skip one generation of estate taxes because the trust leaves the principal to the grantor's grandchildren, not the grantor's children.

gift. Voluntary lifetime or at-death transfer of property, made without compensation.

gift tax. Tax on lifetime transfers of property given without consideration or for less consideration than the property is worth.

grantor. Another term for creator of a trust. *See also donor, settlor.*

grantor trust. Living trust in which the grantor maintains enough control over the assets so that the trust income received is taxed to the grantor, not to the trust or to the beneficiaries of the trust other than the grantor.

gross estate. Property owned by a decedent at death. Value before debts are paid.

guardian. Person legally empowered and appointed by a court to handle the personal affairs or property of another person who is unable to do so because such person is considered incompetent under the law. Incompetency includes physical or mental incapacity or being under the age of 18. The guardian may be appointed to handle financial matters or matters of health and personal care.

H

health care power of attorney. Legal document whereby one person authorizes another to make health care decisions on his or her behalf should illness, incapacity, or disability occur. The power of attorney is designed to avoid a court supervised and controlled guardianship in the event the person becomes ill, incapacitated, or disabled.

heir. Persons entitled by law to receive property from someone who has died without a will.

holographic will. A will that is entirely in the handwriting of the maker and the will is signed by the maker.

incapacitated/incompetent. One who is unable to manage his or her own affairs either temporarily or permanently.

I

income. All financial gains from investments, work, or business.

income beneficiary. A beneficiary of a trust who receives only the income generated by the trust assets.

inheritance tax. A tax imposed on property received by beneficiaries from the estate of a decedent. Rate of tax often depends upon relationship of the beneficiary to decedent.

insurance trust. A trust that owns and manages a life insurance policy. The trust is the beneficiary of the life insurance policy. After receipt of proceeds, the proceeds are distributed to the beneficiaries named in the trust.

inter vivos **trust.** *See living trust.*

intestate. A person who dies without a will or with a will that is not valid under applicable law.

inventory. A list of assets and debts of the estate of the decedent that is prepared by the personal representative of the estate and filed with the probate court.

irrevocable trust. A trust that cannot be changed or canceled after it is created.

J

joint tenancy with right of survivorship (JTWROS). Form of ownership in which property is equally shared by all owners and is automatically transferred to the surviving owners when one of them dies.

L

living trust. A revocable trust separate from a will which may be funded or unfunded during the lifetime of the person who creates the trust. Commonly used to avoid probate and provide a means for the management of assets during incompetency or incapacity.

living will. A document in which a person, while competent to do so, expresses a wish that his or her life not be prolonged by artificial life support systems if his or her medical condition becomes hopeless.

M

marital trust. A trust that is held and administered for the benefit of the surviving spouse of the grantor of the trust. All income from the trust is distributed to the spouse at one or more times during the year and the spouse may also receive principal from the trust.

O

oath. A document signed by the personal representative of an estate stating that the personal representative will perform all of the duties required of him or her.

organ donor cards. Cards that designate anatomical gifts. Such gifts are generally limited to heart, kidneys, liver, pancreas, corneas, and bones for transplantation purposes.

P

payable on death account (POD). An account that is automatically paid to a beneficiary named by the owner of the account upon the death of the owner of the account. The beneficiary has no rights to the account during the lifetime of the account owner.

per capita. Will or trust distribution plan that requires that all living descendants of the grantor, regardless of generation, receive an equal share of the grantor's estate.

personal property. Property that is movable, not land or things attached to land.

personal property memorandum. A document separate from the will or trust that designates distribution of personal effects.

personal representative. Person named in a will or appointed by a court to settle an estate. *See administrator; executor.*

per stirpes. Will or trust distribution plan that requires that descendants of a deceased beneficiary, as a group, inherit equal shares of the amount the deceased beneficiary would have received had he or she lived. (For example, if your child predeceases you, any grandchildren descended from that child would receive equal shares of your deceased child's inheritance.)

pourover will. Will provision that distributes money or property to a trust that already exists.

present interest. Right to use property immediately. Compare with future interest.

principal. Property in a trust; also called corpus.

probate. Legal process of establishing the validity of a deceased person's last will and testament; commonly refers to the process and laws for settling an estate.

probate property. Property that is subject to the probate process such as property that is owned by the decedent in his or her own name, property that is held as tenancy in common, and other property that is not disposed of pursuant to a beneficiary designation such as life insurance policies, retirement plans, annuities, etc.

proceeding to determine heirship. Procedure used when a person dies without a will or if there is property that is not disposed of by the will. The purpose of the proceeding is to identify the persons who are entitled under the law to receive property from the decedent.

Q

qualified terminable interest property trust (QTIP). Trust that qualifies for the unlimited marital deduction and postpones payment of any estate taxes owed until both spouses have died. The surviving spouse receives trust income for life but has little or no legal right to the trust's principal.

R

real property. Property that is immovable, such as land, buildings, and whatever else is attached to or growing on land.

residual beneficiary. A person who receives remaining property that has not been given away in a trust or will, or person who receives property only after the original beneficiary has died.

S

Section 2503(c) trust. A trust that allows a grantor to make gifts of $11,000 a year to a trust for the future benefit of minor children without the grantor incurring gift taxes.

self-proved will. Testator and witnesses sign the document in the presence of one another and each take an oath at the time the will was executed and the statement is included with the will and notarized by a notary public. Such a will can be admitted to probate without further documentation including the testimony of witnesses to the will or family members.

separate property. Property that is owned by a spouse either before marriage and is kept separate during the marriage or property that is acquired by gift, inheritance, or recovered for personal injuries during marriage.

settlor. Another term for creator of a trust. *See grantor, donor.*

small estate. A procedure to administer the estate of a decedent if the value of the gross estate is less than a statutory amount and the value of the property is greater than the liabilities.

sole ownership. Form of ownership where one person owns the entire property in his or her name alone.

spendthrift clause. Provision included in some trusts that prohibits the beneficiary from giving or selling to others the beneficiary's rights to the trust's assets or income.

standby trust. Living trust that takes effect if a grantor becomes ill, incapacitated, or dies. The grantor's assets are transferred to the trust and managed by the designated trustee.

successor executor. Person who takes over the rights and responsibilities of an original executor.

successor trustee. Person who takes over the rights and responsibilities of an original trustee.

T

tenancy by entirety. Form of spousal ownership in which property is equally shared and automatically transferred to the surviving spouse. While both spouses are living, ownership of the property can be altered only by divorce or mutual agreement.

tenancy in common. Way of jointly owning property in which each person's share passes to his or her heirs or beneficiaries, but the ownership shares need not be equal.

testamentary estate. Property that passes to beneficiaries under probate law rather than contract law (such as joint bank accounts, life insurance, or retirement plan beneficiary designations) or trust law (when assets go into a trust rather than directly to beneficiaries).

testamentary trust. Trust established in a person's will.

testate. A person who dies and leaves a valid will.

testator. The person who makes a will.

title. Ownership of property or the document that shows ownership.

Totten trust. Revocable trust created by the owner of a bank account (checking, savings, or other) for the future benefit of another.

trust. Real or personal property held by one party (the trustee) for the benefit of another (the beneficiary). The person establishing the trust is often referred to as the *grantor*, *trustor*, *creator*, *maker*, or *settlor*.

trust A. Another name for the marital trust.

trust B. Another name for bypass trust.

trustee. Person or other agent (such as a bank) who holds legal title to the trust assets and who administers and manages money or property for the benefit of a beneficiary.

U

unlimited marital deduction. Allows a person to transfer all of his or her property to his or her spouse without federal estate tax.

W

will. Legal document that declares how a person wishes property to be distributed to heirs or beneficiaries after death. Can only be enforced through a probate court.

Appendix A:
Tax Explanations and Charts

The following pages contain explanations of the state death taxes and the federal estate tax. In addition, charts depicting various estate planning options are included.

Explanation of Federal Transfer Taxes

Federal Estate and Gift Tax

As discussed throughout the text, all property owned by you at your death, probate and non-probate, is subject to the federal estate tax at your death. The federal estate tax applies to all estates. However, the law grants you a unified credit exemption and your estate does not have to pay tax on an amount up to that credit.

In June, 2001, President Bush signed a new tax law *(Economic Growth and Tax Relief Reconciliation Act of 2001)* that contains drastic changes to the estate and gift tax law. Under the new law, the estate tax is scheduled to be completely repealed in the year 2010. The law provides that unless Congress takes an affirmative step to make the repeal permanent, the estate tax will be reinstated in the year 2011. The new law also reduces the highest estate and gift tax rates. The following table sets forth the increase in the unified credit exemption and the decrease in the estate and gift tax rates.

Year	Estate and Gift Tax Unified Credit Exemption	Highest Estate & Gift Tax Rate
2004	$1,500,000	48%
2005	$1,500,000	47%
2006	$2,000,000	46%
2007	$2,000,000	45%
2008	$2,000,000	45%
2009	$3,500,000	45%
2010	Repealed	—
2011	Reinstated	55%

In addition to the federal estate tax, there is a tax imposed on gifts of property you make to individuals during your lifetime. You can give an unlimited amount of property to your spouse during your lifetime. As of 2002, there is a new $1 million lifetime exemption for gifts. Thus, if you give away gifts totaling more than $1 million during your lifetime, each additional $1.00 of property given away will be subject to gift tax that must be paid to the IRS by April 15 of the year following the most recent gift. Unlike the estate tax, the gift tax is not repealed under the *Economic Growth and Tax Relief Reconciliation Act.* Beginning in 2010, the maximum gift tax rate on gifts in excess of $1 million will be 35%.

Explanation of State Death Taxes

State Death Taxes

Each state imposes some form of death tax on a decedent's estate. There are three types of state death taxes: the *pick-up tax*, the *estate tax*, and the *inheritance tax*.

The Pick-Up Tax

The federal government permits a limited credit against federal estate taxes for death taxes paid to the states. The amount of this state tax credit is calculated through a formula established by the federal government. Several states have a death tax that is equal to the maximum state tax credit that the federal government permits. This type of death tax is referred to as a *pick-up* tax. The following states have a pick-up tax.

Alabama	Georgia	Missouri	Utah
Alaska	Hawaii	Nevada	Vermont
Arizona	Idaho	New Mexico	Virginia
Arkansas	Illinois	North Dakota	Washington
California	Maine	Oregon	West Virginia
Colorado	Massachusetts	Rhode Island	Wisconsin
District of Columbia	Michigan	South Carolina	Wyoming
Florida	Minnesota	Texas	

State Estate Tax

The states listed below impose an *estate tax* on their residents. The estate tax is calculated in the same manner as the federal estate tax. It is a tax on the value of the assets owned by the decedent at the date of his or her death. Often the estate tax imposed by a state is much more than the state death tax credit that the federal government allows. Estate tax states include the following.

Mississippi	Ohio
New York	Oklahoma

State Inheritance Tax

Several states impose an *inheritance tax*. This type of tax is levied directly on the beneficiaries who receive the assets. Often the amount of inheritance tax depends upon the relationship of the beneficiary to the decedent. Spouses, children, grandchildren, and parents are often taxed at a lower rate than sisters, brothers, nieces, nephews, and nonrelatives. The following states use the inheritance tax system.

Connecticut	Louisiana	North Carolina
Delaware	Maryland	Pennsylvania
Indiana	Montana	South Dakota
Iowa	Nebraska	Tennessee
Kansas	New Hampshire	
Kentucky	New Jersey	

No matter which type of tax that a state imposes, you need to be aware of the tax and the potential impact of that tax on your estate. You can obtain specific information on your state's form of tax and the rate of tax by contacting your state treasurer or comptroller or the state tax department.

Appendix B:
State-by-State Laws

The following pages contain an alphabetical listing of states and their statutes governing powers of attorney, both financial and health care, as well as living wills.

NOTE: *The symbol "§" and the abbreviation "s." mean "section" and "§§" means "sections."*

ALABAMA

Financial: Michie's Alabama Code 1975, or Code of Alabama 1975; Title 26, Chapter 1, Section 26-1-2 (C.A. §26-1-2). Durable or springing: "This power of attorney shall not be affected by disability, incompetency, or incapacity of the principal," or "This power of attorney shall become effective upon the disability, incompetency, or incapacity of the principal." No statutory form. Can include a health care power of attorney if it meets the statutory requirements.

Health Care: C.A. §22-8A-1. "Natural Death Act." Health care power of attorney is part of the Advance Directive for Health Care form found at C.A. §22-8A-4, which also includes living will provisions.

ALASKA

Financial: Alaska Statutes, Title 13, Section 13.26.332 (A.S. §13.26.332). Statutory form.

Health Care: Health care is included in the statutory financial power of attorney form. Power of attorney for mental health treatment: A.S. §47.30.950; form at A.S. §47.30.970. Living Will: A.S. §18.12.010. Titled "Living Wills and Do Not Resuscitate Orders."

ARIZONA

Financial: Arizona Revised Statutes, Section 14-5501 (A.R.S. §14-5501). Durable or springing: "This power of attorney is not affected by subsequent disability or incapacity of the principal or lapse of time" or "This power of attorney is effective on the disability or incapacity of the principal." No statutory form. To be valid, must: (1) clearly show intent to make a power of attorney and clearly designate an agent; (2) be dated and signed; (3) be notarized; and, (4) be witnessed by one person other than the agent, the agent's spouse, or the agent's children.

Health Care: A.R.S. §36-3221; form at A.R.S. §36-3224. A separate mental health care power of attorney is provided for in A.R.S. §36-3281; form at A.R.S. §36-3286. Living will form found at A.R.S. §36-3262; and a "Prehospital Medical Care Directive" is found at A.R.S. §36-3251.

ARKANSAS

Financial: Arkansas Code of 1987 Annotated, Title 28, Chapter 68, Section 28-68-201 (A.C.A. §28-68-201). Form found at A.C.A. §28-68-401. Durable or springing: "This power or attorney shall not be affected by subsequent disability or incapacity of the principal" or "This power of attorney shall become effective upon the disability or incapacity of the principal," or similar language. Also see A.C.A. §28-68-301. Titled "Powers of Attorney for Small Property Interests." This is limited to (1) property with a gross value up to $20,000, not including homestead or capitalized value of any annual income or (2) annual income up to $6,000.

Health Care: Living Will: A.C.A. §20-17-201. Form found at A.C.A. §20-17-202.

CALIFORNIA

In General: West's Annotated California Probate Code, Section 4000 et seq. (A.C.P.C. §4000 et seq.)

Financial: A.C.P.C. §4124. "Uniform Durable Power of Attorney Act." Durable or springing: "This power of attorney shall not be affected by subsequent incapacity of the principal" or "This power of attorney shall become effective upon the incapacity of the principal," or similar language. Form may be found at A.C.P.C. §4401.

Health Care: A.C.P.C. §4700, "Advance Health Care Directive Forms." Form may be found at A.C.P.C. §4701, which includes living will provisions.

COLORADO

Financial: West's Colorado Revised Statutes Annotated, Title 15, Section 15-1-1301 (C.R.S.A. §15-1-1301). "Uniform Statutory Form Power of Attorney Act." Form found at C.R.S.A. §15-1-1302. Durable: "This power of attorney will continue to be effective even though I become disabled, incapacitated, or incompetent" or similar language. "Uniform Durable Power of Attorney Act," C.R.S.A. §15-14-501, provides for durable or springing: "This power of attorney shall not be affected by disability of the principal" or "This power of attorney shall become effective upon the disability of the principal" or similar language.

Health Care: C.R.S.A. §15-14-506. Authorizes a "medical durable power of attorney," but no form is provided.

Living Will: C.R.S.A. §15-18-101. "Colorado Medical Treatment Decisions Act." Form may be found at C.R.S.A. §15-18-104. The designation of a "proxy decision-maker" is authorized by C.R.S.A. §15-18.5-103. Organ donation provided for in C.R.S.A. §12-34-105.

CONNECTICUT

Financial: Connecticut General Statutes Annotated, Title 1, Section 1-42 (C.G.S.A. §1-42). "Connecticut Statutory Short Form Power of Attorney Act." Form found at C.G.S.A. §1-43. Durable power of attorney for bank accounts is found at C.G.S.A. §1-56b. Springing powers of attorney authorized by C.G.S.A. §1-56h. Affidavit for agent to certify that power of attorney is in full force and effect is found at C.G.S.A. §1-56i.

Health Care: Health Care Power of Attorney may be found at C.G.S.A. §19a-575a.

Living Will: C.G.S.A. §19a-570, titled "Removal of Life Support Systems." Form may be found at C.G.S.A. §19a-575.

DELAWARE

In General: Delaware Code Annotated, Title 25, Section 171 (D.C.A. 25 §171). This applies to real estate.

Financial: D.C.A. 12 §4901. Durable or springing: "This power of attorney shall not be affected by the subsequent disability or incapacity of the principal" or "This power of attorney shall become effective upon the disability or incapacity of the principal" or similar language.

Health Care: D.C.A. 16 §2501. Form found at D.C.A. 16 §2505. Requires two witnesses, who may not be related to the declarant, not be entitled to a share of the estate, not have any claims against the declarant, not have any financial responsibility for the declarant's medical care, and not be an employee of the hospital or other facility where the declarant is a patient. The witnesses' must state in writing (this can be incorporated into the living will above their signature lines) that they "are not prohibited from being a witness under D.C.A. 16 §2503(b)."

DISTRICT OF COLUMBIA

Financial: District of Columbia Code, Title 21, Section 2081 (D.C.C. §21-2081). The spine of the book reads: "D.C. Official Code." "Uniform Durable Power of Attorney Act." Durable or springing: "This power or attorney shall not be affected by subsequent disability or incapacity of the principal or lapse of time" or "This power of attorney shall become effective upon the disability or incapacity of the principal" or similar language. Also, D.C.C. §21-2102 provides for durable: "This power of attorney will continue to be effective if I become disabled, incapacitated, or incompetent." Form found at D.C.C. §21-2101.

Health Care: D.C.C. §21-2201. Titled "Health-Care Decisions." Form found at D.C.C. §21-2207.

FLORIDA

Financial: Florida Statutes, Chapter 709, Section 709.08 (F.S. §709.08). The language set forth in the statute only provides for a durable power of attorney: "This durable power of attorney is not affected by subsequent incapacity of the principal except as provided in §709.08, Florida Statutes" or similar language. However, the statute also allows for springing power attorney, stating that: "If the durable power of attorney is conditioned upon the principal's lack of capacity to manage property, it is exercisable upon the delivery of an affidavit of the agent that the power of attorney in valid and the affidavit of the principal's primary physician that the principal lacks the capacity to manage property pursuant to Chapter 744, Florida Statutes." Must be executed and witnessed in the same manner as documents for the transfer of real estate. Can incorporate provisions for health care surrogate. Statute also provides for award of attorney fees to party prevailing in a suit for unreasonable refusal to honor a power of attorney.

Health Care: F.S. Chapter 765. Health Care Surrogate form found at F.S. §765.203.

Living Will: Form found at F.S. §765.303.

GEORGIA

Financial: Official Code of Georgia Annotated, Title 10, Chapter 6, Section 10-6-1 (O.C.G.A. §10-6-1). This is titled "Agency" and deals with powers of attorney in general. Durable or springing options in official form. O.C.G.A. §10-6-6 authorizes springing power of attorney and provides that principal can designate any person or persons to have the power to conclusively determine when the disability or other event has occurred that will make the document effective. Such persons must execute a declaration swearing that the event has occurred. Form may be found at O.C.G.A. §§10-6-141 and 10-6-142. (This is not the "Georgia Code," which is a separate and outdated set of books with a completely different numbering system.)

Health Care: O.C.G.A. §31-36-1. "Durable Power of Attorney for Health Care Act." Form found at O.C.G.A. §31-36-10.

HAWAII

In General: Hawaii Revised Statutes, Section 501-174 (H.R.S. §501-174) and §502-84, concern requirements for filing a power of attorney for real estate with the land court and the bureau of conveyances. Ignore "Title" numbers.

Financial: H.R.S. §551D-1, "Uniform Durable Power of Attorney Act." Durable or springing: "This power of attorney shall not be affected by the disability of the principal" or "This power of attorney shall become effective upon the disability of the principal." No form.

Health Care: H.R.S. §327F-3, provides for a mental health care power of attorney.

IDAHO

Financial: Idaho Code, Title 15, Chapter 5, Part 5, Section 15-5-501 (I.C. §15-5-501). "Uniform Durable Power of Attorney Act." Durable or springing: "This power or attorney shall not be affected by subsequent disability or incapacity of the principal" or "This power of attorney shall become effective upon the disability or incapacity of the principal," or similar language.

Health Care: Idaho Code, Title 39, Chapter 45, Section 39-4501 (I.C. §39-4501). "Natural Death Act." Form found at I.C. §39-4505.

ILLINOIS

In General: West's Smith-Hurd Illinois Compiled Statutes Annotated, Chapter 755, Article 45, Section 1-1 (755 ILCS 45/1-1). "Illinois Power of Attorney Act." The financial and health care power of attorney provisions are subparts of this general law.

Financial: 755 ILCS 45/2-1, "Durable Power of Attorney Law" and 755 ILCS 45/3-1, "Statutory Short Form Power of Attorney for Property Law." Statutory form is found at 755 ILCS 45/3-3, which includes durable or springing options.

Health Care: 755 ILCS 45/4-1, "Powers of Attorney for Health Care Law." Form is found at 755 ILCS 45/4-10.

INDIANA

Financial: West's Annotated Indiana Code, Title 30, Article 5, Chapter 1, Section 30-5-1-1 (A.I.C. §30-5-1-1). Durable or springing authorized by A.I.C. §30-5-4-2, but no specific language in statute. Statute does not provide a form, but states that a form can be used that refers to the descriptive language in A.I.C. §§30-5-5-2 to 30-5-5-19 (these sections define each power that is generally referred to, and referenced, in the form). Form 31 in Appendix C is not an official form, but it complies with the statutory requirements. Statute provides that a power of attorney must be notarized.

Health Care: A.I.C. §16-36-1-1. Titled "Health Care Consent." Allows appointment of a "health care representative," but no form is provided. This can also be accomplished with the general power of attorney pursuant to A.I.C. §30-5-5-1, which includes a provision for health care powers.

Living Will: A.I.C. §16-36-4-1. Form for refusing life-prolonging procedures found at A.I.C. §16-36-4-10. Form for requesting life-prolonging procedures found at A.I.C. §16-36-4-11.

IOWA

Financial: Iowa Code Annotated, Section 633.705 (I.C.A. §633.705). Titled "Powers of Attorney." Durable or springing: "This power of attorney shall not be affected by disability of the principal" or "This power of attorney shall become effective upon the disability of the principal," or similar language.

Health Care: I.C.A. §144B.1. Forms may be found at I.C.A. §144B.5 (Durable Power of Attorney for Health Care) and I.C.A. §144A.3 (Living Will).

KANSAS

In General: Kansas Statutes Annotated, Section 58-610 (K.S.A. §58-610). You may find these volumes as either "Vernon's Kansas Statutes Annotated" or "Kansas Statutes Annotated, Official." The supplement is a pocket part in Vernon's and a separate soft-cover volume in the "Official." Both sets have very poor indexing systems.

Financial: K.S.A. §58-610. "Uniform Durable Power of Attorney Act." Durable or springing: "This power of attorney shall not be affected by subsequent disability or incapacity of the principal" or "This power of attorney shall become effective upon the disability or incapacity of the principal" or similar language.

Health Care: K.S.A. §58-625. Called a "Durable Power of Attorney for Health Care Decisions." Form found at K.S.A. §58-632.

KENTUCKY

Financial: Kentucky Revised Statutes, Chapter 386, Section 386.093 (K.R.S. §386.093). Durable or springing: "This power of attorney shall not be affected by subsequent disability or incapacity of the principal or lapse of time" or "This power of attorney shall become effective upon the disability of incapacity of the principal" or similar language. For recording a power of attorney for conveying real estate, see K.R.S. §382.370.

Health Care: Living Will: K.R.S. §311.621, "Kentucky Living Will Directive Act." Form at K.R.S. §311.625.

LOUISIANA

In General: West's Louisiana Statutes Annotated. The set of Louisiana statutes is divided into topics, such as "Civil Code," "Revised Statutes," etc., so be sure you have the correct topic. For example, for the Civil Code, the book spines read "West's LSA Civil Code," and the front covers read "Louisiana Civil Code." In Louisiana a power of attorney is also called a "mandate," "procuration," or "letter of attorney." The agent is also referred to as the "proxy" or "mandatary." L.S.A. Civil Code, Article 2989. No specific form is required, unless specified by a statute relating to a particular type of power of attorney. L.S.A. Civil Code, Art. 2993. Certain powers must be expressly given. L.S.A. Civil Code, Art. 2996 & 2997.

Financial: A financial power of attorney is automatically durable, unless otherwise stated in the document. L.S.A. Civil Code, Art. 3026.

Health Care: L.S.A. Revised Statutes §40:1299.53 provides that health-care decisions can be made by "an agent acting pursuant to a valid mandate, specifically authorizing the agent to make health-care decisions." No statutory form. Living Will: L.S.A. Revised Statutes §40:1299.58.1. "Natural Death Act." Form may be found at L.S.A. Rev. Stat. §40:1299.58.3; special form for military personnel stationed in the state may be found at L.S.A. Rev. Stat. §40:1299.61.

MAINE

Financial: Maine Revised Statutes Annotated, Title 18-A, Section 5-501 (18-A M.R.S.A. §5-501). Durable or springing: "This power of attorney is not affected by subsequent disability or incapacity of the principal or lapse of time" or "This power of attorney becomes effective upon the disability or incapacity of the principal." No statutory form. Notice requirements found at 18-A M.R.S.A. §5-508(c). Power of attorney must be notarized by either a notary public or an attorney.

Health Care: 18-A M.R.S.A. §5-801. "Uniform Health-Care Decisions Act." Form found at 18-A M.R.S.A. §5-804. Also provided for in 18-A M.R.S.A. §5-506, but no form in that statute.

MARYLAND

In General: Annotated Code of Maryland, Real Property, Section 4-107 (A.C.M., RP §4-107). Requires that a power of attorney for conveying real estate must be executed in the same manner as a deed, and must be recorded before or with the deed. These volumes are arranged by subject, so be sure you have the volume marked "Real Property" or whatever other volume is listed below.

Financial: A.C.M., Estates & Trusts §13-601. Durable unless otherwise stated in the document. Be sure you have the volume marked "Estates and Trusts."

Health Care: A.C.M., Health-General §5-601. Titled "Health Care Decision Act." Living Will and Power of Attorney form may be found at A.C.M., HG §5-603. Be sure you have the volume marked "Health-General."

MASSACHUSETTS

Financial: Annotated Laws of Massachusetts, Chapter 201B, Section 1 (A.L.M., C. 201B, §1). "Uniform Durable Power of Attorney Act." Durable or springing: "This power of attorney shall not be affected by subsequent disability or incapacity of the principal" or "This power of attorney shall become effective upon the disability or incapacity of the principal" or similar language.

Health Care: A.L.M., C.201D. No form.

MICHIGAN

Financial: Michigan Compiled Laws Annotated, Section 700.5501 (M.C.L.A. §700.5501). Durable or springing: "This power of attorney is not affected by the principal's subsequent disability or incapacity, or by the lapse of time" or "This power of attorney is effective upon the disability or incapacity of the principal" or similar language.The law specifically states that a general grant of power to buy or sell real estate is sufficient, and the legal property description is not required to be included in the power of attorney (M.C.L.A. §700.5502). Ignore the volume and chapter numbers, and look for section numbers. You may also see it referred to as a "letter of attorney."

Health Care: M.C.L.A. §700.5506. Discusses "Designation of patient advocate," with some details as to what must be in the document; however, no form is provided in the statute. Form 37 in Appendix C of this book is designed to incorporate the legal requirements of this statute. A witness may not be the patient's spouse, parent, child, grandchild, sibling, presumptive heir, known devisee at the time of the witnessing, physician, or patient advocate; nor an employee of a life or health insurance provider for the patient, of a health facility that is treating the patient, or of a home for the aged. The document must be made part of the patient's medical record with the patient's attending physician and, if applicable, with the facility where the patient is located.

MINNESOTA

Financial: Minnesota Statutes Annotated, Chapter 523, Section 523.07 (M.S.A. §523.07). Durable or springing: "This power of attorney shall not be affected by incapacity or incompetence of the principal" or "This power of attorney shall become effective upon the incapacity or disability of the principal." Form may be found at M.S.A. §523.23. Agent's affidavit may be found at M.S.A. §523.17.

Health Care: M.S.A. §145C.01. Titled "Durable Power of Attorney for Health Care." Form may be found at M.S.A. §145C.16.

Living Will: M.S.A. §145B.01. "Minnesota Living Will Act." Form found at M.S.A. §145B.04. Living will can be noted on driver's license. M.S.A. §171.07.

MISSISSIPPI

Financial: Mississippi Code 1972 Annotated, Title 87, Chapter 3, Section 87-3-9 (M.C. §87-3-9). Financial power of attorney: M.C. §§87-3-101 to 87-3-113. Titled "Uniform Durable Power of Attorney Act." Durable or springing: "This power of attorney shall not be affected by subsequent disability or incapacity of the principal or lapse of time" or "This power of attorney shall become effective upon the disability or incapacity of the principal" or similar language.

Health Care: M.C. §41-41-201. "Uniform Health Care Decisions Act." Form may be found at M.C. §41-41-209.

Living Will: M.C. §41-41-101, referred to as "Withdrawal of Life-Saving Mechanism." Form at M.C. §41-41-107. Revocation form at M.C. §41-41-109.

MISSOURI

Financial: Vernon's Annotated Missouri Statutes, Chapter 404, Section 404.700(A.M.S. §404.700). "Durable Power of Attorney Law of Missouri." Specifies which powers must be specifically stated at §404.710, but no form is provided. Durable power of attorney created by either titling the document "Durable Power of Attorney," or by including provision: "THIS IS A DURABLE POWER OF ATTORNEY AND THE AUTHORITY OF MY ATTORNEY IN FACT SHALL NOT TERMINATE IF I BECOME DISABLED OR INCAPACITATED, OR IN THE EVENT OF LATER UNCERTAINTY AS TO WHETHER I AM DEAD OR ALIVE" or "THIS IS A DURABLE POWER OF ATTORNEY AND THE AUTHORITY OF MY ATTORNEY IN FACT, WHEN EFFECTIVE, SHALL NOT TERMINATE OR BE VOID OR VOIDABLE IF I AM OR BECOME DISABLED OR INCAPACITATED OR IN THE EVENT OF LATER UNCERTAINTY AS TO WHETHER I AM DEAD OR ALIVE." A.M.S. §404.705. It must also be executed in the same manner as a deed.

Health Care: A.M.S. §404.800. "Durable Power of Attorney for Health Care Act." No form provided.

Living Will: A.M.S. §459.010. Form found at A.M.S. §459.015.

MONTANA

Financial: Montana Code Annotated, Title 72, Chapter 31, Part 2, Section 72-31-201 (M.C.A. §72-31-201). Form found at M.C.A. §72-31-201. Durable: "This power of attorney will continue to be effective if I become disabled, incapacitated, or incompetent." M.C.A. §72-31-222.

Health Care: No health care power of attorney form.

Living Will: M.C.A. §50-9-103.

NEBRASKA

Financial: Revised Statutes of Nebraska, Chapter 49, Article 15 , Section 49-1501 (R.S.N. §49-1501). "Nebraska Short Form Act." Form found at R.S.N. §49-1522. Durable or springing: "This power of attorney shall not be affected by subsequent disability or incapacity of the principal" or "This power of attorney shall become effective upon the disability or incapacity of the principal" or similar language. R.S.N. §30-2664.

Health Care: R.S.N. §30-3401; form found at R.S.N. §30-3408.

NEVADA

Financial: Nevada Revised Statutes Annotated, Chapter 111, Section 111.460 (N.R.S.A. §111.460). Durable or springing: "This power of attorney is not affected by disability of the principal" or "This power of attorney becomes effective upon the disability of the principal" or similar language. If used to convey real estate, must be executed and recorded in accordance with N.R.S.A. §111.450 (*i.e.*, signed, acknowledged, notarized, and recorded).

Health Care: N.R.S.A. §449.800. Form found at N.R.S.A. §449.830. Form for living will found at N.R.S.A. §449.610.

NEW HAMPSHIRE

Financial: New Hampshire Revised Statutes Annotated 1997, Chapter 506, Section 506:6 (N.H.R.S.A. §506:6). Ignore "title" numbers; look for "chapter" numbers. Durable only: "This power of attorney shall not be affected by the subsequent disability or incompetence of the principal." Statutes have suggested, but not required, disclosure statement. Statute also contains suggested form for acknowledgement by agent.

Health Care: N.H.R.S.A. §137-J:1. Form found at N.H.R.S.A. §137-J:14 & 15.

Living Will: N.H.R.S.A. §137-H:1. Form found at N.H.R.S.A. §137-H:3.

NEW JERSEY

Financial: NJSA (for New Jersey Statutes Annotated), Title 46, Chapter 2B, Section 46:2B-8.1 (NJSA §46:2B-8.1). Durable or springing: "This power of attorney shall not be affected by disability or incapacity of the principal, or lapse of time" or "This power of attorney shall become effective upon the disability or incapacity of the principal" or similar language. NJSA §46:2B-8.2.

Health Care: NJSA §26:2H-53. "New Jersey Advance Directive for Health Care Act." No form. Requires two witnesses or notary. May supplement with video or audio recording. Woman may indicate desires for withholding or withdrawing life support in the event of pregnancy. NJSA §26:2H-56.

NEW MEXICO

Financial: New Mexico Statutes 1978 Annotated, Chapter 45, Section 45-5-501 (N.M.S.A. §45-5-501). Supplement is found at the end of each chapter. Durable or springing: "This power of attorney shall not be affected by subsequent incapacity of the principal or lapse of time," or "This power of attorney shall become effective upon the incapacity of the principal." Form found at N.M.S.A. §45-5-602.

Health Care: N.M.S.A. §24-7A-1. Titled: "Uniform Health-Care Decisions." Form found at N.M.S.A. §24-7A-4. Must be executed in the same manner as a will (with two witnesses and notarized).

NEW YORK

Financial: McKinney's Consolidated Laws of New York Annotated, General Obligation Law, Article 5, Title 15, Section 5-1501 (C.L.N.Y, Gen. Ob. §5-1501). This set of books is divided in subjects, so be sure you have the correct volume, such as "General Obligation Law" or "Public Health." Durable or springing: "This power of attorney shall not be affected by my subsequent disability or incompetence" or similar language (C.L.N.Y., Gen. Obl. §5-1505). Instead of one statutory form with options for various effective dates, New York has created separate forms for each type: Durable (C.L.N.Y., Gen. Ob. §5-1501, 1); Nondurable (§1501, 1-a); and Springing, called "effective at a future date," (§5-1506).

Health Care: C.L.N.Y., Public Health, Article 29-C, §2980. Called "Health Care Agents and Proxies." Form found at §2981(d). Health care proxy may NOT be included in a general power of attorney. C.L.N.Y., Public Health §2981(e).

NORTH CAROLINA

Financial: General Statutes of North Carolina, Chapter 32A, Section 32A-1 (G.S.N.C. §32A-1). Durable or springing: "This power of attorney shall not be affected by my subsequent incapacity or mental incompetence" or "This power of attorney shall become effective after I become incapacitated or incompetent" or similar language (G.S.N.C. §32A-8). G.S.N.C. §32A-9(b) requires the power of attorney to be registered in the office of the register of deeds upon the principal becoming incapacitated or incompetent. G.S.N.C. §32A-11 also requires reporting to the court clerk with periodic accountings, unless this is waived in the power of attorney. Statutory form found at G.S.N.C. §32A-1.

Health Care: G.S.N.C. §32A-15; form found at G.S.N.C. §32A-25. Provisions for "Health Care for Minor" found at G.S.N.C. §32A-34.

NORTH DAKOTA

Financial: North Dakota Century Code Annotated, Title 30.1, Chapter 30, Section 30.1-30-01 (N.D.C.C. §30.1-30-01). UDPAA. Durable or springing: "This power of attorney is not affected by subsequent disability or incapacity of the principal or by lapse of time" or "This power of attorney shall become effective upon the disability or incapacity of the principal."

Health Care: N.D.C.C. §23-06.5-1. Titled "Durable Power of Attorney for Health Care." Form found at N.D.C.C. §23-06.5-17.

OHIO

Financial: Page's Ohio Revised Code Annotated, Title 13, Chapter 1337, Section 1337.09 (O.R.S. §1337.09). Durable only: "This power of attorney shall not be affected by disability of the principal" or "This power of attorney shall not be affected by disability of the principal or lapse of time" or similar language.

Health Care: Discussed at O.R.S. §1337.11, including provisions required signature and date, two witnesses, and setting forth who can be an agent, but no form provided. Also see O.R.S. §2133.01. Titled "Modified Uniform Rights of the Terminally Ill Act."

OKLAHOMA

Financial: Oklahoma Statutes Annotated, Title 58, Section 1071 (58 O.S.A. §1071). "Uniform Durable Power of Attorney Act." Durable or springing: "This power of attorney shall not be affected by subsequent disability or incapacity of the principal or lapse of time" or "This power of attorney shall become effective upon the disability or incapacity of the principal" or similar language.

Health Care: 63 O.S.A. §3101. "Oklahoma Rights of the Terminally Ill or Persistently Unconscious Act." Mandatory form found at 63 O.S.A. §3101.4. Do-not-resuscitate consent form found at 63 O.S.A. §3131.5.

OREGON

Financial: Oregon Revised Statutes, Chapter 127, Section 127.005 (O.R.S. §127.005). A power of attorney is durable unless specifically limited.

Health Care: O.R.S. §127.505. Mandatory form found at §127.531.

PENNSYLVANIA

Financial: Purdon's Pennsylvania Consolidated Statutes Annotated, Title 20, Chapter 56, Section 20-5601 (20 Pa.C.S.A. §5601). A power of attorney is durable unless otherwise stated. 20 Pa.C.S.A. §5601.1. Statute provides forms for required Notice and Acceptance by agent.

Health Care: No health care power of attorney provisions. Living Will: Pa.C.S.A. §20-5401. "Advance Directive for Health Care Act." Living will (called "Declaration") form found at Pa.C.S.A. §20-5404. This allows the appointment of a "surrogate," but only to make decisions if the principal is terminally ill or permanently unconscious, therefore it is not a true power of attorney for health care.

RHODE ISLAND

Financial: General Laws of Rhode Island, Title 34, Chapter 34-22, Section 34-22-6.1 (G.L.R.I. §34-22-6.1). Durable or springing: "This power of attorney shall not be affected by the incompetency of the donor" or "This power of attorney shall become effective upon the incompetency of the donor" or similar language.

Health Care: G.L.R.I. §23-4.10-1, "Health Care Power of Attorney Act." G.L.R.I. §23-4.11-1, "Rights of the Terminally Ill Act." Form found at G.L.R.I. §23-4.10-2.

SOUTH CAROLINA

Financial: Code of Laws of South Carolina, Title 62, Chapter 5, Section 62-5-501 (C.L.S.C. §62-5-501). Durable or springing: "This power of attorney is not affected by physical disability or mental incompetence of the principal which renders the principal incapable of managing his own estate" or "This power of attorney becomes effective upon the physical disability or mental incompetence of the principal" or similar language.

Health Care: C.L.S.C. §62-5-504. Form found at §62-5-504(D). Also see "Adult Health Care Consent Act," at C.L.S.C. §44-66-10 which discusses consent for medical treatment and states that this subject can be included in a durable power of attorney, but no form is provided.

Living Will: Covered in the "Death With Dignity Act," C.L.S.C. §44-77-10. Form found at C.L.S.C. §44-77-50.

SOUTH DAKOTA

Financial: South Dakota Codified Laws, Title 59, Chapter 7, Section 59-7-2.1 (S.D.C.L. §59-7-2.1). Durable or springing: "This power of attorney shall not be affected by disability of the principal" or "This power of attorney shall become effective upon the disability of the principal" or similar language.

Health Care: Authorized by S.D.C.L. §§59-7-2.5 to 59-7-2.8, and 34-12C-3, but no forms are provided.

TENNESSEE

Financial: Tennessee Code Annotated, Title 34, Chapter 6, Section 34-6-101 (T.C.A. §34-6-101). "Uniform Durable Power of Attorney Act." Durable or springing: "This power of attorney shall not be affected by subsequent disability or incapacity of the principal" or "This power of attorney shall become effective upon the disability or incapacity of the principal" or similar language (T.C.A. §34-6-102). No statutory form, but statute provides that a power of attorney may refer generally to the powers listed in the statute (T.C.A. §34-6-109) without restating them. To completely understand what powers are included, and what limitations are placed on an agent, you should read the most current version of T.C.A. §§34-6-108 and 34-6-109. If you want to give your agent full powers over all of your financial matters, you can use form 62 in Appendix C. If there are a few specific things you don't want your agent to do, you may list them on the lines in paragraph 2. You may also use Form 1.

Health Care: T.C.A. §34-6-203. Titled "Durable Power of Attorney for Health Care." No statutory form. T.C.A. §34-6-205 has required warnings if power of attorney is not prepared by the principal.

TEXAS

Financial: Vernon's Texas Civil Statutes, Probate Code (Chapter XII), Section 481 (T.C.S., Probate Code §481). "Durable Power of Attorney Act." The T.C.S. is divided into subjects, so be sure you have the proper subject volume. Durable or springing: "This power of attorney is not affected by subsequent disability or incapacity of the principal" or "This power of attorney shall become effective on the disability or incapacity of the principal." T.C.S., Probate Code §482. Form found at T.C.S., Probate Code §490.

Health Care: Texas Codes Annotated, Health and Safety, Chapter 166, Section 166.151 (T.C.A., Health & Safety §166.151). Titled "Medical Power of Attorney." Form and required notices may be found at T.C.A. §§166.163 & 166.164.

NOTE: *Some of the books containing Texas laws are titled Texas Civil Statutes, and others are titled Texas Codes Ann.*

UTAH

Financial: Pursuant to U.C.A. §75-5-503, a general power of attorney does not allow the agent to do any of the following, unless specifically stated in power of attorney: (1) create, modify, or revoke a revocable living trust created by the principal; (2) use the principal's property to fund a trust not created by the principal or by a person authorized to create a trust on behalf of the principal; (3) make or revoke a gift of the principal's property, in trust or otherwise; or, (4) designate or change the designation of beneficiaries to receive any property, benefit, or contract right on the principal's death.

Health Care: No provisions for a general power of attorney for health care. Living will form provided at U.C.A. §75-2-1104. Under U.C.A. §75-2-1106, you can execute a "Special Power of Attorney" that allows you to appoint someone to execute a living will for you if you are incapacitated. (This form is included in Appendix C.)

VERMONT

In General: Vermont Statutes Annotated, Title 27, (Chapter 5), Section 305 (27 V.S.A. §305). The Chapter number is needed for online access, but is not included in the official statute designation. A power of attorney to convey real estate must be signed, have at least one witness, be acknowledged, and be recorded where a deed would be recorded.

Financial: Vermont Statutes Annotated, Title 14, (Chapter 123), Section 3501 (14 V.S.A. §3501). Durable or springing: Statute states that a power of attorney may become effective upon a future date or occurrence of a specific event, but only provides suggested language for durable: "This power of attorney shall not be affected by the subsequent disability or incapacity of the principal." 14 V.S.A. §3508.

Health Care: Vermont Statutes Annotated, Title 14, (Chapter 121), Section 3451 (14 V.S.A. §3451). Titled "Durable Power of Attorney for Health Care." Form and required notice are found at 14 V.S.A. §§3465 and 3466.

Living Will: Covered at 18 V.S.A. §5252, referred to as a "terminal care document." Form found at 18 V.S.A. §5253.

VIRGINIA

Financial: Code of Virginia 1950, Title 11, Section 11-9.1 (C.V. §11-9.1). Durable or springing: Statute states that a power of attorney may become effective upon a future date or occurrence of a specific event (C.V. §11-9.4), but only provides suggested language for durable: "This power of attorney (or his authority) shall not terminate on disability of the principal."

Health Care: C.V. §54.1-2981, form found at C.V. §54.1-2984.

WASHINGTON

Financial: West's Revised Code of Washington Annotated, Title 11, Chapter 94, Section 11.94.010 (R.C.W. §11.94.010). Found in chapter on "Power of Attorney." Durable or springing: "This power of attorney shall not be affected by disability of the principal" or "This power of attorney shall become effective upon the disability of the principal" or similar language.

Health Care: Health care power of attorney authorized by R.C.W. §11.94.010(3), but no form provided. Mental health power of attorney form found at R.C.W. §71.32.260.

Living Will: Covered at R.C.W. §70.122.010, "Natural Death Act."

WEST VIRGINIA

Financial: West Virginia Code, Chapter 39, Article 4, Section 39-4-1 (W.V.C. §39-4-1). Durable or springing: "This power of attorney shall not be affected by subsequent disability or incapacity of the principal" or "This power of attorney shall become effective upon the disability or incapacity of the principal."

Health Care: W.V.C. §16-30-1. Titled "West Virginia Health Care Decisions Act." Medical power of attorney and living will forms may be found at W.V.C. §16-30-4.

WISCONSIN

Financial: West's Wisconsin Statutes Annotated, Chapter 243, Section 243.01 (W.S.A. §243.01). Statutory form found at W.S.A. §243.10. Durable or springing: "This power of attorney shall not be affected by subsequent disability, incapacity or incompetency of the principal" or "This power of attorney shall become effective upon the subsequent disability, incapacity or incompetency of the principal."

Health Care: W.S.A. §155.01, titled "Power of Attorney for Health Care." Form found at W.S.A. §155.30.

Living Will: Covered in W.S.A. §154.01.

WYOMING

In General: Wyoming Statutes Annotated, Title 34, Chapter 1, Section 34-1-103 (W.S.A. §34-1-103). Referred to as "letter of attorney." For powers of attorney in general see W.S.A. §§34-1-103 & 3-5-101. Husband and wife may give each other power of attorney, W.S.A. §34-1-129.

Financial: W.S.A. §3-5-101. Durable or springing: "This power of attorney shall not become ineffective by my disability" or "This power of attorney shall become effective upon my disability."

Health Care: Health Care: W.S.A. §3-5-201. Titled "Durable Power of Attorney for Health Care." No form, but does contain execution requirements. Must be signed by at least two witnesses, both of whom must sign declaration stating: "I declare under penalty of perjury under the laws of Wyoming that the person who signed or acknowledged this document is personally known to me to be the principal, that the principal signed or acknowledged this durable power of attorney in my presence, that the principal appears to be of sound mind and under no duress, fraud or undue influence, that I am not the person appointed as attorney in fact by this document, and that I am not a treating health care provider, an employee of a treating health care provider, the operator of a community care facility, an employee of an operator of a community care facility, the operator of a residential care facility, nor an employee of an operator of a residential care facility." At least one witness must also sign the following statement: "I further declare under penalty of perjury under the laws of Wyoming that I am not related to the principal by blood, marriage, or adoption, and, to the best of my knowledge, I am not entitled to any part of the estate of the principal upon the death of the principal under a will now existing or by operation of law."

Living Will: W.S.A. §35-22-101.

Appendix C:
The Design of the Forms

No matter whether or not you are an attorney, when you look at a form book it may be difficult to decide which form you should use. When I am looking for a form, I get frustrated when I can't find a brief explanation of the form itself and something telling me why that form is different from other forms in the book. This brief introduction will help you understand the last will and testament and living trust forms in Appendix D.

Keep in mind the following key provisions of the living trust.

Grantor

The living trust must clearly identify the *grantor* (creator) of the trust. All of the forms in this book are written for **one** grantor.

There are a number of living trust promoters (including attorneys) that recommend and use a *joint trust* for married couples. Both husband and wife are the grantors of the trust as well as co-trustees of the trust. Such forms are suggested to streamline the process and to keep the couple's assets consolidated. When a spouse dies, unless all of his or her assets are distributed to the surviving spouse, a portion of the trust becomes irrevocable. After a spouse's death, the provisions of a joint trust governing the disposition and administration of the deceased spouse's assets are irrevocable and cannot be changed or revoked by the surviving spouse. However, provisions governing the disposition and administration of the deceased spouse's assets. The provisions governing the disposition and administration of the surviving spouse's assets remain amendable and revocable during the lifetime of the surviving spouse.

In my experience, clients have a difficult time understanding how a joint trust operates after one spouse dies. Things become more confusing if the surviving spouse wants to amend the trust to respond to changes in family circumstances, tax laws, etc. In some states, if a joint trust is used, upon the death of the first spouse there may be unfavorable income tax consequences to the surviving spouse.

For simplicity, each spouse should have his or her own living trust. There are no additional costs associated with a second trust. In addition, the investment assets of each trust, while kept separate, can be invested in common funds. No investment opportunities are lost.

Trustee

The grantor of the living trust will also be the initial *trustee*. The grantor may elect to have a *co-trustee* serve with him or her. However, this is generally not necessary and can actually complicate the trust administration as the approval and signature of the co-trustee may be required with regard to trust business. A living trust is intended to keep things as simple as they would be without the trust.

Successor Trustee

The individuals designated to serve as *successor trustee* must be clearly identified. For a married person, the successor trustee is the spouse. It is advisable to name at least two individuals who will serve as successor trustee if the spouse cannot serve as successor trustee. The same is true for an unmarried person.

Many times parents name a child to serve as trustee of any trust established by the parents for the benefit of the child. More often than not, a co-trustee is named to serve with the child. This may be another child, a family member, or a trusted friend.

The living trust forms do **not** contain provisions for co-trustees. However, there are sample co-trustee provisions contained in Appendix D that can be used if co-trustees are desired.

Beneficiaries

The grantor will be the primary beneficiary of the living trust during his or her lifetime. If the grantor is married, the spouse will also be a beneficiary of the trust. In addition, if the grantor has minor children, they will also be beneficiaries of the living trust.

Upon the grantor's death, the *beneficiaries* can be any number of individuals, such as:

- surviving spouse;
- minor children;
- adult children;
- parents;
- brothers and sisters;
- other family members and friends; and,
- charities.

The living trust forms assume that the surviving spouse and children will be the beneficiaries of the trust after the grantor's death. Upon the death of the surviving spouse, the children will be the beneficiaries of the trust.

For an unmarried person, his or her children will be the beneficiaries of the trust. If there are no children, the beneficiaries must be designated by name.

NOTE: *All of the living trust forms contain language that automatically include as beneficiaries children born after the creation of the living trust. This avoids the need to amend the living trust whenever a child is born. Also, the living trust forms assume that each child will receive an equal share of the living trust. This allocation can be changed to vary the amounts that will be given to each child.*

The Living Trust Form Documents

The basic living trust forms are included in Appendix D. You are the designer of your living trust. The living trust forms can be customized to address your specific planning goals. Do not feel pigeon-holed into a form document—tailor it to meet your needs.

Unmarried Person

If you are not married, you should use Forms 7, 8, 9, or 10.

FORM 7 An unmarried person with no children. Upon the death of the grantor, assets remaining in the living trust are distributed to designated individuals. No special estate tax planning.

FORM 8 An unmarried person with no children. Upon the death of the grantor, assets remaining in the living trust are held in a *Family Trust* for the benefit of one or more individuals. No special estate tax planning.

FORM 9 An unmarried person with children. Upon the death of the grantor, assets remaining in the living trust are divided into equal shares for each child and the shares are distributed outright to the children. No special estate tax planning.

FORM 10 An unmarried person with children. Upon the death of the grantor, assets remaining in the living trust are divided into equal shares for each child. Each share is held in a *Child's Trust* for the benefit of the child. No special estate tax planning.

Married Person

If you are married, you should use Forms 11, 12, 13, 14, 15, 16, 17, or 18.

FORM 11 A married person with no children. Upon the death of the grantor, assets remaining in the living trust are distributed to the surviving spouse or to the surviving spouse's living trust. No special estate tax planning.

FORM 12 A married person with no children. Upon the death of the grantor, assets remaining in the living trust up to the applicable credit amount are held in a *Family Trust* for the benefit of the surviving spouse. Any assets in excess of the applicable credit amount are distributed to the surviving spouse or to the surviving spouse's living trust. Upon the death of the surviving spouse, assets remaining in the *Family Trust* are distributed to designated individuals. Estate tax planning issues.

FORM 13   A married person with no children. Upon the death of the grantor, assets remaining in the living trust equal to the applicable credit amount are held in a *Family Trust* for the benefit of the surviving spouse. Assets in excess of the applicable credit amount are held in a *Marital Trust* for the benefit of the surviving spouse. Upon the death of the surviving spouse, assets remaining in the *Family Trust* and *Marital Trust* are distributed to designated individuals. No estate tax on the *Marital Trust* until the death of the surviving spouse. Estate tax planning issues.

FORM 14   A married person with children. Upon the death of the grantor, assets remaining in the living trust are distributed to the surviving spouse or to the surviving spouse's living trust. No special estate tax planning.

FORM 15   A married person with children. Upon the death of the grantor, assets remaining in the living trust up to the applicable credit amount are held in a *Family Trust* for the benefit of the surviving spouse and children. Any assets in excess of the applicable credit amount are distributed to the surviving spouse or to the surviving spouse's living trust. Upon the death of the surviving spouse, assets remaining in the *Family Trust* are divided into equal shares for each child and the shares are distributed outright to the children. Estate tax planning issues.

FORM 16   A married person with children. Upon the death of the grantor, assets remaining in the living trust up to the applicable credit amount are held in a *Family Trust* for the benefit of the surviving spouse and children. Any assets in excess of the unified credit amount are distributed to the surviving spouse or to the surviving spouse's living trust. Upon the death of the surviving spouse, assets remaining in the *Family Trust* are divided into equal shares for each child. Each share is held in a *Child's Trust* for the benefit of the child. Estate tax planning issues.

FORM 17   A married person with children. Upon the death of the grantor, assets remaining in the living trust equal to the applicable credit amount are held in a *Family Trust* for the benefit of the surviving spouse and children. Any assets in excess of the applicable credit amount are held in a *Marital Trust* for the benefit of the surviving spouse. Upon the death of the surviving spouse, assets remaining in the *Family Trust* and *Marital Trust* are divided into equal shares for each child and the shares are distributed outright to the children. Estate tax planning issues.

FORM 18   A married person with children. Upon the death of the grantor, assets remaining in the living trust equal to the applicable credit amount are held in a *Family Trust* for the benefit of the surviving spouse and children. Assets in excess of the unified credit amount are held in a *Marital Trust* for the benefit of the surviving spouse. Upon the death of the surviving spouse, assets remaining in the *Family Trust* and *Marital Trust* are divided into equal shares for each child. Each share is held in a *Child's Trust* for the benefit of the child. Estate tax planning issues.

FORM 19   These forms contain provisions that can be used in the event
and   you would like to name co-trustees to serve under the living
FORM 20   trust after your death.

FORM 21   These forms contain alternate provisions for the distribution of
and   a the trust to your children either after the death of you and
FORM22   your spouse or, if a Child's Trust is established, to each child
                when the child attains certain ages.

LAST WILL AND TESTAMENT FORM DOCUMENTS

In addition to your living trust, you should also execute a pourover will. These form documents are relatively simple and are intended to be used in conjunction with your living trust.

> **Warning:** Do not use a pourover will form document without also using a living trust form document.

Unmarried Person

If you are not married, you should use Form 3 or Form 4.

FORM 4   An unmarried person with no children.

FORM 5   An unmarried person with children.

Married Person

If you are married, you should use Form 5 or Form 6.

FORM 5   A married person with no children.

FORM 6   A married person with children.

Unmarried Person

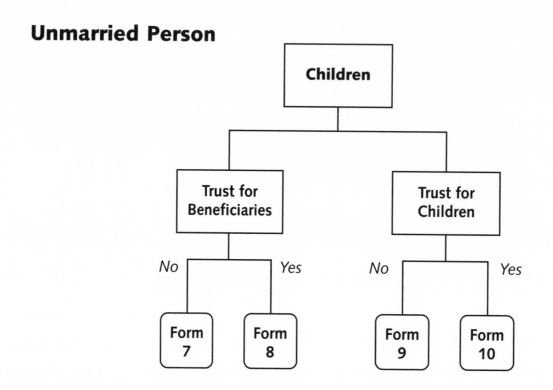

Married Person
with No Children

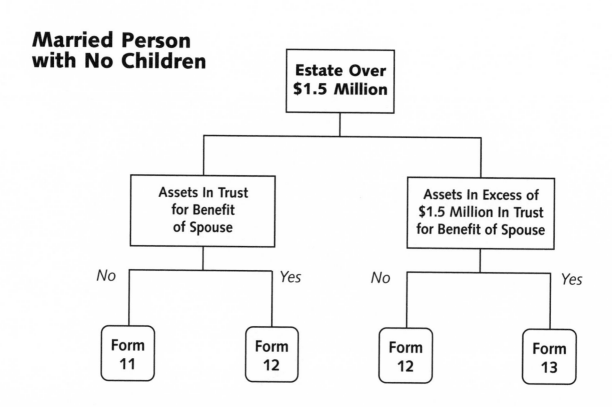

Married Person with Children

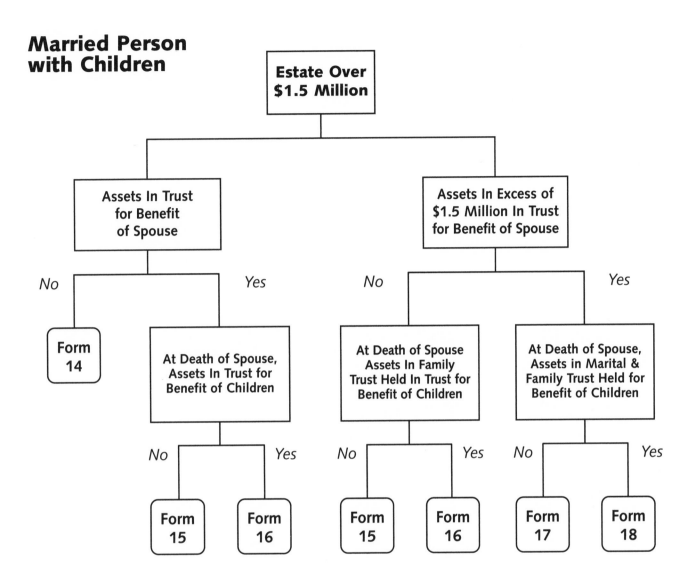

Appendix D:
Blank Forms

The following pages contain forms that can be used to prepare a living trust, a pourover will, and other documents related to the creation, funding, and administration of the living trust. The forms should only be used by persons who have read this book; who do not have any complications in their legal affairs; and, who understand the forms they are using.

The forms may be used directly from the book or they may be photocopied and retyped. Each form is numbered in the upper right hand corner. Be sure you have the correct form number. If there is anything you do not understand, be sure to consult an attorney.

The following is a list of the forms contained in this appendix, along with the page number where each form begins.

Federal Tax Forms

NOTE: *These forms can also be obtained from the Internal Revenue Service website www.irs.gov.*

Net Worth Worksheet
Inventory

Type of Account	# of Shares/ Units	Date(s) Acquired	Cost	Current Market Value*	Husband	Wife
INVESTMENTS						
Stocks						
TOTAL						
Bonds						
TOTAL						
Mutual Funds						
TOTAL						
CDs						
TOTAL						

Net Worth Worksheet
Inventory

Type of Account	# of Shares/ Units	Date(s) Acquired	Cost	Current Market Value*	Husband	Wife
US Bonds						
TOTAL						
US Treasury Notes/Bills						
TOTAL						
CASH						
Checking						
TOTAL						
Savings						
TOTAL						
Money Market						
TOTAL						

Net Worth Worksheet
Inventory

Type of Account	# of Shares/ Units	Date(s) Acquired	Cost	Current Market Value*	Husband	Wife
RETIREMENT PLANS						
Pension/ Profit Shg.						
TOTAL						
401 (k)						
TOTAL						
Keogh/SEP						
TOTAL						
IRAs						
TOTAL						
DEFERRED COMPENSATION						
TOTAL						
ESOP						
TOTAL						
REAL ESTATE						
Home						
Vacation Home						

Net Worth Worksheet
Inventory

Type of Account	# of Shares/ Units	Date(s) Acquired	Cost	Current Market Value*	Husband	Wife
Rental Properties						
TOTAL						
Life Insurance						
Group Term						
Whole Life						
Universal Life						
Variable Life						
TOTAL						
Business Interests						
Corporation						
Sole Prop.						
Ltd. Pshps.						
TOTAL						
Personal Property						
Autos						
Vehicles						
Furnishings						
Jewelry/ Furs						
Artwork						
Antiques						
Collections						
Other						
TOTAL						

Net Worth Worksheet
Inventory

Type of Account	# of Shares/ Units	Date(s) Acquired	Cost	Current Market Value*	Husband	Wife
Misc. Prop.						
Oil & Gas Royalties						
Leases						
Notes Receivable						
Annuities						
Commodity Investments						
TOTAL						

TOTAL ASSETS $_____ $_____ $_____

Liability

Type of Loan	Lender	Balance Due*	Husband	Wife
Home Mortgage				
Home Equity				
Vacation Home Mortgage				
Personal Loans				
Automobile				
Vehicles				
Education Loans				
Life Insurance				
Credit Cards				
Income Taxes				
TOTAL				

TOTAL ASSETS $_____ $_____ $_____

*This column should represent the combined value of the asset/liability. The columns for Husband and Wife reflect the assets that are titled in their individual names. If the investment/account/liability is owned jointly, one-half of the combined value should be included in each column.

Net Worth Summary

ASSETS:

INVESTMENTS:
    Stocks   _____
    Bonds _____
    Mutual Funds _____
    CDs _____
    US Bonds _____
    US Treasury Bills/Notes _____
    TOTAL $_____

CASH:
    Checking   _____
    Savings _____
    Money Market _____
    TOTAL $_____

RETIREMENT PLANS:
    Pension/Profit Sharing   _____
    401(k) _____
    Keogh/SEP _____
    IRA _____
    Deferred Compensation _____
    ESOP _____
    TOTAL $_____

REAL ESTATE:
    Primary Residence   _____
    Vacation Residence _____
    Rental Properties _____
    TOTAL $_____

LIFE INSURANCE: (Cash Value)
    Whole/Universal/Variable Life _____

BUSINESS INTERESTS:
    Corporation/Sole Proprietorship/Limited Partnership _____

PERSONAL PROPERTY:

Automobiles _____

Other Vehicles _____

Household Furnishings/Personal Effects _____

Jewelry/Furs _____

Artwork _____

Antiques _____

Collectibles _____

Other _____

TOTAL $_____

MISCELLANEOUS PROPERTY:

Oil & Gas Royalties _____

Leases _____

Notes Receivable _____

Annuities _____

Commodities _____

TOTAL $_____

TOTAL ASSETS $_____

LIABILITIES:

Mortgage–Primary Residence _____

Mortgage–Vacation Residence _____

Mortgage–Rental Properties _____

Home Equity Loans _____

Personal Loans _____

Automobile _____

Other Vehicles _____

Education _____

Life Insurance _____

Credit Cards _____

Income Taxes _____

TOTAL LIABILITIES $_____

NET WORTH (ASSETS Minus LIABILITIES) $_____

NET WORTH

INCLUDING LIFE INSURANCE DEATH BENEFITS $_____

Form 2:   Self-Proving Affidavit to be used in the following states.

Alabama	Indiana	North Dakota
Alaska	Maine	Oregon
Arizona	Mississippi	South Carolina
Arkansas	Montana	South Dakota
Colorado	Nebraska	Tennessee
Connecticut	Nevada	Utah
Hawaii	New Mexico	Washington
Idaho	New York	West Virginia
Illinois		

Form 2A: Self-Proving Affidavit to be used in the following states.

Delaware	Kentucky	Oklahoma
Florida	Massachusetts	Pennsylvania
Georgia	Missouri	Rhode Island
Iowa	New Jersey	Virginia
Kansas	North Carolina	Wyoming

Self-Proving Affidavit is not used in the following states.

California	Michigan	Vermont
District of Columbia	Ohio	Wisconsin

This page intentionally left blank.

Self-Proving Affidavit for Pourover Will

STATE OF _____§

COUNTY OF_____§

We, _____, and _____,
and _____, the testator and the witnesses, whose names are signed
to the attached or foregoing instrument in those capacities, personally appearing before the undersigned authority and being first duly sworn, declare to the undersigned authority under penalty of perjury that the testator
declared, signed, and executed the instrument as his or her last will and testament; that he or she signed it willingly, or directed another to sign it for him or her; that he or she executed it as his or her free and voluntary act
for the purposes therein expressed; and that each of the witnesses, at the request of the testator, in his or her hearing and presence and in the presence of each other, signed the will as witnesses, and that to the best knowledge the
testator was at that time of legal age, of sound mind, and under no constraint or undue influence.

_____
TESTATOR

_____
WITNESS

_____
WITNESS

SUBSCRIBED, SWORN AND ACKNOWLEDGED before me by _____ testator,
and by _____ and _____, witness-
es, this _____ day of _____, 20____.

_____
Notary Public

My commission expires:_____

This page intentionally left blank.

Self-Proving Affidavit for Pourover Will

STATE OF _____ §

COUNTY OF_____ §

I, the undersigned, an officer authorized to administer oaths, certify that _____,
the testator, and _____ and _____, the witnesses,
whose names are signed to the attached or foregoing instrument and whose signatures appear below, having
appeared before me and having been first duly sworn, each then declared to me that: the attached or foregoing
instrument is the last will and testament of the testator; that the testator willingly and voluntarily declared, signed,
and executed the will in the presence of the witnesses; that the witnesses signed the will upon the request of the testator, in the presence and hearing of the testator and in the presence of each other; to the best knowledge of each
witness, the testator was, at the time of signing, of the age of majority (or otherwise legally competent to make a
will), of sound mind and memory, and under no constraint or undue influence; and that each witness was and is
competent and of proper age to witness a will.

_____
TESTATOR

_____
WITNESS

_____
WITNESS

SUBSCRIBED AND SWORN to before me by , the testator, who is personally known to me or who has produced
_____ as identification, and by _____, a witness, who is per-
sonally known to me or who has produced _____ as identification, and by
_____, a witness, who is personally known to me or who has produced
_____ as identification, on this _____ day of _____, 20_____.

_____
Notary Public

My commission expires:_____

This page intentionally left blank.

LAST WILL AND TESTAMENT

(Pourover Will, Unmarried, No Children)

I, _____, of _____, State of
_____, make this my will and revoke all prior wills and codicils.

I. DEBTS, TAXES AND EXPENSES

My executor shall pay all expenses of my last illness and funeral, costs of administration including ancillary administration, costs of safeguarding and delivering legacies, and other proper charges against my estate (excluding debts
secured by real property or life insurance). My executor shall also pay all estate and inheritance taxes assessed by reason of my death.

II. FAMILY

I am not married and I do not have any children.

III. TANGIBLE PERSONAL PROPERTY

I give all my tangible personal property (including, but not limited to my jewelry, clothing, books, china, crystal, silverware, furniture and household furnishings, objects of art, collections, and automobiles) and any insurance policies
thereon, to _____.

IV. RESIDUE

I give all the rest, remainder, and residue of my estate, real and personal, wherever situated, now owned or hereafter
acquired by me to the then acting Trustee of my Living Trust executed by me on _____ 20____,
before the execution of this will, with myself as trustee and _____ as successor trustee, to be
added to the trust estate subject to the terms of the Living Trust as now provided and as amended from time to time.

V. EXECUTORS

5.1 Appointment. I appoint _____ as executor of this will. If
for any reason _____ is unwilling or unable to act as executor, I appoint _____ as alternate executor of this will.

5.2 Powers. My executor shall have all of the powers conferred on executors under state law including, but not limited to the following:

   (a) **Retain Property.** To retain any property (including stock of any corporate executor hereunder or a parent or affiliate company) originally constituting a part of the estate or subsequently added thereto;

   (b) **Invest.** To invest and reinvest the estate property in bonds, stocks, mortgages, notes, bank deposits, or
other property of any kind, real or personal, domestic or foreign;

   (c) **Sell.** By public offering or private negotiation, to sell, exchange, assign, transfer, or otherwise dispose of all
or any real or personal property for such price and on such terms as the executor deems proper;

   (d) **Employee Benefits.** To elect, pursuant to the terms of any employee benefit plan, individual retirement
plan, or insurance contract, the mode of distribution of the proceeds thereof, and no adjustment shall be made in the
interests of the beneficiaries to compensate for the effect of the election;

(e) Securities. To engage in all actions necessary to the effective administration of securities including, but not limited to, the authority to: vote securities in person or by proxy; engage in a voting trust or voting agreement; exercise any options, rights, or privileges pertaining to any trust property; and consent to or participate in mergers, consolidations, sales of assets, recapitalizations, reorganizations, dissolutions, or other alterations of corporate structure affecting securities held by the executor;

(f) Litigation. To commence or defend at the expense of the estate such litigation with respect to the estate as the executor deems advisable;

(g) Claims. To collect, pay, contest, compromise, settle, renew, or abandon any claims or demands of or against the estate on whatever terms the executor deems advisable;

(h) Agents. To employ attorneys, auditors, brokers, and investment advisors; and

(i) Miscellaneous. To perform other acts necessary or appropriate for the proper administration of the estate, execute and deliver necessary instruments, and give full receipts and discharges.

5.3 Bond. No bond or security shall be required of any executor wherever acting.

5.4 Compensation. The executor shall be reimbursed for all reasonable expenses incurred in the management and protection of the estate, and any corporate executor shall receive compensation for its services in accordance with its schedule of fees in effect from time to time.

5.5 Independent Administration. To the extent provided by applicable state law, the administration of my estate shall be independent of the supervision of any court.

IN WITNESS WHEREOF, I have signed this will, consisting of _____ pages, the following pages included, this _____ day of _____, 20____.

_____

TESTATOR

We certify that the above instrument was on the date thereof signed and declared by the testator as the testator's will in our presence and that we, at the testator's request and in the testator's presence and in the presence of each other, have signed our names as witnesses thereto, believing the testator to be of sound mind and memory at the time of signing.

_____   Residing at: _____

Witness   _____

_____   Residing at: _____

Witness   _____

LAST WILL AND TESTAMENT

(Pourover Will, Unmarried, Children)

I, _____, of _____, State of _____, make this my will and revoke all prior wills and codicils.

I. DEBTS, TAXES AND EXPENSES

My executor shall pay all expenses of my last illness and funeral, costs of administration including ancillary administration, costs of safeguarding and delivering legacies, and other proper charges against my estate (excluding debts secured by real property or life insurance). My executor shall also pay all estate and inheritance taxes assessed by reason of my death.

II. FAMILY

I am not married. I have _____ child(ren) now living, namely: _____.
I intend by this will to provide for all my children, including any hereafter born or adopted.

III. TANGIBLE PERSONAL PROPERTY

I give all my tangible personal property (including, but not limited to my jewelry, clothing, books, china, crystal, silverware, furniture and household furnishings, objects of art, collections, and automobiles) and any insurance policies thereon, to my Children who so survive me to be divided equally among them as they agree. If my Children do not survive me, I give such property to _____.

IV. RESIDUE

I give all the rest, remainder, and residue of my estate, real and personal, wherever situated, now owned or hereafter acquired by me to the then acting Trustee of my Living Trust executed by me on _____ 20____, before the execution of this will, with myself as trustee and _____ as successor trustee, to be added to the trust estate subject to the terms of the Living Trust as now provided and as amended from time to time.

V. GUARDIANS

If I am the surviving natural parent of my minor child(ren), I name _____ as guardian. If for any reason _____ is unable or unwilling to serve as guardian, I name _____ as guardian. No bond or security shall be required of any guardian.

VI. EXECUTORS

6.1 Appointment. I appoint _____ as executor of this will. If for any reason _____ is unwilling or unable to act as executor, I appoint _____ as alternate executor of this will.

6.2 Powers. My executor shall have all of the powers conferred on executors under state law including, but not limited to the following:

(a) **Retain Property.** To retain any property (including stock of any corporate executor hereunder or a parent or affiliate company) originally constituting a part of the estate or subsequently added thereto;

(b) **Invest.** To invest and reinvest the estate property in bonds, stocks, mortgages, notes, bank deposits, or other property of any kind, real or personal, domestic or foreign;

(c) **Sell.** By public offering or private negotiation, to sell, exchange, assign, transfer, or otherwise dispose of all or any real or personal property for such price and on such terms as the executor deems proper;

(d) **Employee Benefits.** To elect, pursuant to the terms of any employee benefit plan, individual retirement plan, or insurance contract, the mode of distribution of the proceeds thereof, and no adjustment shall be made in the interests of the beneficiaries to compensate for the effect of the election;

(e) **Securities.** To engage in all actions necessary to the effective administration of securities including, but not limited to, the authority to: vote securities in person or by proxy; engage in a voting trust or voting agreement; exercise any options, rights, or privileges pertaining to any trust property; and consent to or participate in mergers, consolidations, sales of assets, recapitalizations, reorganizations, dissolutions, or other alterations of corporate structure affecting securities held by the executor;

(f) **Litigation.** To commence or defend at the expense of the estate such litigation with respect to the estate as the executor deems advisable;

(g) **Claims.** To collect, pay, contest, compromise, settle, renew, or abandon any claims or demands of or against the estate on whatever terms the executor deems advisable;

(h) **Agents.** To employ attorneys, auditors, brokers, and investment advisors; and,

(i) **Miscellaneous.** To perform other acts necessary or appropriate for the proper administration of the estate, execute and deliver necessary instruments, and give full receipts and discharges.

6.3 Bond. No bond or security shall be required of any executor wherever acting.

6.4 Compensation. The executor shall be reimbursed for all reasonable expenses incurred in the management and protection of the estate, and any corporate executor shall receive compensation for its services in accordance with its schedule of fees in effect from time to time.

6.5 Independent Administration. To the extent provided by applicable state law, the administration of my estate shall be independent of the supervision of any court.

IN WITNESS WHEREOF, I have signed this will, consisting of _____ pages, the following pages included, this _____ day of _____, 20_____.

_____

TESTATOR

We certify that the above instrument was on the date thereof signed and declared by the testator as the testator's will in our presence and that we, at the testator's request and in the testator's presence and in the presence of each other, have signed our names as witnesses thereto, believing the testator to be of sound mind and memory at the time of signing.

_____   Residing at: _____

Witness   _____

_____   Residing at: _____

Witness   _____

LAST WILL AND TESTAMENT

(Pourover Will, Married, No Children)

I, _____, of _____, State of _____, make this my will and revoke all prior wills and codicils.

I. DEBTS, TAXES AND EXPENSES

My executor shall pay all expenses of my last illness and funeral, costs of administration including ancillary administration, costs of safeguarding and delivering legacies, and other proper charges against my estate (excluding debts secured by real property or life insurance). My executor shall also pay all estate and inheritance taxes assessed by reason of my death.

II. FAMILY

I am married to _____ who is referred to as "my spouse." I do not have any children.

III. TANGIBLE PERSONAL PROPERTY

I give all my tangible personal property (including, but not limited to my jewelry, clothing, books, china, crystal, silverware, furniture and household furnishings, objects of art, collections, and automobiles) and any insurance policies thereon, to my spouse. If my spouse does not survive me, I give such property to _____.

IV. RESIDUE

I give all the rest, remainder, and residue of my estate, real and personal, wherever situated, now owned or hereafter acquired by me to the then acting Trustee of my Living Trust executed by me on _____ 20____, before the execution of this will, with myself as trustee and _____ as successor trustee, to be added to the trust estate subject to the terms of the Living Trust as now provided and as amended from time to time.

V. EXECUTORS

5.1 Appointment. I appoint my spouse as executor of this will. If for any reason my spouse is unwilling or unable to act as executor, I appoint _____ as alternate executor of this will.

5.2 Powers. My executor shall have all of the powers conferred on executors under state law including, but not limited to the following:

(a) **Retain Property.** To retain any property (including stock of any corporate executor hereunder or a parent or affiliate company) originally constituting a part of the estate or subsequently added thereto;

(b) **Invest.** To invest and reinvest the estate property in bonds, stocks, mortgages, notes, bank deposits, or other property of any kind, real or personal, domestic or foreign;

(c) **Sell.** By public offering or private negotiation, to sell, exchange, assign, transfer, or otherwise dispose of all or any real or personal property for such price and on such terms as the executor deems proper;

(d) **Employee Benefits.** To elect, pursuant to the terms of any employee benefit plan, individual retirement plan, or insurance contract, the mode of distribution of the proceeds thereof, and no adjustment shall be made in the interests of the beneficiaries to compensate for the effect of the election;

(e) Securities. To engage in all actions necessary to the effective administration of securities including, but not limited to, the authority to: vote securities in person or by proxy; engage in a voting trust or voting agreement; exercise any options, rights, or privileges pertaining to any trust property; and consent to or participate in mergers, consolidations, sales of assets, recapitalizations, reorganizations, dissolutions, or other alterations of corporate structure affecting securities held by the executor;

(f) Litigation. To commence or defend at the expense of the estate such litigation with respect to the estate as the executor deems advisable;

(g) Claims. To collect, pay, contest, compromise, settle, renew, or abandon any claims or demands of or against the estate on whatever terms the executor deems advisable;

(h) Agents. To employ attorneys, auditors, brokers, and investment advisors; and,

(i) Miscellaneous. To perform other acts necessary or appropriate for the proper administration of the estate, execute and deliver necessary instruments, and give full receipts and discharges.

5.3 Bond. No bond or security shall be required of any executor wherever acting.

5.4 Compensation. The executor shall be reimbursed for all reasonable expenses incurred in the management and protection of the estate, and any corporate executor shall receive compensation for its services in accordance with its schedule of fees in effect from time to time.

5.5 Independent Administration. To the extent provided by applicable state law, the administration of my estate shall be independent of the supervision of any court.

IN WITNESS WHEREOF, I have signed this will, consisting of _____ pages, the following pages included, this _____ day of _____, 20____.

_____
TESTATOR

We certify that the above instrument was on the date thereof signed and declared by the testator as the testator's will in our presence and that we, at the testator's request and in the testator's presence and in the presence of each other, have signed our names as witnesses thereto, believing the testator to be of sound mind and memory at the time of signing.

_____   Residing at: _____

Witness

        _____

_____   Residing at: _____

Witness

        _____

LAST WILL AND TESTAMENT

(Pourover Will, Married, Children)

I, _____, of _____, State of _____, make this my will and revoke all prior wills and codicils.

I. DEBTS, TAXES AND EXPENSES

My executor shall pay all expenses of my last illness and funeral, costs of administration including ancillary administration, costs of safeguarding and delivering legacies, and other proper charges against my estate (excluding debts secured by real property or life insurance). My executor shall also pay all estate and inheritance taxes assessed by reason of my death.

II. FAMILY

I am married to _____ who is referred to as "my spouse." I have _____ child(ren) now living, namely: _____. I intend by this will to provide for all my children, including any hereafter born or adopted.

III. TANGIBLE PERSONAL PROPERTY

I give all my tangible personal property (including, but not limited to my jewelry, clothing, books, china, crystal, silverware, furniture and household furnishings, objects of art, collections, and automobiles) and any insurance policies thereon, to my spouse. If my spouse does not survive me, I give such property to my Children who so survive me to be divided equally among them as they agree. If my children do not survive me, I give such property to _____.

IV. RESIDUE

I give all the rest, remainder, and residue of my estate, real and personal, wherever situated, now owned or hereafter acquired by me to the then acting Trustee of my Living Trust executed by me on _____ 20____, before the execution of this will, with myself as trustee and _____ as successor trustee, to be added to the trust estate subject to the terms of the Living Trust as now provided and as amended from time to time.

V. GUARDIANS

If my spouse does not survive me or dies after my death without providing for the custody of a minor child of mine, I name _____ as guardian. If for any reason _____ is unable or unwilling to serve as guardian, I name _____ as guardian. No bond or security shall be required of any guardian.

VI. EXECUTORS

6.1 Appointment. I appoint my spouse as executor of this will. If for any reason my spouse is unwilling or unable to act as executor, I appoint _____ as alternate executor of this will.

6.2 Powers. My executor shall have all of the powers conferred on executors under state law including, but not limited to the following:

(a) **Retain Property.** To retain any property (including stock of any corporate executor hereunder or a parent or affiliate company) originally constituting a part of the estate or subsequently added thereto;

(b) **Invest.** To invest and reinvest the estate property in bonds, stocks, mortgages, notes, bank deposits, or other property of any kind, real or personal, domestic or foreign;

(c) **Sell.** By public offering or private negotiation, to sell, exchange, assign, transfer, or otherwise dispose of all or any real or personal property for such price and on such terms as the executor deems proper;

(d) Employee Benefits. To elect, pursuant to the terms of any employee benefit plan, individual retirement plan, or insurance contract, the mode of distribution of the proceeds thereof, and no adjustment shall be made in the interests of the beneficiaries to compensate for the effect of the election;

(e) Securities. To engage in all actions necessary to the effective administration of securities including, but not limited to, the authority to: vote securities in person or by proxy; engage in a voting trust or voting agreement; exercise any options, rights, or privileges pertaining to any trust property; and consent to or participate in mergers, consolidations, sales of assets, recapitalizations, reorganizations, dissolutions, or other alterations of corporate structure affecting securities held by the executor;

(f) Litigation. To commence or defend at the expense of the estate such litigation with respect to the estate as the executor deems advisable;

(g) Claims. To collect, pay, contest, compromise, settle, renew, or abandon any claims or demands of or against the estate on whatever terms the executor deems advisable;

(h) Agents. To employ attorneys, auditors, brokers, and investment advisors; and,

(i) Miscellaneous. To perform other acts necessary or appropriate for the proper administration of the estate, execute and deliver necessary instruments, and give full receipts and discharges.

6.3 Bond. No bond or security shall be required of any executor wherever acting.

6.4 Compensation. The executor shall be reimbursed for all reasonable expenses incurred in the management and protection of the estate, and any corporate executor shall receive compensation for its services in accordance with its schedule of fees in effect from time to time.

6.5 Independent Administration. To the extent provided by applicable state law, the administration of my estate shall be independent of the supervision of any court.

IN WITNESS WHEREOF, I have signed this will, consisting of _____ pages, the following pages included, this _____ day of _____, 20____.

_____

TESTATOR

We certify that the above instrument was on the date thereof signed and declared by the testator as the testator's will in our presence and that we, at the testator's request and in the testator's presence and in the presence of each other, have signed our names as witnesses thereto, believing the testator to be of sound mind and memory at the time of signing.

_____   Residing at: _____

Witness   _____

_____   Residing at: _____

Witness   _____

LIVING TRUST

(Unmarried, No Children)

THIS AGREEMENT OF TRUST is entered into at _____, State of _____, this _____ day of _____, 20_____, by and between _____, as Grantor and Trustee. This Trust, as from time to time amended, shall be known as the "_____ LIVING TRUST dated _____, 20_____."

ARTICLE I
FAMILY

I am not married and I do not have any children.

ARTICLE II
FUNDING

Initial Funding. I hereby transfer to the Trustee the sum of Ten Dollars ($10.00).

Additional Funding. From time to time the Trust may be funded with additional property by me or by any other person in any manner. In addition, I may cause the Trustee to be designated as beneficiary of life insurance policies or qualified retirement plans. All property transferred, assigned, conveyed, or delivered to the Trustee and all investment and reinvestment thereof, are herein collectively referred to as the "trust estate" and shall be held, administered, and distributed by the Trustee in accordance with the terms of this Trust Agreement.

ARTICLE III
ADMINISTRATION OF TRUST DURING MY LIFETIME

Distributions of Income. While I am living and not under any incapacity, the Trustee shall distribute the income of the Trust as directed in writing by me from time to time. In the event I do not deliver such direction to the Trustee, the Trustee shall pay to or expend on my behalf such amount of income from the Trust as the Trustee determines is necessary or advisable for my health, education, maintenance, and support. Any income that is not distributed to me or on my behalf shall be added to the principal of the Trust.

Distributions of Principal. While I am living and not under any incapacity, the Trustee shall distribute such part or all of the principal of the Trust as directed in writing by me from time to time. In the event I do not deliver such direction to the Trustee, the Trustee shall pay to or expend on my behalf such part of the principal of the Trust as the Trustee determines is necessary or advisable for my health, education, maintenance, and support.

Use of Residential Property. If any real property used by me for residential purposes (whether on a full-time or part-time basis, including recreational property) becomes part of the trust estate, I shall have the right to use and occupy such property without rental and without accounting to the trust estate. The Trustee shall pay all taxes, debts, and other expenses associated with such residential property from the income of the Trust. To the extent income is insufficient, the Trustee shall use principal of the Trust to pay such taxes, debts, and expenses.

Distribution During My Incapacity. In addition, whenever the Trustee considers that I am incapacitated, the Trustee shall distribute or apply such amounts of the income and principal of the trust estate (even though exhausting the Trust) as the Trustee considers advisable for my health, maintenance, and support, or for any other purpose the Trustee considers to be for my best interests. Any excess income shall be added to principal.

Incapacity. For purposes of this Trust Agreement, I shall be considered to be incapacitated if I: (a) am unable to manage my affairs; (b) am under a legal incapacity; or, (c) by reason of illness or mental or physical incapacity, am unable to give prompt and intelligent consideration to my financial matters. I shall be considered incapacitated upon a good faith determination made by _____ and my physician, or the survivor of them, and the Trustee may rely upon written notice of that determination.

ARTICLE IV
ADMINISTRATION OF TRUST UPON MY DEATH

Payment of Expenses, Claims, and Taxes. Upon my death, if I have no probate estate, or to the extent that the cash and readily marketable assets in the principal of the residue of my probate estate are insufficient, the Trustee shall make the following payments from the principal of the trust estate. The Trustee shall pay the expenses of my last illness and funeral, costs of administration including ancillary administration, costs of safeguarding and delivering legacies, and claims allowable against my estate (excluding debts secured by real property or life insurance). The Trustee shall also pay the estate and inheritance taxes assessed by reason of my death. The Trustee may make payment directly or to the legal representative of my estate, as the Trustee deems advisable. I hereby waive all rights of apportionment or reimbursement for any payments made pursuant to this Article.

Selection of Assets. Assets or funds otherwise excludable from my gross estate for federal estate tax purposes shall not be used to make the foregoing payments. The Trustee's selection of assets to be sold to pay expenses, claims, and taxes shall not be subject to question by any beneficiary.

Tax Elections. The Trustee shall make such elections under the tax laws as the Trustee deems advisable, without regard to the relative interests of the beneficiaries and without liability to any person. No adjustment shall be made between principal and income or in the relative interests of the beneficiaries to compensate for the effect of elections or allocations under the tax laws made by the legal representative of my estate or by the Trustee.

ARTICLE V
DISTRIBUTION OF TRUST ASSETS UPON MY DEATH

Tangible Personal Property. The Trustee shall distribute my tangible personal property in accordance with any written, signed, and dated memorandum prepared by me. Any tangible personal property that is not disposed of by memorandum shall be distributed in equal shares to the following individuals:

Specific Bequest. The Trustee shall distribute the following property to the named individuals:

$ _____ to _____

$ _____ to _____

If any of the individuals named does not survive me, the gift to that person will lapse and the property will pass as provided below. If no specific bequests are set forth in this paragraph, the provisions of this paragraph shall be of no effect.

Distribution to My Beneficiaries. The Trustee shall distribute the remaining trust estate, including any additions to the Trust by reason of my death, to the following individuals in the amounts specified:

_____% to _____

_____% to _____

_____% to _____

_____% to _____

If an individual named herein does not survive me, the gift to such person shall lapse and the share to which such person would have been entitled shall be distributed among the surviving individuals named in this paragraph on a *pro rata* basis.

No Survivors. If none of the individuals named in the preceding paragraph survive me, the remaining trust estate, including any additions to the Trust by reason of my death, shall be distributed to my heirs at law in accordance with the law of descent and distribution in effect on the date of my death.

ARTICLE VI
THE TRUSTEE

Initial Trustee. While I am alive, able, and willing to serve, I shall be the Trustee of the Trust.

Successor Trustee. During my lifetime, if I cannot serve as Trustee, I will appoint a successor Trustee. If I do not appoint a successor Trustee, or in the event of my death, incapacity, or inability to serve as Trustee, the successor Trustee shall be the first of the following individuals who is willing and competent to serve as successor Trustee:

If all of the successor Trustees die, become incapacitated, or otherwise fail or cease to serve as Trustee, a majority in number of the then living income beneficiaries of the Trust shall appoint a successor Trustee. Any appointment made under this Article shall be by a signed, acknowledged instrument delivered to the successor Trustee. A successor Trustee shall have all of the powers granted a Trustee in this Trust Agreement.

Resignation of Trustee. Any Trustee may resign as Trustee as to any one or more of the trusts created hereunder at any time by giving written notice to me if I am living, otherwise to the successor Trustee identified in this Trust Agreement, the current income beneficiaries of the Trust, and to those persons, if any, authorized in this Trust Agreement to appoint the successor Trustee.

Removal of Trustee. During my life, I may remove a Trustee at any time for any reason. After my death or if I am incapacitated and unable to remove the Trustee, a majority in number of the then living income beneficiaries of the Trust shall have the power to remove a Trustee.

Bond. No Trustee wherever acting shall be required to give bond or surety or be appointed by or account for the administration of any trust to any court.

Trustee's Fees. The Trustee shall be entitled to reasonable fees commensurate with the Trustee's duties and responsibilities, taking into account the value and nature of the trust estate and the time and work involved. The Trustee shall be reimbursed for reasonable costs and expenses incurred in connection with the performance of his or her fiduciary duties.

Registration of Trust. The Trustee shall not be required to register the Trust with any federal, state, or local government authority.

Liability of Trustee. A Trustee shall only be liable for willful misconduct or gross negligence and shall not be liable for breach of fiduciary duty by virtue of mistake or error in judgment. No successor Trustee shall be personally liable for any act or omission of any predecessor.

Majority Decision. If more than one Trustee is serving hereunder, the decision of a majority of the Trustees shall control. The dissenting Trustee shall have no liability for participating in or carrying out the acts of the controlling Trustee.

Delegation to Co-Trustee. A Trustee of any trust created hereunder may at any time by written instrument delegate to a Co-Trustee of such trust all or less than all of the powers conferred upon that Trustee, either for a specified time or until the delegation is revoked by a written instrument.

ARTICLE VII
TRUST ADMINISTRATION

Trustee Powers: Investment and Management of Trust Estate. Subject to any limitation stated elsewhere in this Trust Agreement, the Trustee shall hold, manage, care for, and protect the trust property and shall have the following powers and, except to the extent inconsistent herewith, all of the rights, powers, and privileges and be subject to all of the duties, responsibilities, and conditions set forth in applicable state law, as amended from time to time:

(a) **Retain Property.** To retain any property originally constituting the trust or subsequently added thereto, and to invest and reinvest the trust property in bonds, stocks, mortgages, notes, bank deposits, options, futures, limited partnership interests, limited liability company interests, other business organization interests, shares of registered investment companies and real estate investment trusts, or other property of any kind, real or personal, domestic or foreign; the Trustee may retain or make any investment without liability, even though it is not of a type, quality, marketability, or diversification considered proper for trust investments.

(b) **Investment.** To invest in, participate in, form, or cause to be formed (alone or with others, including members of my family) such corporations, partnerships, limited partnerships, limited liability companies, and other business organizations organized under the laws of any state or country and to transfer and convey to such business organizations all or any part of the assets, real or personal, of any trust estate in exchange for such stocks, bonds, notes, other securities, or interests of such business organizations as the Trustee deems best.

(c) **Residential Property.** To acquire, hold, and maintain any residence for the use and benefit of such one or more of the beneficiaries of the trust, including me, and to pay all carrying charges of such residence, including but not limited to, any taxes, assessments, and maintenance thereon, and all expenses of the repair and operation thereof, including the employment of domestic servants and other expenses incident to the maintenance of a household for the benefit of any one or more of the beneficiaries of the trust, all as the Trustee deems best.

(d) **Tangible Personal Property.** To acquire, hold, and maintain as a part of the trust any and all articles of tangible personal property or any other property for the use and benefit of any one or more of the beneficiaries of the trust, without regard to the income productivity of income, and without any duty to convert such property to productive property, and to pay the expenses of safekeeping of any such property, including insurance, and all expenses of the repair and maintenance of such property, and to sell such property and to apply the net proceeds of sale to the purchase of such other property as the Trustee deems best.

(e) **Operate Business.** To continue or participate in the operation of any business or other enterprise, and to effect incorporation, dissolution, or other change in the form of the organization of the business or enterprise.

(f) **Nominee.** To cause any property, real or personal, belonging to the trust to be held or registered in the Trustee's name or in the name of a nominee or in such other form as the Trustee deems best without disclosing the trust relationship.

(g) Real Estate. To operate, maintain, repair, rehabilitate, alter, erect, improve, or remove any improvements on real estate; to subdivide real estate; to grant easements, give consents, and enter into contracts relating to real estate or its use; and to release or dedicate any interest in real estate.

(h) Lease. To enter for any purpose into a lease as lessor or lessee with or without option to purchase or renew for a term within or extending beyond the term of the trust.

(i) Minerals. To enter into a lease or arrangement for exploration and removal of minerals or other natural resources or enter into a pooling or unitization agreement.

(j) Sell. By public offering or private negotiation, to sell, exchange, assign, transfer, or otherwise dispose of all or any real or personal trust property and give options for these purposes, for such price and on such terms, with such covenants of warranty and such security for deferred payment as the Trustee deems proper.

(k) Partition. To partition any property in which the trust owns an undivided interest.

(l) Securities. To engage in all actions necessary to the effective administration of securities including, but not limited to, the authority to vote in person or by general or limited proxy, or refrain from voting, any corporate securities for any purpose; to exercise or sell any subscription or conversion rights; to consent to and join in or oppose any voting trusts, reorganizations, consolidations, mergers, foreclosures, and liquidations and in connection therewith to deposit securities and accept and hold other property received therefore.

(m) Borrow. To borrow money from any lender, and to extend or renew any existing indebtedness to be repaid from trust assets or otherwise; to mortgage or pledge any property in the trust to secure such borrowing; to advance money for the protection of the trust, and for all expenses, losses, and liabilities sustained in the administration of the trust or because of the holding or ownership of any trust assets.

(n) Litigation. To commence or defend actions, claims, or proceedings for the protection of trust assets and of the Trustee in the performance of his or her duties.

(o) Claims. To pay or contest any claim; to settle a claim by or against the trust by compromise, arbitration, or otherwise; and to release, in whole or in part, any claim belonging to the trust to the extent that the claim is uncollectible.

(p) Payments. To pay taxes, assessments, compensation of the Trustee, and other expenses incurred in the collection, care, administration, and protection of the trust.

(q) Beneficiary under Disability. To pay any sum distributable to a beneficiary under legal disability, without liability to the Trustee, by paying the sum to the beneficiary or by paying the sum for the use of the beneficiary either to a legal representative appointed by the court, or if none, to a relative.

(r) Agents. To employ persons, including attorneys, auditors, investment advisors, or agents, even if they are associated with any Trustee, to advise or assist the Trustee in the performance of his or her administrative duties; to act without independent investigation upon their recommendations; and instead of acting personally, to employ one or more agents to perform any act of administration, whether or not discretionary.

(s) **Distributions.** To distribute income and principal in cash or in kind, or partly in each, and to allocate or distribute undivided interests or different assets or disproportionate interests in assets, and no adjustment shall be made to compensate for a disproportionate allocation of unrealized gain for federal income tax purposes; to value the trust property and to sell any part or all thereof in order to make allocation or distribution; no action taken by the Trustee pursuant to this paragraph shall be subject to question by any beneficiary.

(t) **Allocation of Income and Principal.** To allocate items of income or expense to either trust income or principal, as provided by law, including creation of reserves out of income for depreciation, obsolescence, or amortization, or for depletion in mineral or timber properties.

(u) **Employee Benefits.** To elect, pursuant to the terms of any employee benefit plan, individual retirement plan, or insurance contract, the mode of distribution of the proceeds thereof, and no adjustment shall be made in the interests of the beneficiaries to compensate for the effect of the election.

(v) **Division and Distribution.** To divide any trust created under this Trust Agreement into one or more separate trusts for the benefit of one or more of the beneficiaries of the trust so divided, and to allocate to such divided trust some or all of the assets of the trust estate for any reason.

(w) **Tax Elections.** Unless otherwise expressly directed hereunder, to exercise any tax option, allocation, or election permitted by law as the Trustee determines in the Trustee's sole discretion.

(x) **Reliance.** To rely upon any notice, certificate, affidavit, or other document or evidence believed by the Trustee to be genuine and accurate, in making any payment or distribution. The Trustee shall incur no liability for a disbursement or distribution make in good faith and without actual notice or knowledge of a changed condition or status affecting any person's interest in the trust or any other matter.

(y) **Miscellaneous.** To perform other acts necessary or appropriate for the proper administration of the trust, execute and deliver necessary instruments, and give full receipts and discharges.

Common Fund and Consolidation. For convenience of administration or investment, the Trustee may hold separate trusts as a common fund, dividing the income proportionately among them, assign undivided interests to the separate trusts, and make joint investments of the funds belonging to them. The Trustee may consolidate any separate trust with any other trust with similar provisions for the same beneficiary or beneficiaries.

Spendthrift. The interests of beneficiaries in principal or income shall not be subject to the claims of any creditor, any spouse for alimony or support, or others, or to legal process, and may not be voluntarily or involuntarily alienated or encumbered. The rights of beneficiaries to withdraw trust property are personal and may not be exercised by a legal representative, attorney in fact, or others.

Retained Powers. Notwithstanding the foregoing, while I am living and able to manage my affairs:

(a) no sale or investment shall be made without my written approval, unless I fail to indicate my approval or disapproval of any proposed sale or investment within ten days after being requested to do so in writing;

(b) I shall have the power to direct the retention or sale of any trust assets and the purchase of property with any principal cash in the trust. If I direct the retention or purchase of an asset, the Trustee shall have investment, voting, and management responsibility for that asset unless I direct otherwise; and,

(c) I may at any time or times, with or without right of revocation, by a writing delivered to the Trustee, delegate to any other person or to the Trustee or relinquish any or all of the powers reserved to me hereunder.

The statement of the Trustee that he or she is acting according to this paragraph shall fully protect all persons dealing with the Trustee. The Trustee shall have no responsibility for any loss that may result from acting in accordance with this paragraph.

Restriction on Powers. The Trustee shall not lend trust property to me, directly or indirectly, without adequate interest and adequate security. No Trustee who is a beneficiary of any trust, or who is obligated to support a beneficiary of any trust, shall participate in: the exercise of any discretion over distributions of income or principal other than that which is required for the health, education, maintenance and support of a beneficiary provided that such distribution does not satisfy the Trustee's obligation to support the beneficiary; the exercise of discretion to allocate receipts or expenses between principal and income.

Accounts and Compensation. A Trustee (other than myself) shall render an account of trust receipts and disbursements and a statement of assets at least annually to each adult beneficiary then entitled to receive or have the benefit of the income from the trust. An account is binding on each beneficiary who receives it and on all persons claiming by or through the beneficiary, and the Trustee is released, as to all matters stated in the account or shown by it, unless the beneficiary commences a judicial proceeding to assert a claim within five years after the mailing or other delivery of the account.

Small Trust Termination and Perpetuities Savings.

(a) A trustee in its discretion may terminate and distribute any trust hereunder if the corporate trustee determines that the costs of continuance thereof will substantially impair accomplishment of the purposes of the trust.

(b) The trustee shall terminate and forthwith distribute any trust created hereby, or by exercise of a power of appointment hereunder, and still held twenty-one years after the death of the last to die of myself and the beneficiaries in being at my death.

(c) Distribution under this section shall be made to the persons then entitled to receive or have the benefit of the income from the trust in the proportions in which they are entitled thereto, or if their interests are indefinite, then in equal shares.

Merger. If the Trustee deems it best for the beneficiary or beneficiaries of any trust created under this Trust Agreement to merge all of the assets held in such trust with any other trust created by this Trust Agreement or otherwise for the benefit of the same beneficiary or beneficiaries and under substantially similar trusts, terms, and conditions, the Trustee, after giving not less than thirty days written notice to the trust's beneficiaries, may terminate such trust and transfer to or merge all of the assets of such trust to such other trust, regardless of whether the Trustee under this Trust Agreement also is serving as the Trustee of such other trust.

Liability of Third Party. No person dealing with the Trustee of any trust created hereunder shall be obligated to see to the application of any money paid or property transferred to or upon the order of the Trustee; nor shall any person be obligated to inquire into the property of any transaction or the authority of the Trustee to enter into and consummate the same.

Trustee's Judgement Final. Whenever the judgment or discretion of any Trustee may be exercised, it shall be final and binding upon every person interested in the trust estate, and any Trustee exercising any discretionary power relating to the distribution of principal or income shall be responsible only for lack of good faith in the exercise of such power; provided, however, nothing contained in this paragraph shall be construed so as to broaden any standard within which the Trustee is authorized to make distributions of income or principal, so that such standard is no longer considered an ascertainable standard under Code Section 2041 when it would otherwise be ascertainable.

Court Supervision. The Trustee shall not be required to qualify before or be appointed by any court; nor shall the Trustee be required to obtain the order or approval of any court in the exercise of any power or discretion.

Out-of-State Properties. If the Trustee must act in a jurisdiction in which a person or entity serving as Trustee is unwilling or unable to act as to any property, the remaining Trustees or Trustee, if willing and able to act, otherwise such person as the Trustee shall from time to time designate in writing, shall act as ancillary Trustees or Trustee as to that property. Any person or corporation acting as ancillary Trustee may resign at any time by written notice to the Trustees. Each ancillary Trustee shall have the powers, rights, discretions, and duties, exercisable without court order, to act with respect to such matters as the Trustee deems proper. The ancillary Trustee shall be responsible to the Trustee for any property it administers. The Trustee may pay the ancillary Trustee reasonable compensation for services and may absolve the ancillary Trustee from any requirement to furnish bond or other security.

ARTICLE VIII
AMENDMENT AND REVOCATION OF TRUST

While I am living and legally competent, I may from time to time amend or revoke this Trust Agreement and the trusts evidenced by it, in whole or in part, by written instrument (other than by a will) delivered to the Trustee, except that, if amended, the duties, powers, and responsibilities of the Trustee shall not be changed without the Trustee's written consent. During such time as I am not legally competent neither I nor my court appointed guardian may amend or revoke this Trust Agreement or any trust evidenced by it. The trust property to which any revocation relates shall be conveyed to me or otherwise as I direct. This power is personal to me and may not be exercised by my legal representatives, attorneys in fact, or others. After my death, all trusts created under this Trust Agreement shall become irrevocable.

ARTICLE IX
MISCELLANEOUS PROVISIONS

Governing Law. The validity, construction, and administration of each trust created hereunder shall be governed by the laws of the State of _____.

Issue, Child and Children, and Determination of Living Persons. The word "issue," wherever used in this Trust Agreement, means all of the descendants, both by blood and by adoption, of whatever degree of the named ancestor, provided that (a) with respect to descendants by blood, the parents, as determined under applicable state law, of the descendants were married to one another, under the laws of the state in which they resided, either at the time of the descendant's conception or at the time of the descendant's birth, and (b) with respect to descendants by adoption, such adoption is of a person under the age of 21 years and is by court proceedings, the finality of which has not been questioned by the adoptive parent. The words "child" and "children" shall also include persons born or adopted under the same conditions. For the purposes of dividing or distributing any portion of the trust estate among persons who are living at a particular time, any person who has been conceived prior to such time, but has not yet been born, shall be considered to be living at such time if such person is later born and lives at least six months after birth.

Per Stirpes. Wherever this Trust Agreement directs a per stirpes distribution or allocation of assets to a person's descendants, division of those assets is to be made with reference to that person's children, regardless of whether any of them are living. Thus, though a person's children were all deceased the assets to be distributed or allocated would nevertheless be divided into as many equal shares as there were such deceased children with a descendant or descendants surviving at the time of distribution or allocation, and each such share would be divided similarly among the descendants of a deceased child.

Incapacity. For purposes of this Trust Agreement, a person (including any person appointed to act as Trustee hereunder) shall be considered incapacitated if such person has a legal, mental, or physical disability that substantially impairs such person's ability to manage his or her affairs (or the affairs of any trust created hereunder, as the case may be) with reasonable care. Proof that a person has become incapacitated may be conclusively established by the written opinion of two physicians selected by or acceptable to the Trustee of the trust or trusts of which the incapacitated person is a beneficiary (or to the prospective Trustee, if any, if the capacity of any Trustee be at issue) certifying to such fact. The language of such certificate shall be sufficient if acceptable to the Trustee (or the prospective Trustee, as the case may be) as indicating with reasonable certainty that such person is incapacitated. The physicians who issue such certificates, so long as they shall act in good faith in so doing, shall be entitled to indemnification by the trusts created hereunder from any liability rendering the opinion contained in any such certificates. The Trustee (or the prospective Trustee, as the case may be) so long as it shall act in good faith in accepting such certificates, shall be entitled to indemnification by the trusts created hereunder from any liability for acting pursuant to its good faith acceptance of such certificate.

Education. As used in this Trust Agreement, "education" shall include preparatory, collegiate, postgraduate, professional, and vocational education; specialized formal or informal training in music, the stage, handicrafts, the arts, or sports or athletic endeavors, whether by private instruction or otherwise; and any other activity, including foreign or domestic travel, which tends to develop the talents and potential of the beneficiary, regardless of age.

Health. As used in this Trust Agreement, "health" shall include medical, dental, hospital, and nursing care and other expenses of invalidism, and the cost of purchasing or maintaining hospital, medical, or nursing home insurance and disability income insurance coverage.

Code. All references in this trust to the "Code" mean the Internal Revenue Code of 1986, as amended, and shall refer to corresponding provisions of any subsequent federal tax law.

Invalid Provisions. If any part of this Trust Agreement shall be invalid, illegal, or inoperative, for any reason, it is the intention of Grantor that the remaining parts, so far as possible and reasonable, shall be effective and fully operative. The Trustee may seek and obtain court instructions for the purpose of carrying out as nearly as possible the intention of this Trust Agreement as evidenced by the terms hereof, including any term held invalid, illegal, or inoperative.

Survival. Any person must survive by thirty days for a gift made in this Trust Agreement which directly or indirectly requires such person's survival of another to be effective.

Use of Words. As used in this Trust Agreement, the masculine, feminine, and neuter gender, and the singular or plural of any word includes the others unless the context indicates otherwise.

Titles, Headings, and Captions. All titles, headings, and captions used in this Trust Agreement have been included for convenience only and should not be construed in interpreting this Trust Agreement.

IN WITNESS WHEREOF I, as Grantor and Trustee, have signed this Trust Agreement the day and year first above written.

_____   _____
Witness   Grantor and Trustee

_____
Witness

STATE OF _____§

                                        §

COUNTY OF _____§

BEFORE ME, the undersigned authority, on this day personally appeared _____,
Grantor and Trustee, known to me to be the person whose name is subscribed to the foregoing instrument and acknowledged to me that he/she executed the same for the purposes and consideration therein expressed.

GIVEN UNDER MY HAND AND SEAL OF OFFICE this _____ day of _____, 20_____.

                                        _____
                                        Notary Public

                                        My commission expires:_____

_____ LIVING TRUST
(Unmarried, No Children, Family Trust)

THIS AGREEMENT OF TRUST is entered into at _____, State of _____, this _____ day of _____, 20_____, by and between _____, as Grantor and Trustee. This Trust, as from time to time amended, shall be known as the "_____ LIVING TRUST dated _____, 20_____."

ARTICLE I
FAMILY

I am not married and I do not have any children.

ARTICLE II
FUNDING

Initial Funding. I hereby transfer to the Trustee the sum of Ten Dollars ($10.00).

Additional Funding. From time to time the Trust distribute may be funded with additional property by me or by any other person in any manner. In addition, I may cause the Trustee to be designated as beneficiary of life insurance policies or qualified retirement plans. All property transferred, assigned, conveyed, or delivered to the Trustee and all investment and reinvestment thereof, are herein collectively referred to as the "trust estate" and shall be held, administered, and distributed by the Trustee in accordance with the terms of this Trust Agreement.

ARTICLE III
ADMINISTRATION OF TRUST DURING MY LIFETIME

Distributions of Income. While I am living and not under any incapacity, the Trustee shall distribute the income of the Trust as directed in writing by me from time to time. In the event I do not deliver such direction to the Trustee, the Trustee shall pay to or expend on my behalf such amount of income from the Trust as the Trustee determines is necessary or advisable for my health, education, maintenance, and support. Any income that is not distributed to me or on my behalf shall be added to the principal of the Trust.

Distributions of Principal. While I am living and not under any incapacity, the Trustee shall distribute such part or all of the principal of the Trust as directed in writing by me from time to time. In the event I do not deliver such direction to the Trustee, the Trustee shall pay to or expend on my behalf such part of the principal of the Trust as the Trustee determines is necessary or advisable for my health, education, maintenance, and support.

Use of Residential Property. If any real property used by me for residential purposes (whether on a full-time or part-time basis, including recreational property) becomes part of the trust estate, I shall have the right to use and occupy such property without rental and without accounting to the trust estate. The Trustee shall pay all taxes, debts, and other expenses associated with such residential property from the income of the Trust. To the extent income is insufficient, the Trustee shall use principal of the Trust to pay such taxes, debts, and expenses.

Distribution During My Incapacity. In addition, whenever the Trustee considers that I am incapacitated, the Trustee shall distribute or apply such amounts of the income and principal of the trust estate (even though exhausting the Trust) as the Trustee considers advisable for my health, maintenance, and support, or for any other purpose the Trustee considers to be for my best interests. Any excess income shall be added to principal.

Incapacity. For purposes of this Trust Agreement, I shall be considered to be incapacitated if I: (a) am unable to manage my affairs; (b) am under a legal incapacity; or (c) by reason of illness or mental or physical incapacity am unable to give prompt and intelligent consideration to my financial matters. I shall be considered incapacitated upon a good faith determination made by _____ and my physician, or the survivor of them, and the Trustee may rely upon written notice of that determination.

ARTICLE IV
ADMINISTRATION OF TRUST UPON MY DEATH

Payment of Expenses, Claims, and Taxes. Upon my death, if I have no probate estate, or to the extent that the cash and readily marketable assets in the principal of the residue of my probate estate are insufficient, the Trustee shall make the following payments from the principal of the trust estate. The Trustee shall pay the expenses of my last illness and funeral, costs of administration including ancillary administration, costs of safeguarding and delivering legacies, and claims allowable against my estate (excluding debts secured by real property or life insurance). The Trustee shall also pay the estate and inheritance taxes assessed by reason of my death. The Trustee may make payment directly or to the legal representative of my estate, as the Trustee deems advisable. I hereby waive all rights of apportionment or reimbursement for any payments made pursuant to this Article.

Selection of Assets. Assets or funds otherwise excludable from my gross estate for federal estate tax purposes shall not be used to make the foregoing payments. The Trustee's selection of assets to be sold to pay expenses, claims, and taxes shall not be subject to question by any beneficiary.

Tax Elections. The Trustee shall make such elections under the tax laws as the Trustee deems advisable, without regard to the relative interests of the beneficiaries and without liability to any person. No adjustment shall be made between principal and income or in the relative interests of the beneficiaries to compensate for the effect of elections or allocations under the tax laws made by the legal representative of my estate or by the Trustee.

ARTICLE V
DISTRIBUTION OF TRUST ASSETS UPON MY DEATH

Tangible Personal Property. The Trustee shall distribute my tangible personal property in accordance with any written, signed, and dated memorandum prepared by me. Any tangible personal property that is not disposed of by memorandum shall be distributed in equal shares to my surviving Children.

Specific Bequest. The Trustee shall distribute the following property to the named individuals:

$ _____ to _____

$ _____ to _____

If an individual named herein does not survive me, the gift to such person shall lapse and the share to which such person would have been entitled shall be distributed among the surviving individuals named in this paragraph on a pro rata basis.

Distribution for Beneficiaries. The Trustee shall set aside and distribute the trust estate, including any additions to the Trust by reason of my death, in a separate trust designated the Family Trust, and shall hold and distribute the Family Trust in accordance with article VI.

ARTICLE VI
FAMILY TRUST

Family Trust. The trust held under this Article VI shall be referred to as the "Family Trust." The Family Trust shall be administered and distributed upon the following terms:

(a) Distributions of Income. The Trustee may distribute part or all of the income from the Family Trust to any one or more of from time to time living, in equal or unequal proportions and at such times as the Trustee determines to be necessary for the health, education, maintenance, and support of _____. Any income not so paid shall be added to principal.

(b) Distributions of Principal. The Trustee may pay so much or all of the principal from the Family Trust to any one or more of from time to time living, in equal or unequal proportions and at such times as the Trustee determines to be necessary for the health, education, maintenance, and support of _____.

Termination of Trust. When there are no more living beneficiaries of the Family Trust, the Trustee shall distribute the assets remaining in the Family Trust, to the following individuals in the amounts specified:

_____ % to _____
_____ % to _____
_____ % to _____
_____ % to _____

If an individual named herein does not survive me, the gift to such person shall lapse and the share to which such person would have been entitled shall be distributed among the surviving individuals named in this paragraph on a pro rata basis.

No Survivors. If none of the individuals named in the preceding paragraph are then living, the assets remaining in the Family Trust shall be distributed to my heirs at law in accordance with the law of descent and distribution in effect on the date of my death.

ARTICLE VII
THE TRUSTEE

Initial Trustee. While I am alive, able, and willing to serve, I shall be the Trustee of the Trust.

Successor Trustee. During my lifetime, if I cannot serve as Trustee, I will appoint a successor Trustee. If I do not appoint a successor Trustee, or in the event of my death, incapacity, or inability to serve as Trustee, the successor Trustee shall be the first of the following individuals who is willing and competent to serve as successor Trustee:

If all of the successor Trustees die, become incapacitated, or otherwise fail or cease to serve as Trustee, a majority in number of the then living income beneficiaries of the Trust shall appoint a successor Trustee. Any appointment made under this Article shall be by a signed, acknowledged instrument delivered to the successor Trustee. A successor Trustee shall have all of the powers granted a Trustee in this Trust Agreement.

Resignation of Trustee. Any Trustee may resign as Trustee as to any one or more of the trusts created hereunder at any time by giving written notice to me if I am living, otherwise to the successor Trustee identified in this Trust Agreement, the current income beneficiaries of the Trust, and to those persons, if any, authorized in this Trust Agreement to appoint the successor Trustee.

Removal of Trustee. During my life, I may remove a Trustee at any time for any reason. After my death or if I am incapacitated and unable to remove the Trustee, a majority in number of the then living income beneficiaries of the Trust shall have the power to remove a Trustee.

Bond. No Trustee wherever acting shall be required to give bond or surety or be appointed by or account for the administration of any trust to any court.

Trustee's Fees. The Trustee shall be entitled to reasonable fees commensurate with the Trustee's duties and responsibilities, taking into account the value and nature of the trust estate and the time and work involved. The Trustee shall be reimbursed for reasonable costs and expenses incurred in connection with the performance of his or her fiduciary duties.

Registration of Trust. The Trustee shall not be required to register the Trust with any federal, state, or local government authority.

Liability of Trustee. A Trustee shall only be liable for willful misconduct or gross negligence and shall not be liable for breach of fiduciary duty by virtue of mistake or error in judgment. No successor Trustee shall be personally liable for any act or omission of any predecessor.

Majority Decision. If more than one Trustee is serving hereunder, the decision of a majority of the Trustees shall control. The dissenting Trustee shall have no liability for participating in or carrying out the acts of the controlling Trustee.

Delegation to Co-Trustee. A Trustee of any trust created hereunder may at any time by written instrument delegate to a Co-Trustee of such trust all or less than all of the powers conferred upon that Trustee, either for a specified time or until the delegation is revoked by a written instrument.

ARTICLE VIII
TRUST ADMINISTRATION

Trustee Powers: Investment and Management of Trust Estate. Subject to any limitation stated elsewhere in this Trust Agreement, the Trustee shall hold, manage, care for, and protect the trust property and shall have the following powers and, except to the extent inconsistent herewith, all of the rights, powers, and privileges and be subject to all of the duties, responsibilities, and conditions set forth in applicable state law, as amended from time to time:

(a) **Retain Property.** To retain any property originally constituting the trust or subsequently added thereto, and to invest and reinvest the trust property in bonds, stocks, mortgages, notes, bank deposits, options, futures, limited partnership interests, limited liability company interests, other business organization interests, shares of registered investment companies and real estate investment trusts, or other property of any kind, real or personal, domestic or foreign; the Trustee may retain or make any investment without liability, even though it is not of a type, quality, marketability, or diversification considered proper for trust investments.

(b) **Investment.** To invest in, participate in, form, or cause to be formed (alone or with others, including members of my family) such corporations, partnerships, limited partnerships, limited liability companies, and other business organizations organized under the laws of any state or country and to transfer and convey to such business organizations all or any part of the assets, real or personal, of any trust estate in exchange for such stocks, bonds, notes, other securities, or interests of such business organizations as the Trustee deems best.

(c) **Residential Property.** To acquire, hold and maintain any residence for the use and benefit of such one or more of the beneficiaries of the trust, including me, and to pay all carrying charges of such residence, including but not limited to, any taxes, assessments, and maintenance thereon, and all expenses of the repair and operation thereof, including the employment of domestic servants and other expenses incident to the maintenance of a household for the benefit of any one or more of the beneficiaries of the trust, all as the Trustee deems best.

(d) Tangible Personal Property. To acquire, hold, and maintain as a part of the trust any and all articles of tangible personal property or any other property for the use and benefit of any one or more of the beneficiaries of the trust, without regard to the income productivity of income, and without any duty to convert such property to productive property, and to pay the expenses of safekeeping of any such property, including insurance, and all expenses of the repair and maintenance of such property, and to sell such property and to apply the net proceeds of sale to the purchase of such other property as the Trustee deems best.

(e) Operate Business. To continue or participate in the operation of any business or other enterprise, and to effect incorporation, dissolution, or other change in the form of the organization of the business or enterprise.

(f) Nominee. To cause any property, real or personal, belonging to the trust to be held or registered in the Trustee's name or in the name of a nominee or in such other form as the Trustee deems best without disclosing the trust relationship.

(g) Real Estate. To operate, maintain, repair, rehabilitate, alter, erect, improve, or remove any improvements on real estate; to subdivide real estate; to grant easements, give consents, and enter into contracts relating to real estate or its use; and to release or dedicate any interest in real estate.

(h) Lease. To enter for any purpose into a lease as lessor or lessee with or without option to purchase or renew for a term within or extending beyond the term of the trust.

(i) Minerals. To enter into a lease or arrangement for exploration and removal of minerals or other natural resources or enter into a pooling or unitization agreement.

(j) Sell. By public offering or private negotiation, to sell, exchange, assign, transfer, or otherwise dispose of all or any real or personal trust property and give options for these purposes, for such price and on such terms, with such covenants of warranty and such security for deferred payment as the Trustee deems proper.

(k) Partition. To partition any property in which the trust owns an undivided interest.

(l) Securities. To engage in all actions necessary to the effective administration of securities including, but not limited to, the authority to vote in person or by general or limited proxy, or refrain from voting, any corporate securities for any purpose; to exercise or sell any subscription or conversion rights; to consent to and join in or oppose any voting trusts, reorganizations, consolidations, mergers, foreclosures, and liquidations and in connection therewith to deposit securities and accept and hold other property received therefore.

(m) Borrow. To borrow money from any lender, and to extend or renew any existing indebtedness to be repaid from trust assets or otherwise; to mortgage or pledge any property in the trust to secure such borrowing; to advance money for the protection of the trust, and for all expenses, losses, and liabilities sustained in the administration of the trust or because of the holding or ownership of any trust assets.

(n) Litigation. To commence or defend actions, claims, or proceedings for the protection of trust assets and of the Trustee in the performance of his or her duties.

(o) Claims. To pay or contest any claim; to settle a claim by or against the trust by compromise, arbitration, or otherwise; and to release, in whole or in part, any claim belonging to the trust to the extent that the claim is uncollectible.

(p) Payments. To pay taxes, assessments, compensation of the Trustee, and other expenses incurred in the collection, care, administration, and protection of the trust.

(q) Beneficiary under Disability. To pay any sum distributable to a beneficiary under legal disability, without liability to the Trustee, by paying the sum to the beneficiary or by paying the sum for the use of the beneficiary either to a legal representative appointed by the court, or if none, to a relative.

(r) Agents. To employ persons, including attorneys, auditors, investment advisors, or agents, even if they are associated with any Trustee, to advise or assist the Trustee in the performance of his or her administrative duties; to act without independent investigation upon their recommendations; and instead of acting personally, to employ one or more agents to perform any act of administration, whether or not discretionary.

(s) Distributions. To distribute income and principal in cash or in kind, or partly in each, and to allocate or distribute undivided interests or different assets or disproportionate interests in assets, and no adjustment shall be made to compensate for a disproportionate allocation of unrealized gain for federal income tax purposes; to value the trust property and to sell any part or all thereof in order to make allocation or distribution; no action taken by the Trustee pursuant to this paragraph shall be subject to question by any beneficiary.

(t) Allocation of Income and Principal. To allocate items of income or expense to either trust income or principal, as provided by law, including creation of reserves out of income for depreciation, obsolescence, or amortization, or for depletion in mineral or timber properties.

(u) Employee Benefits. To elect, pursuant to the terms of any employee benefit plan, individual retirement plan, or insurance contract, the mode of distribution of the proceeds thereof, and no adjustment shall be made in the interests of the beneficiaries to compensate for the effect of the election.

(v) Division and Distribution. To divide any trust created under this Trust Agreement into one or more separate trusts for the benefit of one or more of the beneficiaries of the trust so divided, and to allocate to such divided trust some or all of the assets of the trust estate for any reason.

(w) Tax Elections. Unless otherwise expressly directed hereunder, to exercise any tax option, allocation, or election permitted by law as the Trustee determines in the Trustee's sole discretion.

(x) Reliance. To rely upon any notice, certificate, affidavit, or other document or evidence believed by the Trustee to be genuine and accurate, in making any payment or distribution. The Trustee shall incur no liability for a disbursement or distribution make in good faith and without actual notice or knowledge of a changed condition or status affecting any person's interest in the trust or any other matter.

(y) Miscellaneous. To perform other acts necessary or appropriate for the proper administration of the trust, execute and deliver necessary instruments, and give full receipts and discharges.

Common Fund and Consolidation. For convenience of administration or investment, the Trustee may hold separate trusts as a common fund, dividing the income proportionately among them, assign undivided interests to the separate trusts, and make joint investments of the funds belonging to them. The Trustee may consolidate any separate trust with any other trust with similar provisions for the same beneficiary or beneficiaries.

Spendthrift. The interests of beneficiaries in principal or income shall not be subject to the claims of any creditor, any spouse for alimony or support, or others, or to legal process, and may not be voluntarily or involuntarily alienated or encumbered. The rights of beneficiaries to withdraw trust property are personal and may not be exercised by a legal representative, attorney in fact, or others.

Retained Powers. Notwithstanding the foregoing, while I am living and able to manage my affairs:

(a) no sale or investment shall be made without my written approval, unless I fail to indicate my approval or disapproval of any proposed sale or investment within ten days after being requested to do so in writing;

(b) I shall have the power to direct the retention or sale of any trust assets and the purchase of property with any principal cash in the trust. If I direct the retention or purchase of an asset, the Trustee shall have investment, voting, and management responsibility for that asset unless I direct otherwise; and,

(c) I may at any time or times, with or without right of revocation, by a writing delivered to the Trustee, delegate to any other person or to the Trustee or relinquish any or all of the powers reserved to me hereunder.

The statement of the Trustee that he or she is acting according to this paragraph shall fully protect all persons dealing with the Trustee. The Trustee shall have no responsibility for any loss that may result from acting in accordance with this paragraph.

Restriction on Powers. The Trustee shall not lend trust property to me, directly or indirectly, without adequate interest and adequate security. No Trustee who is a beneficiary of any trust, or who is obligated to support a beneficiary of any trust, shall participate in: the exercise of any discretion over distributions of income or principal other than that which is required for the health, education, maintenance and support of a beneficiary provided that such distribution does not satisfy the Trustee's obligation to support the beneficiary; the exercise of discretion to allocate receipts or expenses between principal and income.

Accounts and Compensation. A Trustee (other than myself) shall render an account of trust receipts and disbursements and a statement of assets at least annually to each adult beneficiary then entitled to receive or have the benefit of the income from the trust. An account is binding on each beneficiary who receives it and on all persons claiming by or through the beneficiary, and the Trustee is released, as to all matters stated in the account or shown by it, unless the beneficiary commences a judicial proceeding to assert a claim within five years after the mailing or other delivery of the account.

Small Trust Termination and Perpetuities Savings.

(a) A trustee in its discretion may terminate and distribute any trust hereunder if the corporate trustee determines that the costs of continuance thereof will substantially impair accomplishment of the purposes of the trust.

(b) The trustee shall terminate and forthwith distribute any trust created hereby, or by exercise of a power of appointment hereunder, and still held twenty-one years after the death of the last to die of myself and the beneficiaries in being at my death.

(c) Distribution under this section shall be made to the persons then entitled to receive or have the benefit of the income from the trust in the proportions in which they are entitled thereto, or if their interests are indefinite, then in equal shares.

Merger. If the Trustee deems it best for the beneficiary or beneficiaries of any trust created under this Trust Agreement to merge all of the assets held in such trust with any other trust created by this Trust Agreement or otherwise for the benefit of the same beneficiary or beneficiaries and under substantially similar trusts, terms, and conditions, the Trustee, after giving not less than thirty days written notice to the trust's beneficiaries, may terminate such trust and transfer to or merge all of the assets of such trust to such other trust, regardless of whether the Trustee under this Trust Agreement also is serving as the Trustee of such other trust.

Liability of Third Party. No person dealing with the Trustee of any trust created hereunder shall be obligated to see to the application of any money paid or property transferred to or upon the order of the Trustee; nor shall any person be obligated to inquire into the property of any transaction or the authority of the Trustee to enter into and consummate the same.

Trustee's Judgement Final. Whenever the judgment or discretion of any Trustee may be exercised, it shall be final and binding upon every person interested in the trust estate, and any Trustee exercising any discretionary power relating to the distribution of principal or income shall be responsible only for lack of good faith in the exercise of such power; provided, however, nothing contained in this paragraph shall be construed so as to broaden any standard within which the Trustee is authorized to make distributions of income or principal, so that such standard is no longer considered an ascertainable standard under Code Trustee 2041 when it would otherwise be ascertainable.

Court Supervision. The Trustee shall not be required to qualify before or be appointed by any court; nor shall the Trustee be required to obtain the order or approval of any court in the exercise of any power or discretion.

Out-of-State Properties. If the Trustee must act in a jurisdiction in which a person or entity serving as Trustee is unwilling or unable to act as to any property, the remaining Trustees or Trustee, if willing and able to act, otherwise such person as the Trustee shall from time to time designate in writing, shall act as ancillary Trustees or Trustee as to that property. Any person or corporation acting as ancillary Trustee may resign at any time by written notice to the Trustees. Each ancillary Trustee shall have the powers, rights, discretions, and duties, exercisable without court order, to act with respect to such matters as the Trustee deems proper. The ancillary Trustee shall be responsible to the Trustee for any property it administers. The Trustee may pay the ancillary Trustee reasonable compensation for services and may absolve the ancillary Trustee from any requirement to furnish bond or other security.

ARTICLE IX
AMENDMENT AND REVOCATION OF TRUST

While I am living and legally competent, I may from time to time amend or revoke this Trust Agreement and the trusts evidenced by it, in whole or in part, by written instrument (other than by a will) delivered to the Trustee, except that, if amended, the duties, powers, and responsibilities of the Trustee shall not be changed without the Trustee's written consent. During such time as I am not legally competent neither I nor my court appointed guardian may amend or revoke this Trust Agreement or any trust evidenced by it. The trust property to which any revocation relates shall be conveyed to me or otherwise as I direct. This power is personal to me and may not be exercised by my legal representatives, attorneys in fact, or others. After my death, all trusts created under this Trust Agreement shall become irrevocable.

ARTICLE X
MISCELLANEOUS PROVISIONS

Governing Law. The validity, construction, and administration of each trust created hereunder shall be governed by the laws of the State of _____.

Issue, Child and Children, and Determination of Living Persons. The word "issue," wherever used in this Trust Agreement, means all of the descendants, both by blood and by adoption, of whatever degree of the named ancestor, provided that (a) with respect to descendants by blood, the parents, as determined under applicable state law, of the descendants were married to one another, under the laws of the state in which they resided, either at the time of the descendant's conception or at the time of the descendant's birth, and (b) with respect to descendants by adoption, such adoption is of a person under the age of 21 years and is by court proceedings, the finality of which has not been questioned by the adoptive parent. The words "child" and "children" shall also include persons born or adopted under the same conditions. For the purposes of dividing or distributing any portion of the trust estate among persons who are living at a particular time, any person who has been conceived prior to such time, but has not yet been born, shall be considered to be living at such time if such person is later born and lives at least six months after birth.

Per Stirpes. Wherever this Trust Agreement directs a per stirpes distribution or allocation of assets to a person's descendants, division of those assets is to be made with reference to that person's children, regardless of whether any of them are living. Thus, though a person's children were all deceased the assets to be distributed or allocated would nevertheless be divided into as many equal shares as there were such deceased children with a descendant or descendants surviving at the time of distribution or allocation, and each such share would be divided similarly among the descendants of a deceased child.

Incapacity. For purposes of this Trust Agreement, a person (including any person appointed to act as Trustee hereunder) shall be considered incapacitated if such person has a legal, mental, or physical disability that substantially impairs such person's ability to manage his or her affairs (or the affairs of any trust created hereunder, as the case may be) with reasonable care. Proof that a person has become incapacitated may be conclusively established by the written opinion of two physicians selected by or acceptable to the Trustee of the trust or trusts of which the incapacitated person is a beneficiary (or to the prospective Trustee, if any, if the capacity of any Trustee be at issue) certifying to such fact. The language of such certificate shall be sufficient if acceptable to the Trustee (or the prospective Trustee, as the case may be) as indicating with reasonable certainty that such person is incapacitated. The physicians who issue such certificates, so long as they shall act in good faith in so doing, shall be entitled to indemnification by the trusts created hereunder from any liability rendering the opinion contained in any such certificates. The Trustee (or the prospective Trustee, as the case may be) so long as it shall act in good faith in accepting such certificates, shall be entitled to indemnification by the trusts created hereunder from any liability for acting pursuant to its good faith acceptance of such certificate.

Education. As used in this Trust Agreement, "education" shall include preparatory, collegiate, postgraduate, professional, and vocational education; specialized formal or informal training in music, the stage, handicrafts, the arts, or sports or athletic endeavors, whether by private instruction or otherwise; and any other activity, including foreign or domestic travel, which tends to develop the talents and potential of the beneficiary, regardless of age.

Health. As used in this Trust Agreement, "health" shall include medical, dental, hospital, and nursing care and other expenses of invalidism, and the cost of purchasing or maintaining hospital, medical, or nursing home insurance and disability income insurance coverage.

Code. All references in this trust to the "Code" mean the Internal Revenue Code of 1986, as amended, and shall refer to corresponding provisions of any subsequent federal tax law.

Invalid Provisions. If any part of this Trust Agreement shall be invalid, illegal, or inoperative, for any reason, it is the intention of Grantor that the remaining parts, so far as possible and reasonable, shall be effective and fully operative. The Trustee may seek and obtain court instructions for the purpose of carrying out as nearly as possible the intention of this Trust Agreement as evidenced by the terms hereof, including any term held invalid, illegal, or inoperative.

Survival. Any person must survive by thirty days for a gift made in this Trust Agreement which directly or indirectly requires such person's survival of another to be effective.

Use of Words. As used in this Trust Agreement, the masculine, feminine, and neuter gender, and the singular or plural of any word includes the others unless the context indicates otherwise.

Titles, Headings, and Captions. All titles, headings, and captions used in this Trust Agreement have been included for convenience only and should not be construed in interpreting this Trust Agreement.

IN WITNESS WHEREOF I, as Grantor and Trustee, have signed this Trust Agreement the day and year first above written.

_____   _____
Witness   Grantor and Trustee

_____
Witness

STATE OF _____ §

§

COUNTY OF _____ §

BEFORE ME, the undersigned authority, on this day personally appeared _____,
Grantor and Trustee, known to me to be the person whose name is subscribed to the foregoing instrument and acknowledged to me that he/she executed the same for the purposes and consideration therein expressed.

GIVEN UNDER MY HAND AND SEAL OF OFFICE this _____ day of _____, 20_____.

_____
Notary Public

My commission expires:_____

_____ LIVING TRUST

(Unmarried, Children Outright)

THIS AGREEMENT OF TRUST is entered into at _____, State of _____, this _____ day of _____, 20_____, by and between _____, as Grantor and Trustee. This Trust, as from time to time amended, shall be known as the "_____ LIVING TRUST dated _____, 20_____."

ARTICLE I
FAMILY

I am not married. I have _____ children now living, namely: _____.
I intend by this Trust Agreement to provide for all my children, including any hereafter born or adopted.

ARTICLE II
FUNDING

Initial Funding. I hereby transfer to the Trustee the sum of Ten Dollars ($10.00).

Additional Funding. From time to time the Trust may be funded with additional property by me or by any other person in any manner. In addition, I may cause the Trustee to be designated as beneficiary of life insurance policies or qualified retirement plans. All property transferred, assigned, conveyed, or delivered to the Trustee and all investment and reinvestment thereof, are herein collectively referred to as the "trust estate" and shall be held, administered, and distributed by the Trustee in accordance with the terms of this Trust Agreement.

ARTICLE III
ADMINISTRATION OF TRUST DURING MY LIFETIME

Distributions of Income. While I am living and not under any incapacity, the Trustee shall distribute the income of the Trust as directed in writing by me from time to time. In the event I do not deliver such direction to the Trustee, the Trustee shall pay to or expend on my behalf such amount of income from the Trust as the Trustee determines is necessary or advisable for my health, education, maintenance, and support. Any income that is not distributed to me or on my behalf shall be added to the principal of the Trust.

Distributions of Principal. While I am living and not under any incapacity, the Trustee shall distribute such part or all of the principal of the Trust as directed in writing by me from time to time. In the event I do not deliver such direction to the Trustee, the Trustee shall pay to or expend on my behalf such part of the principal of the Trust as the Trustee determines is necessary or advisable for my health, education, maintenance, and support.

Use of Residential Property. If any real property used by me for residential purposes (whether on a full-time or part-time basis, including recreational property) becomes part of the trust estate, I shall have the right to use and occupy such property without rental and without accounting to the trust estate. The Trustee shall pay all taxes, debts, and other expenses associated with such residential property from the income of the Trust. To the extent income is insufficient, the Trustee shall use principal of the Trust to pay such taxes, debts, and expenses.

Distributions to My Children. The Trustee shall pay to or expend for the benefit of my minor Children, so much of the income and principal of the Trust as the Trustee, in his or her sole discretion, determines to be necessary for the health, education, maintenance, and support of my Children. The Trustee shall make such discretionary distributions only after conferring with me. The distributions from the Trust to my children do not need to be equal.

Distribution During My Incapacity. In addition, whenever the Trustee considers that I am incapacitated, the Trustee shall distribute or apply such amounts of the income and principal of the trust estate (even though exhausting the Trust) as the Trustee considers advisable for my health, maintenance, and support, or for any other purpose the Trustee considers to be for my best interests. Any excess income shall be added to principal.

Incapacity. For purposes of this Trust Agreement, I shall be considered to be incapacitated if I: (a) am unable to manage my affairs; (b) am under a legal incapacity; or, (c) by reason of illness or mental or physical incapacity am unable to give prompt and intelligent consideration to my financial matters. I shall be considered incapacitated upon a good faith determination made by _____ and my physician, or the survivor of them, and the Trustee may rely upon written notice of that determination.

ARTICLE IV
ADMINISTRATION OF TRUST UPON MY DEATH

Payment of Expenses, Claims, and Taxes. Upon my death, if I have no probate estate, or to the extent that the cash and readily marketable assets in the principal of the residue of my probate estate are insufficient, the Trustee shall make the following payments from the principal of the trust estate. The Trustee shall pay the expenses of my last illness and funeral, costs of administration including ancillary administration, costs of safeguarding and delivering legacies, and claims allowable against my estate (excluding debts secured by real property or life insurance). The Trustee shall also pay the estate and inheritance taxes assessed by reason of my death. The Trustee may make payment directly or to the legal representative of my estate, as the Trustee deems advisable. I hereby waive all rights of apportionment or reimbursement for any payments made pursuant to this Article.

Selection of Assets. Assets or funds otherwise excludable from my gross estate for federal estate tax purposes shall not be used to make the foregoing payments. The Trustee's selection of assets to be sold to pay expenses, claims, and taxes shall not be subject to question by any beneficiary.

Tax Elections. The Trustee shall make such elections under the tax laws as the Trustee deems advisable, without regard to the relative interests of the beneficiaries and without liability to any person. No adjustment shall be made between principal and income or in the relative interests of the beneficiaries to compensate for the effect of elections or allocations under the tax laws made by the legal representative of my estate or by the Trustee.

ARTICLE V
DISTRIBUTION OF TRUST ASSETS UPON MY DEATH

Tangible Personal Property. The Trustee shall distribute my tangible personal property in accordance with any written, signed, and dated memorandum prepared by me. Any tangible personal property that is not disposed of by memorandum shall be distributed in equal shares to my surviving Children.

Specific Bequest. The Trustee shall distribute the following property to the named individuals:

$ _____ to _____

$ _____ to _____

If an individual named herein does not survive me, the gift to such person shall lapse and the share to which such person would have been entitled shall be distributed among the surviving individuals named in this paragraph on a pro rata basis.

Distribution to My Children. The Trustee shall divide the remaining trust estate, including any additions to the Trust by reason of my death, into separate equal shares to create one share for each Child of mine who is then living, and one share for the then living descendants, collectively, of each deceased Child of mine with one or more descendants then living. The

Trustee shall distribute the share created for each Child to such Child outright and free of trust. The share for the descendants of each deceased Child shall be distributed, per stirpes, to those descendants living at my death.

Contingent Distribution. If none of my Children or their descendants survive me, the remaining trust estate, including any additions to the Trust by reason of my death, shall be distributed to the following individuals in the amounts specified:

_____ % to _____

_____ % to _____

_____ % to _____

_____ % to _____

If an individual named herein does not survive me, the share to which he or she would be entitled under this paragraph shall be distributed in equal shares to the individuals named in this paragraph who survive me.

No Survivors. If none of my Children, their descendants, or the individuals named in the preceding paragraph survive me, the remaining trust estate, including any additions to the Trust by reason of my death, shall be distributed to my heirs at law in accordance with the law of descent and distribution in effect on the date of my death.

ARTICLE VI
THE TRUSTEE

Initial Trustee. While I am alive, able, and willing to serve, I shall be the Trustee of the Trust.

Successor Trustee. During my lifetime, if I cannot serve as Trustee, I will appoint a successor Trustee. If I do not appoint a successor Trustee, or in the event of my death, incapacity, or inability to serve as Trustee, the successor Trustee shall be the first of the following individuals who is willing and competent to serve as successor Trustee:

If all of the successor Trustees die, become incapacitated, or otherwise fail or cease to serve as Trustee, a majority in number of the then living income beneficiaries of the Trust shall appoint a successor Trustee. Any appointment made under this Article shall be by a signed, acknowledged instrument delivered to the successor Trustee. A successor Trustee shall have all of the powers granted a Trustee in this Trust Agreement.

Resignation of Trustee. Any Trustee may resign as Trustee as to any one or more of the trusts created hereunder at any time by giving written notice to me if I am living, otherwise to the successor Trustee identified in this Trust Agreement, the current income beneficiaries of the Trust, and to those persons, if any, authorized in this Trust Agreement to appoint the successor Trustee.

Removal of Trustee. During my life, I may remove a Trustee at any time for any reason. After my death or if I am incapacitated and unable to remove the Trustee, a majority in number of the then living income beneficiaries of the Trust shall have the power to remove a Trustee.

Bond. No Trustee wherever acting shall be required to give bond or surety or be appointed by or account for the administration of any trust to any court.

Trustee's Fees. The Trustee shall be entitled to reasonable fees commensurate with the Trustee's duties and responsibilities, taking into account the value and nature of the trust estate and the time and work involved. The Trustee shall be reimbursed for reasonable costs and expenses incurred in connection with the performance of his or her fiduciary duties.

Registration of Trust. The Trustee shall not be required to register the Trust with any federal, state, or local government authority.

Liability of Trustee. A Trustee shall only be liable for willful misconduct or gross negligence and shall not be liable for breach of fiduciary duty by virtue of mistake or error in judgment. No successor Trustee shall be personally liable for any act or omission of any predecessor.

Majority Decision. If more than one Trustee is serving hereunder, the decision of a majority of the Trustees shall control. The dissenting Trustee shall have no liability for participating in or carrying out the acts of the controlling Trustee.

Delegation to Co-Trustee. A Trustee of any trust created hereunder may at any time by written instrument delegate to a Co-Trustee of such trust all or less than all of the powers conferred upon that Trustee, either for a specified time or until the delegation is revoked by a written instrument.

ARTICLE VII
TRUST ADMINISTRATION

Trustee Powers: Investment and Management of Trust Estate. Subject to any limitation stated elsewhere in this Trust Agreement, the Trustee shall hold, manage, care for, and protect the trust property and shall have the following powers and, except to the extent inconsistent herewith, all of the rights, powers, and privileges and be subject to all of the duties, responsibilities, and conditions set forth in applicable state law, as amended from time to time:

(a) **Retain Property.** To retain any property originally constituting the trust or subsequently added thereto, and to invest and reinvest the trust property in bonds, stocks, mortgages, notes, bank deposits, options, futures, limited partnership interests, limited liability company interests, other business organization interests, shares of registered investment companies and real estate investment trusts, or other property of any kind, real or personal, domestic or foreign; the Trustee may retain or make any investment without liability, even though it is not of a type, quality, marketability, or diversification considered proper for trust investments.

(b) **Investment.** To invest in, participate in, form, or cause to be formed (alone or with others, including members of my family) such corporations, partnerships, limited partnerships, limited liability companies, and other business organizations organized under the laws of any state or country and to transfer and convey to such business organizations all or any part of the assets, real or personal, of any trust estate in exchange for such stocks, bonds, notes, other securities, or interests of such business organizations as the Trustee deems best.

(c) **Residential Property.** To acquire, hold and maintain any residence for the use and benefit of such one or more of the beneficiaries of the trust, including me, and to pay all carrying charges of such residence, including but not limited to, any taxes, assessments, and maintenance thereon, and all expenses of the repair and operation thereof, including the employment of domestic servants and other expenses incident to the maintenance of a household for the benefit of any one or more of the beneficiaries of the trust, all as the Trustee deems best.

(d) **Tangible Personal Property.** To acquire, hold, and maintain as a part of the trust any and all articles of tangible personal property or any other property for the use and benefit of any one or more of the beneficiaries of the trust, without regard to the income productivity of income, and without any duty to convert such property to productive property, and to pay the expenses of safekeeping of any such property, including insurance, and all expenses of the repair and maintenance of such property, and to sell such property and to apply the net proceeds of sale to the purchase of such other property as the Trustee deems best.

(e) Operate Business. To continue or participate in the operation of any business or other enterprise, and to effect incorporation, dissolution, or other change in the form of the organization of the business or enterprise.

(f) Nominee. To cause any property, real or personal, belonging to the trust to be held or registered in the Trustee's name or in the name of a nominee or in such other form as the Trustee deems best without disclosing the trust relationship.

(g) Real Estate. To operate, maintain, repair, rehabilitate, alter, erect, improve, or remove any improvements on real estate; to subdivide real estate; to grant easements, give consents, and enter into contracts relating to real estate or its use; and to release or dedicate any interest in real estate.

(h) Lease. To enter for any purpose into a lease as lessor or lessee with or without option to purchase or renew for a term within or extending beyond the term of the trust.

(i) Minerals. To enter into a lease or arrangement for exploration and removal of minerals or other natural resources or enter into a pooling or unitization agreement.

(j) Sell. By public offering or private negotiation, to sell, exchange, assign, transfer, or otherwise dispose of all or any real or personal trust property and give options for these purposes, for such price and on such terms, with such covenants of warranty and such security for deferred payment as the Trustee deems proper.

(k) Partition. To partition any property in which the trust owns an undivided interest.

(l) Securities. To engage in all actions necessary to the effective administration of securities including, but not limited to, the authority to vote in person or by general or limited proxy, or refrain from voting, any corporate securities for any purpose; to exercise or sell any subscription or conversion rights; to consent to and join in or oppose any voting trusts, reorganizations, consolidations, mergers, foreclosures, and liquidations and in connection therewith to deposit securities and accept and hold other property received therefore.

(m) Borrow. To borrow money from any lender, and to extend or renew any existing indebtedness to be repaid from trust assets or otherwise; to mortgage or pledge any property in the trust to secure such borrowing; to advance money for the protection of the trust, and for all expenses, losses, and liabilities sustained in the administration of the trust or because of the holding or ownership of any trust assets.

(n) Litigation. To commence or defend actions, claims, or proceedings for the protection of trust assets and of the Trustee in the performance of his or her duties.

(o) Claims. To pay or contest any claim; to settle a claim by or against the trust by compromise, arbitration, or otherwise; and to release, in whole or in part, any claim belonging to the trust to the extent that the claim is uncollectible.

(p) Payments. To pay taxes, assessments, compensation of the Trustee, and other expenses incurred in the collection, care, administration, and protection of the trust.

(q) Beneficiary under Disability. To pay any sum distributable to a beneficiary under legal disability, without liability to the Trustee, by paying the sum to the beneficiary or by paying the sum for the use of the beneficiary either to a legal representative appointed by the court, or if none, to a relative.

(r) **Agents.** To employ persons, including attorneys, auditors, investment advisors, or agents, even if they are associated with any Trustee, to advise or assist the Trustee in the performance of his or her administrative duties; to act without independent investigation upon their recommendations; and instead of acting personally, to employ one or more agents to perform any act of administration, whether or not discretionary.

(s) **Distributions.** To distribute income and principal in cash or in kind, or partly in each, and to allocate or distribute undivided interests or different assets or disproportionate interests in assets, and no adjustment shall be made to compensate for a disproportionate allocation of unrealized gain for federal income tax purposes; to value the trust property and to sell any part or all thereof in order to make allocation or distribution; no action taken by the Trustee pursuant to this paragraph shall be subject to question by any beneficiary.

(t) **Allocation of Income and Principal.** To allocate items of income or expense to either trust income or principal, as provided by law, including creation of reserves out of income for depreciation, obsolescence, or amortization, or for depletion in mineral or timber properties.

(u) **Employee Benefits.** To elect, pursuant to the terms of any employee benefit plan, individual retirement plan, or insurance contract, the mode of distribution of the proceeds thereof, and no adjustment shall be made in the interests of the beneficiaries to compensate for the effect of the election.

(v) **Division and Distribution.** To divide any trust created under this Trust Agreement into one or more separate trusts for the benefit of one or more of the beneficiaries of the trust so divided, and to allocate to such divided trust some or all of the assets of the trust estate for any reason.

(w) **Tax Elections.** Unless otherwise expressly directed hereunder, to exercise any tax option, allocation, or election permitted by law as the Trustee determines in the Trustee's sole discretion.

(x) **Reliance.** To rely upon any notice, certificate, affidavit, or other document or evidence believed by the Trustee to be genuine and accurate, in making any payment or distribution. The Trustee shall incur no liability for a disbursement or distribution make in good faith and without actual notice or knowledge of a changed condition or status affecting any person's interest in the trust or any other matter.

(y) **Miscellaneous.** To perform other acts necessary or appropriate for the proper administration of the trust, execute and deliver necessary instruments, and give full receipts and discharges.

Common Fund and Consolidation. For convenience of administration or investment, the Trustee may hold separate trusts as a common fund, dividing the income proportionately among them, assign undivided interests to the separate trusts, and make joint investments of the funds belonging to them. The Trustee may consolidate any separate trust with any other trust with similar provisions for the same beneficiary or beneficiaries.

Spendthrift. The interests of beneficiaries in principal or income shall not be subject to the claims of any creditor, any spouse for alimony or support, or others, or to legal process, and may not be voluntarily or involuntarily alienated or encumbered. The rights of beneficiaries to withdraw trust property are personal and may not be exercised by a legal representative, attorney in fact, or others.

Retained Powers. Notwithstanding the foregoing, while I am living and able to manage my affairs:

(a) no sale or investment shall be made without my written approval, unless I fail to indicate my approval or disapproval of any proposed sale or investment within ten days after being requested to do so in writing;

(b) I shall have the power to direct the retention or sale of any trust assets and the purchase of property with any principal cash in the trust. If I direct the retention or purchase of an asset, the Trustee shall have investment, voting, and management responsibility for that asset unless I direct otherwise; and,

(c) I may at any time or times, with or without right of revocation, by a writing delivered to the Trustee, delegate to any other person or to the Trustee or relinquish any or all of the powers reserved to me hereunder.

The statement of the Trustee that he or she is acting according to this paragraph shall fully protect all persons dealing with the Trustee. The Trustee shall have no responsibility for any loss that may result from acting in accordance with this paragraph.

Restriction on Powers. The Trustee shall not lend trust property to me, directly or indirectly, without adequate interest and adequate security. No Trustee who is a beneficiary of any trust, or who is obligated to support a beneficiary of any trust, shall participate in: the exercise of any discretion over distributions of income or principal other than that which is required for the health, education, maintenance and support of a beneficiary provided that such distribution does not satisfy the Trustee's obligation to support the beneficiary; the exercise of discretion to allocate receipts or expenses between principal and income.

Accounts and Compensation. A Trustee (other than myself) shall render an account of trust receipts and disbursements and a statement of assets at least annually to each adult beneficiary then entitled to receive or have the benefit of the income from the trust. An account is binding on each beneficiary who receives it and on all persons claiming by or through the beneficiary, and the Trustee is released, as to all matters stated in the account or shown by it, unless the beneficiary commences a judicial proceeding to assert a claim within five years after the mailing or other delivery of the account.

Small Trust Termination and Perpetuities Savings.

(a) A trustee in its discretion may terminate and distribute any trust hereunder if the corporate trustee determines that the costs of continuance thereof will substantially impair accomplishment of the purposes of the trust.

(b) The trustee shall terminate and forthwith distribute any trust created hereby, or by exercise of a power of appointment hereunder, and still held twenty-one years after the death of the last to die of myself and the beneficiaries in being at my death.

(c) Distribution under this section shall be made to the persons then entitled to receive or have the benefit of the income from the trust in the proportions in which they are entitled thereto, or if their interests are indefinite, then in equal shares.

Merger. If the Trustee deems it best for the beneficiary or beneficiaries of any trust created under this Trust Agreement to merge all of the assets held in such trust with any other trust created by this Trust Agreement or otherwise for the benefit of the same beneficiary or beneficiaries and under substantially similar trusts, terms, and conditions, the Trustee, after giving not less than thirty days written notice to the trust's beneficiaries, may terminate such trust and transfer to or merge all of the assets of such trust to such other trust, regardless of whether the Trustee under this Trust Agreement also is serving as the Trustee of such other trust.

Liability of Third Party. No person dealing with the Trustee of any trust created hereunder shall be obligated to see to the application of any money paid or property transferred to or upon the order of the Trustee; nor shall any person be obligated to inquire into the property of any transaction or the authority of the Trustee to enter into and consummate the same.

Trustee's Judgement Final. Whenever the judgment or discretion of any Trustee may be exercised, it shall be final and binding upon every person interested in the trust estate, and any Trustee exercising any discretionary power relating to the distribution of principal or income shall be responsible only for lack of good faith in the exercise of such power; provided, however, nothing contained in this paragraph shall be construed so as to broaden any standard within which the Trustee is authorized to make distributions of income or principal, so that such standard is no longer considered an ascertainable standard under Code Section 2041 when it would otherwise be ascertainable.

Court Supervision. The Trustee shall not be required to qualify before or be appointed by any court; nor shall the Trustee be required to obtain the order or approval of any court in the exercise of any power or discretion.

Out-of-State Properties. If the Trustee must act in a jurisdiction in which a person or entity serving as Trustee is unwilling or unable to act as to any property, the remaining Trustees or Trustee, if willing and able to act, otherwise such person as the Trustee shall from time to time designate in writing, shall act as ancillary Trustees or Trustee as to that property. Any person or corporation acting as ancillary Trustee may resign at any time by written notice to the Trustees. Each ancillary Trustee shall have the powers, rights, discretions, and duties, exercisable without court order, to act with respect to such matters as the Trustee deems proper. The ancillary Trustee shall be responsible to the Trustee for any property it administers. The Trustee may pay the ancillary Trustee reasonable compensation for services and may absolve the ancillary Trustee from any requirement to furnish bond or other security.

ARTICLE VIII
AMENDMENT AND REVOCATION OF TRUST

While I am living and legally competent, I may from time to time amend or revoke this Trust Agreement and the trusts evidenced by it, in whole or in part, by written instrument (other than by a will) delivered to the Trustee, except that, if amended, the duties, powers, and responsibilities of the Trustee shall not be changed without the Trustee's written consent. During such time as I am not legally competent neither I nor my court appointed guardian may amend or revoke this Trust Agreement or any trust evidenced by it. The trust property to which any revocation relates shall be conveyed to me or otherwise as I direct. This power is personal to me and may not be exercised by my legal representatives, attorneys in fact, or others. After my death, all trusts created under this Trust Agreement shall become irrevocable.

ARTICLE IX
MISCELLANEOUS PROVISIONS

Governing Law. The validity, construction, and administration of each trust created hereunder shall be governed by the laws of the State of _____.

Issue, Child and Children, and Determination of Living Persons. The word "issue," wherever used in this Trust Agreement, means all of the descendants, both by blood and by adoption, of whatever degree of the named ancestor, provided that (a) with respect to descendants by blood, the parents, as determined under applicable state law, of the descendants were married to one another, under the laws of the state in which they resided, either at the time of the descendant's conception or at the time of the descendant's birth, and (b) with respect to descendants by adoption, such adoption is of a person under the age of 21 years and is by court proceedings, the finality of which has not been questioned by the adoptive parent. The words "child" and "children" shall also include persons born or adopted under the same conditions. For the purposes of dividing or distributing any portion of the trust estate among persons who are living at a particular time, any person who has been conceived prior to such time, but has not yet been born, shall be considered to be living at such time if such person is later born and lives at least six months after birth.

Per Stirpes. Wherever this Trust Agreement directs a per stirpes distribution or allocation of assets to a person's descendants, division of those assets is to be made with reference to that person's children, regardless of whether any of them are living. Thus, though a person's children were all deceased the assets to be distributed or allocated would nevertheless be divided into as many equal shares as there were such deceased children with a descendant or descendants surviving at the time of distribution or allocation, and each such share would be divided similarly among the descendants of a deceased child.

Incapacity. For purposes of this Trust Agreement, a person (including any person appointed to act as Trustee hereunder) shall be considered incapacitated if such person has a legal, mental, or physical disability that substantially impairs such person's ability to manage his or her affairs (or the affairs of any trust created hereunder, as the case may be) with reasonable care. Proof that a person has become incapacitated may be conclusively established by the written opinion of two physicians selected by or acceptable to the Trustee of the trust or trusts of which the incapacitated person is a beneficiary (or to the prospective Trustee, if any, if the capacity of any Trustee be at issue) certifying to such fact. The language of such certificate shall be sufficient if acceptable to the Trustee (or the prospective Trustee, as the case may be) as indicating with reasonable certainty that such person is incapacitated. The physicians who issue such certificates, so long as they shall act in good faith in so doing, shall be entitled to indemnification by the trusts created hereunder from any liability rendering the opinion contained in any such certificates. The Trustee (or the prospective Trustee, as the case may be) so long as it shall act in good faith in accepting such certificates, shall be entitled to indemnification by the trusts created hereunder from any liability for acting pursuant to its good faith acceptance of such certificate.

Education. As used in this Trust Agreement, "education" shall include preparatory, collegiate, postgraduate, professional, and vocational education; specialized formal or informal training in music, the stage, handicrafts, the arts, or sports or athletic endeavors, whether by private instruction or otherwise; and any other activity, including foreign or domestic travel, which tends to develop the talents and potential of the beneficiary, regardless of age.

Health. As used in this Trust Agreement, "health" shall include medical, dental, hospital, and nursing care and other expenses of invalidism, and the cost of purchasing or maintaining hospital, medical, or nursing home insurance and disability income insurance coverage.

Code. All references in this trust to the "Code" mean the Internal Revenue Code of 1986, as amended, and shall refer to corresponding provisions of any subsequent federal tax law.

Invalid Provisions. If any part of this Trust Agreement shall be invalid, illegal or inoperative, for any reason, it is the intention of Grantor that the remaining parts, so far as possible and reasonable, shall be effective and fully operative. The Trustee may seek and obtain court instructions for the purpose of carrying out as nearly as possible the intention of this Trust Agreement as evidenced by the terms hereof, including any term held invalid, illegal, or inoperative.

Survival. Any person must survive by thirty days for a gift made in this Trust Agreement which directly or indirectly requires such person's survival of another to be effective.

Use of Words. As used in this Trust Agreement, the masculine, feminine, and neuter gender, and the singular or plural of any word includes the others unless the context indicates otherwise.

Titles, Headings, and Captions. All titles, headings, and captions used in this Trust Agreement have been included for convenience only and should not be construed in interpreting this Trust Agreement.

IN WITNESS WHEREOF I, as Grantor and Trustee, have signed this Trust Agreement the day and year first above written.

_____

Witness

_____   _____

Witness   Grantor and Trustee

STATE OF _____ §

§

COUNTY OF _____ §

BEFORE ME, the undersigned authority, on this day personally appeared _____,
Grantor and Trustee, known to me to be the person whose name is subscribed to the foregoing instrument and acknowledged to me that he/she executed the same for the purposes and consideration therein expressed.

GIVEN UNDER MY HAND AND SEAL OF OFFICE this _____ day of _____, 20_____.

_____

Notary Public

My commission expires:_____

_____ LIVING TRUST

(Unmarried, Children, Child's Trust)

THIS AGREEMENT OF TRUST is entered into at _____, State of _____, this _____ day of _____, 20_____, by and between _____, as Grantor and Trustee. This Trust, as from time to time amended, shall be known as the "_____ LIVING TRUST dated _____, 20_____."

ARTICLE I
FAMILY

I am not married. I have _____children now living, namely: _____. I intend by this Trust Agreement to provide for all my children, including any hereafter born or adopted.

ARTICLE II
FUNDING

Initial Funding. I hereby transfer to the Trustee the sum of Ten Dollars ($10.00).

Additional Funding. From time to time the Trust may be funded with additional property by me or by any other person in any manner. In addition, I may cause the Trustee to be designated as beneficiary of life insurance policies or qualified retirement plans. All property transferred, assigned, conveyed, or delivered to the Trustee and all investment and reinvestment thereof, are herein collectively referred to as the "trust estate" and shall be held, administered, and distributed by the Trustee in accordance with the terms of this Trust Agreement.

ARTICLE III
ADMINISTRATION OF TRUST DURING MY LIFETIME

Distributions of Income. While I am living and not under any incapacity, the Trustee shall distribute the income of the Trust as directed in writing by me from time to time. In the event I do not deliver such direction to the Trustee, the Trustee shall pay to or expend on my behalf such amount of income from the Trust as the Trustee determines is necessary or advisable for my health, education, maintenance, and support. Any income that is not distributed to me or on my behalf shall be added to the principal of the Trust.

Distributions of Principal. While I am living and not under any incapacity, the Trustee shall distribute such part or all of the principal of the Trust as directed in writing by me from time to time. In the event I do not deliver such direction to the Trustee, the Trustee shall pay to or expend on my behalf such part of the principal of the Trust as the Trustee determines is necessary or advisable for my health, education, maintenance, and support.

Use of Residential Property. If any real property used by me for residential purposes (whether on a full-time or part-time basis, including recreational property) becomes part of the trust estate, I shall have the right to use and occupy such property without rental and without accounting to the trust estate. The Trustee shall pay all taxes, debts, and other expenses associated with such residential property from the income of the Trust. To the extent income is insufficient, the Trustee shall use principal of the Trust to pay such taxes, debts, and expenses.

Distributions to My Children. The Trustee shall pay to or expend for the benefit of my minor Children, so much of the income and principal of the Trust as the Trustee, in his or her sole discretion, determines to be necessary for the health, education, maintenance, and support of my Children. The Trustee shall make such discretionary distributions only after conferring with me. The distributions from the Trust to my Children do not need to be equal.

Distribution During My Incapacity. In addition, whenever the Trustee considers that I am incapacitated, the Trustee shall distribute or apply such amounts of the income and principal of the trust estate (even though exhausting the Trust) as the Trustee considers advisable for my health, maintenance, and support, or for any other purpose the Trustee considers to be for my best interests. Any excess income shall be added to principal.

Incapacity. For purposes of this Trust Agreement, I shall be considered to be incapacitated if I: (a) am unable to manage my affairs; (b) am under a legal incapacity; or, (c) by reason of illness or mental or physical incapacity am unable to give prompt and intelligent consideration to my financial matters. I shall be considered incapacitated upon a good faith determination made by _____ and my physician, or the survivor of them, and the Trustee may rely upon written notice of that determination.

ARTICLE IV
ADMINISTRATION OF TRUST UPON MY DEATH

Payment of Expenses, Claims, and Taxes. Upon my death, if I have no probate estate, or to the extent that the cash and readily marketable assets in the principal of the residue of my probate estate are insufficient, the Trustee shall make the following payments from the principal of the trust estate. The Trustee shall pay the expenses of my last illness and funeral, costs of administration including ancillary administration, costs of safeguarding and delivering legacies, and claims allowable against my estate (excluding debts secured by real property or life insurance). The Trustee shall also pay the estate and inheritance taxes assessed by reason of my death. The Trustee may make payment directly or to the legal representative of my estate, as the Trustee deems advisable. I hereby waive all rights of apportionment or reimbursement for any payments made pursuant to this Article.

Selection of Assets. Assets or funds otherwise excludable from my gross estate for federal estate tax purposes shall not be used to make the foregoing payments. The Trustee's selection of assets to be sold to pay expenses, claims, and taxes shall not be subject to question by any beneficiary.

Tax Elections. The Trustee shall make such elections under the tax laws as the Trustee deems advisable, without regard to the relative interests of the beneficiaries and without liability to any person. No adjustment shall be made between principal and income or in the relative interests of the beneficiaries to compensate for the effect of elections or allocations under the tax laws made by the legal representative of my estate or by the Trustee.

ARTICLE V
DISTRIBUTION OF TRUST ASSETS UPON MY DEATH

Tangible Personal Property. The Trustee shall distribute my tangible personal property in accordance with any written, signed, and dated memorandum prepared by me. Any tangible personal property that is not disposed of by memorandum shall be distributed in equal shares to my surviving Children.

Specific Bequest. The Trustee shall distribute the following property to the named individuals:

$ _____ to _____

$ _____ to _____

If an individual named herein does not survive me, the gift to such person shall lapse and the share to which such person would have been entitled shall be distributed among the surviving individuals named in this paragraph on a pro rata basis.

Distribution to My Children. The Trustee shall divide the remaining trust estate, including any additions to the Trust by reason of my death, into separate equal shares to create one share for each Child of mine who is then living, and one share for the then living descendants, collectively, of each deceased Child of mine with one or more descendants then living. The

Trustee shall administer a share for each Child in a separate trust, pursuant to the provisions of Article VI. The share for the descendants of each deceased Child shall be distributed, per stirpes, to those descendants living at my death.

Contingent Distribution. If none of my Children or their descendants survive me, the remaining trust estate, including any additions to the Trust by reason of my death, shall be distributed to the following individuals in the amounts specified:

_____% to _____

_____% to _____

_____% to _____

_____% to _____

If an individual named herein does not survive me, the share to which he or she would be entitled under this paragraph shall be distributed in equal shares to the individuals named in this paragraph who survive me.

No Survivors. If none of my Children, their descendants, or the individuals named in the preceding paragraph survive me, the remaining trust estate, including any additions to the Trust by reason of my death, shall be distributed to my heirs at law in accordance with the law of descent and distribution in effect on the date of my death.

ARTICLE VI
TRUSTS FOR CHILDREN

Separate Trust for Child. Each trust for the benefit of a Child shall be administered and distributed upon the following terms:

(a) **Distributions of Income.** The Trustee may pay so much or all of the income from a Child's Trust to any one or more of the Child and his or her descendants from time to time living, in equal or unequal proportions and at such times as the Trustee determines to be necessary for the health, education, maintenance, and support of the Child and his or her descendants. Any income not so paid shall be added to principal.

(b) **Distributions of Principal.** The Trustee may pay so much or all of the principal from a Child's Trust to any one or more of the Child and his or her descendants from time to time living, in equal or unequal proportions and at such times as the Trustee determines to be necessary for the health, education, maintenance, and support of the Child and his or her descendants.

(c) **Distribution of Child's Trust.** After creation of a Child's Trust and after a Child has reached _____ years of age, the Trustee shall distribute to the Child the balance of his or her Child's Trust.

(d) **Termination of Trust.** Upon the death of a Child, any part of his or her Child's Trust that has not been distributed to the Child shall be distributed per stirpes to his or her then living descendants, or if none, then per stirpes to my then living descendants, except that each portion otherwise distributable to a Child of mine for whom a Child's Trust is then held under this Article VI shall be added to that trust. If none of my descendants are then living, the deceased Child's Trust shall be distributed in accordance with Article V.

ARTICLE VII
THE TRUSTEE

Initial Trustee. While I am alive, able, and willing to serve, I shall be the Trustee of the Trust.

Successor Trustee. During my lifetime, if I cannot serve as Trustee, I will appoint a successor Trustee. If I do not appoint a successor Trustee, or in the event of my death, incapacity, or inability to serve as Trustee, the successor Trustee shall be the first of the following individuals who is willing and competent to serve as successor Trustee:

If all of the successor Trustees die, become incapacitated, or otherwise fail or cease to serve as Trustee, a majority in number of the then living income beneficiaries of the Trust shall appoint a successor Trustee. Any appointment made under this Article shall be by a signed, acknowledged instrument delivered to the successor Trustee. A successor Trustee shall have all of the powers granted a Trustee in this Trust Agreement.

Resignation of Trustee. Any Trustee may resign as Trustee as to any one or more of the trusts created hereunder at any time by giving written notice to me if I am living, otherwise to the successor Trustee identified in this Trust Agreement, the current income beneficiaries of the Trust, and to those persons, if any, authorized in this Trust Agreement to appoint the successor Trustee.

Removal of Trustee. During my life, I may remove a Trustee at any time for any reason. After my death or if I am incapacitated and unable to remove the Trustee, a majority in number of the then living income beneficiaries of the Trust shall have the power to remove a Trustee.

Bond. No Trustee wherever acting shall be required to give bond or surety or be appointed by or account for the administration of any trust to any court.

Trustee's Fees. The Trustee shall be entitled to reasonable fees commensurate with the Trustee's duties and responsibilities, taking into account the value and nature of the trust estate and the time and work involved. The Trustee shall be reimbursed for reasonable costs and expenses incurred in connection with the performance of his or her fiduciary duties.

Registration of Trust. The Trustee shall not be required to register the Trust with any federal, state, or local government authority.

Liability of Trustee. A Trustee shall only be liable for willful misconduct or gross negligence and shall not be liable for breach of fiduciary duty by virtue of mistake or error in judgment. No successor Trustee shall be personally liable for any act or omission of any predecessor.

Majority Decision. If more than one Trustee is serving hereunder, the decision of a majority of the Trustees shall control. The dissenting Trustee shall have no liability for participating in or carrying out the acts of the controlling Trustee.

Delegation to Co-Trustee. A Trustee of any trust created hereunder may at any time by written instrument delegate to a Co-Trustee of such trust all or less than all of the powers conferred upon that Trustee, either for a specified time or until the delegation is revoked by a written instrument.

ARTICLE VIII
TRUST ADMINISTRATION

Trustee Powers: Investment and Management of Trust Estate. Subject to any limitation stated elsewhere in this Trust Agreement, the Trustee shall hold, manage, care for, and protect the trust property and shall have the following powers and, except to the extent inconsistent herewith, all of the rights, powers, and privileges and be subject to all of the duties, responsibilities, and conditions set forth in applicable state law, as amended from time to time:

(a) **Retain Property.** To retain any property originally constituting the trust or subsequently added thereto, and to invest and reinvest the trust property in bonds, stocks, mortgages, notes, bank deposits, options, futures, limited partnership interests, limited liability company interests, other business organization interests, shares of registered investment companies and real estate investment trusts, or other property of any kind, real or personal, domestic or foreign; the Trustee may retain or make any investment without liability, even though it is not of a type, quality, marketability, or diversification considered proper for trust investments.

(b) **Investment.** To invest in, participate in, form, or cause to be formed (alone or with others, including members of my family) such corporations, partnerships, limited partnerships, limited liability companies, and other business organizations organized under the laws of any state or country and to transfer and convey to such business organizations all or any part of the assets, real or personal, of any trust estate in exchange for such stocks, bonds, notes, other securities, or interests of such business organizations as the Trustee deems best.

(c) **Residential Property.** To acquire, hold, and maintain any residence for the use and benefit of such one or more of the beneficiaries of the trust, including me, and to pay all carrying charges of such residence, including but not limited to, any taxes, assessments, and maintenance thereon, and all expenses of the repair and operation thereof, including the employment of domestic servants and other expenses incident to the maintenance of a household for the benefit of any one or more of the beneficiaries of the trust, all as the Trustee deems best.

(d) **Tangible Personal Property.** To acquire, hold, and maintain as a part of the trust any and all articles of tangible personal property or any other property for the use and benefit of any one or more of the beneficiaries of the trust, without regard to the income productivity of income, and without any duty to convert such property to productive property, and to pay the expenses of safekeeping of any such property, including insurance, and all expenses of the repair and maintenance of such property, and to sell such property and to apply the net proceeds of sale to the purchase of such other property as the Trustee deems best.

(e) **Operate Business.** To continue or participate in the operation of any business or other enterprise, and to effect incorporation, dissolution, or other change in the form of the organization of the business or enterprise.

(f) **Nominee.** To cause any property, real or personal, belonging to the trust to be held or registered in the Trustee's name or in the name of a nominee or in such other form as the Trustee deems best without disclosing the trust relationship.

(g) **Real Estate.** To operate, maintain, repair, rehabilitate, alter, erect, improve, or remove any improvements on real estate; to subdivide real estate; to grant easements, give consents, and enter into contracts relating to real estate or its use; and to release or dedicate any interest in real estate.

(h) Lease. To enter for any purpose into a lease as lessor or lessee with or without option to purchase or renew for a term within or extending beyond the term of the trust.

(i) Minerals. To enter into a lease or arrangement for exploration and removal of minerals or other natural resources or enter into a pooling or unitization agreement.

(j) Sell. By public offering or private negotiation, to sell, exchange, assign, transfer, or otherwise dispose of all or any real or personal trust property and give options for these purposes, for such price and on such terms, with such covenants of warranty and such security for deferred payment as the Trustee deems proper.

(k) Partition. To partition any property in which the trust owns an undivided interest.

(l) Securities. To engage in all actions necessary to the effective administration of securities including, but not limited to, the authority to vote in person or by general or limited proxy, or refrain from voting, any corporate securities for any purpose; to exercise or sell any subscription or conversion rights; to consent to and join in or oppose any voting trusts, reorganizations, consolidations, mergers, foreclosures, and liquidations and in connection therewith to deposit securities and accept and hold other property received therefore.

(m) Borrow. To borrow money from any lender, and to extend or renew any existing indebtedness to be repaid from trust assets or otherwise; to mortgage or pledge any property in the trust to secure such borrowing; to advance money for the protection of the trust, and for all expenses, losses, and liabilities sustained in the administration of the trust or because of the holding or ownership of any trust assets.

(n) Litigation. To commence or defend actions, claims, or proceedings for the protection of trust assets and of the Trustee in the performance of his or her duties.

(o) Claims. To pay or contest any claim; to settle a claim by or against the trust by compromise, arbitration, or otherwise; and to release, in whole or in part, any claim belonging to the trust to the extent that the claim is uncollectible.

(p) Payments. To pay taxes, assessments, compensation of the Trustee, and other expenses incurred in the collection, care, administration, and protection of the trust.

(q) Beneficiary under Disability. To pay any sum distributable to a beneficiary under legal disability, without liability to the Trustee, by paying the sum to the beneficiary or by paying the sum for the use of the beneficiary either to a legal representative appointed by the court, or if none, to a relative.

(r) Agents. To employ persons, including attorneys, auditors, investment advisors, or agents, even if they are associated with any Trustee, to advise or assist the Trustee in the performance of his or her administrative duties; to act without independent investigation upon their recommendations; and instead of acting personally, to employ one or more agents to perform any act of administration, whether or not discretionary.

(s) Distributions. To distribute income and principal in cash or in kind, or partly in each, and to allocate or distribute undivided interests or different assets or disproportionate interests in assets, and no adjustment shall be made to compensate for a disproportionate allocation of unrealized gain for federal income tax purposes;

to value the trust property and to sell any part or all thereof in order to make allocation or distribution; no action taken by the Trustee pursuant to this paragraph shall be subject to question by any beneficiary.

(t) Allocation of Income and Principal. To allocate items of income or expense to either trust income or principal, as provided by law, including creation of reserves out of income for depreciation, obsolescence, or amortization, or for depletion in mineral or timber properties.

(u) Employee Benefits. To elect, pursuant to the terms of any employee benefit plan, individual retirement plan, or insurance contract, the mode of distribution of the proceeds thereof, and no adjustment shall be made in the interests of the beneficiaries to compensate for the effect of the election.

(v) Division and Distribution. To divide any trust created under this Trust Agreement into one or more separate trusts for the benefit of one or more of the beneficiaries of the trust so divided, and to allocate to such divided trust some or all of the assets of the trust estate for any reason.

(w) Tax Elections. Unless otherwise expressly directed hereunder, to exercise any tax option, allocation, or election permitted by law as the Trustee determines in the Trustee's sole discretion.

(x) Reliance. To rely upon any notice, certificate, affidavit, or other document or evidence believed by the Trustee to be genuine and accurate, in making any payment or distribution. The Trustee shall incur no liability for a disbursement or distribution make in good faith and without actual notice or knowledge of a changed condition or status affecting any person's interest in the trust or any other matter.

(y) Miscellaneous. To perform other acts necessary or appropriate for the proper administration of the trust, execute and deliver necessary instruments, and give full receipts and discharges.

Common Fund and Consolidation. For convenience of administration or investment, the Trustee may hold separate trusts as a common fund, dividing the income proportionately among them, assign undivided interests to the separate trusts, and make joint investments of the funds belonging to them. The Trustee may consolidate any separate trust with any other trust with similar provisions for the same beneficiary or beneficiaries.

Spendthrift. The interests of beneficiaries in principal or income shall not be subject to the claims of any creditor, any spouse for alimony or support, or others, or to legal process, and may not be voluntarily or involuntarily alienated or encumbered. The rights of beneficiaries to withdraw trust property are personal and may not be exercised by a legal representative, attorney in fact, or others.

Retained Powers. Notwithstanding the foregoing, while I am living and able to manage my affairs:

(a) no sale or investment shall be made without my written approval, unless I fail to indicate my approval or disapproval of any proposed sale or investment within ten days after being requested to do so in writing;

(b) I shall have the power to direct the retention or sale of any trust assets and the purchase of property with any principal cash in the trust. If I direct the retention or purchase of an asset, the Trustee shall have investment, voting, and management responsibility for that asset unless I direct otherwise; and,

(c) I may at any time or times, with or without right of revocation, by a writing delivered to the Trustee, delegate to any other person or to the Trustee or relinquish any or all of the powers reserved to me hereunder.

The statement of the Trustee that he or she is acting according to this paragraph shall fully protect all persons dealing with the Trustee. The Trustee shall have no responsibility for any loss that may result from acting in accordance with this paragraph.

Restriction on Powers. The Trustee shall not lend trust property to me, directly or indirectly, without adequate interest and adequate security. No Trustee who is a beneficiary of any trust, or who is obligated to support a beneficiary of any trust, shall participate in: the exercise of any discretion over distributions of income or principal other than that which is required for the health, education, maintenance and support of a beneficiary provided that such distribution does not satisfy the Trustee's obligation to support the beneficiary; the exercise of discretion to allocate receipts or expenses between principal and income.

Accounts and Compensation. A Trustee (other than myself) shall render an account of trust receipts and disbursements and a statement of assets at least annually to each adult beneficiary then entitled to receive or have the benefit of the income from the trust. An account is binding on each beneficiary who receives it and on all persons claiming by or through the beneficiary, and the Trustee is released, as to all matters stated in the account or shown by it, unless the beneficiary commences a judicial proceeding to assert a claim within five years after the mailing or other delivery of the account.

Small Trust Termination and Perpetuities Savings.

(a) A trustee in its discretion may terminate and distribute any trust hereunder if the corporate trustee determines that the costs of continuance thereof will substantially impair accomplishment of the purposes of the trust.

(b) The trustee shall terminate and forthwith distribute any trust created hereby, or by exercise of a power of appointment hereunder, and still held twenty-one years after the death of the last to die of myself and the beneficiaries in being at my death.

(c) Distribution under this section shall be made to the persons then entitled to receive or have the benefit of the income from the trust in the proportions in which they are entitled thereto, or if their interests are indefinite, then in equal shares.

Merger. If the Trustee deems it best for the beneficiary or beneficiaries of any trust created under this Trust Agreement to merge all of the assets held in such trust with any other trust created by this Trust Agreement or otherwise for the benefit of the same beneficiary or beneficiaries and under substantially similar trusts, terms, and conditions, the Trustee, after giving not less than thirty days written notice to the trust's beneficiaries, may terminate such trust and transfer to or merge all of the assets of such trust to such other trust, regardless of whether the Trustee under this Trust Agreement also is serving as the Trustee of such other trust.

Liability of Third Party. No person dealing with the Trustee of any trust created hereunder shall be obligated to see to the application of any money paid or property transferred to or upon the order of the Trustee; nor shall any person be obligated to inquire into the property of any transaction or the authority of the Trustee to enter into and consummate the same.

Trustee's Judgement Final. Whenever the judgment or discretion of any Trustee may be exercised, it shall be final and binding upon every person interested in the trust estate, and any Trustee exercising any discretionary power relating to the distribution of principal or income shall be responsible only for lack of good faith in the exercise of such power; provided, however, nothing contained in this paragraph shall be construed so as to broaden any standard within which the Trustee is authorized to make distributions of income or principal, so that such standard is no longer considered an ascertainable standard under Code Section 2041 when it would otherwise be ascertainable.

Court Supervision. The Trustee shall not be required to qualify before or be appointed by any court; nor shall the Trustee be required to obtain the order or approval of any court in the exercise of any power or discretion.

Out-of-State Properties. If the Trustee must act in a jurisdiction in which a person or entity serving as Trustee is unwilling or unable to act as to any property, the remaining Trustees or Trustee, if willing and able to act, otherwise such person as the Trustee shall from time to time designate in writing, shall act as ancillary Trustees or Trustee as to that property. Any person or corporation acting as ancillary Trustee may resign at any time by written notice to the Trustees. Each ancillary Trustee shall have the powers, rights, discretions, and duties, exercisable without court order, to act with respect to such matters as the Trustee deems proper. The ancillary Trustee shall be responsible to the Trustee for any property it administers. The Trustee may pay the ancillary Trustee reasonable compensation for services and may absolve the ancillary Trustee from any requirement to furnish bond or other security.

ARTICLE IX
AMENDMENT AND REVOCATION OF TRUST

While I am living and legally competent, I may from time to time amend or revoke this Trust Agreement and the trusts evidenced by it, in whole or in part, by written instrument (other than by a will) delivered to the Trustee, except that, if amended, the duties, powers, and responsibilities of the Trustee shall not be changed without the Trustee's written consent. During such time as I am not legally competent neither I nor my court appointed guardian may amend or revoke this Trust Agreement or any trust evidenced by it. The trust property to which any revocation relates shall be conveyed to me or otherwise as I direct. This power is personal to me and may not be exercised by my legal representatives, attorneys in fact, or others. After my death, all trusts created under this Trust Agreement shall become irrevocable.

ARTICLE X
MISCELLANEOUS PROVISIONS

Governing Law. The validity, construction, and administration of each trust created hereunder shall be governed by the laws of the State of _____.

Issue, Child and Children, and Determination of Living Persons. The word "issue," wherever used in this Trust Agreement, means all of the descendants, both by blood and by adoption, of whatever degree of the named ancestor, provided that (a) with respect to descendants by blood, the parents, as determined under applicable state law, of the descendants were married to one another, under the laws of the state in which they resided, either at the time of the descendant's conception or at the time of the descendant's birth, and (b) with respect to descendants by adoption, such adoption is of a person under the age of 21 years and is by court proceedings, the finality of which has not been questioned by the adoptive parent. The words "child" and "children" shall also include persons born or adopted under the same conditions. For the purposes of dividing or distributing any portion of the trust estate among persons who are living at a particular time, any person who has been conceived prior to such time, but has not yet been born, shall be considered to be living at such time if such person is later born and lives at least six months after birth.

Per Stirpes. Wherever this Trust Agreement directs a per stirpes distribution or allocation of assets to a person's descendants, division of those assets is to be made with reference to that person's children, regardless of whether any of them are living. Thus, though a person's children were all deceased the assets to be distributed or allocated would nevertheless be divided into as many equal shares as there were such deceased children with a descendant or descendants surviving at the time of distribution or allocation, and each such share would be divided similarly among the descendants of a deceased child.

Incapacity. For purposes of this Trust Agreement, a person (including any person appointed to act as Trustee hereunder) shall be considered incapacitated if such person has a legal, mental, or physical disability that substantially impairs such person's ability to manage his or her affairs (or the affairs of any trust created hereunder, as the case may be) with reasonable care. Proof that a person has become incapacitated may be conclusively established by the written opinion of two physicians selected by or acceptable to the Trustee of the trust or trusts of which the incapacitated person is a beneficiary (or to the prospective Trustee, if any, if the capacity of any Trustee be at issue) certifying to such fact. The language of such certificate shall be sufficient if acceptable to the Trustee (or the prospective Trustee, as the case may be) as indicating with reasonable certainty that such person is incapacitated. The physicians who issue such certificates, so long as they shall act in good faith in so doing, shall be entitled to indemnification by the trusts created hereunder from any liability rendering the opinion contained in any such certificates. The Trustee (or the prospective Trustee, as the case may be) so long as it shall act in good faith in accepting such certificates, shall be entitled to indemnification by the trusts created hereunder from any liability for acting pursuant to its good faith acceptance of such certificate.

Education. As used in this Trust Agreement, "education" shall include preparatory, collegiate, postgraduate, professional, and vocational education; specialized formal or informal training in music, the stage, handicrafts, the arts, or sports or athletic endeavors, whether by private instruction or otherwise; and any other activity, including foreign or domestic travel, which tends to develop the talents and potential of the beneficiary, regardless of age.

Health. As used in this Trust Agreement, "health" shall include medical, dental, hospital, and nursing care and other expenses of invalidism, and the cost of purchasing or maintaining hospital, medical, or nursing home insurance and disability income insurance coverage.

Code. All references in this trust to the "Code" mean the Internal Revenue Code of 1986, as amended, and shall refer to corresponding provisions of any subsequent federal tax law.

Invalid Provisions. If any part of this Trust Agreement shall be invalid, illegal, or inoperative, for any reason, it is the intention of Grantor that the remaining parts, so far as possible and reasonable, shall be effective and fully operative. The Trustee may seek and obtain court instructions for the purpose of carrying out as nearly as possible the intention of this Trust Agreement as evidenced by the terms hereof, including any term held invalid, illegal, or inoperative.

Survival. Any person must survive by thirty days for a gift made in this Trust Agreement which directly or indirectly requires such person's survival of another to be effective.

Use of Words. As used in this Trust Agreement, the masculine, feminine, and neuter gender, and the singular or plural of any word includes the others unless the context indicates otherwise.

Titles, Headings, and Captions. All titles, headings, and captions used in this Trust Agreement have been included for convenience only and should not be construed in interpreting this Trust Agreement.

IN WITNESS WHEREOF I, as Grantor and Trustee, have signed this Trust Agreement the day and year first above written.

_____   _____
Witness   Grantor and Trustee

_____
Witness

STATE OF _____§

§

COUNTY OF _____§

BEFORE ME, the undersigned authority, on this day personally appeared _____, Grantor and Trustee, known to me to be the person whose name is subscribed to the foregoing instrument and acknowledged to me that he/she executed the same for the purposes and consideration therein expressed.

GIVEN UNDER MY HAND AND SEAL OF OFFICE this _____ day of _____, 20_____.

_____
Notary Public

My commission expires:_____

This page intentionally left blank.

LIVING TRUST

(Married, No Children, Outright to Spouse)

THIS AGREEMENT OF TRUST is entered into at _____, State of _____, this _____ day of _____, 20_____, by and between _____, as Grantor and Trustee. This Trust, as from time to time amended, shall be known as the "_____ LIVING TRUST dated _____, 20_____."

ARTICLE I
FAMILY

I am married to _____ who is hereafter referred to as my spouse. I do not have any children.

ARTICLE II
FUNDING

Initial Funding. I hereby transfer to the Trustee the sum of Ten Dollars ($10.00).

Additional Funding. From time to time the Trust may be funded with additional property by me or by any other person in any manner. In addition, I may cause the Trustee to be designated as beneficiary of life insurance policies or qualified retirement plans. All property transferred, assigned, conveyed, or delivered to the Trustee and all investment and reinvestment thereof, are herein collectively referred to as the "trust estate" and shall be held, administered, and distributed by the Trustee in accordance with the terms of this Trust Agreement.

ARTICLE III
ADMINISTRATION OF TRUST DURING MY LIFETIME

Distributions of Income. While I am living and not under any incapacity, the Trustee shall distribute the income of the Trust as directed in writing by me from time to time. In the event I do not deliver such direction to the Trustee, the Trustee shall pay to or expend on my behalf such amount of income from the Trust as the Trustee determines is necessary or advisable for my health, education, maintenance, and support. Any income that is not distributed to me or on my behalf shall be added to the principal of the Trust.

Distributions of Principal. While I am living and not under any incapacity, the Trustee shall distribute such part or all of the principal of the Trust as directed in writing by me from time to time. In the event I do not deliver such direction to the Trustee, the Trustee shall pay to or expend on my behalf such part of the principal of the Trust as the Trustee determines is necessary or advisable for my health, education, maintenance, and support.

Use of Residential Property. If any real property used by me for residential purposes (whether on a full-time or part time basis, including recreational property) becomes part of the trust estate, I shall have the right to use and occupy such property without rental and without accounting to the trust estate. The Trustee shall pay all taxes, debts, and other expenses associated with such residential property from the income of the Trust. To the extent income is insufficient, the Trustee shall use principal of the Trust to pay such taxes, debts, and expenses.

Distribution During My Incapacity. In addition, whenever the Trustee considers that I am incapacitated, the Trustee shall distribute or apply such amounts of the income and principal of the trust estate (even though exhausting the Trust) as the Trustee considers advisable for my health, maintenance, and support, or for any other purpose the Trustee considers to be for my best interests. Any excess income shall be added to principal.

Distributions to My Spouse. The Trustee shall pay to or expend for the benefit of my spouse so much of the income and principal of the trust estate as the Trustee, in his or her sole discretion, determines to be necessary for the education, health, maintenance, and support of my spouse. The Trustee shall make such discretionary distributions only after conferring with me.

Incapacity. For purposes of this Trust Agreement, I shall be considered to be incapacitated if I: (a) am unable to manage my affairs; (b) am under a legal incapacity; or, (c) by reason of illness or mental or physical incapacity am unable to give prompt and intelligent consideration to my financial matters. I shall be considered incapacitated upon a good faith determination made by spouse and my physician, or the survivor of them, and the Trustee may rely upon written notice of that determination.

ARTICLE IV
ADMINISTRATION OF TRUST UPON MY DEATH

Payment of Expenses, Claims, and Taxes. Upon my death, if I have no probate estate, or to the extent that the cash and readily marketable assets in the principal of the residue of my probate estate are insufficient, the Trustee shall make the following payments from the principal of the trust estate. The Trustee shall pay the expenses of my last illness and funeral, costs of administration including ancillary administration, costs of safeguarding and delivering legacies, and claims allowable against my estate (excluding debts secured by real property or life insurance). The Trustee shall also pay the estate and inheritance taxes assessed by reason of my death. The Trustee may make payment directly or to the legal representative of my estate, as the Trustee deems advisable. I hereby waive all rights of apportionment or reimbursement for any payments made pursuant to this Article.

Selection of Assets. Assets or funds otherwise excludable from my gross estate for federal estate tax purposes shall not be used to make the foregoing payments. The Trustee's selection of assets to be sold to pay expenses, claims, and taxes shall not be subject to question by any beneficiary.

Tax Elections. The Trustee shall make such elections under the tax laws as the Trustee deems advisable, without regard to the relative interests of the beneficiaries and without liability to any person. No adjustment shall be made between principal and income or in the relative interests of the beneficiaries to compensate for the effect of elections or allocations under the tax laws made by the legal representative of my estate or by the Trustee.

ARTICLE V
DISTRIBUTION OF TRUST ASSETS UPON MY DEATH

Tangible Personal Property. The Trustee shall distribute my tangible personal property in accordance with any written, signed, and dated memorandum prepared by me. Any tangible personal property that is not disposed of by memorandum shall be distributed in to my spouse if he/she survives me otherwise in equal shares to the following individuals:

Specific Bequest. The Trustee shall distribute the following property to the named individuals:

$ _____ to _____

$ _____ to _____

If an individual named herein does not survive me, the gift to such person shall lapse and the share to which such person would have been entitled shall be distributed among the surviving individuals named in this paragraph on a pro rata basis.

Distribution to My Spouse. If my spouse survives me, the Trustee shall distribute the remaining trust estate, including any additions to the Trust by reason of my death, to my spouse outright and free of trust or, if my spouse chooses, to the Living Trust dated _____, 20____, established by my spouse.

Contingent Distribution. If my spouse does not survive me, the Trustee shall distribute the remaining trust estate, including any additions to the Trust by reason of my death, to the following individuals in the amounts specified:

_____% to _____

_____% to _____

_____% to _____

_____% to _____

If an individual named herein does not survive me, the share to which he or she would be entitled under this paragraph shall be distributed in equal shares to the individuals named in this paragraph who survive me.

No Survivors. If none of the individuals named in the preceding paragraph survive me, the remaining trust estate, including any additions to the Trust by reason of my death, shall be distributed to my heirs at law in accordance with the law of descent and distribution in effect on the date of my death.

ARTICLE VI
THE TRUSTEE

Initial Trustee. While I am alive, able, and willing to serve, I shall be the Trustee of the Trust.

Successor Trustee. During my lifetime, if I cannot serve as Trustee, I will appoint a successor Trustee. If I do not appoint a successor Trustee, or in the event of my death, incapacity, or inability to serve as Trustee, the successor Trustee shall be my spouse. In the event of the death, incapacity, or inability of my spouse to serve as Trustee, the successor Trustee shall be the first of the following individuals who is willing and competent to serve as successor Trustee:

If all of the successor Trustees die, become incapacitated, or otherwise fail or cease to serve as Trustee, a majority in number of the then living income beneficiaries of the Trust shall appoint a successor Trustee. Any appointment made under this Article shall be by a signed, acknowledged instrument delivered to the successor Trustee. A successor Trustee shall have all of the powers granted a Trustee in this Trust Agreement.

Resignation of Trustee. Any Trustee may resign as Trustee as to any one or more of the trusts created hereunder at any time by giving written notice to me if I am living, otherwise to the successor Trustee identified in this Trust Agreement, the current income beneficiaries of the Trust, and to those persons, if any, authorized in this Trust Agreement to appoint the successor Trustee.

Removal of Trustee. During my life, I may remove a Trustee at any time for any reason. After my death or if I am incapacitated and unable to remove the Trustee, my spouse shall have the power to remove a Trustee. If neither I nor my spouse are able to exercise the power to remove the Trustee, a majority in number of the then living income beneficiaries of the Trust shall have the power to remove a Trustee.

Bond. No Trustee wherever acting shall be required to give bond or surety or be appointed by or account for the administration of any trust to any court.

Trustee's Fees. The Trustee shall be entitled to reasonable fees commensurate with the Trustee's duties and responsibilities, taking into account the value and nature of the trust estate and the time and work involved. The Trustee shall be reimbursed for reasonable costs and expenses incurred in connection with the performance of his or her fiduciary duties.

Registration of Trust. The Trustee shall not be required to register the Trust with any federal, state, or local government authority.

Liability of Trustee. A Trustee shall only be liable for willful misconduct or gross negligence and shall not be liable for breach of fiduciary duty by virtue of mistake or error in judgment. No successor Trustee shall be personally liable for any act or omission of any predecessor.

Majority Decision. If more than one Trustee is serving hereunder, the decision of a majority of the Trustees shall control. The dissenting Trustee shall have no liability for participating in or carrying out the acts of the controlling Trustee.

Delegation to Co-Trustee. A Trustee of any trust created hereunder may at any time by written instrument delegate to a Co-Trustee of such trust all or less than all of the powers conferred upon that Trustee, either for a specified time or until the delegation is revoked by a written instrument.

ARTICLE VII
TRUST ADMINISTRATION

Trustee Powers: Investment and Management of Trust Estate. Subject to any limitation stated elsewhere in this Trust Agreement, the Trustee shall hold, manage, care for, and protect the trust property and shall have the following powers and, except to the extent inconsistent herewith, all of the rights, powers, and privileges and be subject to all of the duties, responsibilities, and conditions set forth in applicable state law, as amended from time to time:

(a) **Retain Property.** To retain any property originally constituting the trust or subsequently added thereto, and to invest and reinvest the trust property in bonds, stocks, mortgages, notes, bank deposits, options, futures, limited partnership interests, limited liability company interests, other business organization interests, shares of registered investment companies and real estate investment trusts, or other property of any kind, real or personal, domestic or foreign; the Trustee may retain or make any investment without liability, even though it is not of a type, quality, marketability, or diversification considered proper for trust investments.

(b) **Investment.** To invest in, participate in, form, or cause to be formed (alone or with others, including members of my family) such corporations, partnerships, limited partnerships, limited liability companies, and other business organizations organized under the laws of any state or country and to transfer and convey to such business organizations all or any part of the assets, real or personal, of any trust estate in exchange for such stocks, bonds, notes, other securities, or interests of such business organizations as the Trustee deems best.

(c) **Residential Property.** To acquire, hold, and maintain any residence for the use and benefit of such one or more of the beneficiaries of the trust, including me, and to pay all carrying charges of such residence, including but not limited to, any taxes, assessments, and maintenance thereon, and all expenses of the repair and operation thereof, including the employment of domestic servants and other expenses incident to the maintenance of a household for the benefit of any one or more of the beneficiaries of the trust, all as the Trustee deems best.

(d) **Tangible Personal Property.** To acquire, hold, and maintain as a part of the trust any and all articles of tangible personal property or any other property for the use and benefit of any one or more of the beneficiaries of the trust, without regard to the income productivity of income, and without any duty to convert such property to productive property, and to pay the expenses of safekeeping of any such property, including insurance, and all expenses of the repair and maintenance of such property, and to sell such property and to apply the net proceeds of sale to the purchase of such other property as the Trustee deems best.

(e) Operate Business. To continue or participate in the operation of any business or other enterprise, and to effect incorporation, dissolution, or other change in the form of the organization of the business or enterprise.

(f) Nominee. To cause any property, real or personal, belonging to the trust to be held or registered in the Trustee's name or in the name of a nominee or in such other form as the Trustee deems best without disclosing the trust relationship.

(g) Real Estate. To operate, maintain, repair, rehabilitate, alter, erect, improve, or remove any improvements on real estate; to subdivide real estate; to grant easements, give consents, and enter into contracts relating to real estate or its use; and to release or dedicate any interest in real estate.

(h) Lease. To enter for any purpose into a lease as lessor or lessee with or without option to purchase or renew for a term within or extending beyond the term of the trust.

(i) Minerals. To enter into a lease or arrangement for exploration and removal of minerals or other natural resources or enter into a pooling or unitization agreement.

(j) Sell. By public offering or private negotiation, to sell, exchange, assign, transfer, or otherwise dispose of all or any real or personal trust property and give options for these purposes, for such price and on such terms, with such covenants of warranty and such security for deferred payment as the Trustee deems proper.

(k) Partition. To partition any property in which the trust owns an undivided interest.

(l) Securities. To engage in all actions necessary to the effective administration of securities including, but not limited to, the authority to vote in person or by general or limited proxy, or refrain from voting, any corporate securities for any purpose; to exercise or sell any subscription or conversion rights; to consent to and join in or oppose any voting trusts, reorganizations, consolidations, mergers, foreclosures, and liquidations and in connection therewith to deposit securities and accept and hold other property received therefore.

(m) Borrow. To borrow money from any lender, and to extend or renew any existing indebtedness to be repaid from trust assets or otherwise; to mortgage or pledge any property in the trust to secure such borrowing; to advance money for the protection of the trust, and for all expenses, losses, and liabilities sustained in the administration of the trust or because of the holding or ownership of any trust assets.

(n) Litigation. To commence or defend actions, claims, or proceedings for the protection of trust assets and of the Trustee in the performance of his or her duties.

(o) Claims. To pay or contest any claim; to settle a claim by or against the trust by compromise, arbitration, or otherwise; and to release, in whole or in part, any claim belonging to the trust to the extent that the claim is uncollectible.

(p) Payments. To pay taxes, assessments, compensation of the Trustee, and other expenses incurred in the collection, care, administration, and protection of the trust.

(q) Beneficiary Under Disability. To pay any sum distributable to a beneficiary under legal disability, without liability to the Trustee, by paying the sum to the beneficiary or by paying the sum for the use of the beneficiary either to a legal representative appointed by the court, or if none, to a relative.

(r) Agents. To employ persons, including attorneys, auditors, investment advisors, or agents, even if they are associated with any Trustee, to advise or assist the Trustee in the performance of his or her administrative duties; to act without independent investigation upon their recommendations; and instead of acting personally, to employ one or more agents to perform any act of administration, whether or not discretionary.

(s) Distributions. To distribute income and principal in cash or in kind, or partly in each, and to allocate or distribute undivided interests or different assets or disproportionate interests in assets, and no adjustment shall be made to compensate for a disproportionate allocation of unrealized gain for federal income tax purposes; to value the trust property and to sell any part or all thereof in order to make allocation or distribution; no action taken by the Trustee pursuant to this paragraph shall be subject to question by any beneficiary.

(t) Allocation of Income and Principal. To allocate items of income or expense to either trust income or principal, as provided by law, including creation of reserves out of income for depreciation, obsolescence, or amortization, or for depletion in mineral or timber properties.

(u) Employee Benefits. To elect, pursuant to the terms of any employee benefit plan, individual retirement plan, or insurance contract, the mode of distribution of the proceeds thereof, and no adjustment shall be made in the interests of the beneficiaries to compensate for the effect of the election.

(v) Division and Distribution. To divide any trust created under this Trust Agreement into one or more separate trusts for the benefit of one or more of the beneficiaries of the trust so divided, and to allocate to such divided trust some or all of the assets of the trust estate for any reason.

(w) Tax Elections. Unless otherwise expressly directed hereunder, to exercise any tax option, allocation, or election permitted by law as the Trustee determines in the Trustee's sole discretion.

(x) Reliance. To rely upon any notice, certificate, affidavit, or other document or evidence believed by the Trustee to be genuine and accurate, in making any payment or distribution. The Trustee shall incur no liability for a disbursement or distribution make in good faith and without actual notice or knowledge of a changed condition or status affecting any person's interest in the trust or any other matter.

(y) Miscellaneous. To perform other acts necessary or appropriate for the proper administration of the trust, execute and deliver necessary instruments, and give full receipts and discharges.

Common Fund and Consolidation. For convenience of administration or investment, the Trustee may hold separate trusts as a common fund, dividing the income proportionately among them, assign undivided interests to the separate trusts, and make joint investments of the funds belonging to them. The Trustee may consolidate any separate trust with any other trust with similar provisions for the same beneficiary or beneficiaries.

Spendthrift. The interests of beneficiaries in principal or income shall not be subject to the claims of any creditor, any spouse for alimony or support, or others, or to legal process, and may not be voluntarily or involuntarily alienated or encumbered. The rights of beneficiaries to withdraw trust property are personal and may not be exercised by a legal representative, attorney in fact, or others.

Retained Powers. Notwithstanding the foregoing, while I am living and able to manage my affairs:

(**a**) no sale or investment shall be made without my written approval, unless I fail to indicate my approval or disapproval of any proposed sale or investment within ten days after being requested to do so in writing;

(**b**) I shall have the power to direct the retention or sale of any trust assets and the purchase of property with any principal cash in the trust. If I direct the retention or purchase of an asset, the Trustee shall have investment, voting, and management responsibility for that asset unless I direct otherwise; and,

(**c**) I may at any time or times, with or without right of revocation, by a writing delivered to the Trustee, delegate to any other person or to the Trustee or relinquish any or all of the powers reserved to me hereunder.

The statement of the Trustee that he or she is acting according to this paragraph shall fully protect all persons dealing with the Trustee. The Trustee shall have no responsibility for any loss that may result from acting in accordance with this paragraph.

Restriction on Powers. The Trustee shall not lend trust property to me, directly or indirectly, without adequate interest and adequate security. No Trustee who is a beneficiary of any trust, or who is obligated to support a beneficiary of any trust, shall participate in: the exercise of any discretion over distributions of income or principal other than that which is required for the health, education, maintenance and support of a beneficiary provided that such distribution does not satisfy the Trustee's obligation to support the beneficiary; the exercise of discretion to allocate receipts or expenses between principal and income.

Accounts and Compensation. A Trustee (other than myself) shall render an account of trust receipts and disbursements and a statement of assets at least annually to each adult beneficiary then entitled to receive or have the benefit of the income from the trust. An account is binding on each beneficiary who receives it and on all persons claiming by or through the beneficiary, and the Trustee is released, as to all matters stated in the account or shown by it, unless the beneficiary commences a judicial proceeding to assert a claim within five years after the mailing or other delivery of the account.

Small Trust Termination and Perpetuities Savings.

(**a**) A trustee in its discretion may terminate and distribute any trust hereunder if the corporate trustee determines that the costs of continuance thereof will substantially impair accomplishment of the purposes of the trust.

(**b**) The trustee shall terminate and forthwith distribute any trust created hereby, or by exercise of a power of appointment hereunder, and still held twenty-one years after the death of the last to die of myself and the beneficiaries in being at my death.

(**c**) Distribution under this section shall be made to the persons then entitled to receive or have the benefit of the income from the trust in the proportions in which they are entitled thereto, or if their interests are indefinite, then in equal shares.

Merger. If the Trustee deems it best for the beneficiary or beneficiaries of any trust created under this Trust Agreement to merge all of the assets held in such trust with any other trust created by this Trust Agreement or otherwise for the benefit of the same beneficiary or beneficiaries and under substantially similar trusts, terms, and conditions, the Trustee, after giving not less than thirty days written notice to the trust's beneficiaries, may terminate such trust and transfer to or merge all of the assets of such trust to such other trust, regardless of whether the Trustee under this Trust Agreement also is serving as the Trustee of such other trust.

Liability of Third Party. No person dealing with the Trustee of any trust created hereunder shall be obligated to see to the application of any money paid or property transferred to or upon the order of the Trustee; nor shall any person be obligated to inquire into the property of any transaction or the authority of the Trustee to enter into and consummate the same.

Trustee's Judgement Final. Whenever the judgment or discretion of any Trustee may be exercised, it shall be final and binding upon every person interested in the trust estate, and any Trustee exercising any discretionary power relating to the distribution of principal or income shall be responsible only for lack of good faith in the exercise of such power; provided, however, nothing contained in this paragraph shall be construed so as to broaden any standard within which the Trustee is authorized to make distributions of income or principal, so that such standard is no longer considered an ascertainable standard under Code Section 2041 when it would otherwise be ascertainable.

Court Supervision. The Trustee shall not be required to qualify before or be appointed by any court; nor shall the Trustee be required to obtain the order or approval of any court in the exercise of any power or discretion.

Out-of-State Properties. If the Trustee must act in a jurisdiction in which a person or entity serving as Trustee is unwilling or unable to act as to any property, the remaining Trustees or Trustee, if willing and able to act, otherwise such person as the Trustee shall from time to time designate in writing, shall act as ancillary Trustees or Trustee as to that property. Any person or corporation acting as ancillary Trustee may resign at any time by written notice to the Trustees. Each ancillary Trustee shall have the powers, rights, discretions, and duties, exercisable without court order, to act with respect to such matters as the Trustee deems proper. The ancillary Trustee shall be responsible to the Trustee for any property it administers. The Trustee may pay the ancillary Trustee reasonable compensation for services and may absolve the ancillary Trustee from any requirement to furnish bond or other security.

ARTICLE VIII
AMENDMENT AND REVOCATION OF TRUST

While I am living and legally competent, I may from time to time amend or revoke this Trust Agreement and the trusts evidenced by it, in whole or in part, by written instrument (other than by a will) delivered to the Trustee, except that, if amended, the duties, powers, and responsibilities of the Trustee shall not be changed without the Trustee's written consent. During such time as I am not legally competent neither I nor my court appointed guardian may amend or revoke this Trust Agreement or any trust evidenced by it. The trust property to which any revocation relates shall be conveyed to me or otherwise as I direct. This power is personal to me and may not be exercised by my legal representatives, attorneys in fact, or others. After my death, all trusts created under this Trust Agreement shall become irrevocable.

ARTICLE IX
MISCELLANEOUS PROVISIONS

Governing Law. The validity, construction, and administration of each trust created hereunder shall be governed by the laws of the State of _____.

Issue, Child and Children, and Determination of Living Persons. The word "issue," wherever used in this Trust Agreement, means all of the descendants, both by blood and by adoption, of whatever degree of the named ancestor, provided that (a) with respect to descendants by blood, the parents, as determined under applicable state law, of the descendants were married to one another, under the laws of the state in which they resided, either at the time of the descendant's conception or at the time of the descendant's birth, and (b) with respect to descendants by adoption, such adoption is of a person under the age of 21 years and is by court proceedings, the finality of which has not been questioned by the adoptive parent. The words "child" and "children" shall also include persons born or adopted under the same conditions. For the purposes of dividing or distributing any portion of the trust estate among persons who are living at a particular time, any person who has been conceived prior to such time, but has not yet been born, shall be considered to be living at such time if such person is later born and lives at least six months after birth.

Per Stirpes. Wherever this Trust Agreement directs a per stirpes distribution or allocation of assets to a person's descendants, division of those assets is to be made with reference to that person's children, regardless of whether any of them are living. Thus, though a person's children were all deceased the assets to be distributed or allocated would nevertheless be divided into as many equal shares as there were such deceased children with a descendant or descendants surviving at the time of distribution or allocation, and each such share would be divided similarly among the descendants of a deceased child.

Incapacity. For purposes of this Trust Agreement, a person (including any person appointed to act as Trustee hereunder) shall be considered incapacitated if such person has a legal, mental, or physical disability that substantially impairs such person's ability to manage his or her affairs (or the affairs of any trust created hereunder, as the case may be) with reasonable care. Proof that a person has become incapacitated may be conclusively established by the written opinion of two physicians selected by or acceptable to the Trustee of the trust or trusts of which the incapacitated person is a beneficiary (or to the prospective Trustee, if any, if the capacity of any Trustee be at issue) certifying to such fact. The language of such certificate shall be sufficient if acceptable to the Trustee (or the prospective Trustee, as the case may be) as indicating with reasonable certainty that such person is incapacitated. The physicians who issue such certificates, so long as they shall act in good faith in so doing, shall be entitled to indemnification by the trusts created hereunder from any liability rendering the opinion contained in any such certificates. The Trustee (or the prospective Trustee, as the case may be) so long as it shall act in good faith in accepting such certificates, shall be entitled to indemnification by the trusts created hereunder from any liability for acting pursuant to its good faith acceptance of such certificate.

Education. As used in this Trust Agreement, "education" shall include preparatory, collegiate, postgraduate, professional, and vocational education; specialized formal or informal training in music, the stage, handicrafts, the arts, or sports or athletic endeavors, whether by private instruction or otherwise; and any other activity, including foreign or domestic travel, which tends to develop the talents and potential of the beneficiary, regardless of age.

Health. As used in this Trust Agreement, "health" shall include medical, dental, hospital, and nursing care and other expenses of invalidism, and the cost of purchasing or maintaining hospital, medical, or nursing home insurance and disability income insurance coverage.

Code. All references in this trust to the "Code" mean the Internal Revenue Code of 1986, as amended, and shall refer to corresponding provisions of any subsequent federal tax law.

Invalid Provisions. If any part of this Trust Agreement shall be invalid, illegal, or inoperative, for any reason, it is the intention of Grantor that the remaining parts, so far as possible and reasonable, shall be effective and fully operative. The Trustee may seek and obtain court instructions for the purpose of carrying out as nearly as possible the intention of this Trust Agreement as evidenced by the terms hereof, including any term held invalid, illegal, or inoperative.

Survival. Any person must survive by thirty days for a gift made in this Trust Agreement which directly or indirectly requires such person's survival of another to be effective.

Use of Words. As used in this Trust Agreement, the masculine, feminine, and neuter gender, and the singular or plural of any word includes the others unless the context indicates otherwise.

Titles, Headings, and Captions. All titles, headings, and captions used in this Trust Agreement have been included for convenience only and should not be construed in interpreting this Trust Agreement.

IN WITNESS WHEREOF I, as Grantor and Trustee, have signed this Trust Agreement the day and year first above written.

_____ _____

Witness   Grantor and Trustee

_____

Witness

STATE OF _____§

§

COUNTY OF _____§

BEFORE ME, the undersigned authority, on this day personally appeared _____, Grantor and Trustee, known to me to be the person whose name is subscribed to the foregoing instrument and acknowledged to me that he/she executed the same for the purposes and consideration therein expressed.

GIVEN UNDER MY HAND AND SEAL OF OFFICE this _____ day of _____, 20_____.

_____

Notary Public

My commission expires:_____

_____ LIVING TRUST

(Married, No Children, Family Trust for Spouse)

THIS AGREEMENT OF TRUST is entered into at _____, State of _____, this _____ day of _____, 20_____, by and between _____, as Grantor and Trustee. This Trust, as from time to time amended, shall be known as the "_____ LIVING TRUST dated _____, 20_____."

ARTICLE I
FAMILY

I am married to _____ who is hereafter referred to as my spouse. I do not have any children.

ARTICLE II
FUNDING

Initial Funding. I hereby transfer to the Trustee the sum of Ten Dollars ($10.00).

Additional Funding. From time to time the Trust may be funded with additional property by me or by any other person in any manner. In addition, I may cause the Trustee to be designated as beneficiary of life insurance policies or qualified retirement plans. All property transferred, assigned, conveyed, or delivered to the Trustee and all investment and reinvestment thereof, are herein collectively referred to as the "trust estate" and shall be held, administered, and distributed by the Trustee in accordance with the terms of this Trust Agreement.

ARTICLE III
ADMINISTRATION OF TRUST DURING MY LIFETIME

Distributions of Income. While I am living and not under any incapacity, the Trustee shall distribute the income of the Trust as directed in writing by me from time to time. In the event I do not deliver such direction to the Trustee, the Trustee shall pay to or expend on my behalf such amount of income from the Trust as the Trustee determines is necessary or advisable for my health, education, maintenance, and support. Any income that is not distributed to me or on my behalf shall be added to the principal of the Trust.

Distributions of Principal. While I am living and not under any incapacity, the Trustee shall distribute such part or all of the principal of the Trust as directed in writing by me from time to time. In the event I do not deliver such direction to the Trustee, the Trustee shall pay to or expend on my behalf such part of the principal of the Trust as the Trustee determines is necessary or advisable for my health, education, maintenance, and support.

Use of Residential Property. If any real property used by me for residential purposes (whether on a full-time or part time basis, including recreational property) becomes part of the trust estate, I shall have the right to use and occupy such property without rental and without accounting to the trust estate. The Trustee shall pay all taxes, debts, and other expenses associated with such residential property from the income of the Trust. To the extent income is insufficient, the Trustee shall use principal of the Trust to pay such taxes, debts, and expenses.

Distribution During My Incapacity. In addition, whenever the Trustee considers that I am incapacitated, the Trustee shall distribute or apply such amounts of the income and principal of the trust estate (even though exhausting the Trust) as the Trustee considers advisable for my health, maintenance, and support, or for any other purpose the Trustee considers to be for my best interests. Any excess income shall be added to principal.

Distributions to My Spouse. The Trustee shall pay to or expend for the benefit of my spouse so much of the income and principal of the trust estate as the Trustee, in his or her sole discretion, determines to be necessary for the education, health, maintenance, and support of my spouse. The Trustee shall make such discretionary distributions only after conferring with me.

Incapacity. For purposes of this Trust Agreement, I shall be considered to be incapacitated if I: (a) am unable to manage my affairs; (b) am under a legal incapacity; or, (c) by reason of illness or mental or physical incapacity am unable to give prompt and intelligent consideration to my financial matters. I shall be considered incapacitated upon a good faith determination made by spouse and my physician, or the survivor of them, and the Trustee may rely upon written notice of that determination.

ARTICLE IV
ADMINISTRATION OF TRUST UPON MY DEATH

Payment of Expenses, Claims, and Taxes. Upon my death, if I have no probate estate, or to the extent that the cash and readily marketable assets in the principal of the residue of my probate estate are insufficient, the Trustee shall make the following payments from the principal of the trust estate. The Trustee shall pay the expenses of my last illness and funeral, costs of administration including ancillary administration, costs of safeguarding and delivering legacies, and claims allowable against my estate (excluding debts secured by real property or life insurance). The Trustee shall also pay the estate and inheritance taxes assessed by reason of my death. The Trustee may make payment directly or to the legal representative of my estate, as the Trustee deems advisable. I hereby waive all rights of apportionment or reimbursement for any payments made pursuant to this Article.

Selection of Assets. Assets or funds otherwise excludable from my gross estate for federal estate tax purposes shall not be used to make the foregoing payments. The Trustee's selection of assets to be sold to pay expenses, claims, and taxes shall not be subject to question by any beneficiary.

Tax Elections. The Trustee shall make such elections under the tax laws as the Trustee deems advisable, without regard to the relative interests of the beneficiaries and without liability to any person. No adjustment shall be made between principal and income or in the relative interests of the beneficiaries to compensate for the effect of elections or allocations under the tax laws made by the legal representative of my estate or by the Trustee.

ARTICLE V
DISTRIBUTION OF TRUST ASSETS UPON MY DEATH

Tangible Personal Property. The Trustee shall distribute my tangible personal property in accordance with any written, signed, and dated memorandum prepared by me. Any tangible personal property that is not disposed of by memorandum shall be distributed in to my spouse if he or she survives me otherwise in equal shares to the following individuals:

Specific Bequest. The Trustee shall distribute the following property to the named individuals:

$ _____ to _____

$ _____ to _____

If an individual named herein does not survive me, the gift to such person shall lapse and the share to which such person would have been entitled shall be distributed among the surviving individuals named in this paragraph on a pro rata basis.

Distribution if My Spouse Survives Me. If my spouse survives me, the Trustee shall set aside and distribute the trust estate, including any additions to the Trust by reason of my death, as follows:

(a) All property in the trust estate as to which a federal estate tax marital deduction would not be allowed if it were distributed outright to my spouse, plus the largest pecuniary amount that will not result in or increase federal estate tax payable by reason of my death, shall be set aside in a separate trust designated the Family Trust, and shall be held and distributed in accordance with article VI. In determining the pecuniary amount, the trustee shall consider the credit for state death taxes only to the extent those taxes are not thereby incurred or increased, shall assume that none of this trust qualifies for a federal estate tax deduction, and shall assume that the Marital Trust hereinafter established (including any part thereof disclaimed by my spouse) qualifies in full for the federal estate tax marital deduction.

(b) The balance, if any, shall be distributed to my spouse outright and free of trust.

Contingent Distribution. If my spouse does not survive me, the Trustee shall distribute the remaining trust estate, including any additions to the Trust by reason of my death, to the following individuals in the amounts specified:

_____% to _____
_____% to _____
_____% to _____
_____% to _____

If an individual named herein does not survive me, the gift to such person shall lapse and the share to which such person would have been entitled shall be distributed among the surviving individuals named in this paragraph on a *pro rata* basis.

No Survivors. If none of the individuals named in the preceding paragraph survive me, the remaining trust estate, including any additions to the Trust by reason of my death, shall be distributed to my heirs at law in accordance with the law of descent and distribution in effect on the date of my death.

ARTICLE VI
FAMILY TRUST

Family Trust. The trust held under this Article VI shall be referred to as the "Family Trust." The Family Trust shall be administered and distributed upon the following terms:

(a) **Distributions of Income**. The Trustee may distribute part or all of the income from the Family Trust to my spouse as the Trustee, in his or her sole discretion, determines to be necessary for the health, education, maintenance, and support of my spouse. Any income not so paid shall be added to principal.

(b) **Distributions of Principal**. The Trustee may pay so much or all of the principal from the Family Trust my spouse as the Trustee, in his or her sole discretion, determines to be necessary for the health, education, maintenance, and support of my spouse.

Termination of Trust. Upon the death of my spouse, the Trustee shall distribute the assets remaining in the Family Trust, to the following individuals in the amounts specified:

_____% to _____
_____% to _____
_____% to _____
_____% to _____

If an individual named herein does not survive me, the gift to such person shall lapse and the share to which such person would have been entitled shall be distributed among the surviving individuals named in this paragraph on a pro rata basis.

No Survivors. If none of the individuals named in the preceding paragraph are then living, the assets remaining in the Family Trust shall be distributed to my heirs at law in accordance with the law of descent and distribution in effect on the date of my death.

ARTICLE VII
THE TRUSTEE

Initial Trustee. While I am alive, able, and willing to serve, I shall be the Trustee of the Trust.

Successor Trustee. During my lifetime, if I cannot serve as Trustee, I will appoint a successor Trustee. If I do not appoint a successor Trustee, or in the event of my death, incapacity, or inability to serve as Trustee, the successor Trustee shall be my spouse. In the event of the death, incapacity, or inability of my spouse to serve as Trustee, the successor Trustee shall be the first of the following individuals who is willing and competent to serve as successor Trustee:

If all of the successor Trustees die, become incapacitated, or otherwise fail or cease to serve as Trustee, a majority in number of the then living income beneficiaries of the Trust shall appoint a successor Trustee. Any appointment made under this Article shall be by a signed, acknowledged instrument delivered to the successor Trustee. A successor Trustee shall have all of the powers granted a Trustee in this Trust Agreement.

Resignation of Trustee. Any Trustee may resign as Trustee as to any one or more of the trusts created hereunder at any time by giving written notice to me if I am living, otherwise to the successor Trustee identified in this Trust Agreement, the current income beneficiaries of the Trust, and to those persons, if any, authorized in this Trust Agreement to appoint the successor Trustee.

Removal of Trustee. During my life, I may remove a Trustee at any time for any reason. After my death or if I am incapacitated and unable to remove the Trustee, my spouse shall have the power to remove a Trustee. If neither I nor my spouse are able to exercise the power to remove the Trustee, a majority in number of the then living income beneficiaries of the Trust shall have the power to remove a Trustee.

Bond. No Trustee wherever acting shall be required to give bond or surety or be appointed by or account for the administration of any trust to any court.

Trustee's Fees. The Trustee shall be entitled to reasonable fees commensurate with the Trustee's duties and responsibilities, taking into account the value and nature of the trust estate and the time and work involved. The Trustee shall be reimbursed for reasonable costs and expenses incurred in connection with the performance of his or her fiduciary duties.

Registration of Trust. The Trustee shall not be required to register the Trust with any federal, state, or local government authority.

Liability of Trustee. A Trustee shall only be liable for willful misconduct or gross negligence and shall not be liable for breach of fiduciary duty by virtue of mistake or error in judgment. No successor Trustee shall be personally liable for any act or omission of any predecessor.

Majority Decision. If more than one Trustee is serving hereunder, the decision of a majority of the Trustees shall control. The dissenting Trustee shall have no liability for participating in or carrying out the acts of the controlling Trustee.

Delegation to Co-Trustee. A Trustee of any trust created hereunder may at any time by written instrument delegate to a Co-Trustee of such trust all or less than all of the powers conferred upon that Trustee, either for a specified time or until the delegation is revoked by a written instrument.

ARTICLE VIII
TRUST ADMINISTRATION

Trustee Powers: Investment and Management of Trust Estate. Subject to any limitation stated elsewhere in this Trust Agreement, the Trustee shall hold, manage, care for, and protect the trust property and shall have the following powers and, except to the extent inconsistent herewith, all of the rights, powers, and privileges and be subject to all of the duties, responsibilities, and conditions set forth in applicable state law, as amended from time to time:

(a) **Retain Property.** To retain any property originally constituting the trust or subsequently added thereto, and to invest and reinvest the trust property in bonds, stocks, mortgages, notes, bank deposits, options, futures, limited partnership interests, limited liability company interests, other business organization interests, shares of registered investment companies and real estate investment trusts, or other property of any kind, real or personal, domestic or foreign; the Trustee may retain or make any investment without liability, even though it is not of a type, quality, marketability, or diversification considered proper for trust investments.

(b) **Investment.** To invest in, participate in, form, or cause to be formed (alone or with others, including members of my family) such corporations, partnerships, limited partnerships, limited liability companies, and other business organizations organized under the laws of any state or country and to transfer and convey to such business organizations all or any part of the assets, real or personal, of any trust estate in exchange for such stocks, bonds, notes, other securities, or interests of such business organizations as the Trustee deems best.

(c) **Residential Property.** To acquire, hold, and maintain any residence for the use and benefit of such one or more of the beneficiaries of the trust, including me, and to pay all carrying charges of such residence, including but not limited to, any taxes, assessments, and maintenance thereon, and all expenses of the repair and operation thereof, including the employment of domestic servants and other expenses incident to the maintenance of a household for the benefit of any one or more of the beneficiaries of the trust, all as the Trustee deems best.

(d) **Tangible Personal Property.** To acquire, hold, and maintain as a part of the trust any and all articles of tangible personal property or any other property for the use and benefit of any one or more of the beneficiaries of the trust, without regard to the income productivity of income, and without any duty to convert such property to productive property, and to pay the expenses of safekeeping of any such property, including insurance, and all expenses of the repair and maintenance of such property, and to sell such property and to apply the net proceeds of sale to the purchase of such other property as the Trustee deems best.

(e) **Operate Business.** To continue or participate in the operation of any business or other enterprise, and to effect incorporation, dissolution, or other change in the form of the organization of the business or enterprise.

(f) Nominee. To cause any property, real or personal, belonging to the trust to be held or registered in the Trustee's name or in the name of a nominee or in such other form as the Trustee deems best without disclosing the trust relationship.

(g) Real Estate. To operate, maintain, repair, rehabilitate, alter, erect, improve, or remove any improvements on real estate; to subdivide real estate; to grant easements, give consents, and enter into contracts relating to real estate or its use; and to release or dedicate any interest in real estate.

(h) Lease. To enter for any purpose into a lease as lessor or lessee with or without option to purchase or renew for a term within or extending beyond the term of the trust.

(i) Minerals. To enter into a lease or arrangement for exploration and removal of minerals or other natural resources or enter into a pooling or unitization agreement.

(j) Sell. By public offering or private negotiation, to sell, exchange, assign, transfer, or otherwise dispose of all or any real or personal trust property and give options for these purposes, for such price and on such terms, with such covenants of warranty and such security for deferred payment as the Trustee deems proper.

(k) Partition. To partition any property in which the trust owns an undivided interest.

(l) Securities. To engage in all actions necessary to the effective administration of securities including, but not limited to, the authority to vote in person or by general or limited proxy, or refrain from voting, any corporate securities for any purpose; to exercise or sell any subscription or conversion rights; to consent to and join in or oppose any voting trusts, reorganizations, consolidations, mergers, foreclosures, and liquidations and in connection therewith to deposit securities and accept and hold other property received therefore.

(m) Borrow. To borrow money from any lender, and to extend or renew any existing indebtedness to be repaid from trust assets or otherwise; to mortgage or pledge any property in the trust to secure such borrowing; to advance money for the protection of the trust, and for all expenses, losses, and liabilities sustained in the administration of the trust or because of the holding or ownership of any trust assets.

(n) Litigation. To commence or defend actions, claims, or proceedings for the protection of trust assets and of the Trustee in the performance of his or her duties.

(o) Claims. To pay or contest any claim; to settle a claim by or against the trust by compromise, arbitration, or otherwise; and to release, in whole or in part, any claim belonging to the trust to the extent that the claim is uncollectible.

(p) Payments. To pay taxes, assessments, compensation of the Trustee, and other expenses incurred in the collection, care, administration, and protection of the trust.

(q) Beneficiary Under Disability. To pay any sum distributable to a beneficiary under legal disability, without liability to the Trustee, by paying the sum to the beneficiary or by paying the sum for the use of the beneficiary either to a legal representative appointed by the court, or if none, to a relative.

(r) **Agents.** To employ persons, including attorneys, auditors, investment advisors, or agents, even if they are associated with any Trustee, to advise or assist the Trustee in the performance of his or her administrative duties; to act without independent investigation upon their recommendations; and instead of acting personally, to employ one or more agents to perform any act of administration, whether or not discretionary.

(s) **Distributions.** To distribute income and principal in cash or in kind, or partly in each, and to allocate or distribute undivided interests or different assets or disproportionate interests in assets, and no adjustment shall be made to compensate for a disproportionate allocation of unrealized gain for federal income tax purposes; to value the trust property and to sell any part or all thereof in order to make allocation or distribution; no action taken by the Trustee pursuant to this paragraph shall be subject to question by any beneficiary.

(t) **Allocation of Income and Principal.** To allocate items of income or expense to either trust income or principal, as provided by law, including creation of reserves out of income for depreciation, obsolescence, or amortization, or for depletion in mineral or timber properties.

(u) **Employee Benefits.** To elect, pursuant to the terms of any employee benefit plan, individual retirement plan, or insurance contract, the mode of distribution of the proceeds thereof, and no adjustment shall be made in the interests of the beneficiaries to compensate for the effect of the election.

(v) **Division and Distribution.** To divide any trust created under this Trust Agreement into one or more separate trusts for the benefit of one or more of the beneficiaries of the trust so divided, and to allocate to such divided trust some or all of the assets of the trust estate for any reason.

(w) **Tax Elections.** Unless otherwise expressly directed hereunder, to exercise any tax option, allocation, or election permitted by law as the Trustee determines in the Trustee's sole discretion.

(x) **Reliance.** To rely upon any notice, certificate, affidavit, or other document or evidence believed by the Trustee to be genuine and accurate, in making any payment or distribution. The Trustee shall incur no liability for a disbursement or distribution make in good faith and without actual notice or knowledge of a changed condition or status affecting any person's interest in the trust or any other matter.

(y) **Miscellaneous.** To perform other acts necessary or appropriate for the proper administration of the trust, execute and deliver necessary instruments, and give full receipts and discharges.

Common Fund and Consolidation. For convenience of administration or investment, the Trustee may hold separate trusts as a common fund, dividing the income proportionately among them, assign undivided interests to the separate trusts, and make joint investments of the funds belonging to them. The Trustee may consolidate any separate trust with any other trust with similar provisions for the same beneficiary or beneficiaries.

Spendthrift. The interests of beneficiaries in principal or income shall not be subject to the claims of any creditor, any spouse for alimony or support, or others, or to legal process, and may not be voluntarily or involuntarily alienated or encumbered. The rights of beneficiaries to withdraw trust property are personal and may not be exercised by a legal representative, attorney in fact, or others.

Retained Powers. Notwithstanding the foregoing, while I am living and able to manage my affairs:

(**a**) no sale or investment shall be made without my written approval, unless I fail to indicate my approval or disapproval of any proposed sale or investment within ten days after being requested to do so in writing;

(b) I shall have the power to direct the retention or sale of any trust assets and the purchase of property with any principal cash in the trust. If I direct the retention or purchase of an asset, the Trustee shall have investment, voting, and management responsibility for that asset unless I direct otherwise; and,

(c) I may at any time or times, with or without right of revocation, by a writing delivered to the Trustee, delegate to any other person or to the Trustee or relinquish any or all of the powers reserved to me hereunder.

The statement of the Trustee that he or she is acting according to this paragraph shall fully protect all persons dealing with the Trustee. The Trustee shall have no responsibility for any loss that may result from acting in accordance with this paragraph.

Restriction on Powers. The Trustee shall not lend trust property to me, directly or indirectly, without adequate interest and adequate security. No Trustee who is a beneficiary of any trust, or who is obligated to support a beneficiary of any trust, shall participate in: the exercise of any discretion over distributions of income or principal other than that which is required for the health, education, maintenance and support of a beneficiary provided that such distribution does not satisfy the Trustee's obligation to support the beneficiary; the exercise of discretion to allocate receipts or expenses between principal and income.

Accounts and Compensation. A Trustee (other than myself) shall render an account of trust receipts and disbursements and a statement of assets at least annually to each adult beneficiary then entitled to receive or have the benefit of the income from the trust. An account is binding on each beneficiary who receives it and on all persons claiming by or through the beneficiary, and the Trustee is released, as to all matters stated in the account or shown by it, unless the beneficiary commences a judicial proceeding to assert a claim within five years after the mailing or other delivery of the account.

Small Trust Termination and Perpetuities Savings.

(a) A trustee in its discretion may terminate and distribute any trust hereunder if the corporate trustee determines that the costs of continuance thereof will substantially impair accomplishment of the purposes of the trust.

(b) The trustee shall terminate and forthwith distribute any trust created hereby, or by exercise of a power of appointment hereunder, and still held twenty-one years after the death of the last to die of myself and the beneficiaries in being at my death.

(c) Distribution under this section shall be made to the persons then entitled to receive or have the benefit of the income from the trust in the proportions in which they are entitled thereto, or if their interests are indefinite, then in equal shares.

Merger. If the Trustee deems it best for the beneficiary or beneficiaries of any trust created under this Trust Agreement to merge all of the assets held in such trust with any other trust created by this Trust Agreement or otherwise for the benefit of the same beneficiary or beneficiaries and under substantially similar trusts, terms, and conditions, the Trustee, after giving not less than thirty days written notice to the trust's beneficiaries, may terminate such trust and transfer to or merge all of the assets of such trust to such other trust, regardless of whether the Trustee under this Trust Agreement also is serving as the Trustee of such other trust.

Liability of Third Party. No person dealing with the Trustee of any trust created hereunder shall be obligated to see to the application of any money paid or property transferred to or upon the order of the Trustee; nor shall any person be obligated to inquire into the property of any transaction or the authority of the Trustee to enter into and consummate the same.

Trustee's Judgement Final. Whenever the judgment or discretion of any Trustee may be exercised, it shall be final and binding upon every person interested in the trust estate, and any Trustee exercising any discretionary power relating to the distribution of principal or income shall be responsible only for lack of good faith in the exercise of such power; provided, however, nothing contained in this paragraph shall be construed so as to broaden any standard within which the Trustee is authorized to make distributions of income or principal, so that such standard is no longer considered an ascertainable standard under Code Section 2041 when it would otherwise be ascertainable.

Court Supervision. The Trustee shall not be required to qualify before or be appointed by any court; nor shall the Trustee be required to obtain the order or approval of any court in the exercise of any power or discretion.

Out-of-State Properties. If the Trustee must act in a jurisdiction in which a person or entity serving as Trustee is unwilling or unable to act as to any property, the remaining Trustees or Trustee, if willing and able to act, otherwise such person as the Trustee shall from time to time designate in writing, shall act as ancillary Trustees or Trustee as to that property. Any person or corporation acting as ancillary Trustee may resign at any time by written notice to the Trustees. Each ancillary Trustee shall have the powers, rights, discretions, and duties, exercisable without court order, to act with respect to such matters as the Trustee deems proper. The ancillary Trustee shall be responsible to the Trustee for any property it administers. The Trustee may pay the ancillary Trustee reasonable compensation for services and may absolve the ancillary Trustee from any requirement to furnish bond or other security.

ARTICLE IX
AMENDMENT AND REVOCATION OF TRUST

While I am living and legally competent, I may from time to time amend or revoke this Trust Agreement and the trusts evidenced by it, in whole or in part, by written instrument (other than by a will) delivered to the Trustee, except that, if amended, the duties, powers and responsibilities of the Trustee shall not be changed without the Trustee's written consent. During such time as I am not legally competent neither I nor my court appointed guardian may amend or revoke this Trust Agreement or any trust evidenced by it. The trust property to which any revocation relates shall be conveyed to me or otherwise as I direct. This power is personal to me and may not be exercised by my legal representatives, attorneys in fact, or others. After my death, all trusts created under this Trust Agreement shall become irrevocable.

ARTICLE X
MISCELLANEOUS PROVISIONS

Governing Law. The validity, construction, and administration of each trust created hereunder shall be governed by the laws of the State of _____.

Issue, Child and Children, and Determination of Living Persons. The word "issue," wherever used in this Trust Agreement, means all of the descendants, both by blood and by adoption, of whatever degree of the named ancestor, provided that (a) with respect to descendants by blood, the parents, as determined under applicable state law, of the descendants were married to one another, under the laws of the state in which they resided, either at the time of the descendant's conception or at the time of the descendant's birth, and (b) with respect to descendants by adoption, such adoption is of a person under the age of 21 years and is by court proceedings, the finality of which has not been questioned by the adoptive parent. The words "child" and "children" shall also include persons born or adopted under the same conditions. For the purposes of dividing or distributing any portion of the trust estate among persons who are living at a particular time, any person who has been conceived prior to such time, but has not yet been born, shall be considered to be living at such time if such person is later born and lives at least six months after birth.

Per Stirpes. Wherever this Trust Agreement directs a per stirpes distribution or allocation of assets to a person's descendants, division of those assets is to be made with reference to that person's children, regardless of whether any of them are living. Thus, though a person's children were all deceased the assets to be distributed or allocated would nevertheless be divided into as many equal shares as there were such deceased children with a descendant or descendants surviving at the time of distribution or allocation, and each such share would be divided similarly among the descendants of a deceased child.

Incapacity. For purposes of this Trust Agreement, a person (including any person appointed to act as Trustee hereunder) shall be considered incapacitated if such person has a legal, mental, or physical disability that substantially impairs such person's ability to manage his or her affairs (or the affairs of any trust created hereunder, as the case may be) with reasonable care. Proof that a person has become incapacitated may be conclusively established by the written opinion of two physicians selected by or acceptable to the Trustee of the trust or trusts of which the incapacitated person is a beneficiary (or to the prospective Trustee, if any, if the capacity of any Trustee be at issue) certifying to such fact. The language of such certificate shall be sufficient if acceptable to the Trustee (or the prospective Trustee, as the case may be) as indicating with reasonable certainty that such person is incapacitated. The physicians who issue such certificates, so long as they shall act in good faith in so doing, shall be entitled to indemnification by the trusts created hereunder from any liability rendering the opinion contained in any such certificates. The Trustee (or the prospective Trustee, as the case may be) so long as it shall act in good faith in accepting such certificates, shall be entitled to indemnification by the trusts created hereunder from any liability for acting pursuant to its good faith acceptance of such certificate.

Education. As used in this Trust Agreement, "education" shall include preparatory, collegiate, postgraduate, professional, and vocational education; specialized formal or informal training in music, the stage, handicrafts, the arts, or sports or athletic endeavors, whether by private instruction or otherwise; and any other activity, including foreign or domestic travel, which tends to develop the talents and potential of the beneficiary, regardless of age.

Health. As used in this Trust Agreement, "health" shall include medical, dental, hospital, and nursing care and other expenses of invalidism, and the cost of purchasing or maintaining hospital, medical, or nursing home insurance and disability income insurance coverage.

Code. All references in this trust to the "Code" mean the Internal Revenue Code of 1986, as amended, and shall refer to corresponding provisions of any subsequent federal tax law.

Invalid Provisions. If any part of this Trust Agreement shall be invalid, illegal, or inoperative, for any reason, it is the intention of Grantor that the remaining parts, so far as possible and reasonable, shall be effective and fully operative. The Trustee may seek and obtain court instructions for the purpose of carrying out as nearly as possible the intention of this Trust Agreement as evidenced by the terms hereof, including any term held invalid, illegal, or inoperative.

Survival. Any person must survive by thirty days for a gift made in this Trust Agreement which directly or indirectly requires such person's survival of another to be effective.

Use of Words. As used in this Trust Agreement, the masculine, feminine, and neuter gender, and the singular or plural of any word includes the others unless the context indicates otherwise.

Titles, Headings, and Captions. All titles, headings, and captions used in this Trust Agreement have been included for convenience only and should not be construed in interpreting this Trust Agreement.

IN WITNESS WHEREOF I, as Grantor and Trustee, have signed this Trust Agreement the day and year first above written.

_____   _____
Witness   Grantor and Trustee

_____
Witness

STATE OF _____§

§

COUNTY OF _____§

BEFORE ME, the undersigned authority, on this day personally appeared _____, Grantor and Trustee, known to me to be the person whose name is subscribed to the foregoing instrument and acknowledged to me that he/she executed the same for the purposes and consideration therein expressed.

GIVEN UNDER MY HAND AND SEAL OF OFFICE this _____ day of _____, 20_____.

_____
Notary Public

My commission expires:_____

This page intentionally left blank.

LIVING TRUST

(Married, No Children, Marital and Family Trusts for Spouse)

THIS AGREEMENT OF TRUST is entered into at _____, State of _____, this _____ day of _____, 20_____, by and between _____, as Grantor and Trustee. This Trust, as from time to time amended, shall be known as the "_____ LIVING TRUST dated _____, 20_____."

ARTICLE I
FAMILY

I am married to _____ who is hereafter referred to as my spouse. I do not have any children.

ARTICLE II
FUNDING

Initial Funding. I hereby transfer to the Trustee the sum of Ten Dollars ($10.00).

Additional Funding. From time to time the Trust may be funded with additional property by me or by any other person in any manner. In addition, I may cause the Trustee to be designated as beneficiary of life insurance policies or qualified retirement plans. All property transferred, assigned, conveyed, or delivered to the Trustee and all investment and reinvestment thereof, are herein collectively referred to as the "trust estate" and shall be held, administered, and distributed by the Trustee in accordance with the terms of this Trust Agreement.

ARTICLE III
ADMINISTRATION OF TRUST DURING MY LIFETIME

Distributions of Income. While I am living and not under any incapacity, the Trustee shall distribute the income of the Trust as directed in writing by me from time to time. In the event I do not deliver such direction to the Trustee, the Trustee shall pay to or expend on my behalf such amount of income from the Trust as the Trustee determines is necessary or advisable for my health, education, maintenance, and support. Any income that is not distributed to me or on my behalf shall be added to the principal of the Trust.

Distributions of Principal. While I am living and not under any incapacity, the Trustee shall distribute such part or all of the principal of the Trust as directed in writing by me from time to time. In the event I do not deliver such direction to the Trustee, the Trustee shall pay to or expend on my behalf such part of the principal of the Trust as the Trustee determines is necessary or advisable for my health, education, maintenance, and support.

Use of Residential Property. If any real property used by me for residential purposes (whether on a full-time or part-time basis, including recreational property) becomes part of the trust estate, I shall have the right to use and occupy such property without rental and without accounting to the trust estate. The Trustee shall pay all taxes, debts, and other expenses associated with such residential property from the income of the Trust. To the extent income is insufficient, the Trustee shall use principal of the Trust to pay such taxes, debts, and expenses.

Distribution During My Incapacity. In addition, whenever the Trustee considers that I am incapacitated, the Trustee shall distribute or apply such amounts of the income and principal of the trust estate (even though exhausting the Trust) as the Trustee considers advisable for my health, maintenance, and support, or for any other purpose the Trustee considers to be for my best interests. Any excess income shall be added to principal.

Distributions to My Spouse. The Trustee shall pay to or expend for the benefit of my spouse so much of the income and principal of the trust estate as the Trustee, in his or her sole discretion, determines to be necessary for the education, health, maintenance, and support of my spouse. The Trustee shall make such discretionary distributions only after conferring with me.

Incapacity. For purposes of this Trust Agreement, I shall be considered to be incapacitated if I: (a) am unable to manage my affairs; (b) am under a legal incapacity; or, (c) by reason of illness or mental or physical incapacity am unable to give prompt and intelligent consideration to my financial matters. I shall be considered incapacitated upon a good faith determination made by spouse and my physician, or the survivor of them, and the Trustee may rely upon written notice of that determination.

ARTICLE IV
ADMINISTRATION OF TRUST UPON MY DEATH

Payment of Expenses, Claims, and Taxes. Upon my death, if I have no probate estate, or to the extent that the cash and readily marketable assets in the principal of the residue of my probate estate are insufficient, the Trustee shall make the following payments from the principal of the trust estate. The Trustee shall pay the expenses of my last illness and funeral, costs of administration including ancillary administration, costs of safeguarding and delivering legacies, and claims allowable against my estate (excluding debts secured by real property or life insurance). The trustee shall also pay the estate and inheritance taxes assessed by reason of my death. The trustee may make payment directly or to the legal representative of my estate, as the trustee deems advisable. I hereby waive all rights of apportionment or reimbursement for any payments made pursuant to this Article.

Selection of Assets. Assets or funds otherwise excludable from my gross estate for federal estate tax purposes shall not be used to make the foregoing payments. The Trustee's selection of assets to be sold to pay expenses, claims, and taxes shall not be subject to question by any beneficiary.

Tax Elections. The Trustee shall make such elections under the tax laws as the Trustee deems advisable, without regard to the relative interests of the beneficiaries and without liability to any person. No adjustment shall be made between principal and income or in the relative interests of the beneficiaries to compensate for the effect of elections or allocations under the tax laws made by the legal representative of my estate or by the Trustee.

ARTICLE V
DISTRIBUTION OF TRUST ASSETS UPON MY DEATH

Tangible Personal Property. The Trustee shall distribute my tangible personal property in accordance with any written, signed, and dated memorandum prepared by me. Any tangible personal property that is not disposed of by memorandum shall be distributed in to my spouse if he or she survives me otherwise in equal shares to the following individuals:

Specific Bequest. The Trustee shall distribute the following property to the named individuals:

$ _____ to _____

$ _____ to _____

If an individual named herein does not survive me, the gift to such person shall lapse and the share to which such person would have been entitled shall be distributed among the surviving individuals named in this paragraph on a pro rata basis.

Distribution if My Spouse Survives Me. If my spouse survives me, the Trustee shall set aside and distribute the trust estate, including any additions to the Trust by reason of my death, as follows:

(a) All property in the trust estate as to which a federal estate tax marital deduction would not be allowed if it were distributed outright to my spouse, plus the largest pecuniary amount that will not result in or increase federal estate tax payable by reason of my death, shall be set aside in a separate trust designated the Family Trust, and shall be held and distributed in accordance with article VII. In determining the pecuniary amount, the trustee shall consider the credit for state death taxes only to the extent those taxes are not thereby incurred or increased, shall assume that none of this trust qualifies for a federal estate tax deduction, and shall assume that the Marital Trust hereinafter established (including any part thereof disclaimed by my spouse) qualifies in full for the federal estate tax marital deduction.

(b) The balance, if any, shall be set aside in a separate trust designated the Marital Trust, and shall be held and distributed in accordance with article VI.

Contingent Distribution. If my spouse does not survive me, the Trustee shall distribute the remaining trust estate, including any additions to the Trust by reason of my death, to the following individuals in the amounts specified:

_____ % to _____

_____ % to _____

_____ % to _____

_____ % to _____

If an individual named herein does not survive me, the gift to such person shall lapse and the share to which such person would have been entitled shall be distributed among the surviving individuals named in this paragraph on a *pro rata* basis.

No Survivors. If none of the individuals named in the preceding paragraph survive me, the remaining trust estate, including any additions to the Trust by reason of my death, shall be distributed to my heirs at law in accordance with the law of descent and distribution in effect on the date of my death.

ARTICLE VI
TRUST FOR SPOUSE

Marital Trust. The trust for the benefit of my spouse shall be referred to as the "Marital Trust." The Marital Trust shall be administered and distributed upon the following terms:

(a) **Distributions of Income.** The Trustee may distribute all of the income from the Marital Trust to my spouse at such times as the Trustee determines to be necessary for the health, education, maintenance, and support of my spouse. Any income not so paid shall be added to principal.

(b) **Distributions of Principal.** The Trustee may pay so much or all of the principal from the Marital Trust to my spouse at such times as the Trustee determines to be necessary for the health, education, maintenance, and support of my spouse.

Termination of Trust. Upon the death of my spouse, the assets remaining in the Marital Trust shall be distributed to the following individuals in the amounts specified:

_____ % to _____

_____ % to _____

_____ % to _____

_____ % to _____

If an individual named herein does not survive me, the gift to such person shall lapse and the share to which such person would have been entitled shall be distributed among the surviving individuals named in this paragraph on a pro rata basis.

No Survivors. If none of the individuals named in the preceding paragraph is not then living, the assets remaining in the Marital Trust shall be distributed to my heirs at law in accordance with the law of descent and distribution in effect on the date of my death.

ARTICLE VII
FAMILY TRUST

Family Trust. The trust held under this Article VII shall be referred to as the "Family Trust." The Family Trust shall be administered and distributed upon the following terms:

> **(a) Distributions of Income.** The Trustee may distribute part or all of the income from the Family Trust to my spouse as the Trustee, in his or her sole discretion, determines to be necessary for the health, education, maintenance, and support of my spouse. Any income not so paid shall be added to principal.

> **(b) Distributions of Principal.** The Trustee may pay so much or all of the principal from the Family Trust my spouse as the Trustee, in his or her sole discretion, determines to be necessary for the health, education, maintenance, and support of my spouse

Termination of Trust. Upon the death of my spouse, the Trustee shall distribute the assets remaining in the Family Trust to the following individuals in the amounts specified:

_____% to _____
_____% to _____
_____% to _____
_____% to _____

If an individual named herein is not then living, the share to which he or she would be entitled under this paragraph shall be distributed in equal shares to the individuals named in this paragraph who is then living.

No Survivors. If none of the individuals named in the preceding paragraph survive me, the assets remaining in the Family Trust shall be distributed to my heirs at law in accordance with the law of descent and distribution in effect on the date of my death.

ARTICLE VII
THE TRUSTEE

Initial Trustee. While I am alive, able, and willing to serve, I shall be the Trustee of the Trust.

Successor Trustee. During my lifetime, if I cannot serve as Trustee, I will appoint a successor Trustee. If I do not appoint a successor Trustee, or in the event of my death, incapacity, or inability to serve as Trustee, the successor Trustee shall be my spouse. In the event of the death, incapacity, or inability of my spouse to serve as Trustee, the successor Trustee shall be the first of the following individuals who is willing and competent to serve as successor Trustee:

If all of the successor Trustees die, become incapacitated, or otherwise fail or cease to serve as Trustee, a majority in number of the then living income beneficiaries of the Trust shall appoint a successor Trustee. Any appointment made under this Article shall be by a signed, acknowledged instrument delivered to the successor Trustee. A successor Trustee shall have all of the powers granted a Trustee in this Trust Agreement.

Resignation of Trustee. Any Trustee may resign as Trustee as to any one or more of the trusts created hereunder at any time by giving written notice to me if I am living, otherwise to the successor Trustee identified in this Trust Agreement, the current income beneficiaries of the Trust, and to those persons, if any, authorized in this Trust Agreement to appoint the successor Trustee.

Removal of Trustee. During my life, I may remove a Trustee at any time for any reason. After my death or if I am incapacitated and unable to remove the Trustee, my spouse shall have the power to remove a Trustee. If neither I nor my spouse are able to exercise the power to remove the Trustee, a majority in number of the then living income beneficiaries of the Trust shall have the power to remove a Trustee.

Bond. No Trustee wherever acting shall be required to give bond or surety or be appointed by or account for the administration of any trust to any court.

Trustee's Fees. The Trustee shall be entitled to reasonable fees commensurate with the Trustee's duties and responsibilities, taking into account the value and nature of the trust estate and the time and work involved. The Trustee shall be reimbursed for reasonable costs and expenses incurred in connection with the performance of his or her fiduciary duties.

Registration of Trust. The Trustee shall not be required to register the Trust with any federal, state, or local government authority.

Liability of Trustee. A Trustee shall only be liable for willful misconduct or gross negligence and shall not be liable for breach of fiduciary duty by virtue of mistake or error in judgment. No successor Trustee shall be personally liable for any act or omission of any predecessor.

Majority Decision. If more than one Trustee is serving hereunder, the decision of a majority of the Trustees shall control. The dissenting Trustee shall have no liability for participating in or carrying out the acts of the controlling Trustee.

Delegation to Co-Trustee. A Trustee of any trust created hereunder may at any time by written instrument delegate to a Co-Trustee of such trust all or less than all of the powers conferred upon that Trustee, either for a specified time or until the delegation is revoked by a written instrument.

ARTICLE VIII
TRUST ADMINISTRATION

Trustee Powers: Investment and Management of Trust Estate. Subject to any limitation stated elsewhere in this Trust Agreement, the Trustee shall hold, manage, care for, and protect the trust property and shall have the following powers and, except to the extent inconsistent herewith, all of the rights, powers, and privileges and be subject to all of the duties, responsibilities, and conditions set forth in applicable state law, as amended from time to time:

(a) **Retain Property.** To retain any property originally constituting the trust or subsequently added thereto, and to invest and reinvest the trust property in bonds, stocks, mortgages, notes, bank deposits, options, futures, limited partnership interests, limited liability company interests, other business organization interests, shares of registered investment companies and real estate investment trusts, or other property of any kind, real or personal, domestic or foreign; the Trustee may retain or make any investment without liability, even though it is not of a type, quality, marketability, or diversification considered proper for trust investments.

(b) Investment. To invest in, participate in, form, or cause to be formed (alone or with others, including members of my family) such corporations, partnerships, limited partnerships, limited liability companies, and other business organizations organized under the laws of any state or country and to transfer and convey to such business organizations all or any part of the assets, real or personal, of any trust estate in exchange for such stocks, bonds, notes, other securities, or interests of such business organizations as the Trustee deems best.

(c) Residential Property. To acquire, hold, and maintain any residence for the use and benefit of such one or more of the beneficiaries of the trust, including me, and to pay all carrying charges of such residence, including but not limited to, any taxes, assessments, and maintenance thereon, and all expenses of the repair and operation thereof, including the employment of domestic servants and other expenses incident to the maintenance of a household for the benefit of any one or more of the beneficiaries of the trust, all as the Trustee deems best.

(d) Tangible Personal Property. To acquire, hold, and maintain as a part of the trust any and all articles of tangible personal property or any other property for the use and benefit of any one or more of the beneficiaries of the trust, without regard to the income productivity of income, and without any duty to convert such property to productive property, and to pay the expenses of safekeeping of any such property, including insurance, and all expenses of the repair and maintenance of such property, and to sell such property and to apply the net proceeds of sale to the purchase of such other property as the Trustee deems best.

(e) Operate Business. To continue or participate in the operation of any business or other enterprise, and to effect incorporation, dissolution, or other change in the form of the organization of the business or enterprise.

(f) Nominee. To cause any property, real or personal, belonging to the trust to be held or registered in the Trustee's name or in the name of a nominee or in such other form as the Trustee deems best without disclosing the trust relationship.

(g) Real Estate. To operate, maintain, repair, rehabilitate, alter, erect, improve, or remove any improvements on real estate; to subdivide real estate; to grant easements, give consents, and enter into contracts relating to real estate or its use; and to release or dedicate any interest in real estate.

(h) Lease. To enter for any purpose into a lease as lessor or lessee with or without option to purchase or renew for a term within or extending beyond the term of the trust.

(i) Minerals. To enter into a lease or arrangement for exploration and removal of minerals or other natural resources or enter into a pooling or unitization agreement.

(j) Sell. By public offering or private negotiation, to sell, exchange, assign, transfer, or otherwise dispose of all or any real or personal trust property and give options for these purposes, for such price and on such terms, with such covenants of warranty and such security for deferred payment as the Trustee deems proper.

(k) Partition. To partition any property in which the trust owns an undivided interest.

(l) Securities. To engage in all actions necessary to the effective administration of securities including, but not limited to, the authority to vote in person or by general or limited proxy, or refrain from voting, any corporate securities for any purpose; to exercise or sell any subscription or conversion rights; to consent to and join in or oppose any voting trusts, reorganizations, consolidations, mergers, foreclosures, and liquidations and in connection therewith to deposit securities and accept and hold other property received therefore.

(m) Borrow. To borrow money from any lender, and to extend or renew any existing indebtedness to be repaid from trust assets or otherwise; to mortgage or pledge any property in the trust to secure such borrowing; to advance money for the protection of the trust, and for all expenses, losses, and liabilities sustained in the administration of the trust or because of the holding or ownership of any trust assets.

(n) Litigation. To commence or defend actions, claims, or proceedings for the protection of trust assets and of the Trustee in the performance of his or her duties.

(o) Claims. To pay or contest any claim; to settle a claim by or against the trust by compromise, arbitration, or otherwise; and to release, in whole or in part, any claim belonging to the trust to the extent that the claim is uncollectible.

(p) Payments. To pay taxes, assessments, compensation of the Trustee, and other expenses incurred in the collection, care, administration, and protection of the trust.

(q) Beneficiary Under Disability. To pay any sum distributable to a beneficiary under legal disability, without liability to the Trustee, by paying the sum to the beneficiary or by paying the sum for the use of the beneficiary either to a legal representative appointed by the court, or if none, to a relative.

(r) Agents. To employ persons, including attorneys, auditors, investment advisors, or agents, even if they are associated with any Trustee, to advise or assist the Trustee in the performance of his or her administrative duties; to act without independent investigation upon their recommendations; and instead of acting personally, to employ one or more agents to perform any act of administration, whether or not discretionary.

(s) Distributions. To distribute income and principal in cash or in kind, or partly in each, and to allocate or distribute undivided interests or different assets or disproportionate interests in assets, and no adjustment shall be made to compensate for a disproportionate allocation of unrealized gain for federal income tax purposes; to value the trust property and to sell any part or all thereof in order to make allocation or distribution; no action taken by the Trustee pursuant to this paragraph shall be subject to question by any beneficiary.

(t) Allocation of Income and Principal. To allocate items of income or expense to either trust income or principal, as provided by law, including creation of reserves out of income for depreciation, obsolescence, or amortization, or for depletion in mineral or timber properties.

(u) Employee Benefits. To elect, pursuant to the terms of any employee benefit plan, individual retirement plan, or insurance contract, the mode of distribution of the proceeds thereof, and no adjustment shall be made in the interests of the beneficiaries to compensate for the effect of the election.

(v) Division and Distribution. To divide any trust created under this Trust Agreement into one or more separate trusts for the benefit of one or more of the beneficiaries of the trust so divided, and to allocate to such divided trust some or all of the assets of the trust estate for any reason.

(w) **Tax Elections.** Unless otherwise expressly directed hereunder, to exercise any tax option, allocation, or election permitted by law as the Trustee determines in the Trustee's sole discretion.

(x) **Reliance.** To rely upon any notice, certificate, affidavit, or other document or evidence believed by the Trustee to be genuine and accurate, in making any payment or distribution. The Trustee shall incur no liability for a disbursement or distribution make in good faith and without actual notice or knowledge of a changed condition or status affecting any person's interest in the trust or any other matter.

(y) **Miscellaneous.** To perform other acts necessary or appropriate for the proper administration of the trust, execute and deliver necessary instruments, and give full receipts and discharges.

Common Fund and Consolidation. For convenience of administration or investment, the Trustee may hold separate trusts as a common fund, dividing the income proportionately among them, assign undivided interests to the separate trusts, and make joint investments of the funds belonging to them. The Trustee may consolidate any separate trust with any other trust with similar provisions for the same beneficiary or beneficiaries.

Spendthrift. The interests of beneficiaries in principal or income shall not be subject to the claims of any creditor, any spouse for alimony or support, or others, or to legal process, and may not be voluntarily or involuntarily alienated or encumbered. The rights of beneficiaries to withdraw trust property are personal and may not be exercised by a legal representative, attorney in fact, or others.

Retained Powers. Notwithstanding the foregoing, while I am living and able to manage my affairs:

(a) no sale or investment shall be made without my written approval, unless I fail to indicate my approval or disapproval of any proposed sale or investment within ten days after being requested to do so in writing;

(b) I shall have the power to direct the retention or sale of any trust assets and the purchase of property with any principal cash in the trust. If I direct the retention or purchase of an asset, the Trustee shall have investment, voting, and management responsibility for that asset unless I direct otherwise; and,

(c) I may at any time or times, with or without right of revocation, by a writing delivered to the Trustee, delegate to any other person or to the Trustee or relinquish any or all of the powers reserved to me hereunder.

The statement of the Trustee that he or she is acting according to this paragraph shall fully protect all persons dealing with the Trustee. The Trustee shall have no responsibility for any loss that may result from acting in accordance with this paragraph.

Restriction on Powers. The Trustee shall not lend trust property to me, directly or indirectly, without adequate interest and adequate security. No Trustee who is a beneficiary of any trust, or who is obligated to support a beneficiary of any trust, shall participate in: the exercise of any discretion over distributions of income or principal other than that which is required for the health, education, maintenance and support of a beneficiary provided that such distribution does not satisfy the Trustee's obligation to support the beneficiary; the exercise of discretion to allocate receipts or expenses between principal and income.

Accounts and Compensation. A Trustee (other than myself) shall render an account of trust receipts and disbursements and a statement of assets at least annually to each adult beneficiary then entitled to receive or have the benefit of the income from the trust. An account is binding on each beneficiary who receives it and on all persons claiming by or through the beneficiary, and the Trustee is released, as to all matters stated in the account or shown by it, unless the beneficiary commences a judicial proceeding to assert a claim within five years after the mailing or other delivery of the account.

Small Trust Termination and Perpetuities Savings.

(a) A trustee in its discretion may terminate and distribute any trust hereunder if the corporate trustee determines that the costs of continuance thereof will substantially impair accomplishment of the purposes of the trust.

(b) The trustee shall terminate and forthwith distribute any trust created hereby, or by exercise of a power of appointment hereunder, and still held twenty-one years after the death of the last to die of myself and the beneficiaries in being at my death.

(c) Distribution under this section shall be made to the persons then entitled to receive or have the benefit of the income from the trust in the proportions in which they are entitled thereto, or if their interests are indefinite, then in equal shares.

Merger. If the Trustee deems it best for the beneficiary or beneficiaries of any trust created under this Trust Agreement to merge all of the assets held in such trust with any other trust created by this Trust Agreement or otherwise for the benefit of the same beneficiary or beneficiaries and under substantially similar trusts, terms, and conditions, the Trustee, after giving not less than thirty days written notice to the trust's beneficiaries, may terminate such trust and transfer to or merge all of the assets of such trust to such other trust, regardless of whether the Trustee under this Trust Agreement also is serving as the Trustee of such other trust.

Liability of Third Party. No person dealing with the Trustee of any trust created hereunder shall be obligated to see to the application of any money paid or property transferred to or upon the order of the Trustee; nor shall any person be obligated to inquire into the property of any transaction or the authority of the Trustee to enter into and consummate the same.

Trustee's Judgement Final. Whenever the judgment or discretion of any Trustee may be exercised, it shall be final and binding upon every person interested in the trust estate, and any Trustee exercising any discretionary power relating to the distribution of principal or income shall be responsible only for lack of good faith in the exercise of such power; provided, however, nothing contained in this paragraph shall be construed so as to broaden any standard within which the Trustee is authorized to make distributions of income or principal, so that such standard is no longer considered an ascertainable standard under Code Section 2041 when it would otherwise be ascertainable.

Court Supervision. The Trustee shall not be required to qualify before or be appointed by any court; nor shall the Trustee be required to obtain the order or approval of any court in the exercise of any power or discretion.

Out-of-State Properties. If the Trustee must act in a jurisdiction in which a person or entity serving as Trustee is unwilling or unable to act as to any property, the remaining Trustees or Trustee, if willing and able to act, otherwise such person as the Trustee shall from time to time designate in writing, shall act as ancillary Trustees or Trustee as to that property. Any person or corporation acting as ancillary Trustee may resign at any time by written notice to the Trustees. Each ancillary Trustee shall have the powers, rights, discretions, and duties, exercisable without court order, to act with respect to such matters as the Trustee deems proper. The ancillary Trustee shall be responsible to the Trustee for any property it administers. The Trustee may pay the ancillary Trustee reasonable compensation for services and may absolve the ancillary Trustee from any requirement to furnish bond or other security.

ARTICLE IX
AMENDMENT AND REVOCATION OF TRUST

While I am living and legally competent, I may from time to time amend or revoke this instrument and the trusts evidenced by it, in whole or in part, by written instrument (other than by a will) delivered to the Trustee, except that, if amended, the duties, powers and responsibilities of the Trustee shall not be changed without the Trustee's written consent. During such time as I am not legally competent neither I nor my court appointed guardian may amend or revoke this instrument or any trust evidenced by it. The trust property to which any revocation relates shall be conveyed to me or otherwise as I direct. This power is personal to me and may not be exercised by my legal representatives, attorneys in fact, or others. After my death, all trusts created under this instrument shall become irrevocable.

ARTICLE X
MISCELLANEOUS PROVISIONS

Governing Law. The validity, construction, and administration of each trust created hereunder shall be governed by the laws of the State of _____.

Issue, Child and Children, and Determination of Living Persons. The word "issue," wherever used in this Trust Agreement, means all of the descendants, both by blood and by adoption, of whatever degree of the named ancestor, provided that (a) with respect to descendants by blood, the parents, as determined under applicable state law, of the descendants were married to one another, under the laws of the state in which they resided, either at the time of the descendant's conception or at the time of the descendant's birth, and (b) with respect to descendants by adoption, such adoption is of a person under the age of twenty-one (21) years and is by court proceedings, the finality of which has not been questioned by the adoptive parent. The words "child" and "children" shall also include persons born or adopted under the same conditions. For the purposes of dividing or distributing any portion of the trust estate among persons who are living at a particular time, any person who has been conceived prior to such time, but has not yet been born, shall be considered to be living at such time if such person is later born and lives at least six (6) months after birth.

Per Stirpes. Wherever this Trust Agreement directs a per stirpes distribution or allocation of assets to a person's descendants, division of those assets is to be made with reference to that person's children, regardless of whether any of them are living. Thus, though a person's children were all deceased the assets to be distributed or allocated would nevertheless be divided into as many equal shares as there were such deceased children with a descendant or descendants surviving at the time of distribution or allocation, and each such share would be divided similarly among the descendants of a deceased child.

Incapacity. For purposes of this Trust Agreement, a person (including any person appointed to act as Trustee hereunder) shall be considered incapacitated if such person has a legal, mental, or physical disability that substantially impairs such person's ability to manage his or her affairs (or the affairs of any trust created hereunder, as the case may be) with reasonable care. Proof that a person has become incapacitated may be conclusively established by the written opinion of two (2) physicians selected by or acceptable to the Trustee of the trust or trusts of which the incapacitated person is a beneficiary (or to the prospective Trustee, if any, if the capacity of any Trustee be at issue) certifying to such fact. The language of such certificate shall be sufficient if acceptable to the Trustee (or the prospective Trustee, as the case may be) as indicating with reasonable certainty that such person is incapacitated. The physicians who issue such certificates, so long as they shall act in good faith in so doing, shall be entitled to indemnification by the trusts created hereunder from any liability rendering the opinion contained in any such certificates. The Trustee (or the prospective Trustee, as the case may be) so long as it shall act in good faith in accepting such certificates, shall be entitled to indemnification by the trusts created hereunder from any liability for acting pursuant to its good faith acceptance of such certificate.

Education. As used in this Trust Agreement, "education" shall include preparatory, collegiate, postgraduate, professional, and vocational education; specialized formal or informal training in music, the stage, handicrafts, the arts, or sports or athletic endeavors, whether by private instruction or otherwise; and any other activity, including foreign or domestic travel, which tends to develop the talents and potential of the beneficiary, regardless of age.

Health. As used in this Trust Agreement, "health" shall include medical, dental, hospital, and nursing care and other expenses of invalidism, and the cost of purchasing or maintaining hospital, medical, or nursing home insurance and disability income insurance coverage.

Code. All references in this trust to the "Code" mean the Internal Revenue Code of 1986, as amended, and shall refer to corresponding provisions of any subsequent federal tax law.

Invalid Provisions. If any part of this Trust Agreement shall be invalid, illegal, or inoperative, for any reason, it is the intention of Grantor that the remaining parts, so far as possible and reasonable, shall be effective and fully operative. The Trustee may seek and obtain court instructions for the purpose of carrying out as nearly as possible the intention of this Trust Agreement as evidenced by the terms hereof, including any term held invalid, illegal, or inoperative.

Survival. Any person must survive by thirty days for a gift made in this Trust Agreement which directly or indirectly requires such person's survival of another to be effective.

Use of Words. As used in this Trust Agreement, the masculine, feminine, and neuter gender, and the singular or plural of any word includes the others unless the context indicates otherwise.

Titles, Headings, and Captions. All titles, headings, and captions used in this Trust Agreement have been included for convenience only and should not be construed in interpreting this Trust Agreement.

IN WITNESS WHEREOF I, as Grantor and Trustee, have signed this Trust Agreement the day and year first above written.

_____   _____

Witness   Grantor and Trustee

_____

Witness

STATE OF _____§

                                                §

COUNTY OF _____§

BEFORE ME, the undersigned authority, on this day personally appeared _____, Grantor and Trustee, known to me to be the person whose name is subscribed to the foregoing instrument and acknowledged to me that he/she executed the same for the purposes and consideration therein expressed.

GIVEN UNDER MY HAND AND SEAL OF OFFICE this _____ day of _____, 20_____.

_____

Notary Public

My commission expires:_____

This page intentionally left blank.

_____ LIVING TRUST
(Married, Children, Outright to Spouse)

THIS AGREEMENT OF TRUST is entered into at _____, State of _____, this _____ day of _____, 20_____, by and between _____, as Grantor and Trustee. This Trust, as from time to time amended, shall be known as the "_____ LIVING TRUST dated _____, 20_____."

ARTICLE I
FAMILY

I am married to _____ who is hereafter referred to as my spouse. I have _____children now living, namely: _____. I intend by this Trust Agreement to provide for all my children, including any hereafter born or adopted.

ARTICLE II
FUNDING

Initial Funding. I hereby transfer to the Trustee the sum of Ten Dollars ($10.00).

Additional Funding. From time to time the Trust may be funded with additional property by me or by any other person in any manner. In addition, I may cause the Trustee to be designated as beneficiary of life insurance policies or qualified retirement plans. All property transferred, assigned, conveyed, or delivered to the Trustee and all investment and reinvestment thereof, are herein collectively referred to as the "trust estate" and shall be held, administered, and distributed by the Trustee in accordance with the terms of this Trust Agreement.

ARTICLE III
ADMINISTRATION OF TRUST DURING MY LIFETIME

Distributions of Income. While I am living and not under any incapacity, the Trustee shall distribute the income of the Trust as directed in writing by me from time to time. In the event I do not deliver such direction to the Trustee, the Trustee shall pay to or expend on my behalf such amount of income from the Trust as the Trustee determines is necessary or advisable for my health, education, maintenance, and support. Any income that is not distributed to me or on my behalf shall be added to the principal of the Trust.

Distributions of Principal. While I am living and not under any incapacity, the Trustee shall distribute such part or all of the principal of the Trust as directed in writing by me from time to time. In the event I do not deliver such direction to the Trustee, the Trustee shall pay to or expend on my behalf such part of the principal of the Trust as the Trustee determines is necessary or advisable for my health, education, maintenance, and support.

Use of Residential Property. If any real property used by me for residential purposes (whether on a full-time or part-time basis, including recreational property) becomes part of the trust estate, I shall have the right to use and occupy such property without rental and without accounting to the trust estate. The Trustee shall pay all taxes, debts, and other expenses associated with such residential property from the income of the Trust. To the extent income is insufficient, the Trustee shall use principal of the Trust to pay such taxes, debts, and expenses.

Distribution During My Incapacity. In addition, whenever the Trustee considers that I am incapacitated, the Trustee shall distribute or apply such amounts of the income and principal of the trust estate (even though exhausting the Trust) as the Trustee considers advisable for my health, maintenance, and support, or for any other purpose the Trustee considers to be for my best interests. Any excess income shall be added to principal.

Distributions to My Spouse and Children. The Trustee shall pay to or expend for the benefit of my spouse and minor Children so much of the principal of the trust estate as the Trustee, in his or her sole discretion, determines to be necessary for the education, health, maintenance, and support of my spouse and Children. The Trustee shall make such discretionary distributions only after conferring with me. The distributions from the Trust to my spouse and Children do not need to be equal.

Incapacity. For purposes of this Trust Agreement, I shall be considered to be incapacitated if I: (a) am unable to manage my affairs; (b) am under a legal incapacity; or, (c) by reason of illness or mental or physical incapacity am unable to give prompt and intelligent consideration to my financial matters. I shall be considered incapacitated upon a good faith determination made by spouse and my physician, or the survivor of them, and the Trustee may rely upon written notice of that determination.

ARTICLE IV
ADMINISTRATION OF TRUST UPON MY DEATH

Payment of Expenses, Claims, and Taxes. Upon my death, if I have no probate estate, or to the extent that the cash and readily marketable assets in the principal of the residue of my probate estate are insufficient, the Trustee shall make the following payments from the principal of the trust estate. The Trustee shall pay the expenses of my last illness and funeral, costs of administration including ancillary administration, costs of safeguarding and delivering legacies, and claims allowable against my estate (excluding debts secured by real property or life insurance). The Trustee shall also pay the estate and inheritance taxes assessed by reason of my death. The Trustee may make payment directly or to the legal representative of my estate, as the Trustee deems advisable. I hereby waive all rights of apportionment or reimbursement for any payments made pursuant to this Article.

Selection of Assets. Assets or funds otherwise excludable from my gross estate for federal estate tax purposes shall not be used to make the foregoing payments. The Trustee's selection of assets to be sold to pay expenses, claims, and taxes shall not be subject to question by any beneficiary.

Tax Elections. The Trustee shall make such elections under the tax laws as the Trustee deems advisable, without regard to the relative interests of the beneficiaries and without liability to any person. No adjustment shall be made between principal and income or in the relative interests of the beneficiaries to compensate for the effect of elections or allocations under the tax laws made by the legal representative of my estate or by the Trustee.

ARTICLE V
DISTRIBUTION OF TRUST ASSETS UPON MY DEATH

Tangible Personal Property. The Trustee shall distribute my tangible personal property in accordance with any written, signed, and dated memorandum prepared by me. Any tangible personal property that is not disposed of by memorandum shall be distributed in to my spouse if he or she survives me otherwise in equal shares to the following individuals:

Specific Bequest. The Trustee shall distribute the following property to the named individuals:

$ _____ to _____

$ _____ to _____

If an individual named herein does not survive me, the gift to such person shall lapse and the share to which such person would have been entitled shall be distributed among the surviving individuals named in this paragraph on a pro rata basis.

Distribution to My Spouse. If my spouse survives me, the Trustee shall distribute the remaining trust estate, including any additions to the Trust by reason of my death, to my spouse outright and free of trust or, if my spouse chooses, to the Living Trust dated _____, 20___, established by my spouse.

Distribution to My Children. If my spouse does not survive me, the Trustee shall divide the remaining trust estate, including any additions to the Trust by reason of my death, into separate equal shares to create one share for each Child of mine who is then living, and one share for the then living descendants, collectively, of each deceased Child of mine with one or more descendants then living. The Trustee shall distribute the share created for each Child to such Child outright and free of trust. The share for the descendants of each deceased Child shall be distributed, per stirpes, to those descendants living at my death.

Contingent Distribution. If my spouse, Children, and descendants do not survive me, the Trustee shall distribute the remaining trust estate, including any additions to the Trust by reason of my death, to the following individuals in the amounts specified:

_____% to _____

_____% to _____

_____% to _____

_____% to _____

If an individual named herein does not survive me, the share to which he or she would be entitled under this paragraph shall be distributed in equal shares to the individuals named in this paragraph who survive me.

No Survivors. If none of the individuals named in the preceding paragraph survive me, the remaining trust estate, including any additions to the Trust by reason of my death, shall be distributed to my heirs at law in accordance with the law of descent and distribution in effect on the date of my death.

ARTICLE VI
THE TRUSTEE

Initial Trustee. While I am alive, able, and willing to serve, I shall be the Trustee of the Trust.

Successor Trustee. During my lifetime, if I cannot serve as Trustee, I will appoint a successor Trustee. If I do not appoint a successor Trustee, or in the event of my death, incapacity, or inability to serve as Trustee, the successor Trustee shall be my spouse. In the event of the death, incapacity, or inability of my spouse to serve as Trustee, the successor Trustee shall be the first of the following individuals who is willing and competent to serve as successor Trustee:

If all of the successor Trustees die, become incapacitated, or otherwise fail or cease to serve as Trustee, a majority in number of the then living income beneficiaries of the Trust shall appoint a successor Trustee. Any appointment made under this Article shall be by a signed, acknowledged instrument delivered to the successor Trustee. A successor Trustee shall have all of the powers granted a Trustee in this Trust Agreement.

Resignation of Trustee. Any Trustee may resign as Trustee as to any one or more of the trusts created hereunder at any time by giving written notice to me if I am living, otherwise to the successor Trustee identified in this Trust Agreement, the current income beneficiaries of the Trust, and to those persons, if any, authorized in this Trust Agreement to appoint the successor Trustee.

Removal of Trustee. During my life, I may remove a Trustee at any time for any reason. After my death or if I am incapacitated and unable to remove the Trustee, my spouse shall have the power to remove a Trustee. If neither I nor my spouse are able to exercise the power to remove the Trustee, a majority in number of the then living income beneficiaries of the Trust shall have the power to remove a Trustee.

Bond. No Trustee wherever acting shall be required to give bond or surety or be appointed by or account for the administration of any trust to any court.

Trustee's Fees. The Trustee shall be entitled to reasonable fees commensurate with the Trustee's duties and responsibilities, taking into account the value and nature of the trust estate and the time and work involved. The Trustee shall be reimbursed for reasonable costs and expenses incurred in connection with the performance of his or her fiduciary duties.

Registration of Trust. The Trustee shall not be required to register the Trust with any federal, state, or local government authority.

Liability of Trustee. A Trustee shall only be liable for willful misconduct or gross negligence and shall not be liable for breach of fiduciary duty by virtue of mistake or error in judgment. No successor Trustee shall be personally liable for any act or omission of any predecessor.

Majority Decision. If more than one Trustee is serving hereunder, the decision of a majority of the Trustees shall control. The dissenting Trustee shall have no liability for participating in or carrying out the acts of the controlling Trustee.

Delegation to Co-Trustee. A Trustee of any trust created hereunder may at any time by written instrument delegate to a Co-Trustee of such trust all or less than all of the powers conferred upon that Trustee, either for a specified time or until the delegation is revoked by a written instrument.

ARTICLE VII
TRUST ADMINISTRATION

Trustee Powers: Investment and Management of Trust Estate. Subject to any limitation stated elsewhere in this Trust Agreement, the Trustee shall hold, manage, care for, and protect the trust property and shall have the following powers and, except to the extent inconsistent herewith, all of the rights, powers, and privileges and be subject to all of the duties, responsibilities, and conditions set forth in applicable state law, as amended from time to time:

(a) **Retain Property.** To retain any property originally constituting the trust or subsequently added thereto, and to invest and reinvest the trust property in bonds, stocks, mortgages, notes, bank deposits, options, futures, limited partnership interests, limited liability company interests, other business organization interests, shares of registered investment companies and real estate investment trusts, or other property of any kind, real or personal, domestic or foreign; the Trustee may retain or make any investment without liability, even though it is not of a type, quality, marketability, or diversification considered proper for trust investments.

(b) **Investment.** To invest in, participate in, form, or cause to be formed (alone or with others, including members of my family) such corporations, partnerships, limited partnerships, limited liability companies, and other business organizations organized under the laws of any state or country and to transfer and convey to such business organizations all or any part of the assets, real or personal, of any trust estate in exchange for such stocks, bonds, notes, other securities, or interests of such business organizations as the Trustee deems best.

(c) **Residential Property.** To acquire, hold, and maintain any residence for the use and benefit of such one or more of the beneficiaries of the trust, including me, and to pay all carrying charges of such residence, including but not limited to, any taxes, assessments, and maintenance thereon, and all expenses of the repair and operation thereof, including the employment of domestic servants and other expenses incident to the maintenance of a household for the benefit of any one or more of the beneficiaries of the trust, all as the Trustee deems best.

(d) Tangible Personal Property. To acquire, hold, and maintain as a part of the trust any and all articles of tangible personal property or any other property for the use and benefit of any one or more of the beneficiaries of the trust, without regard to the income productivity of income, and without any duty to convert such property to productive property, and to pay the expenses of safekeeping of any such property, including insurance, and all expenses of the repair and maintenance of such property, and to sell such property and to apply the net proceeds of sale to the purchase of such other property as the Trustee deems best.

(e) Operate Business. To continue or participate in the operation of any business or other enterprise, and to effect incorporation, dissolution, or other change in the form of the organization of the business or enterprise.

(f) Nominee. To cause any property, real or personal, belonging to the trust to be held or registered in the Trustee's name or in the name of a nominee or in such other form as the Trustee deems best without disclosing the trust relationship.

(g) Real Estate. To operate, maintain, repair, rehabilitate, alter, erect, improve, or remove any improvements on real estate; to subdivide real estate; to grant easements, give consents, and enter into contracts relating to real estate or its use; and to release or dedicate any interest in real estate.

(h) Lease. To enter for any purpose into a lease as lessor or lessee with or without option to purchase or renew for a term within or extending beyond the term of the trust.

(i) Minerals. To enter into a lease or arrangement for exploration and removal of minerals or other natural resources or enter into a pooling or unitization agreement.

(j) Sell. By public offering or private negotiation, to sell, exchange, assign, transfer, or otherwise dispose of all or any real or personal trust property and give options for these purposes, for such price and on such terms, with such covenants of warranty and such security for deferred payment as the Trustee deems proper.

(k) Partition. To partition any property in which the trust owns an undivided interest.

(l) Securities. To engage in all actions necessary to the effective administration of securities including, but not limited to, the authority to vote in person or by general or limited proxy, or refrain from voting, any corporate securities for any purpose; to exercise or sell any subscription or conversion rights; to consent to and join in or oppose any voting trusts, reorganizations, consolidations, mergers, foreclosures, and liquidations and in connection therewith to deposit securities and accept and hold other property received therefore.

(m) Borrow. To borrow money from any lender, and to extend or renew any existing indebtedness to be repaid from trust assets or otherwise; to mortgage or pledge any property in the trust to secure such borrowing; to advance money for the protection of the trust, and for all expenses, losses, and liabilities sustained in the administration of the trust or because of the holding or ownership of any trust assets.

(n) Litigation. To commence or defend actions, claims, or proceedings for the protection of trust assets and of the Trustee in the performance of his or her duties.

(o) Claims. To pay or contest any claim; to settle a claim by or against the trust by compromise, arbitration, or otherwise; and to release, in whole or in part, any claim belonging to the trust to the extent that the claim is uncollectible.

(p) Payments. To pay taxes, assessments, compensation of the Trustee, and other expenses incurred in the collection, care, administration, and protection of the trust.

(q) Beneficiary Under Disability. To pay any sum distributable to a beneficiary under legal disability, without liability to the Trustee, by paying the sum to the beneficiary or by paying the sum for the use of the beneficiary either to a legal representative appointed by the court, or if none, to a relative.

(r) Agents. To employ persons, including attorneys, auditors, investment advisors, or agents, even if they are associated with any Trustee, to advise or assist the Trustee in the performance of his or her administrative duties; to act without independent investigation upon their recommendations; and instead of acting personally, to employ one or more agents to perform any act of administration, whether or not discretionary.

(s) Distributions. To distribute income and principal in cash or in kind, or partly in each, and to allocate or distribute undivided interests or different assets or disproportionate interests in assets, and no adjustment shall be made to compensate for a disproportionate allocation of unrealized gain for federal income tax purposes; to value the trust property and to sell any part or all thereof in order to make allocation or distribution; no action taken by the Trustee pursuant to this paragraph shall be subject to question by any beneficiary.

(t) Allocation of Income and Principal. To allocate items of income or expense to either trust income or principal, as provided by law, including creation of reserves out of income for depreciation, obsolescence, or amortization, or for depletion in mineral or timber properties.

(u) Employee Benefits. To elect, pursuant to the terms of any employee benefit plan, individual retirement plan, or insurance contract, the mode of distribution of the proceeds thereof, and no adjustment shall be made in the interests of the beneficiaries to compensate for the effect of the election.

(v) Division and Distribution. To divide any trust created under this Trust Agreement into one or more separate trusts for the benefit of one or more of the beneficiaries of the trust so divided, and to allocate to such divided trust some or all of the assets of the trust estate for any reason.

(w) Tax Elections. Unless otherwise expressly directed hereunder, to exercise any tax option, allocation, or election permitted by law as the Trustee determines in the Trustee's sole discretion.

(x) Reliance. To rely upon any notice, certificate, affidavit, or other document or evidence believed by the Trustee to be genuine and accurate, in making any payment or distribution. The Trustee shall incur no liability for a disbursement or distribution make in good faith and without actual notice or knowledge of a changed condition or status affecting any person's interest in the trust or any other matter.

(y) Miscellaneous. To perform other acts necessary or appropriate for the proper administration of the trust, execute and deliver necessary instruments, and give full receipts and discharges.

Common Fund and Consolidation. For convenience of administration or investment, the Trustee may hold separate trusts as a common fund, dividing the income proportionately among them, assign undivided interests to the separate trusts, and make joint investments of the funds belonging to them. The Trustee may consolidate any separate trust with any other trust with similar provisions for the same beneficiary or beneficiaries.

Spendthrift. The interests of beneficiaries in principal or income shall not be subject to the claims of any creditor, any spouse for alimony or support, or others, or to legal process, and may not be voluntarily or involuntarily alienated or encumbered. The rights of beneficiaries to withdraw trust property are personal and may not be exercised by a legal representative, attorney in fact, or others.

Retained Powers. Notwithstanding the foregoing, while I am living and able to manage my affairs:

(a) no sale or investment shall be made without my written approval, unless I fail to indicate my approval or disapproval of any proposed sale or investment within ten days after being requested to do so in writing;

(b) I shall have the power to direct the retention or sale of any trust assets and the purchase of property with any principal cash in the trust. If I direct the retention or purchase of an asset, the Trustee shall have investment, voting, and management responsibility for that asset unless I direct otherwise; and,

(c) I may at any time or times, with or without right of revocation, by a writing delivered to the Trustee, delegate to any other person or to the Trustee or relinquish any or all of the powers reserved to me hereunder.

The statement of the Trustee that he or she is acting according to this paragraph shall fully protect all persons dealing with the Trustee. The Trustee shall have no responsibility for any loss that may result from acting in accordance with this paragraph.

Restriction on Powers. The Trustee shall not lend trust property to me, directly or indirectly, without adequate interest and adequate security. No Trustee who is a beneficiary of any trust, or who is obligated to support a beneficiary of any trust, shall participate in: the exercise of any discretion over distributions of income or principal other than that which is required for the health, education, maintenance and support of a beneficiary provided that such distribution does not satisfy the Trustee's obligation to support the beneficiary; the exercise of discretion to allocate receipts or expenses between principal and income.

Accounts and Compensation. A Trustee (other than myself) shall render an account of trust receipts and disbursements and a statement of assets at least annually to each adult beneficiary then entitled to receive or have the benefit of the income from the trust. An account is binding on each beneficiary who receives it and on all persons claiming by or through the beneficiary, and the Trustee is released, as to all matters stated in the account or shown by it, unless the beneficiary commences a judicial proceeding to assert a claim within five years after the mailing or other delivery of the account.

Small Trust Termination and Perpetuities Savings.

(a) A trustee in its discretion may terminate and distribute any trust hereunder if the corporate trustee determines that the costs of continuance thereof will substantially impair accomplishment of the purposes of the trust.

(b) The trustee shall terminate and forthwith distribute any trust created hereby, or by exercise of a power of appointment hereunder, and still held twenty-one years after the death of the last to die of myself and the beneficiaries in being at my death.

(c) Distribution under this section shall be made to the persons then entitled to receive or have the benefit of the income from the trust in the proportions in which they are entitled thereto, or if their interests are indefinite, then in equal shares.

Merger. If the Trustee deems it best for the beneficiary or beneficiaries of any trust created under this Trust Agreement to merge all of the assets held in such trust with any other trust created by this Trust Agreement or otherwise for the benefit of the same beneficiary or beneficiaries and under substantially similar trusts, terms, and conditions, the Trustee, after giving not less than thirty days written notice to the trust's beneficiaries, may terminate such trust and transfer to or merge all of the assets of such trust to such other trust, regardless of whether the Trustee under this Trust Agreement also is serving as the Trustee of such other trust.

Liability of Third Party. No person dealing with the Trustee of any trust created hereunder shall be obligated to see to the application of any money paid or property transferred to or upon the order of the Trustee; nor shall any person be obligated to inquire into the property of any transaction or the authority of the Trustee to enter into and consummate the same.

Trustee's Judgement Final. Whenever the judgment or discretion of any Trustee may be exercised, it shall be final and binding upon every person interested in the trust estate, and any Trustee exercising any discretionary power relating to the distribution of principal or income shall be responsible only for lack of good faith in the exercise of such power; provided, however, nothing contained in this paragraph shall be construed so as to broaden any standard within which the Trustee is authorized to make distributions of income or principal, so that such standard is no longer considered an ascertainable standard under Code Trustee 2041 when it would otherwise be ascertainable.

Court Supervision. The Trustee shall not be required to qualify before or be appointed by any court; nor shall the Trustee be required to obtain the order or approval of any court in the exercise of any power or discretion.

Out-of-State Properties. If the Trustee must act in a jurisdiction in which a person or entity serving as Trustee is unwilling or unable to act as to any property, the remaining Trustees or Trustee, if willing and able to act, otherwise such person as the Trustee shall from time to time designate in writing, shall act as ancillary Trustees or Trustee as to that property. Any person or corporation acting as ancillary Trustee may resign at any time by written notice to the Trustees. Each ancillary Trustee shall have the powers, rights, discretions, and duties, exercisable without court order, to act with respect to such matters as the Trustee deems proper. The ancillary Trustee shall be responsible to the Trustee for any property it administers. The Trustee may pay the ancillary Trustee reasonable compensation for services and may absolve the ancillary Trustee from any requirement to furnish bond or other security.

ARTICLE VIII
AMENDMENT AND REVOCATION OF TRUST

While I am living and legally competent, I may from time to time amend or revoke this Trust Agreement and the trusts evidenced by it, in whole or in part, by written instrument (other than by a will) delivered to the Trustee, except that, if amended, the duties, powers and responsibilities of the Trustee shall not be changed without the Trustee's written consent. During such time as I am not legally competent neither I nor my court appointed guardian may amend or revoke this Trust Agreement or any trust evidenced by it. The trust property to which any revocation relates shall be conveyed to me or otherwise as I direct. This power is personal to me and may not be exercised by my legal representatives, attorneys in fact, or others. After my death, all trusts created under this Trust Agreement shall become irrevocable.

ARTICLE IX
MISCELLANEOUS PROVISIONS

Governing Law. The validity, construction, and administration of each trust created hereunder shall be governed by the laws of the State of _____.

Issue, Child and Children, and Determination of Living Persons. The word "issue," wherever used in this Trust Agreement, means all of the descendants, both by blood and by adoption, of whatever degree of the named ancestor, provided that (a) with respect to descendants by blood, the parents, as determined under applicable state law, of the descendants were married to one another, under the laws of the state in which they resided, either at the time of the descendant's conception or at the time of the descendant's birth, and (b) with respect to descendants by adoption, such adoption is of a person under the age of 21 years and is by court proceedings, the finality of which has not been questioned by the adoptive parent. The words "child" and "children" shall also include persons born or adopted under the same conditions. For the purposes of dividing or distributing any portion of the trust estate among persons who are living at a particular time, any person who has been conceived prior to such time, but has not yet been born, shall be considered to be living at such time if such person is later born and lives at least six months after birth.

Per Stirpes. Wherever this Trust Agreement directs a per stirpes distribution or allocation of assets to a person's descendants, division of those assets is to be made with reference to that person's children, regardless of whether any of them are living. Thus, though a person's children were all deceased the assets to be distributed or allocated would nevertheless be divided into as many equal shares as there were such deceased children with a descendant or descendants surviving at the time of distribution or allocation, and each such share would be divided similarly among the descendants of a deceased child.

Incapacity. For purposes of this Trust Agreement, a person (including any person appointed to act as Trustee hereunder) shall be considered incapacitated if such person has a legal, mental, or physical disability that substantially impairs such person's ability to manage his or her affairs (or the affairs of any trust created hereunder, as the case may be) with reasonable care. Proof that a person has become incapacitated may be conclusively established by the written opinion of two physicians selected by or acceptable to the Trustee of the trust or trusts of which the incapacitated person is a beneficiary (or to the prospective Trustee, if any, if the capacity of any Trustee be at issue) certifying to such fact. The language of such certificate shall be sufficient if acceptable to the Trustee (or the prospective Trustee, as the case may be) as indicating with reasonable certainty that such person is incapacitated. The physicians who issue such certificates, so long as they shall act in good faith in so doing, shall be entitled to indemnification by the trusts created hereunder from any liability rendering the opinion contained in any such certificates. The Trustee (or the prospective Trustee, as the case may be) so long as it shall act in good faith in accepting such certificates, shall be entitled to indemnification by the trusts created hereunder from any liability for acting pursuant to its good faith acceptance of such certificate.

Education. As used in this Trust Agreement, "education" shall include preparatory, collegiate, postgraduate, professional, and vocational education; specialized formal or informal training in music, the stage, handicrafts, the arts, or sports or athletic endeavors, whether by private instruction or otherwise; and any other activity, including foreign or domestic travel, which tends to develop the talents and potential of the beneficiary, regardless of age.

Health. As used in this Trust Agreement, "health" shall include medical, dental, hospital, and nursing care and other expenses of invalidism, and the cost of purchasing or maintaining hospital, medical, or nursing home insurance and disability income insurance coverage.

Code. All references in this trust to the "Code" mean the Internal Revenue Code of 1986, as amended, and shall refer to corresponding provisions of any subsequent federal tax law.

Invalid Provisions. If any part of this Trust Agreement shall be invalid, illegal, or inoperative, for any reason, it is the intention of Grantor that the remaining parts, so far as possible and reasonable, shall be effective and fully operative. The Trustee may seek and obtain court instructions for the purpose of carrying out as nearly as possible the intention of this Trust Agreement as evidenced by the terms hereof, including any term held invalid, illegal, or inoperative.

Survival. Any person must survive by thirty days for a gift made in this Trust Agreement which directly or indirectly requires such person's survival of another to be effective.

Use of Words. As used in this Trust Agreement, the masculine, feminine, and neuter gender, and the singular or plural of any word includes the others unless the context indicates otherwise.

Titles, Headings, and Captions. All titles, headings, and captions used in this Trust Agreement have been included for convenience only and should not be construed in interpreting this Trust Agreement.

IN WITNESS WHEREOF I, as Grantor and Trustee, have signed this Trust Agreement the day and year first above written.

_____   _____

Witness   Grantor and Trustee

_____

Witness

STATE OF _____§

§

COUNTY OF _____§

BEFORE ME, the undersigned authority, on this day personally appeared _____,
Grantor and Trustee, known to me to be the person whose name is subscribed to the foregoing instrument and acknowledged to me that he/she executed the same for the purposes and consideration therein expressed.

GIVEN UNDER MY HAND AND SEAL OF OFFICE this _____ day of _____, 20_____.

_____

Notary Public

My commission expires:_____

LIVING TRUST

(Married, Children, Family Trust for Spouse & Children, Outright to Children)

THIS AGREEMENT OF TRUST is entered into at _____, State of _____, this _____ day of _____, 20_____, by and between _____, as Grantor and Trustee. This Trust, as from time to time amended, shall be known as the "_____ LIVING TRUST dated _____, 20_____."

ARTICLE I
FAMILY

I am married to _____ who is hereafter referred to as my spouse. I have _____ Children now living, namely: _____. I intend by this Trust Agreement to provide for all my Children, including any hereafter born or adopted.

ARTICLE II
FUNDING

Initial Funding. I hereby transfer to the Trustee the sum of Ten Dollars ($10.00).

Additional Funding. From time to time the Trust may be funded with additional property by me or by any other person in any manner. In addition, I may cause the Trustee to be designated as beneficiary of life insurance policies or qualified retirement plans. All property transferred, assigned, conveyed, or delivered to the Trustee and all investment and reinvestment thereof, are herein collectively referred to as the "trust estate" and shall be held, administered, and distributed by the Trustee in accordance with the terms of this Trust Agreement.

ARTICLE III
ADMINISTRATION OF TRUST DURING MY LIFETIME

Distributions of Income. While I am living and not under any incapacity, the Trustee shall distribute the income of the Trust as directed in writing by me from time to time. In the event I do not deliver such direction to the Trustee, the Trustee shall pay to or expend on my behalf such amount of income from the Trust as the Trustee determines is necessary or advisable for my health, education, maintenance, and support. Any income that is not distributed to me or on my behalf shall be added to the principal of the Trust.

Distributions of Principal. While I am living and not under any incapacity, the Trustee shall distribute such part or all of the principal of the Trust as directed in writing by me from time to time. In the event I do not deliver such direction to the Trustee, the Trustee shall pay to or expend on my behalf such part of the principal of the Trust as the Trustee determines is necessary or advisable for my health, education, maintenance, and support.

Use of Residential Property. If any real property used by me for residential purposes (whether on a full-time or part-time basis, including recreational property) becomes part of the trust estate, I shall have the right to use and occupy such property without rental and without accounting to the trust estate. The Trustee shall pay all taxes, debts, and other expenses associated with such residential property from the income of the Trust. To the extent income is insufficient, the Trustee shall use principal of the Trust to pay such taxes, debts, and expenses.

Distribution During My Incapacity. In addition, whenever the Trustee considers that I am incapacitated, the Trustee shall distribute or apply such amounts of the income and principal of the trust estate (even though exhausting the Trust) as the Trustee considers advisable for my health, maintenance, and support, or for any other purpose the Trustee considers to be for my best interests. Any excess income shall be added to principal.

Distributions to My Spouse and Children. The Trustee shall pay to or expend for the benefit of my spouse and minor Children so much of the principal of the trust estate as the Trustee, in his or her sole discretion, determines to be necessary for the education, health, maintenance, and support of my spouse and Children. The Trustee shall make such discretionary distributions only after conferring with me. The distributions from the Trust to my spouse and Children do not need to be equal.

Incapacity. For purposes of this Trust Agreement, I shall be considered to be incapacitated if I: (a) am unable to manage my affairs; (b) am under a legal incapacity; or, (c) by reason of illness or mental or physical incapacity am unable to give prompt and intelligent consideration to my financial matters. I shall be considered incapacitated upon a good faith determination made by spouse and my physician, or the survivor of them, and the Trustee may rely upon written notice of that determination.

ARTICLE IV
ADMINISTRATION OF TRUST UPON MY DEATH

Payment of Expenses, Claims, and Taxes. Upon my death, if I have no probate estate, or to the extent that the cash and readily marketable assets in the principal of the residue of my probate estate are insufficient, the Trustee shall make the following payments from the principal of the trust estate. The Trustee shall pay the expenses of my last illness and funeral, costs of administration including ancillary administration, costs of safeguarding and delivering legacies, and claims allowable against my estate (excluding debts secured by real property or life insurance). The Trustee shall also pay the estate and inheritance taxes assessed by reason of my death. The Trustee may make payment directly or to the legal representative of my estate, as the Trustee deems advisable. I hereby waive all rights of apportionment or reimbursement for any payments made pursuant to this Article.

Selection of Assets. Assets or funds otherwise excludable from my gross estate for federal estate tax purposes shall not be used to make the foregoing payments. The Trustee's selection of assets to be sold to pay expenses, claims, and taxes shall not be subject to question by any beneficiary.

Tax Elections. The Trustee shall make such elections under the tax laws as the Trustee deems advisable, without regard to the relative interests of the beneficiaries and without liability to any person. No adjustment shall be made between principal and income or in the relative interests of the beneficiaries to compensate for the effect of elections or allocations under the tax laws made by the legal representative of my estate or by the Trustee.

ARTICLE V
DISTRIBUTION OF TRUST ASSETS UPON MY DEATH

Tangible Personal Property. The Trustee shall distribute my tangible personal property in accordance with any written, signed, and dated memorandum prepared by me. Any tangible personal property that is not disposed of by memorandum shall be distributed in to my spouse if he or she survives me otherwise in equal shares to the following individuals:

Specific Bequest. The Trustee shall distribute the following property to the named individuals:

$ _____ to _____

$ _____ to _____

If an individual named herein does not survive me, the gift to such person shall lapse and the share to which such person would have been entitled shall be distributed among the surviving individuals named in this paragraph on a pro rata basis.

Distribution if My Spouse Survives Me. If my spouse survives me, the Trustee shall set aside and distribute the trust estate, including any additions to the Trust by reason of my death, as follows:

(a) All property in the trust estate as to which a federal estate tax marital deduction would not be allowed if it were distributed outright to my spouse, plus the largest pecuniary amount which will not result in or increase federal estate tax payable by reason of my death, shall be set aside in a separate trust designated the Family Trust, and shall be held and distributed in accordance with article VI. In determining the pecuniary amount, the trustee shall consider the credit for state death taxes only to the extent those taxes are not thereby incurred or increased, shall assume that none of this trust qualifies for a federal estate tax deduction, and shall assume that the Marital Trust hereinafter established (including any part thereof disclaimed by my spouse) qualifies in full for the federal estate tax marital deduction.

(b) The balance, if any, shall be distributed to my spouse outright and free of trust.

Distribution if My Spouse Does Not Survive. If my spouse does not survive me, the Trustee shall divide the remaining trust estate, including any additions to the Trust by reason of my death, into separate equal shares to create one share for each Child of mine who is then living, and one share for the then living descendants, collectively, of each deceased Child of mine with one or more descendants then living. The Trustee shall distribute the share created for each Child to such Child outright and free of trust. The share for the descendants of each deceased Child shall be distributed, per stirpes, to those descendants living at my death.

Contingent Distribution. If my spouse, Children, and descendants do not survive me, the Trustee shall distribute the remaining trust estate, including any additions to the Trust by reason of my death, to the following individuals in the amounts specified:

_____ % to _____
_____ % to _____
_____ % to _____
_____ % to _____

If an individual named herein does not survive me, the gift to such person shall lapse and the share to which such person would have been entitled shall be distributed among the surviving individuals named in this paragraph on a pro rata basis.

No Survivors. If none of the individuals named in the preceding paragraph survive me, the remaining trust estate, including any additions to the Trust by reason of my death, shall be distributed to my heirs at law in accordance with the law of descent and distribution in effect on the date of my death.

ARTICLE VI
FAMILY TRUST

Family Trust. The trust held under this Article VI shall be referred to as the "Family Trust." The Family Trust shall be administered and distributed upon the following terms:

(a) **Distributions of Income**. The Trustee may distribute part or all of the income from the Family Tr~ to any one or more of my spouse and Children from time to time living, in equal or unequal ~ tions and at such times as the Trustee determines to be necessary for the education, he~ nance, and support of my spouse and Children. The distributions from the Trust t~ Children do not need to be equal. Any income not so paid shall be added to pr~

(b) Distributions of Principal. The Trustee may pay so much or all of the principal from the Family Trust to any one or more of my spouse and Children from time to time living, in equal or unequal proportions and at such times as the Trustee determines to be necessary for the education, health, maintenance, and support of my spouse and Children. The distributions from the Trust to my spouse and Children do not need to be equal.

Termination of Trust. Upon the death of my spouse, the Trustee shall divide the assets remaining in the Family Trust into separate equal shares to create one share for each Child of mine who is then living, and one share for the then living descendants, collectively, of each deceased Child of mine with one or more descendants then living. The Trustee shall distribute the share created for each Child to such Child outright and free of trust. The share for the descendants of each deceased Child shall be distributed, per stirpes, to those descendants living at my death.

Contingent Distribution. If my spouse, Children, and descendants are not then living, the Trustee shall distribute the assets remaining in the Family Trust to the following individuals in the amounts specified:

_____% to _____

_____% to _____

_____% to _____

_____% to _____

If an individual named herein is not then living, the share to which he or she would be entitled under this paragraph shall be distributed in equal shares to the individuals named in this paragraph who are then living.

No Survivors. If none of the individuals named in the preceding paragraph survive me, the assets remaining in the Family Trust shall be distributed to my heirs at law in accordance with the law of descent and distribution in effect on the date of my death.

ARTICLE VII
THE TRUSTEE

Initial Trustee. While I am alive, able, and willing to serve, I shall be the Trustee of the Trust.

Successor Trustee. During my lifetime, if I cannot serve as Trustee, I will appoint a successor Trustee. If I do not appoint a successor Trustee, or in the event of my death, incapacity, or inability to serve as Trustee, the successor Trustee shall be my spouse. In the event of the death, incapacity, or inability of my spouse to serve as Trustee, the successor Trustee shall be the first of the following individuals who is willing and competent to serve as successor Trustee:

If all of the successor Trustees die, become incapacitated, or otherwise fail or cease to serve as Trustee, a majority in number of the then living income beneficiaries of the Trust shall appoint a successor Trustee. Any appointment made under this Article shall be by a signed, acknowledged instrument delivered to the successor Trustee. A successor Trustee shall have all of the powers granted a Trustee in this Trust Agreement.

Resignation of Trustee. Any Trustee may resign as Trustee as to any one or more of the trusts created hereunder at any time by giving written notice to me if I am living, otherwise to the successor Trustee identified in this Trust Agreement, the current income beneficiaries of the Trust, and to those persons, if any, authorized in this Trust Agreement to appoint the successor Trustee.

Removal of Trustee. During my life, I may remove a Trustee at any time for any reason. After my death or if I am incapacitated and unable to remove the Trustee, my spouse shall have the power to remove a Trustee. If neither I nor my spouse are able to exercise the power to remove the Trustee, a majority in number of the then living income beneficiaries of the Trust shall have the power to remove a Trustee.

Bond. No Trustee wherever acting shall be required to give bond or surety or be appointed by or account for the administration of any trust to any court.

Trustee's Fees. The Trustee shall be entitled to reasonable fees commensurate with the Trustee's duties and responsibilities, taking into account the value and nature of the trust estate and the time and work involved. The Trustee shall be reimbursed for reasonable costs and expenses incurred in connection with the performance of his or her fiduciary duties.

Registration of Trust. The Trustee shall not be required to register the Trust with any federal, state, or local government authority.

Liability of Trustee. A Trustee shall only be liable for willful misconduct or gross negligence and shall not be liable for breach of fiduciary duty by virtue of mistake or error in judgment. No successor Trustee shall be personally liable for any act or omission of any predecessor.

Majority Decision. If more than one Trustee is serving hereunder, the decision of a majority of the Trustees shall control. The dissenting Trustee shall have no liability for participating in or carrying out the acts of the controlling Trustee.

Delegation to Co-Trustee. A Trustee of any trust created hereunder may at any time by written instrument delegate to a Co-Trustee of such trust all or less than all of the powers conferred upon that Trustee, either for a specified time or until the delegation is revoked by a written instrument.

ARTICLE VIII
TRUST ADMINISTRATION

Trustee Powers: Investment and Management of Trust Estate. Subject to any limitation stated elsewhere in this Trust Agreement, the Trustee shall hold, manage, care for, and protect the trust property and shall have the following powers and, except to the extent inconsistent herewith, all of the rights, powers, and privileges and be subject to all of the duties, responsibilities, and conditions set forth in applicable state law, as amended from time to time:

(a) **Retain Property.** To retain any property originally constituting the trust or subsequently added thereto, and to invest and reinvest the trust property in bonds, stocks, mortgages, notes, bank deposits, options, futures, limited partnership interests, limited liability company interests, other business organization interests, shares of registered investment companies and real estate investment trusts, or other property of any kind, real or personal, domestic or foreign; the Trustee may retain or make any investment without liability, even though it is not of a type, quality, marketability, or diversification considered proper for trust investments.

(b) **Investment.** To invest in, participate in, form, or cause to be formed (alone or with others, including members of my family) such corporations, partnerships, limited partnerships, limited liability companies, and other business organizations organized under the laws of any state or country and to transfer and convey to such business organizations all or any part of the assets, real or personal, of any trust estate in exchange for such stocks, bonds, notes, other securities, or interests of such business organizations as the Trustee deems best.

(c) Residential Property. To acquire, hold, and maintain any residence for the use and benefit of such one or more of the beneficiaries of the trust, including me, and to pay all carrying charges of such residence, including but not limited to, any taxes, assessments, and maintenance thereon, and all expenses of the repair and operation thereof, including the employment of domestic servants and other expenses incident to the maintenance of a household for the benefit of any one or more of the beneficiaries of the trust, all as the Trustee deems best.

(d) Tangible Personal Property. To acquire, hold, and maintain as a part of the trust any and all articles of tangible personal property or any other property for the use and benefit of any one or more of the beneficiaries of the trust, without regard to the income productivity of income, and without any duty to convert such property to productive property, and to pay the expenses of safekeeping of any such property, including insurance, and all expenses of the repair and maintenance of such property, and to sell such property and to apply the net proceeds of sale to the purchase of such other property as the Trustee deems best.

(e) Operate Business. To continue or participate in the operation of any business or other enterprise, and to effect incorporation, dissolution, or other change in the form of the organization of the business or enterprise.

(f) Nominee. To cause any property, real or personal, belonging to the trust to be held or registered in the Trustee's name or in the name of a nominee or in such other form as the Trustee deems best without disclosing the trust relationship.

(g) Real Estate. To operate, maintain, repair, rehabilitate, alter, erect, improve, or remove any improvements on real estate; to subdivide real estate; to grant easements, give consents, and enter into contracts relating to real estate or its use; and to release or dedicate any interest in real estate.

(h) Lease. To enter for any purpose into a lease as lessor or lessee with or without option to purchase or renew for a term within or extending beyond the term of the trust.

(i) Minerals. To enter into a lease or arrangement for exploration and removal of minerals or other natural resources or enter into a pooling or unitization agreement.

(j) Sell. By public offering or private negotiation, to sell, exchange, assign, transfer, or otherwise dispose of all or any real or personal trust property and give options for these purposes, for such price and on such terms, with such covenants of warranty and such security for deferred payment as the Trustee deems proper.

(k) Partition. To partition any property in which the trust owns an undivided interest.

(l) Securities. To engage in all actions necessary to the effective administration of securities including, but not limited to, the authority to vote in person or by general or limited proxy, or refrain from voting, any corporate securities for any purpose; to exercise or sell any subscription or conversion rights; to consent to and join in or oppose any voting trusts, reorganizations, consolidations, mergers, foreclosures, and liquidations and in connection therewith to deposit securities and accept and hold other property received therefore.

(m) Borrow. To borrow money from any lender, and to extend or renew any existing indebtedness to be repaid from trust assets or otherwise; to mortgage or pledge any property in the trust to secure such borrowing; to advance money for the protection of the trust, and for all expenses, losses, and liabilities sustained in the administration of the trust or because of the holding or ownership of any trust assets.

(n) Litigation. To commence or defend actions, claims, or proceedings for the protection of trust assets and of the Trustee in the performance of his or her duties.

(o) Claims. To pay or contest any claim; to settle a claim by or against the trust by compromise, arbitration, or otherwise; and to release, in whole or in part, any claim belonging to the trust to the extent that the claim is uncollectible.

(p) Payments. To pay taxes, assessments, compensation of the Trustee, and other expenses incurred in the collection, care, administration, and protection of the trust.

(q) Beneficiary Under Disability. To pay any sum distributable to a beneficiary under legal disability, without liability to the Trustee, by paying the sum to the beneficiary or by paying the sum for the use of the beneficiary either to a legal representative appointed by the court, or if none, to a relative.

(r) Agents. To employ persons, including attorneys, auditors, investment advisors, or agents, even if they are associated with any Trustee, to advise or assist the Trustee in the performance of his or her administrative duties; to act without independent investigation upon their recommendations; and instead of acting personally, to employ one or more agents to perform any act of administration, whether or not discretionary.

(s) Distributions. To distribute income and principal in cash or in kind, or partly in each, and to allocate or distribute undivided interests or different assets or disproportionate interests in assets, and no adjustment shall be made to compensate for a disproportionate allocation of unrealized gain for federal income tax purposes; to value the trust property and to sell any part or all thereof in order to make allocation or distribution; no action taken by the Trustee pursuant to this paragraph shall be subject to question by any beneficiary.

(t) Allocation of Income and Principal. To allocate items of income or expense to either trust income or principal, as provided by law, including creation of reserves out of income for depreciation, obsolescence, or amortization, or for depletion in mineral or timber properties.

(u) Employee Benefits. To elect, pursuant to the terms of any employee benefit plan, individual retirement plan, or insurance contract, the mode of distribution of the proceeds thereof, and no adjustment shall be made in the interests of the beneficiaries to compensate for the effect of the election.

(v) Division and Distribution. To divide any trust created under this Trust Agreement into one or more separate trusts for the benefit of one or more of the beneficiaries of the trust so divided, and to allocate to such divided trust some or all of the assets of the trust estate for any reason.

(w) Tax Elections. Unless otherwise expressly directed hereunder, to exercise any tax option, allocation, or election permitted by law as the Trustee determines in the Trustee's sole discretion.

(**x**) **Reliance.** To rely upon any notice, certificate, affidavit, or other document or evidence believed by the Trustee to be genuine and accurate, in making any payment or distribution. The Trustee shall incur no liability for a disbursement or distribution make in good faith and without actual notice or knowledge of a changed condition or status affecting any person's interest in the trust or any other matter.

(**y**) **Miscellaneous.** To perform other acts necessary or appropriate for the proper administration of the trust, execute and deliver necessary instruments, and give full receipts and discharges.

Common Fund and Consolidation. For convenience of administration or investment, the Trustee may hold separate trusts as a common fund, dividing the income proportionately among them, assign undivided interests to the separate trusts, and make joint investments of the funds belonging to them. The Trustee may consolidate any separate trust with any other trust with similar provisions for the same beneficiary or beneficiaries.

Spendthrift. The interests of beneficiaries in principal or income shall not be subject to the claims of any creditor, any spouse for alimony or support, or others, or to legal process, and may not be voluntarily or involuntarily alienated or encumbered. The rights of beneficiaries to withdraw trust property are personal and may not be exercised by a legal representative, attorney in fact, or others.

Retained Powers. Notwithstanding the foregoing, while I am living and able to manage my affairs:

(**a**) no sale or investment shall be made without my written approval, unless I fail to indicate my approval or disapproval of any proposed sale or investment within ten days after being requested to do so in writing;

(**b**) I shall have the power to direct the retention or sale of any trust assets and the purchase of property with any principal cash in the trust. If I direct the retention or purchase of an asset, the Trustee shall have investment, voting, and management responsibility for that asset unless I direct otherwise; and,

(**c**) I may at any time or times, with or without right of revocation, by a writing delivered to the Trustee, delegate to any other person or to the Trustee or relinquish any or all of the powers reserved to me hereunder.

The statement of the Trustee that he or she is acting according to this paragraph shall fully protect all persons dealing with the Trustee. The Trustee shall have no responsibility for any loss that may result from acting in accordance with this paragraph.

Restriction on Powers. The Trustee shall not lend trust property to me, directly or indirectly, without adequate interest and adequate security. No Trustee who is a beneficiary of any trust, or who is obligated to support a beneficiary of any trust, shall participate in: the exercise of any discretion over distributions of income or principal other than that which is required for the health, education, maintenance and support of a beneficiary provided that such distribution does not satisfy the Trustee's obligation to support the beneficiary; the exercise of discretion to allocate receipts or expenses between principal and income.

Accounts and Compensation. A Trustee (other than myself) shall render an account of trust receipts and disbursements and a statement of assets at least annually to each adult beneficiary then entitled to receive or have the benefit of the income from the trust. An account is binding on each beneficiary who receives it and on all persons claiming by or through the beneficiary, and the Trustee is released, as to all matters stated in the account or shown by it, unless the beneficiary commences a judicial proceeding to assert a claim within five years after the mailing or other delivery of the account.

Small Trust Termination and Perpetuities Savings.

(a) A trustee in its discretion may terminate and distribute any trust hereunder if the corporate trustee determines that the costs of continuance thereof will substantially impair accomplishment of the purposes of the trust.

(b) The trustee shall terminate and forthwith distribute any trust created hereby, or by exercise of a power of appointment hereunder, and still held twenty-one years after the death of the last to die of myself and the beneficiaries in being at my death.

(c) Distribution under this section shall be made to the persons then entitled to receive or have the benefit of the income from the trust in the proportions in which they are entitled thereto, or if their interests are indefinite, then in equal shares.

Merger. If the Trustee deems it best for the beneficiary or beneficiaries of any trust created under this Trust Agreement to merge all of the assets held in such trust with any other trust created by this Trust Agreement or otherwise for the benefit of the same beneficiary or beneficiaries and under substantially similar trusts, terms, and conditions, the Trustee, after giving not less than thirty days written notice to the trust's beneficiaries, may terminate such trust and transfer to or merge all of the assets of such trust to such other trust, regardless of whether the Trustee under this Trust Agreement also is serving as the Trustee of such other trust.

Liability of Third Party. No person dealing with the Trustee of any trust created hereunder shall be obligated to see to the application of any money paid or property transferred to or upon the order of the Trustee; nor shall any person be obligated to inquire into the property of any transaction or the authority of the Trustee to enter into and consummate the same.

Trustee's Judgement Final. Whenever the judgment or discretion of any Trustee may be exercised, it shall be final and binding upon every person interested in the trust estate, and any Trustee exercising any discretionary power relating to the distribution of principal or income shall be responsible only for lack of good faith in the exercise of such power; provided, however, nothing contained in this paragraph shall be construed so as to broaden any standard within which the Trustee is authorized to make distributions of income or principal, so that such standard is no longer considered an ascertainable standard under Code Section 2041 when it would otherwise be ascertainable.

Court Supervision. The Trustee shall not be required to qualify before or be appointed by any court; nor shall the Trustee be required to obtain the order or approval of any court in the exercise of any power or discretion.

Out-of-State Properties. If the Trustee must act in a jurisdiction in which a person or entity serving as Trustee is unwilling or unable to act as to any property, the remaining Trustees or Trustee, if willing and able to act, otherwise such person as the Trustee shall from time to time designate in writing, shall act as ancillary Trustees or Trustee as to that property. Any person or corporation acting as ancillary Trustee may resign at any time by written notice to the Trustees. Each ancillary Trustee shall have the powers, rights, discretions, and duties, exercisable without court order, to act with respect to such matters as the Trustee deems proper. The ancillary Trustee shall be responsible to the Trustee for any property it administers. The Trustee may pay the ancillary Trustee reasonable compensation for services and may absolve the ancillary Trustee from any requirement to furnish bond or other security.

ARTICLE IX
AMENDMENT AND REVOCATION OF TRUST

While I am living and legally competent, I may from time to time amend or revoke this Trust Agreement and the trusts evidenced by it, in whole or in part, by written instrument (other than by a will) delivered to the Trustee, except that, if amended, the duties, powers and responsibilities of the Trustee shall not be changed without the Trustee's written consent. During such time as I am not legally competent neither I nor my court appointed guardian may amend or revoke this Trust Agreement or any trust evidenced by it. The trust property to which any revocation relates shall be conveyed to me or otherwise as I direct. This power is personal to me and may not be exercised by my legal representatives, attorneys in fact, or others. After my death, all trusts created under this Trust Agreement shall become irrevocable.

ARTICLE X
MISCELLANEOUS PROVISIONS

Governing Law. The validity, construction, and administration of each trust created hereunder shall be governed by the laws of the State of _____.

Issue, Child and Children, and Determination of Living Persons. The word "issue," wherever used in this Trust Agreement, means all of the descendants, both by blood and by adoption, of whatever degree of the named ancestor, provided that (a) with respect to descendants by blood, the parents, as determined under applicable state law, of the descendants were married to one another, under the laws of the state in which they resided, either at the time of the descendant's conception or at the time of the descendant's birth, and (b) with respect to descendants by adoption, such adoption is of a person under the age of 21 years and is by court proceedings, the finality of which has not been questioned by the adoptive parent. The words "child" and "children" shall also include persons born or adopted under the same conditions. For the purposes of dividing or distributing any portion of the trust estate among persons who are living at a particular time, any person who has been conceived prior to such time, but has not yet been born, shall be considered to be living at such time if such person is later born and lives at least six months after birth.

Per Stirpes. Wherever this Trust Agreement directs a per stirpes distribution or allocation of assets to a person's descendants, division of those assets is to be made with reference to that person's children, regardless of whether any of them are living. Thus, though a person's children were all deceased the assets to be distributed or allocated would nevertheless be divided into as many equal shares as there were such deceased children with a descendant or descendants surviving at the time of distribution or allocation, and each such share would be divided similarly among the descendants of a deceased child.

Incapacity. For purposes of this Trust Agreement, a person (including any person appointed to act as Trustee hereunder) shall be considered incapacitated if such person has a legal, mental, or physical disability that substantially impairs such person's ability to manage his or her affairs (or the affairs of any trust created hereunder, as the case may be) with reasonable care. Proof that a person has become incapacitated may be conclusively established by the written opinion of two (2) physicians selected by or acceptable to the Trustee of the trust or trusts of which the incapacitated person is a beneficiary (or to the prospective Trustee, if any, if the capacity of any Trustee be at issue) certifying to such fact. The language of such certificate shall be sufficient if acceptable to the Trustee (or the prospective Trustee, as the case may be) as indicating with reasonable certainty that such person is incapacitated. The physicians who issue such certificates, so long as they shall act in good faith in so doing, shall be entitled to indemnification by the trusts created hereunder from any liability rendering the opinion contained in any such certificates. The Trustee (or the prospective Trustee, as the case may be) so long as it shall act in good faith in accepting such certificates, shall be entitled to indemnification by the trusts created hereunder from any liability for acting pursuant to its good faith acceptance of such certificate.

Education. As used in this Trust Agreement, "education" shall include preparatory, collegiate, postgraduate, professional, and vocational education; specialized formal or informal training in music, the stage, handicrafts, the arts, or sports or athletic endeavors, whether by private instruction or otherwise; and any other activity, including foreign or domestic travel, which tends to develop the talents and potential of the beneficiary, regardless of age.

Health. As used in this Trust Agreement, "health" shall include medical, dental, hospital, and nursing care and other expenses of invalidism, and the cost of purchasing or maintaining hospital, medical, or nursing home insurance and disability income insurance coverage.

Code. All references in this trust to the "Code" mean the Internal Revenue Code of 1986, as amended, and shall refer to corresponding provisions of any subsequent federal tax law.

Invalid Provisions. If any part of this Trust Agreement shall be invalid, illegal, or inoperative, for any reason, it is the intention of Grantor that the remaining parts, so far as possible and reasonable, shall be effective and fully operative. The Trustee may seek and obtain court instructions for the purpose of carrying out as nearly as possible the intention of this Trust Agreement as evidenced by the terms hereof, including any term held invalid, illegal, or inoperative.

Survival. Any person must survive by thirty days for a gift made in this Trust Agreement which directly or indirectly requires such person's survival of another to be effective.

Use of Words. As used in this Trust Agreement, the masculine, feminine, and neuter gender, and the singular or plural of any word includes the others unless the context indicates otherwise.

Titles, Headings, and Captions. All titles, headings, and captions used in this Trust Agreement have been included for convenience only and should not be construed in interpreting this Trust Agreement.

IN WITNESS WHEREOF I, as Grantor and Trustee, have signed this Trust Agreement the day and year first above written.

_____   _____
Witness   Grantor and Trustee

_____
Witness

STATE OF _____ §
§
COUNTY OF _____ §

BEFORE ME, the undersigned authority, on this day personally appeared _____, Grantor and Trustee, known to me to be the person whose name is subscribed to the foregoing instrument and acknowledged to me that he/she executed the same for the purposes and consideration therein expressed.

GIVEN UNDER MY HAND AND SEAL OF OFFICE this _____ day of _____, 20_____.

_____
Notary Public

My commission expires:_____

This page intentionally left blank.

LIVING TRUST

(Married, Children, Family Trust for Spouse and Children, Child's Trust)

THIS AGREEMENT OF TRUST is entered into at _____, State of _____, this _____ day of _____, 20_____, by and between _____, as Grantor and Trustee. This Trust, as from time to time amended, shall be known as the "_____ LIVING TRUST dated _____, 20_____."

ARTICLE I
FAMILY

I am married to _____ who is hereafter referred to as my spouse. I have_____ Children now living, namely: _____. I intend by this Trust Agreement to provide for all my Children, including any hereafter born or adopted.

ARTICLE II
FUNDING

Initial Funding. I hereby transfer to the Trustee the sum of Ten Dollars ($10.00).

Additional Funding. From time to time the Trust may be funded with additional property by me or by any other person in any manner. In addition, I may cause the Trustee to be designated as beneficiary of life insurance policies or qualified retirement plans. All property transferred, assigned, conveyed, or delivered to the Trustee and all investment and reinvestment thereof, are herein collectively referred to as the "trust estate" and shall be held, administered, and distributed by the Trustee in accordance with the terms of this Trust Agreement.

ARTICLE III
ADMINISTRATION OF TRUST DURING MY LIFETIME

Distributions of Income. While I am living and not under any incapacity, the Trustee shall distribute the income of the Trust as directed in writing by me from time to time. In the event I do not deliver such direction to the Trustee, the Trustee shall pay to or expend on my behalf such amount of income from the Trust as the Trustee determines is necessary or advisable for my health, education, maintenance, and support. Any income that is not distributed to me or on my behalf shall be added to the principal of the Trust.

Distributions of Principal. While I am living and not under any incapacity, the Trustee shall distribute such part or all of the principal of the Trust as directed in writing by me from time to time. In the event I do not deliver such direction to the Trustee, the Trustee shall pay to or expend on my behalf such part of the principal of the Trust as the Trustee determines is necessary or advisable for my health, education, maintenance, and support.

Use of Residential Property. If any real property used by me for residential purposes (whether on a full-time or part-time basis, including recreational property) becomes part of the trust estate, I shall have the right to use and occupy such property without rental and without accounting to the trust estate. The Trustee shall pay all taxes, debts, and other expenses associated with such residential property from the income of the Trust. To the extent income is insufficient, the Trustee shall use principal of the Trust to pay such taxes, debts, and expenses.

Distribution During My Incapacity. In addition, whenever the Trustee considers that I am incapacitated, the Trustee shall distribute or apply such amounts of the income and principal of the trust estate (even though exhausting the Trust) as the Trustee considers advisable for my health, maintenance, and support, or for any other purpose the Trustee considers to be for my best interests. Any excess income shall be added to principal.

Distributions to My Spouse and Children. The Trustee shall pay to or expend for the benefit of my spouse and minor Children so much of the principal of the trust estate as the Trustee, in his or her sole discretion, determines to be necessary for the education, health, maintenance, and support of my spouse and Children. The Trustee shall make such discretionary distributions only after conferring with me. The distributions from the Trust to my spouse and Children do not need to be equal.

Incapacity. For purposes of this Trust Agreement, I shall be considered to be incapacitated if I: (a) am unable to manage my affairs; (b) am under a legal incapacity; or, (c) by reason of illness or mental or physical incapacity am unable to give prompt and intelligent consideration to my financial matters. I shall be considered incapacitated upon a good faith determination made by spouse and my physician, or the survivor of them, and the Trustee may rely upon written notice of that determination.

ARTICLE IV
ADMINISTRATION OF TRUST UPON MY DEATH

Payment of Expenses, Claims, and Taxes. Upon my death, if I have no probate estate, or to the extent that the cash and readily marketable assets in the principal of the residue of my probate estate are insufficient, the Trustee shall make the following payments from the principal of the trust estate. The Trustee shall pay the expenses of my last illness and funeral, costs of administration including ancillary administration, costs of safeguarding and delivering legacies, and claims allowable against my estate (excluding debts secured by real property or life insurance). The Trustee shall also pay the estate and inheritance taxes assessed by reason of my death. The Trustee may make payment directly or to the legal representative of my estate, as the Trustee deems advisable. I hereby waive all rights of apportionment or reimbursement for any payments made pursuant to this Article.

Selection of Assets. Assets or funds otherwise excludable from my gross estate for federal estate tax purposes shall not be used to make the foregoing payments. The Trustee's selection of assets to be sold to pay expenses, claims, and taxes shall not be subject to question by any beneficiary.

Tax Elections. The Trustee shall make such elections under the tax laws as the Trustee deems advisable, without regard to the relative interests of the beneficiaries and without liability to any person. No adjustment shall be made between principal and income or in the relative interests of the beneficiaries to compensate for the effect of elections or allocations under the tax laws made by the legal representative of my estate or by the Trustee.

ARTICLE V
DISTRIBUTION OF TRUST ASSETS UPON MY DEATH

Tangible Personal Property. The Trustee shall distribute my tangible personal property in accordance with any written, signed, and dated memorandum prepared by me. Any tangible personal property that is not disposed of by memorandum shall be distributed in to my spouse if he or she survives me otherwise in equal shares to the following individuals:

Specific Bequest. The Trustee shall distribute the following property to the named individuals:

$ _____ to _____

$ _____ to _____

If an individual named herein does not survive me, the gift to such person shall lapse and the share to which such person would have been entitled shall be distributed among the surviving individuals named in this paragraph on a pro rata basis.

Distribution if My Spouse Survives Me. If my spouse survives me, the Trustee shall set aside and distribute the trust estate, including any additions to the Trust by reason of my death, as follows:

(a) All property in the trust estate as to which a federal estate tax marital deduction would not be allowed if it were distributed outright to my spouse, plus the largest pecuniary amount that will not result in or increase federal estate tax payable by reason of my death, shall be set aside in a separate trust designated the Family Trust, and shall be held and distributed in accordance with article VII. In determining the pecuniary amount, the trustee shall consider the credit for state death taxes only to the extent those taxes are not thereby incurred or increased, shall assume that none of this trust qualifies for a federal estate tax deduction, and shall assume that the Marital Trust hereinafter established (including any part thereof disclaimed by my spouse) qualifies in full for the federal estate tax marital deduction.

(b) The balance, if any, shall be distributed to my spouse outright and free of trust.

Distribution if My Spouse Does Not Survive. If my spouse does not survive me, the Trustee shall divide the remaining trust estate, including any additions to the Trust by reason of my death, into separate equal shares to create one share for each Child of mine who is then living, and one share for the then living descendants, collectively, of each deceased Child of mine with one or more descendants then living. The Trustee shall administer a share for each Child in a separate trust, pursuant to the provisions of Article VII. The share for the descendants of each deceased Child shall be distributed, per stirpes, to those descendants living at my death.

Contingent Distribution. If my spouse, Children, and descendants do not survive me, the Trustee shall distribute the remaining trust estate, including any additions to the Trust by reason of my death, to the following individuals in the amounts specified:

_____ % to _____

_____ % to _____

_____ % to _____

_____ % to _____

If an individual named herein does not survive me, the gift to such person shall lapse and the share to which such person would have been entitled shall be distributed among the surviving individuals named in this paragraph on a *pro rata* basis.

No Survivors. If none of the individuals named in the preceding paragraph survive me, the remaining trust estate, including any additions to the Trust by reason of my death, shall be distributed to my heirs at law in accordance with the law of descent and distribution in effect on the date of my death.

ARTICLE VI
FAMILY TRUST

Family Trust. The trust held under this Article VI shall be referred to as the "Family Trust." The Family Trust shall be administered and distributed upon the following terms:

(a) **Distributions of Income.** The Trustee may distribute part or all of the income from the Family Trust to any one or more of my spouse and Children from time to time living, in equal or unequal proportions and at such times as the Trustee determines to be necessary for the education, health, maintenance, and support of my spouse and Children. The distributions from the Trust to my spouse and Children do not need to be equal. Any income not so paid shall be added to principal.

(b) Distributions of Principal. The Trustee may pay so much or all of the principal from the Family Trust to any one or more of my spouse and Children from time to time living, in equal or unequal proportions and at such times as the Trustee determines to be necessary for the education, health, maintenance, and support of my spouse and Children. The distributions from the Trust to my spouse and Children do not need to be equal.

Termination of Trust. Upon the death of my spouse, the Trustee shall divide the assets remaining in the Family Trust, into separate equal shares to create one share for each Child of mine who is then living, and one share for the then living descendants, collectively, of each deceased Child of mine with one or more descendants then living. The Trustee shall administer a share for each Child in a separate trust, pursuant to the provisions of Article VII. The share for the descendants of each deceased Child shall be distributed, per stirpes, to those descendants who are then living.

Contingent Distribution. Upon the death of my spouse, if no Children or lineal descendants are then living, the Trustee shall distribute the assets remaining in the Family Trust to the following individuals in the amounts specified:

_____% to _____

_____% to _____

_____% to _____

_____% to _____

If an individual named herein is not then living, the share to which he or she would be entitled under this paragraph shall be distributed in equal shares to the individuals named in this paragraph who is then living.

No Survivors. If none of the individuals named in the preceding paragraph are then living, the assets remaining in the Family Trust shall be distributed to my heirs at law in accordance with the law of descent and distribution in effect on the date of my death.

ARTICLE VII
TRUSTS FOR CHILDREN

Separate Trust for Child. Each trust for the benefit of a Child shall be administered and distributed upon the following terms:

(a) Distributions of Income. The Trustee may pay so much or all of the income from a Child's Trust to any one or more of the Child and his or her descendants from time to time living, in equal or unequal proportions and at such times as the Trustee determines to be necessary best, for the health, education, maintenance, and support of the Child and his or her descendants. Any income not so paid shall be added to principal.

(b) Distributions of Principal. The Trustee may pay so much or all of the principal from a Child's Trust to any one or more of the Child and his or her descendants from time to time living, in equal or unequal proportions and at such times as the Trustee determines to be necessary best, for the health, education, maintenance, and support of the Child and his or her descendants.

(c) Distribution of Child's Trust. After creation of a Child's Trust and after a Child has reached _____ years of age, the Trustee shall distribute to the Child the balance of his or her Child's Trust.

(d) Termination of Trust. Upon the death of a Child, any part of his or her Child's Trust that has not been distributed to the Child shall be distributed per stirpes to his or her then living descendants, or if none, then per stirpes to my then living descendants, except that each portion otherwise distributable to a Child of mine for whom a Child's Trust is then held under this Article VII shall be added to that trust. If none of my descendants are then living, the deceased Child's Trust shall be distributed in accordance with Article V.

ARTICLE VIII
THE TRUSTEE

Initial Trustee. While I am alive, able, and willing to serve, I shall be the Trustee of the Trust.

Successor Trustee. During my lifetime, if I cannot serve as Trustee, I will appoint a successor Trustee. If I do not appoint a successor Trustee, or in the event of my death, incapacity, or inability to serve as Trustee, the successor Trustee shall be my spouse. In the event of the death, incapacity, or inability of my spouse to serve as Trustee, the successor Trustee shall be the first of the following individuals who is willing and competent to serve as successor Trustee:

If all of the successor Trustees die, become incapacitated, or otherwise fail or cease to serve as Trustee, a majority in number of the then living income beneficiaries of the Trust shall appoint a successor Trustee. Any appointment made under this Article shall be by a signed, acknowledged instrument delivered to the successor Trustee. A successor Trustee shall have all of the powers granted a Trustee in this Trust Agreement.

Resignation of Trustee. Any Trustee may resign as Trustee as to any one or more of the trusts created hereunder at any time by giving written notice to me if I am living, otherwise to the successor Trustee identified in this Trust Agreement, the current income beneficiaries of the Trust, and to those persons, if any, authorized in this Trust Agreement to appoint the successor Trustee.

Removal of Trustee. During my life, I may remove a Trustee at any time for any reason. After my death or if I am incapacitated and unable to remove the Trustee, my spouse shall have the power to remove a Trustee. If neither I nor my spouse are able to exercise the power to remove the Trustee, a majority in number of the then living income beneficiaries of the Trust shall have the power to remove a Trustee.

Bond. No Trustee wherever acting shall be required to give bond or surety or be appointed by or account for the administration of any trust to any court.

Trustee's Fees. The Trustee shall be entitled to reasonable fees commensurate with the Trustee's duties and responsibilities, taking into account the value and nature of the trust estate and the time and work involved. The Trustee shall be reimbursed for reasonable costs and expenses incurred in connection with the performance of his or her fiduciary duties.

Registration of Trust. The Trustee shall not be required to register the Trust with any federal, state, or local government authority.

Liability of Trustee. A Trustee shall only be liable for willful misconduct or gross negligence and shall not be liable for breach of fiduciary duty by virtue of mistake or error in judgment. No successor Trustee shall be personally liable for any act or omission of any predecessor.

Majority Decision. If more than one Trustee is serving hereunder, the decision of a majority of the Trustees shall control. The dissenting Trustee shall have no liability for participating in or carrying out the acts of the controlling Trustee.

Delegation to Co-Trustee. A Trustee of any trust created hereunder may at any time by written instrument delegate to a Co-Trustee of such trust all or less than all of the powers conferred upon that Trustee, either for a specified time or until the delegation is revoked by a written instrument.

ARTICLE IX
TRUST ADMINISTRATION

Trustee Powers: Investment and Management of Trust Estate. Subject to any limitation stated elsewhere in this Trust Agreement, the Trustee shall hold, manage, care for and protect the trust property and shall have the following powers and, except to the extent inconsistent herewith, all of the rights, powers, and privileges and be subject to all of the duties, responsibilities, and conditions set forth in applicable state law, as amended from time to time:

(a) **Retain Property.** To retain any property originally constituting the trust or subsequently added thereto, and to invest and reinvest the trust property in bonds, stocks, mortgages, notes, bank deposits, options, futures, limited partnership interests, limited liability company interests, other business organization interests, shares of registered investment companies and real estate investment trusts, or other property of any kind, real or personal, domestic or foreign; the Trustee may retain or make any investment without liability, even though it is not of a type, quality, marketability, or diversification considered proper for trust investments.

(b) **Investment.** To invest in, participate in, form, or cause to be formed (alone or with others, including members of my family) such corporations, partnerships, limited partnerships, limited liability companies, and other business organizations organized under the laws of any state or country and to transfer and convey to such business organizations all or any part of the assets, real or personal, of any trust estate in exchange for such stocks, bonds, notes, other securities, or interests of such business organizations as the Trustee deems best.

(c) **Residential Property.** To acquire, hold, and maintain any residence for the use and benefit of such one or more of the beneficiaries of the trust, including me, and to pay all carrying charges of such residence, including but not limited to, any taxes, assessments, and maintenance thereon, and all expenses of the repair and operation thereof, including the employment of domestic servants and other expenses incident to the maintenance of a household for the benefit of any one or more of the beneficiaries of the trust, all as the Trustee deems best.

(d) **Tangible Personal Property.** To acquire, hold, and maintain as a part of the trust any and all articles of tangible personal property or any other property for the use and benefit of any one or more of the beneficiaries of the trust, without regard to the income productivity of income, and without any duty to convert such property to productive property, and to pay the expenses of safekeeping of any such property, including insurance, and all expenses of the repair and maintenance of such property, and to sell such property and to apply the net proceeds of sale to the purchase of such other property as the Trustee deems best.

(e) **Operate Business.** To continue or participate in the operation of any business or other enterprise, and to effect incorporation, dissolution, or other change in the form of the organization of the business or enterprise.

(f) **Nominee.** To cause any property, real or personal, belonging to the trust to be held or registered in the Trustee's name or in the name of a nominee or in such other form as the Trustee deems best without disclosing the trust relationship.

(g) Real Estate. To operate, maintain, repair, rehabilitate, alter, erect, improve, or remove any improvements on real estate; to subdivide real estate; to grant easements, give consents, and enter into contracts relating to real estate or its use; and to release or dedicate any interest in real estate.

(h) Lease. To enter for any purpose into a lease as lessor or lessee with or without option to purchase or renew for a term within or extending beyond the term of the trust.

(i) Minerals. To enter into a lease or arrangement for exploration and removal of minerals or other natural resources or enter into a pooling or unitization agreement.

(j) Sell. By public offering or private negotiation, to sell, exchange, assign, transfer, or otherwise dispose of all or any real or personal trust property and give options for these purposes, for such price and on such terms, with such covenants of warranty and such security for deferred payment as the Trustee deems proper.

(k) Partition. To partition any property in which the trust owns an undivided interest.

(l) Securities. To engage in all actions necessary to the effective administration of securities including, but not limited to, the authority to vote in person or by general or limited proxy, or refrain from voting, any corporate securities for any purpose; to exercise or sell any subscription or conversion rights; to consent to and join in or oppose any voting trusts, reorganizations, consolidations, mergers, foreclosures, and liquidations and in connection therewith to deposit securities and accept and hold other property received therefore.

(m) Borrow. To borrow money from any lender, and to extend or renew any existing indebtedness to be repaid from trust assets or otherwise; to mortgage or pledge any property in the trust to secure such borrowing; to advance money for the protection of the trust, and for all expenses, losses, and liabilities sustained in the administration of the trust or because of the holding or ownership of any trust assets.

(n) Litigation. To commence or defend actions, claims, or proceedings for the protection of trust assets and of the Trustee in the performance of his or her duties.

(o) Claims. To pay or contest any claim; to settle a claim by or against the trust by compromise, arbitration, or otherwise; and to release, in whole or in part, any claim belonging to the trust to the extent that the claim is uncollectible.

(p) Payments. To pay taxes, assessments, compensation of the Trustee, and other expenses incurred in the collection, care, administration, and protection of the trust.

(q) Beneficiary Under Disability. To pay any sum distributable to a beneficiary under legal disability, without liability to the Trustee, by paying the sum to the beneficiary or by paying the sum for the use of the beneficiary either to a legal representative appointed by the court, or if none, to a relative.

(r) Agents. To employ persons, including attorneys, auditors, investment advisors, or agents, even if they are associated with any Trustee, to advise or assist the Trustee in the performance of his or her administrative duties; to act without independent investigation upon their recommendations; and instead of acting personally, to employ one or more agents to perform any act of administration, whether or not discretionary.

(s) Distributions. To distribute income and principal in cash or in kind, or partly in each, and to allocate or distribute undivided interests or different assets or disproportionate interests in assets, and no adjustment shall be made to compensate for a disproportionate allocation of unrealized gain for federal income tax purposes; to value the trust property and to sell any part or all thereof in order to make allocation or distribution; no action taken by the Trustee pursuant to this paragraph shall be subject to question by any beneficiary.

(t) Allocation of Income and Principal. To allocate items of income or expense to either trust income or principal, as provided by law, including creation of reserves out of income for depreciation, obsolescence, or amortization, or for depletion in mineral or timber properties.

(u) Employee Benefits. To elect, pursuant to the terms of any employee benefit plan, individual retirement plan, or insurance contract, the mode of distribution of the proceeds thereof, and no adjustment shall be made in the interests of the beneficiaries to compensate for the effect of the election.

(v) Division and Distribution. To divide any trust created under this Trust Agreement into one or more separate trusts for the benefit of one or more of the beneficiaries of the trust so divided, and to allocate to such divided trust some or all of the assets of the trust estate for any reason.

(w) Tax Elections. Unless otherwise expressly directed hereunder, to exercise any tax option, allocation, or election permitted by law as the Trustee determines in the Trustee's sole discretion.

(x) Reliance. To rely upon any notice, certificate, affidavit, or other document or evidence believed by the Trustee to be genuine and accurate, in making any payment or distribution. The Trustee shall incur no liability for a disbursement or distribution make in good faith and without actual notice or knowledge of a changed condition or status affecting any person's interest in the trust or any other matter.

(y) Miscellaneous. To perform other acts necessary or appropriate for the proper administration of the trust, execute and deliver necessary instruments, and give full receipts and discharges.

Common Fund and Consolidation. For convenience of administration or investment, the Trustee may hold separate trusts as a common fund, dividing the income proportionately among them, assign undivided interests to the separate trusts, and make joint investments of the funds belonging to them. The Trustee may consolidate any separate trust with any other trust with similar provisions for the same beneficiary or beneficiaries.

Spendthrift. The interests of beneficiaries in principal or income shall not be subject to the claims of any creditor, any spouse for alimony or support, or others, or to legal process, and may not be voluntarily or involuntarily alienated or encumbered. The rights of beneficiaries to withdraw trust property are personal and may not be exercised by a legal representative, attorney in fact, or others.

Retained Powers. Notwithstanding the foregoing, while I am living and able to manage my affairs:

(a) no sale or investment shall be made without my written approval, unless I fail to indicate my approval or disapproval of any proposed sale or investment within ten days after being requested to do so in writing;

(**b**) I shall have the power to direct the retention or sale of any trust assets and the purchase of property with any principal cash in the trust. If I direct the retention or purchase of an asset, the Trustee shall have investment, voting, and management responsibility for that asset unless I direct otherwise; and,

(**c**) I may at any time or times, with or without right of revocation, by a writing delivered to the Trustee, delegate to any other person or to the Trustee or relinquish any or all of the powers reserved to me hereunder.

The statement of the Trustee that he or she is acting according to this paragraph shall fully protect all persons dealing with the Trustee. The Trustee shall have no responsibility for any loss that may result from acting in accordance with this paragraph.

Restriction on Powers. The Trustee shall not lend trust property to me, directly or indirectly, without adequate interest and adequate security. No Trustee who is a beneficiary of any trust, or who is obligated to support a beneficiary of any trust, shall participate in: the exercise of any discretion over distributions of income or principal other than that which is required for the health, education, maintenance and support of a beneficiary provided that such distribution does not satisfy the Trustee's obligation to support the beneficiary; the exercise of discretion to allocate receipts or expenses between principal and income.

Accounts and Compensation. A Trustee (other than myself) shall render an account of trust receipts and disbursements and a statement of assets at least annually to each adult beneficiary then entitled to receive or have the benefit of the income from the trust. An account is binding on each beneficiary who receives it and on all persons claiming by or through the beneficiary, and the Trustee is released, as to all matters stated in the account or shown by it, unless the beneficiary commences a judicial proceeding to assert a claim within five years after the mailing or other delivery of the account.

Small Trust Termination and Perpetuities Savings.

(**a**) A trustee in its discretion may terminate and distribute any trust hereunder if the corporate trustee determines that the costs of continuance thereof will substantially impair accomplishment of the purposes of the trust.

(**b**) The trustee shall terminate and forthwith distribute any trust created hereby, or by exercise of a power of appointment hereunder, and still held 21 years after the death of the last to die of myself and the beneficiaries in being at my death.

(**c**) Distribution under this section shall be made to the persons then entitled to receive or have the benefit of the income from the trust in the proportions in which they are entitled thereto, or if their interests are indefinite, then in equal shares.

Merger. If the Trustee deems it best for the beneficiary or beneficiaries of any trust created under this Trust Agreement to merge all of the assets held in such trust with any other trust created by this Trust Agreement or otherwise for the benefit of the same beneficiary or beneficiaries and under substantially similar trusts, terms, and conditions, the Trustee, after giving not less than thirty days written notice to the trust's beneficiaries, may terminate such trust and transfer to or merge all of the assets of such trust to such other trust, regardless of whether the Trustee under this Trust Agreement also is serving as the Trustee of such other trust.

Liability of Third Party. No person dealing with the Trustee of any trust created hereunder shall be obligated to see to the application of any money paid or property transferred to or upon the order of the Trustee; nor shall any person be obligated to inquire into the property of any transaction or the authority of the Trustee to enter into and consummate the same.

Trustee's Judgement Final. Whenever the judgment or discretion of any Trustee may be exercised, it shall be final and binding upon every person interested in the trust estate, and any Trustee exercising any discretionary power relating to the distribution of principal or income shall be responsible only for lack of good faith in the exercise of such power; provided, however, nothing contained in this paragraph shall be construed so as to broaden any standard within which the Trustee is authorized to make distributions of income or principal, so that such standard is no longer considered an ascertainable standard under Code Section 2041 when it would otherwise be ascertainable.

Court Supervision. The Trustee shall not be required to qualify before or be appointed by any court; nor shall the Trustee be required to obtain the order or approval of any court in the exercise of any power or discretion.

Out-of-State Properties. If the Trustee must act in a jurisdiction in which a person or entity serving as Trustee is unwilling or unable to act as to any property, the remaining Trustees or Trustee, if willing and able to act, otherwise such person as the Trustee shall from time to time designate in writing, shall act as ancillary Trustees or Trustee as to that property. Any person or corporation acting as ancillary Trustee may resign at any time by written notice to the Trustees. Each ancillary Trustee shall have the powers, rights, discretions, and duties, exercisable without court order, to act with respect to such matters as the Trustee deems proper. The ancillary Trustee shall be responsible to the Trustee for any property it administers. The Trustee may pay the ancillary Trustee reasonable compensation for services and may absolve the ancillary Trustee from any requirement to furnish bond or other security.

ARTICLE X
AMENDMENT AND REVOCATION OF TRUST

While I am living and legally competent, I may from time to time amend or revoke this Trust Agreement and the trusts evidenced by it, in whole or in part, by written instrument (other than by a will) delivered to the Trustee, except that, if amended, the duties, powers and responsibilities of the Trustee shall not be changed without the Trustee's written consent. During such time as I am not legally competent neither I nor my court appointed guardian may amend or revoke this Trust Agreement or any trust evidenced by it. The trust property to which any revocation relates shall be conveyed to me or otherwise as I direct. This power is personal to me and may not be exercised by my legal representatives, attorneys in fact, or others. After my death, all trusts created under this Trust Agreement shall become irrevocable.

ARTICLE XI
MISCELLANEOUS PROVISIONS

Governing Law. The validity, construction, and administration of each trust created hereunder shall be governed by the laws of the State of _____.

Issue, Child and Children, and Determination of Living Persons. The word "issue," wherever used in this Trust Agreement, means all of the descendants, both by blood and by adoption, of whatever degree of the named ancestor, provided that (a) with respect to descendants by blood, the parents, as determined under applicable state law, of the descendants were married to one another, under the laws of the state in which they resided, either at the time of the descendant's conception or at the time of the descendant's birth, and (b) with respect to descendants by adoption, such adoption is of a person under the age of 21 years and is by court proceedings, the finality of which has not been questioned by the adoptive parent. The words "child" and "children" shall also include persons born or adopted under the same conditions. For the purposes of dividing or distributing any portion of the trust estate among persons who are living at a particular time, any person who has been conceived prior to such time, but has not yet been born, shall be considered to be living at such time if such person is later born and lives at least six months after birth.

Per Stirpes. Wherever this Trust Agreement directs a per stirpes distribution or allocation of assets to a person's descendants, division of those assets is to be made with reference to that person's children, regardless of whether any of them are living. Thus, though a person's children were all deceased the assets to be distributed or allocated would nevertheless be divided into as many equal shares as there were such deceased children with a descendant or descendants surviving at the time of distribution or allocation, and each such share would be divided similarly among the descendants of a deceased child.

Incapacity. For purposes of this Trust Agreement, a person (including any person appointed to act as Trustee hereunder) shall be considered incapacitated if such person has a legal, mental, or physical disability that substantially impairs such person's ability to manage his or her affairs (or the affairs of any trust created hereunder, as the case may be) with reasonable care. Proof that a person has become incapacitated may be conclusively established by the written opinion of two physicians selected by or acceptable to the Trustee of the trust or trusts of which the incapacitated person is a beneficiary (or to the prospective Trustee, if any, if the capacity of any Trustee be at issue) certifying to such fact. The language of such certificate shall be sufficient if acceptable to the Trustee (or the prospective Trustee, as the case may be) as indicating with reasonable certainty that such person is incapacitated. The physicians who issue such certificates, so long as they shall act in good faith in so doing, shall be entitled to indemnification by the trusts created hereunder from any liability rendering the opinion contained in any such certificates. The Trustee (or the prospective Trustee, as the case may be) so long as it shall act in good faith in accepting such certificates, shall be entitled to indemnification by the trusts created hereunder from any liability for acting pursuant to its good faith acceptance of such certificate.

Education. As used in this Trust Agreement, "education" shall include preparatory, collegiate, postgraduate, professional, and vocational education; specialized formal or informal training in music, the stage, handicrafts, the arts, or sports or athletic endeavors, whether by private instruction or otherwise; and any other activity, including foreign or domestic travel, which tends to develop the talents and potential of the beneficiary, regardless of age.

Health. As used in this Trust Agreement, "health" shall include medical, dental, hospital, and nursing care and other expenses of invalidism, and the cost of purchasing or maintaining hospital, medical, or nursing home insurance and disability income insurance coverage.

Code. All references in this trust to the "Code" mean the Internal Revenue Code of 1986, as amended, and shall refer to corresponding provisions of any subsequent federal tax law.

Invalid Provisions. If any part of this Trust Agreement shall be invalid, illegal, or inoperative, for any reason, it is the intention of Grantor that the remaining parts, so far as possible and reasonable, shall be effective and fully operative. The Trustee may seek and obtain court instructions for the purpose of carrying out as nearly as possible the intention of this Trust Agreement as evidenced by the terms hereof, including any term held invalid, illegal, or inoperative.

Survival. Any person must survive by thirty days for a gift made in this Trust Agreement which directly or indirectly requires such person's survival of another to be effective.

Use of Words. As used in this Trust Agreement, the masculine, feminine, and neuter gender, and the singular or plural of any word includes the others unless the context indicates otherwise.

Titles, Headings, and Captions. All titles, headings, and captions used in this Trust Agreement have been included for convenience only and should not be construed in interpreting this Trust Agreement.

IN WITNESS WHEREOF I, as Grantor and Trustee, have signed this Trust Agreement the day and year first above written.

_____   _____
Witness   Grantor and Trustee

_____
Witness

STATE OF _____§

                                                                          §

COUNTY OF _____§

BEFORE ME, the undersigned authority, on this day personally appeared _____,
Grantor and Trustee, known to me to be the person whose name is subscribed to the foregoing instrument and acknowledged to me that he/she executed the same for the purposes and consideration therein expressed.

GIVEN UNDER MY HAND AND SEAL OF OFFICE this _____ day of _____, 20_____.

                                                    _____
                                                                                              Notary Public

                                                    My commission expires:_____

_____ LIVING TRUST

(Married, Children, Marital & Family Trust for Spouse & Children, Outright to Children)

THIS AGREEMENT OF TRUST is entered into at _____, State of _____, this _____ day of _____, 20_____, by and between _____, as Grantor and Trustee. This Trust, as from time to time amended, shall be known as the "_____ LIVING TRUST dated _____, 20_____."

ARTICLE I
FAMILY

I am married to _____ who is hereafter referred to as my spouse. I have _____ Children now living, namely: _____. I intend by this Trust Agreement to provide for all my Children, including any hereafter born or adopted.

ARTICLE II
FUNDING

Initial Funding. I hereby transfer to the Trustee the sum of Ten Dollars ($10.00).

Additional Funding. From time to time the Trust may be funded with additional property by me or by any other person in any manner. In addition, I may cause the Trustee to be designated as beneficiary of life insurance policies or qualified retirement plans. All property transferred, assigned, conveyed, or delivered to the Trustee and all investment and reinvestment thereof, are herein collectively referred to as the "trust estate" and shall be held, administered, and distributed by the Trustee in accordance with the terms of this Trust Agreement.

ARTICLE III
ADMINISTRATION OF TRUST DURING MY LIFETIME

Distributions of Income. While I am living and not under any incapacity, the Trustee shall distribute the income of the Trust as directed in writing by me from time to time. In the event I do not deliver such direction to the Trustee, the Trustee shall pay to or expend on my behalf such amount of income from the Trust as the Trustee determines is necessary or advisable for my health, education, maintenance, and support. Any income that is not distributed to me or on my behalf shall be added to the principal of the Trust.

Distributions of Principal. While I am living and not under any incapacity, the Trustee shall distribute such part or all of the principal of the Trust as directed in writing by me from time to time. In the event I do not deliver such direction to the Trustee, the Trustee shall pay to or expend on my behalf such part of the principal of the Trust as the Trustee determines is necessary or advisable for my health, education, maintenance, and support.

Use of Residential Property. If any real property used by me for residential purposes (whether on a full-time or part-time basis, including recreational property) becomes part of the trust estate, I shall have the right to use and occupy such property without rental and without accounting to the trust estate. The Trustee shall pay all taxes, debts, and other expenses associated with such residential property from the income of the Trust. To the extent income is insufficient, the Trustee shall use principal of the Trust to pay such taxes, debts, and expenses.

Distribution During My Incapacity. In addition, whenever the Trustee considers that I am incapacitated, the Trustee shall distribute or apply such amounts of the income and principal of the trust estate (even though exhausting the Trust) as the Trustee considers advisable for my health, maintenance, and support, or for any other purpose the Trustee considers to be for my best interests. Any excess income shall be added to principal.

Distributions to My Spouse and Children. The Trustee shall pay to or expend for the benefit of my spouse and minor Children so much of the principal of the trust estate as the Trustee, in his or her sole discretion, determines to be necessary for the education, health, maintenance, and support of my spouse and Children. The Trustee shall make such discretionary distributions only after conferring with me. The distributions from the Trust to my spouse and Children do not need to be equal.

Incapacity. For purposes of this Trust Agreement, I shall be considered to be incapacitated if I: (a) am unable to manage my affairs; (b) am under a legal incapacity; or, (c) by reason of illness or mental or physical incapacity am unable to give prompt and intelligent consideration to my financial matters. I shall be considered incapacitated upon a good faith determination made by spouse and my physician, or the survivor of them, and the Trustee may rely upon written notice of that determination.

ARTICLE IV
ADMINISTRATION OF TRUST UPON MY DEATH

Payment of Expenses, Claims, and Taxes. Upon my death, if I have no probate estate, or to the extent that the cash and readily marketable assets in the principal of the residue of my probate estate are insufficient, the Trustee shall make the following payments from the principal of the trust estate. The Trustee shall pay the expenses of my last illness and funeral, costs of administration including ancillary administration, costs of safeguarding and delivering legacies, and claims allowable against my estate (excluding debts secured by real property or life insurance). The Trustee shall also pay the estate and inheritance taxes assessed by reason of my death. The Trustee may make payment directly or to the legal representative of my estate, as the Trustee deems advisable. I hereby waive all rights of apportionment or reimbursement for any payments made pursuant to this Article.

Selection of Assets. Assets or funds otherwise excludable from my gross estate for federal estate tax purposes shall not be used to make the foregoing payments. The Trustee's selection of assets to be sold to pay expenses, claims, and taxes shall not be subject to question by any beneficiary.

Tax Elections. The Trustee shall make such elections under the tax laws as the Trustee deems advisable, without regard to the relative interests of the beneficiaries and without liability to any person. No adjustment shall be made between principal and income or in the relative interests of the beneficiaries to compensate for the effect of elections or allocations under the tax laws made by the legal representative of my estate or by the Trustee.

ARTICLE V
DISTRIBUTION OF TRUST ASSETS UPON MY DEATH

Tangible Personal Property. The Trustee shall distribute my tangible personal property in accordance with any written, signed, and dated memorandum prepared by me. Any tangible personal property that is not disposed of by memorandum shall be distributed in to my spouse if he or she survives me otherwise in equal shares to the following individuals:

Specific Bequest. The Trustee shall distribute the following property to the named individuals:

$ _____ to _____

$ _____ to _____

If an individual named herein does not survive me, the gift to such person shall lapse and the share to which such person would have been entitled shall be distributed among the surviving individuals named in this paragraph on a pro rata basis.

Distribution if My Spouse Survives Me. If my spouse survives me, the Trustee shall set aside and distribute the trust estate, including any additions to the Trust by reason of my death, as follows:

(a) All property in the trust estate as to which a federal estate tax marital deduction would not be allowed if it were distributed outright to my spouse, plus the largest pecuniary amount that will not result in or increase federal estate tax payable by reason of my death, shall be set aside in a separate trust designated the Family Trust, and shall be held and distributed in accordance with article VII. In determining the pecuniary amount, the Trustee shall consider the credit for state death taxes only to the extent those taxes are not thereby incurred or increased, shall assume that none of this trust qualifies for a federal estate tax deduction, and shall assume that the Marital Trust hereinafter established (including any part thereof disclaimed by my spouse) qualifies in full for the federal estate tax marital deduction.

(b) The balance, if any, shall be set aside in a separate trust designated the Marital Trust, and shall be held and distributed in accordance with article VI.

Distribution if My Spouse Does Not Survive. If my spouse does not survive me but Children of mine survive me, the Trustee shall divide the remaining trust estate, including any additions to the Trust by reason of my death, into separate equal shares to create one share for each Child of mine who is then living, and one share for the then living descendants, collectively, of each deceased Child of mine with one or more descendants then living. The Trustee shall distribute the share created for each Child to such Child outright and free of trust. The share for the descendants of each deceased Child shall be distributed, per stirpes, to those descendants living at my death.

Contingent Distribution. If my spouse, Children, and descendants do not survive me, the Trustee shall distribute the remaining trust estate, including any additions to the Trust by reason of my death, to the following individuals in the amounts specified:

_____ % to _____
_____ % to _____
_____ % to _____
_____ % to _____

If an individual named herein does not survive me, the gift to such person shall lapse and the share to which such person would have been entitled shall be distributed among the surviving individuals named in this paragraph on a *pro rata* basis.

No Survivors. If none of the individuals named in the preceding paragraph survive me, the remaining trust estate, including any additions to the Trust by reason of my death, shall be distributed to my heirs at law in accordance with the law of descent and distribution in effect on the date of my death.

ARTICLE VI
TRUST FOR SPOUSE

Marital Trust. The trust for the benefit of my spouse shall be referred to as the "Marital Trust." The Marital Trust shall be administered and distributed upon the following terms:

(a) **Distributions of Income**. The Trustee may distribute all of the income from the Marital Trust to my spouse at such times as the Trustee deems necessary for the health, education, maintenance, and support of my spouse. Any income not so paid shall be added to principal.

(b) Distributions of Principal. The Trustee may pay so much or all of the principal from the Marital Trust to my spouse at such times as the Trustee deems necessary for the health, education, maintenance, and support of my spouse.

Termination of Trust. Upon the death of my spouse, the Trustee shall divide the assets remaining in the Marital Trust, into separate equal shares to create one share for each Child of mine who is then living, and one share for the then living descendants, collectively, of each deceased Child of mine with one or more descendants then living. The Trustee shall distribute the share created for each Child to such Child outright and free of trust. The share for the descendants of each deceased Child shall be distributed, per stirpes, to those descendants who are then living.

Contingent Distribution. If none of my Children or descendants are living at the death of my spouse, the Trustee shall distribute the assets remaining in the Marital Trust to the following individuals in the amounts specified:

_____% to _____
_____% to _____
_____% to _____
_____% to _____

If an individual named herein does not survive me, the gift to such person shall lapse and the share to which such person would have been entitled shall be distributed among the surviving individuals named in this paragraph on a pro rata basis.

No Survivors. If none of the individuals named in the preceding paragraph are living at the death of my spouse, the assets remaining in the Marital Trust shall be distributed to my heirs at law in accordance with the law of descent and distribution in effect on the date of my death.

ARTICLE VII
FAMILY TRUST

Family Trust. The trust held under this Article VII shall be referred to as the "Family Trust." The Family Trust shall be administered and distributed upon the following terms:

(a) Distributions of Income. The Trustee may distribute part or all of the income from the Family Trust to any one or more of my spouse and Children from time to time living, in equal or unequal proportions and at such times as the Trustee determines to be necessary for the education, health, maintenance, and support of my spouse and Children. The distributions from the Trust to my spouse and Children do not need to be equal. Any income not so paid shall be added to principal.

(b) Distributions of Principal. The Trustee may pay so much or all of the principal from the Family Trust to any one or more of my spouse and Children from time to time living, in equal or unequal proportions and at such times as the Trustee determines to be necessary for the education, health, maintenance, and support of my spouse and Children. The distributions from the Trust to my spouse and Children do not need to be equal.

Termination of Trust. Upon the death of my spouse, the Trustee shall divide the assets remaining in the Family Trust, into separate equal shares to create one share for each Child of mine who is then living, and one share for the then living descendants, collectively, of each deceased Child of mine with one or more descendants then living. The Trustee shall distribute the share created for each Child to such Child outright and free of trust. The share for the descendants of each deceased Child shall be distributed, per stirpes, to those descendants who are then living.

Contingent Distribution. Upon the death of my spouse, if no Children or lineal descendants are then living, the Trustee shall distribute the assets remaining in the Family Trust to the following individuals in the amounts specified:

_____% to _____

_____% to _____

_____% to _____

_____% to _____

If an individual named herein does not survive me, the gift to such person shall lapse and the share to which such person would have been entitled shall be distributed among the surviving individuals named in this paragraph on a *pro rata* basis.

No Survivors. If none of the individuals named in the preceding paragraph are then living, the assets remaining in the Family Trust shall be distributed to my heirs at law in accordance with the law of descent and distribution in effect on the date of my death.

ARTICLE VIII
THE TRUSTEE

Initial Trustee. While I am alive, able, and willing to serve, I shall be the Trustee of the Trust.

Successor Trustee. During my lifetime, if I cannot serve as Trustee, I will appoint a successor Trustee. If I do not appoint a successor Trustee, or in the event of my death, incapacity, or inability to serve as Trustee, the successor Trustee shall be my spouse. In the event of the death, incapacity, or inability of my spouse to serve as Trustee, the successor Trustee shall be the first of the following individuals who is willing and competent to serve as successor Trustee:

If all of the successor Trustees die, become incapacitated, or otherwise fail or cease to serve as Trustee, a majority in number of the then living income beneficiaries of the Trust shall appoint a successor Trustee. Any appointment made under this Article shall be by a signed, acknowledged instrument delivered to the successor Trustee. A successor Trustee shall have all of the powers granted a Trustee in this Trust Agreement.

Resignation of Trustee. Any Trustee may resign as Trustee as to any one or more of the trusts created hereunder at any time by giving written notice to me if I am living, otherwise to the successor Trustee identified in this Trust Agreement, the current income beneficiaries of the Trust, and to those persons, if any, authorized in this Trust Agreement to appoint the successor Trustee.

Removal of Trustee. During my life, I may remove a Trustee at any time for any reason. After my death or if I am incapacitated and unable to remove the Trustee, my spouse shall have the power to remove a Trustee. If neither I nor my spouse are able to exercise the power to remove the Trustee, a majority in number of the then living income beneficiaries of the Trust shall have the power to remove a Trustee.

Bond. No Trustee wherever acting shall be required to give bond or surety or be appointed by or account for the administration of any trust to any court.

Trustee's Fees. The Trustee shall be entitled to reasonable fees commensurate with the Trustee's duties and responsibilities, taking into account the value and nature of the trust estate and the time and work involved. The Trustee shall be reimbursed for reasonable costs and expenses incurred in connection with the performance of his or her fiduciary duties.

Registration of Trust. The Trustee shall not be required to register the Trust with any federal, state, or local government authority.

Liability of Trustee. A Trustee shall only be liable for willful misconduct or gross negligence and shall not be liable for breach of fiduciary duty by virtue of mistake or error in judgment. No successor Trustee shall be personally liable for any act or omission of any predecessor.

Majority Decision. If more than one Trustee is serving hereunder, the decision of a majority of the Trustees shall control. The dissenting Trustee shall have no liability for participating in or carrying out the acts of the controlling Trustee.

Delegation to Co-Trustee. A Trustee of any trust created hereunder may at any time by written instrument delegate to a Co-Trustee of such trust all or less than all of the powers conferred upon that Trustee, either for a specified time or until the delegation is revoked by a written instrument.

ARTICLE IX
TRUST ADMINISTRATION

Trustee Powers: Investment and Management of Trust Estate. Subject to any limitation stated elsewhere in this Trust Agreement, the Trustee shall hold, manage, care for and protect the trust property and shall have the following powers and, except to the extent inconsistent herewith, all of the rights, powers, and privileges and be subject to all of the duties, responsibilities, and conditions set forth in applicable state law, as amended from time to time:

(a) **Retain Property.** To retain any property originally constituting the trust or subsequently added thereto, and to invest and reinvest the trust property in bonds, stocks, mortgages, notes, bank deposits, options, futures, limited partnership interests, limited liability company interests, other business organization interests, shares of registered investment companies and real estate investment trusts, or other property of any kind, real or personal, domestic or foreign; the Trustee may retain or make any investment without liability, even though it is not of a type, quality, marketability, or diversification considered proper for trust investments.

(b) **Investment.** To invest in, participate in, form, or cause to be formed (alone or with others, including members of my family) such corporations, partnerships, limited partnerships, limited liability companies, and other business organizations organized under the laws of any state or country and to transfer and convey to such business organizations all or any part of the assets, real or personal, of any trust estate in exchange for such stocks, bonds, notes, other securities, or interests of such business organizations as the Trustee deems best.

(c) **Residential Property.** To acquire, hold, and maintain any residence for the use and benefit of such one or more of the beneficiaries of the trust, including me, and to pay all carrying charges of such residence, including but not limited to, any taxes, assessments, and maintenance thereon, and all expenses of the repair and operation thereof, including the employment of domestic servants and other expenses incident to the maintenance of a household for the benefit of any one or more of the beneficiaries of the trust, all as the Trustee deems best.

(d) **Tangible Personal Property.** To acquire, hold, and maintain as a part of the trust any and all articles of tangible personal property or any other property for the use and benefit of any one or more of the beneficiaries of the trust, without regard to the income productivity of income, and without any duty to convert such property to productive property, and to pay the expenses of safekeeping of any such property, including insurance, and all expenses of the repair and maintenance of such property, and to sell such property and to apply the net proceeds of sale to the purchase of such other property as the Trustee deems best.

(e) **Operate Business.** To continue or participate in the operation of any business or other enterprise, and to effect incorporation, dissolution, or other change in the form of the organization of the business or enterprise.

(f) **Nominee.** To cause any property, real or personal, belonging to the trust to be held or registered in the Trustee's name or in the name of a nominee or in such other form as the Trustee deems best without disclosing the trust relationship.

(g) **Real Estate.** To operate, maintain, repair, rehabilitate, alter, erect, improve, or remove any improvements on real estate; to subdivide real estate; to grant easements, give consents, and enter into contracts relating to real estate or its use; and to release or dedicate any interest in real estate.

(h) **Lease.** To enter for any purpose into a lease as lessor or lessee with or without option to purchase or renew for a term within or extending beyond the term of the trust.

(i) **Minerals.** To enter into a lease or arrangement for exploration and removal of minerals or other natural resources or enter into a pooling or unitization agreement.

(j) **Sell.** By public offering or private negotiation, to sell, exchange, assign, transfer, or otherwise dispose of all or any real or personal trust property and give options for these purposes, for such price and on such terms, with such covenants of warranty and such security for deferred payment as the Trustee deems proper.

(k) **Partition.** To partition any property in which the trust owns an undivided interest.

(l) **Securities.** To engage in all actions necessary to the effective administration of securities including, but not limited to, the authority to vote in person or by general or limited proxy, or refrain from voting, any corporate securities for any purpose; to exercise or sell any subscription or conversion rights; to consent to and join in or oppose any voting trusts, reorganizations, consolidations, mergers, foreclosures, and liquidations and in connection therewith to deposit securities and accept and hold other property received therefore.

(m) **Borrow.** To borrow money from any lender, and to extend or renew any existing indebtedness to be repaid from trust assets or otherwise; to mortgage or pledge any property in the trust to secure such borrowing; to advance money for the protection of the trust, and for all expenses, losses, and liabilities sustained in the administration of the trust or because of the holding or ownership of any trust assets.

(n) **Litigation.** To commence or defend actions, claims, or proceedings for the protection of trust assets and of the Trustee in the performance of his or her duties.

(o) **Claims.** To pay or contest any claim; to settle a claim by or against the trust by compromise, arbitration, or otherwise; and to release, in whole or in part, any claim belonging to the trust to the extent that the claim is uncollectible.

(p) Payments. To pay taxes, assessments, compensation of the Trustee, and other expenses incurred in the collection, care, administration, and protection of the trust.

(q) Beneficiary Under Disability. To pay any sum distributable to a beneficiary under legal disability, without liability to the Trustee, by paying the sum to the beneficiary or by paying the sum for the use of the beneficiary either to a legal representative appointed by the court, or if none, to a relative.

(r) Agents. To employ persons, including attorneys, auditors, investment advisors, or agents, even if they are associated with any Trustee, to advise or assist the Trustee in the performance of his or her administrative duties; to act without independent investigation upon their recommendations; and instead of acting personally, to employ one or more agents to perform any act of administration, whether or not discretionary.

(s) Distributions. To distribute income and principal in cash or in kind, or partly in each, and to allocate or distribute undivided interests or different assets or disproportionate interests in assets, and no adjustment shall be made to compensate for a disproportionate allocation of unrealized gain for federal income tax purposes; to value the trust property and to sell any part or all thereof in order to make allocation or distribution; no action taken by the Trustee pursuant to this paragraph shall be subject to question by any beneficiary.

(t) Allocation of Income and Principal. To allocate items of income or expense to either trust income or principal, as provided by law, including creation of reserves out of income for depreciation, obsolescence, or amortization, or for depletion in mineral or timber properties.

(u) Employee Benefits. To elect, pursuant to the terms of any employee benefit plan, individual retirement plan, or insurance contract, the mode of distribution of the proceeds thereof, and no adjustment shall be made in the interests of the beneficiaries to compensate for the effect of the election.

(v) Division and Distribution. To divide any trust created under this Trust Agreement into one or more separate trusts for the benefit of one or more of the beneficiaries of the trust so divided, and to allocate to such divided trust some or all of the assets of the trust estate for any reason.

(w) Tax Elections. Unless otherwise expressly directed hereunder, to exercise any tax option, allocation, or election permitted by law as the Trustee determines in the Trustee's sole discretion.

(x) Reliance. To rely upon any notice, certificate, affidavit, or other document or evidence believed by the Trustee to be genuine and accurate, in making any payment or distribution. The Trustee shall incur no liability for a disbursement or distribution make in good faith and without actual notice or knowledge of a changed condition or status affecting any person's interest in the trust or any other matter.

(y) Miscellaneous. To perform other acts necessary or appropriate for the proper administration of the trust, execute and deliver necessary instruments, and give full receipts and discharges.

Common Fund and Consolidation. For convenience of administration or investment, the Trustee may hold separate trusts as a common fund, dividing the income proportionately among them, assign undivided interests to the separate trusts, and make joint investments of the funds belonging to them. The Trustee may consolidate any separate trust with any other trust with similar provisions for the same beneficiary or beneficiaries.

Spendthrift. The interests of beneficiaries in principal or income shall not be subject to the claims of any creditor, any spouse for alimony or support, or others, or to legal process, and may not be voluntarily or involuntarily alienated or encumbered. The rights of beneficiaries to withdraw trust property are personal and may not be exercised by a legal representative, attorney in fact, or others.

Retained Powers. Notwithstanding the foregoing, while I am living and able to manage my affairs:

(**a**) no sale or investment shall be made without my written approval, unless I fail to indicate my approval or disapproval of any proposed sale or investment within ten days after being requested to do so in writing;

(**b**) I shall have the power to direct the retention or sale of any trust assets and the purchase of property with any principal cash in the trust. If I direct the retention or purchase of an asset, the Trustee shall have investment, voting, and management responsibility for that asset unless I direct otherwise; and,

(**c**) I may at any time or times, with or without right of revocation, by a writing delivered to the Trustee, delegate to any other person or to the Trustee or relinquish any or all of the powers reserved to me hereunder.

The statement of the Trustee that he or she is acting according to this paragraph shall fully protect all persons dealing with the Trustee. The Trustee shall have no responsibility for any loss that may result from acting in accordance with this paragraph.

Restriction on Powers. The Trustee shall not lend trust property to me, directly or indirectly, without adequate interest and adequate security. No Trustee who is a beneficiary of any trust, or who is obligated to support a beneficiary of any trust, shall participate in: the exercise of any discretion over distributions of income or principal other than that which is required for the health, education, maintenance and support of a beneficiary provided that such distribution does not satisfy the Trustee's obligation to support the beneficiary; the exercise of discretion to allocate receipts or expenses between principal and income.

Accounts and Compensation. A Trustee (other than myself) shall render an account of trust receipts and disbursements and a statement of assets at least annually to each adult beneficiary then entitled to receive or have the benefit of the income from the trust. An account is binding on each beneficiary who receives it and on all persons claiming by or through the beneficiary, and the Trustee is released, as to all matters stated in the account or shown by it, unless the beneficiary commences a judicial proceeding to assert a claim within five years after the mailing or other delivery of the account.

Small Trust Termination and Perpetuities Savings.

(**a**) A trustee in its discretion may terminate and distribute any trust hereunder if the corporate trustee determines that the costs of continuance thereof will substantially impair accomplishment of the purposes of the trust.

(**b**) The trustee shall terminate and forthwith distribute any trust created hereby, or by exercise of a power of appointment hereunder, and still held twenty-one years after the death of the last to die of myself and the beneficiaries in being at my death.

(c) Distribution under this section shall be made to the persons then entitled to receive or have the benefit of the income from the trust in the proportions in which they are entitled thereto, or if their interests are indefinite, then in equal shares.

Merger. If the Trustee deems it best for the beneficiary or beneficiaries of any trust created under this Trust Agreement to merge all of the assets held in such trust with any other trust created by this Trust Agreement or otherwise for the benefit of the same beneficiary or beneficiaries and under substantially similar trusts, terms, and conditions, the Trustee, after giving not less than thirty days written notice to the trust's beneficiaries, may terminate such trust and transfer to or merge all of the assets of such trust to such other trust, regardless of whether the Trustee under this Trust Agreement also is serving as the Trustee of such other trust.

Liability of Third Party. No person dealing with the Trustee of any trust created hereunder shall be obligated to see to the application of any money paid or property transferred to or upon the order of the Trustee; nor shall any person be obligated to inquire into the property of any transaction or the authority of the Trustee to enter into and consummate the same.

Trustee's Judgement Final. Whenever the judgment or discretion of any Trustee may be exercised, it shall be final and binding upon every person interested in the trust estate, and any Trustee exercising any discretionary power relating to the distribution of principal or income shall be responsible only for lack of good faith in the exercise of such power; provided, however, nothing contained in this paragraph shall be construed so as to broaden any standard within which the Trustee is authorized to make distributions of income or principal, so that such standard is no longer considered an ascertainable standard under Code Section 2041 when it would otherwise be ascertainable.

Court Supervision. The Trustee shall not be required to qualify before or be appointed by any court; nor shall the Trustee be required to obtain the order or approval of any court in the exercise of any power or discretion.

Out-of-State Properties. If the Trustee must act in a jurisdiction in which a person or entity serving as Trustee is unwilling or unable to act as to any property, the remaining Trustees or Trustee, if willing and able to act, otherwise such person as the Trustee shall from time to time designate in writing, shall act as ancillary Trustees or Trustee as to that property. Any person or corporation acting as ancillary Trustee may resign at any time by written notice to the Trustees. Each ancillary Trustee shall have the powers, rights, discretions, and duties, exercisable without court order, to act with respect to such matters as the Trustee deems proper. The ancillary Trustee shall be responsible to the Trustee for any property it administers. The Trustee may pay the ancillary Trustee reasonable compensation for services and may absolve the ancillary Trustee from any requirement to furnish bond or other security.

ARTICLE X
AMENDMENT AND REVOCATION OF TRUST

While I am living and legally competent, I may from time to time amend or revoke this Trust Agreement and the trusts evidenced by it, in whole or in part, by written instrument (other than by a will) delivered to the Trustee, except that, if amended, the duties, powers and responsibilities of the Trustee shall not be changed without the Trustee's written consent. During such time as I am not legally competent neither I nor my court appointed guardian may amend or revoke this Trust Agreement or any trust evidenced by it. The trust property to which any revocation relates shall be conveyed to me or otherwise as I direct. This power is personal to me and may not be exercised by my legal representatives, attorneys in fact, or others. After my death, all trusts created under this Trust Agreement shall become irrevocable.

ARTICLE XI
MISCELLANEOUS PROVISIONS

Governing Law. The validity, construction, and administration of each trust created hereunder shall be governed by the laws of the State of _____.

Issue, Child and Children, and Determination of Living Persons. The word "issue," wherever used in this Trust Agreement, means all of the descendants, both by blood and by adoption, of whatever degree of the named ancestor, provided that (a) with respect to descendants by blood, the parents, as determined under applicable state law, of the descendants were married to one another, under the laws of the state in which they resided, either at the time of the descendant's conception or at the time of the descendant's birth, and (b) with respect to descendants by adoption, such adoption is of a person under the age of 21 years and is by court proceedings, the finality of which has not been questioned by the adoptive parent. The words "child" and "children" shall also include persons born or adopted under the same conditions. For the purposes of dividing or distributing any portion of the trust estate among persons who are living at a particular time, any person who has been conceived prior to such time, but has not yet been born, shall be considered to be living at such time if such person is later born and lives at least six months after birth.

Per Stirpes. Wherever this Trust Agreement directs a per stirpes distribution or allocation of assets to a person's descendants, division of those assets is to be made with reference to that person's children, regardless of whether any of them are living. Thus, though a person's children were all deceased the assets to be distributed or allocated would nevertheless be divided into as many equal shares as there were such deceased children with a descendant or descendants surviving at the time of distribution or allocation, and each such share would be divided similarly among the descendants of a deceased child.

Incapacity. For purposes of this Trust Agreement, a person (including any person appointed to act as Trustee hereunder) shall be considered incapacitated if such person has a legal, mental, or physical disability that substantially impairs such person's ability to manage his or her affairs (or the affairs of any trust created hereunder, as the case may be) with reasonable care. Proof that a person has become incapacitated may be conclusively established by the written opinion of two physicians selected by or acceptable to the Trustee of the trust or trusts of which the incapacitated person is a beneficiary (or to the prospective Trustee, if any, if the capacity of any Trustee be at issue) certifying to such fact. The language of such certificate shall be sufficient if acceptable to the Trustee (or the prospective Trustee, as the case may be) as indicating with reasonable certainty that such person is incapacitated. The physicians who issue such certificates, so long as they shall act in good faith in so doing, shall be entitled to indemnification by the trusts created hereunder from any liability rendering the opinion contained in any such certificates. The Trustee (or the prospective Trustee, as the case may be) so long as it shall act in good faith in accepting such certificates, shall be entitled to indemnification by the trusts created hereunder from any liability for acting pursuant to its good faith acceptance of such certificate.

Education. As used in this Trust Agreement, "education" shall include preparatory, collegiate, postgraduate, professional, and vocational education; specialized formal or informal training in music, the stage, handicrafts, the arts, or sports or athletic endeavors, whether by private instruction or otherwise; and any other activity, including foreign or domestic travel, which tends to develop the talents and potential of the beneficiary, regardless of age.

Health. As used in this Trust Agreement, "health" shall include medical, dental, hospital, and nursing care and other expenses of invalidism, and the cost of purchasing or maintaining hospital, medical, or nursing home insurance and disability income insurance coverage.

Code. All references in this trust to the "Code" mean the Internal Revenue Code of 1986, as amended, and shall refer to corresponding provisions of any subsequent federal tax law.

Invalid Provisions. If any part of this Trust Agreement shall be invalid, illegal, or inoperative, for any reason, it is the intention of Grantor that the remaining parts, so far as possible and reasonable, shall be effective and fully operative. The Trustee may seek and obtain court instructions for the purpose of carrying out as nearly as possible the intention of this Trust Agreement as evidenced by the terms hereof, including any term held invalid, illegal, or inoperative.

Survival. Any person must survive by thirty days for a gift made in this Trust Agreement which directly or indirectly requires such person's survival of another to be effective.

Use of Words. As used in this Trust Agreement, the masculine, feminine, and neuter gender, and the singular or plural of any word includes the others unless the context indicates otherwise.

Titles, Headings, and Captions. All titles, headings, and captions used in this Trust Agreement have been included for convenience only and should not be construed in interpreting this Trust Agreement.

IN WITNESS WHEREOF I, as Grantor and Trustee, have signed this Trust Agreement the day and year first above written.

_____   _____
Witness   Grantor and Trustee

_____
Witness

STATE OF _____§

§

COUNTY OF _____§

BEFORE ME, the undersigned authority, on this day personally appeared _____,
Grantor and Trustee, known to me to be the person whose name is subscribed to the foregoing instrument and acknowledged to me that he/she executed the same for the purposes and consideration therein expressed.

GIVEN UNDER MY HAND AND SEAL OF OFFICE this _____ day of _____, 20_____.

_____
Notary Public

My commission expires:_____

_____ LIVING TRUST

(Married, Children, Marital & Family Trusts for Spouse & Children, Child's Trust)

THIS AGREEMENT OF TRUST is entered into at _____, State of _____, this _____ day of _____, 20_____, by and between _____, as Grantor and Trustee. This Trust, as from time to time amended, shall be known as the "_____ LIVING TRUST dated _____, 20_____."

ARTICLE I
FAMILY

I am married to _____ who is hereafter referred to as my spouse. I have_____Children now living, namely: _____. I intend by this Trust Agreement to provide for all my Children, including any hereafter born or adopted.

ARTICLE II
FUNDING

Initial Funding. I hereby transfer to the Trustee the sum of Ten Dollars ($10.00).

Additional Funding. From time to time the Trust may be funded with additional property by me or by any other person in any manner. In addition, I may cause the Trustee to be designated as beneficiary of life insurance policies or qualified retirement plans. All property transferred, assigned, conveyed, or delivered to the Trustee and all investment and reinvestment thereof, are herein collectively referred to as the "trust estate" and shall be held, administered, and distributed by the Trustee in accordance with the terms of this Trust Agreement.

ARTICLE III
ADMINISTRATION OF TRUST DURING MY LIFETIME

Distributions of Income. While I am living and not under any incapacity, the Trustee shall distribute the income of the Trust as directed in writing by me from time to time. In the event I do not deliver such direction to the Trustee, the Trustee shall pay to or expend on my behalf such amount of income from the Trust as the Trustee determines is necessary or advisable for my health, education, maintenance, and support. Any income that is not distributed to me or on my behalf shall be added to the principal of the Trust.

Distributions of Principal. While I am living and not under any incapacity, the Trustee shall distribute such part or all of the principal of the Trust as directed in writing by me from time to time. In the event I do not deliver such direction to the Trustee, the Trustee shall pay to or expend on my behalf such part of the principal of the Trust as the Trustee determines is necessary or advisable for my health, education, maintenance, and support.

Use of Residential Property. If any real property used by me for residential purposes (whether on a full-time or part-time basis, including recreational property) becomes part of the trust estate, I shall have the right to use and occupy such property without rental and without accounting to the trust estate. The Trustee shall pay all taxes, debts, and other expenses associated with such residential property from the income of the Trust. To the extent income is insufficient, the Trustee shall use principal of the Trust to pay such taxes, debts, and expenses.

Distribution During My Incapacity. In addition, whenever the Trustee considers that I am incapacitated, the Trustee shall distribute or apply such amounts of the income and principal of the trust estate (even though exhausting the Trust) as the Trustee considers advisable for my health, maintenance, and support, or for any other purpose the Trustee considers to be for my best interests. Any excess income shall be added to principal.

Distributions to My Spouse and Children. The Trustee shall pay to or expend for the benefit of my spouse and minor Children so much of the principal of the trust estate as the Trustee, in his or her sole discretion, determines to be necessary for the education, health, maintenance, and support of my spouse and Children. The Trustee shall make such discretionary distributions only after conferring with me. The distributions from the Trust to my spouse and Children do not need to be equal.

Incapacity. For purposes of this Trust Agreement, I shall be considered to be incapacitated if I: (a) am unable to manage my affairs; (b) am under a legal incapacity; or, (c) by reason of illness or mental or physical incapacity am unable to give prompt and intelligent consideration to my financial matters. I shall be considered incapacitated upon a good faith determination made by spouse and my physician, or the survivor of them, and the Trustee may rely upon written notice of that determination.

ARTICLE IV
ADMINISTRATION OF TRUST UPON MY DEATH

Payment of Expenses, Claims, and Taxes. Upon my death, if I have no probate estate, or to the extent that the cash and readily marketable assets in the principal of the residue of my probate estate are insufficient, the Trustee shall make the following payments from the principal of the trust estate. The Trustee shall pay the expenses of my last illness and funeral, costs of administration including ancillary administration, costs of safeguarding and delivering legacies, and claims allowable against my estate (excluding debts secured by real property or life insurance). The Trustee shall also pay the estate and inheritance taxes assessed by reason of my death. The Trustee may make payment directly or to the legal representative of my estate, as the Trustee deems advisable. I hereby waive all rights of apportionment or reimbursement for any payments made pursuant to this Article.

Selection of Assets. Assets or funds otherwise excludable from my gross estate for federal estate tax purposes shall not be used to make the foregoing payments. The Trustee's selection of assets to be sold to pay expenses, claims, and taxes shall not be subject to question by any beneficiary.

Tax Elections. The Trustee shall make such elections under the tax laws as the Trustee deems advisable, without regard to the relative interests of the beneficiaries and without liability to any person. No adjustment shall be made between principal and income or in the relative interests of the beneficiaries to compensate for the effect of elections or allocations under the tax laws made by the legal representative of my estate or by the Trustee.

ARTICLE V
DISTRIBUTION OF TRUST ASSETS UPON MY DEATH

Tangible Personal Property. The Trustee shall distribute my tangible personal property in accordance with any written, signed, and dated memorandum prepared by me. Any tangible personal property that is not disposed of by memorandum shall be distributed in to my spouse if he or she survives me otherwise in equal shares to the following individuals:

Specific Bequest. The Trustee shall distribute the following property to the named individuals:

$ _____ to _____

$ _____ to _____

If an individual named herein does not survive me, the gift to such person shall lapse and the share to which such person would have been entitled shall be distributed among the surviving individuals named in this paragraph on a pro rata basis.

Distribution if My Spouse Survives Me. If my spouse survives me, the Trustee shall set aside and distribute the trust estate, including any additions to the Trust by reason of my death, as follows:

(a) All property in the trust estate as to which a federal estate tax marital deduction would not be allowed if it were distributed outright to my spouse, plus the largest pecuniary amount that will not result in or increase federal estate tax payable by reason of my death, shall be set aside in a separate trust designated the Family Trust, and shall be held and distributed in accordance with article VII. In determining the pecuniary amount, the Trustee shall consider the credit for state death taxes only to the extent those taxes are not thereby incurred or increased, shall assume that none of this trust qualifies for a federal estate tax deduction, and shall assume that the Marital Trust hereinafter established (including any part thereof disclaimed by my spouse) qualifies in full for the federal estate tax marital deduction.

(b) The balance, if any, shall be set aside in a separate trust designated the Marital Trust, and shall be held and distributed in accordance with article VI.

Distribution if My Spouse Does Not Survive. If my spouse does not survive me but Children of mine survive me, the Trustee shall divide the remaining trust estate, including any additions to the Trust by reason of my death, into separate equal shares to create one share for each Child of mine who is then living, and one share for the then living descendants, collectively, of each deceased Child of mine with one or more descendants then living. The Trustee shall administer a share for each Child in a separate trust, pursuant to the provisions of Article VIII The share for the descendants of each deceased Child shall be distributed, per stirpes, to those descendants living at my death.

Contingent Distribution. If my spouse, Children, and descendants do not survive me, The Trustee shall distribute the remaining trust estate, including any additions to the Trust by reason of my death, to the following individuals in the amounts specified:

_____ % to _____

_____ % to _____

_____ % to _____

_____ % to _____

If an individual named herein does not survive me, the gift to such person shall lapse and the share to which such person would have been entitled shall be distributed among the surviving individuals named in this paragraph on a pro rata basis.

No Survivors. If none of the individuals named in the preceding paragraph survive me, the remaining trust estate, including any additions to the Trust by reason of my death, shall be distributed to my heirs at law in accordance with the law of descent and distribution in effect on the date of my death.

ARTICLE VI
TRUST FOR SPOUSE

Marital Trust. The trust for the benefit of my spouse shall be referred to as the "Marital Trust." The Marital Trust shall be administered and distributed upon the following terms:

(a) **Distributions of Income.** The Trustee may distribute all of the income from the Marital Trust to my spouse at such times as the Trustee deems necessary for the health, education, maintenance, and support of my spouse. Any income not so paid shall be added to principal.

(b) Distributions of Principal. The Trustee may pay so much or all of the principal from the Marital Trust to my spouse at such times as the Trustee deems necessary for the health, education, maintenance, and support of my spouse.

Termination of Trust. Upon the death of my spouse, the Trustee shall divide the assets remaining in the Marital Trust, into separate equal shares to create one share for each Child of mine who is then living, and one share for the then living descendants, collectively, of each deceased Child of mine with one or more descendants then living. The Trustee shall administer a share for each Child in a separate trust, pursuant to the provisions of Article VIII The share for the descendants of each deceased Child shall be distributed, per stirpes, to those descendants who are then living.

Contingent Distribution. If none of my Children or descendants are living at the death of my spouse, the Trustee shall distribute the assets remaining in the Marital Trust to the following individuals in the amounts specified:

_____ % to _____
_____ % to _____
_____ % to _____
_____ % to _____

If an individual named herein does not survive me, the gift to such person shall lapse and the share to which such person would have been entitled shall be distributed among the surviving individuals named in this paragraph on a *pro rata* basis.

No Survivors. If none of the individuals named in the preceding paragraph are living at the death of my spouse, the assets remaining in the Martial Trust shall be distributed to my heirs at law in accordance with the law of descent and distribution in effect on the date of my death.

ARTICLE VII
FAMILY TRUST

Family Trust. The trust held under this Article VII shall be referred to as the "Family Trust." The Family Trust shall be administered and distributed upon the following terms:

(a) Distributions of Income. The Trustee may distribute part or all of the income from the Family Trust to any one or more of my spouse and Children from time to time living, in equal or unequal proportions and at such times as the Trustee determines to be necessary for the education, health, maintenance, and support of my spouse and Children. The distributions from the Trust to my spouse and Children do not need to be equal. Any income not so paid shall be added to principal.

(b) Distributions of Principal. The Trustee may pay so much or all of the principal from the Family Trust to any one or more of my spouse and Children from time to time living, in equal or unequal proportions and at such times as the Trustee determines to be necessary for the education, health, maintenance, and support of my spouse and Children. The distributions from the Trust to my spouse and Children do not need to be equal.

Termination of Trust. Upon the death of my spouse, the Trustee shall divide the assets remaining in the Family Trust, into separate equal shares to create one share for each Child of mine who is then living, and one share for the then living descendants, collectively, of each deceased Child of mine with one or more descendants then living. The Trustee shall administer a share for each Child in a separate trust, pursuant to the provisions of Article VIII. The share for the descendants of each deceased Child shall be distributed, per stirpes, to those descendants who are then living.

Contingent Distribution. Upon the death of my spouse, if no Children or lineal descendants are then living, the Trustee shall distribute the assets remaining in the Family Trust to the following individuals in the amounts specified:

_____% to _____

_____% to _____

_____% to _____

_____% to _____

If an individual named herein does not survive me, the gift to such person shall lapse and the share to which such person would have been entitled shall be distributed among the surviving individuals named in this paragraph on a pro rata basis.

No Survivors. If none of the individuals named in the preceding paragraph are then living, the assets remaining in the Family Trust shall be distributed to my heirs at law in accordance with the law of descent and distribution in effect on the date of my death.

ARTICLE VIII
TRUSTS FOR CHILDREN

Separate Trust for Child. Each trust for the benefit of a Child shall be administered and distributed upon the following terms:

(a) **Distributions of Income.** The Trustee may pay so much or all of the income from a Child's Trust to any one or more of the Child and his or her descendants from time to time living, in equal or unequal proportions and at such times as the Trustee determines to be necessary for the health, education, maintenance, and support of the Child and his or her descendants. Any income not so paid shall be added to principal.

(b) **Distributions of Principal.** The Trustee may pay so much or all of the principal from a Child's Trust to any one or more of the Child and his or her descendants from time to time living, in equal or unequal proportions and at such times as the Trustee determines to be necessary for the health, education, maintenance, and support of the Child and his or her descendants.

(c) **Distribution of Child's Trust.** After creation of a Child's Trust and after a Child has reached _____ years of age, the Trustee shall distribute to the Child the balance of his or her Child's Trust.

(d) **Termination of Trust.** Upon the death of a Child, any part of his or her Child's Trust that has not been distributed to the Child shall be distributed per stirpes to his or her then living descendants, or if none, then per stirpes to my then living descendants, except that each portion otherwise distributable to a Child of mine for whom a Child's Trust is then held under this Article VIII shall be added to that trust. If none of my descendants are then living, the deceased Child's Trust shall be distributed in accordance with Article V.

ARTICLE IX
THE TRUSTEE

Initial Trustee. While I am alive, able, and willing to serve, I shall be the Trustee of the Trust.

Successor Trustee. During my lifetime, if I cannot serve as Trustee, I will appoint a successor Trustee. If I do not appoint a successor Trustee, or in the event of my death, incapacity, or inability to serve as Trustee, the successor Trustee shall be my spouse. In the event of the death, incapacity, or inability of my spouse to serve as Trustee, the successor Trustee shall be the first of the following individuals who is willing and competent to serve as successor Trustee:

_____

_____

_____

If all of the successor Trustees die, become incapacitated, or otherwise fail or cease to serve as Trustee, a majority in number of the then living income beneficiaries of the Trust shall appoint a successor Trustee. Any appointment made under this Article shall be by a signed, acknowledged instrument delivered to the successor Trustee. A successor Trustee shall have all of the powers granted a Trustee in this Trust Agreement.

Resignation of Trustee. Any Trustee may resign as Trustee as to any one or more of the trusts created hereunder at any time by giving written notice to me if I am living, otherwise to the successor Trustee identified in this Trust Agreement, the current income beneficiaries of the Trust, and to those persons, if any, authorized in this Trust Agreement to appoint the successor Trustee.

Removal of Trustee. During my life, I may remove a Trustee at any time for any reason. After my death or if I am incapacitated and unable to remove the Trustee, my spouse shall have the power to remove a Trustee. If neither I nor my spouse are able to exercise the power to remove the Trustee, a majority in number of the then living income beneficiaries of the Trust shall have the power to remove a Trustee.

Bond. No Trustee wherever acting shall be required to give bond or surety or be appointed by or account for the administration of any trust to any court.

Trustee's Fees. The Trustee shall be entitled to reasonable fees commensurate with the Trustee's duties and responsibilities, taking into account the value and nature of the trust estate and the time and work involved. The Trustee shall be reimbursed for reasonable costs and expenses incurred in connection with the performance of his or her fiduciary duties.

Registration of Trust. The Trustee shall not be required to register the Trust with any federal, state, or local government authority.

Liability of Trustee. A Trustee shall only be liable for willful misconduct or gross negligence and shall not be liable for breach of fiduciary duty by virtue of mistake or error in judgment. No successor Trustee shall be personally liable for any act or omission of any predecessor.

Majority Decision. If more than one Trustee is serving hereunder, the decision of a majority of the Trustees shall control. The dissenting Trustee shall have no liability for participating in or carrying out the acts of the controlling Trustee.

Delegation to Co-Trustee. A Trustee of any trust created hereunder may at any time by written instrument delegate to a Co-Trustee of such trust all or less than all of the powers conferred upon that Trustee, either for a specified time or until the delegation is revoked by a written instrument.

ARTICLE X
TRUST ADMINISTRATION

Trustee Powers: Investment and Management of Trust Estate. Subject to any limitation stated elsewhere in this Trust Agreement, the Trustee shall hold, manage, care for and protect the trust property and shall have the following powers and, except to the extent inconsistent herewith, all of the rights, powers, and privileges and be subject to all of the duties, responsibilities, and conditions set forth in applicable state law, as amended from time to time:

(a) **Retain Property.** To retain any property originally constituting the trust or subsequently added thereto, and to invest and reinvest the trust property in bonds, stocks, mortgages, notes, bank deposits, options, futures, limited partnership interests, limited liability company interests, other business organization interests, shares of registered investment companies and real estate investment trusts, or other property of any kind, real or personal, domestic or foreign; the Trustee may retain or make any investment without liability, even though it is not of a type, quality, marketability, or diversification considered proper for trust investments.

(b) **Investment.** To invest in, participate in, form, or cause to be formed (alone or with others, including members of my family) such corporations, partnerships, limited partnerships, limited liability companies, and other business organizations organized under the laws of any state or country and to transfer and convey to such business organizations all or any part of the assets, real or personal, of any trust estate in exchange for such stocks, bonds, notes, other securities, or interests of such business organizations as the Trustee deems best.

(c) **Residential Property.** To acquire, hold, and maintain any residence for the use and benefit of such one or more of the beneficiaries of the trust, including me, and to pay all carrying charges of such residence, including but not limited to, any taxes, assessments, and maintenance thereon, and all expenses of the repair and operation thereof, including the employment of domestic servants and other expenses incident to the maintenance of a household for the benefit of any one or more of the beneficiaries of the trust, all as the Trustee deems best.

(d) **Tangible Personal Property.** To acquire, hold, and maintain as a part of the trust any and all articles of tangible personal property or any other property for the use and benefit of any one or more of the beneficiaries of the trust, without regard to the income productivity of income, and without any duty to convert such property to productive property, and to pay the expenses of safekeeping of any such property, including insurance, and all expenses of the repair and maintenance of such property, and to sell such property and to apply the net proceeds of sale to the purchase of such other property as the Trustee deems best.

(e) **Operate Business.** To continue or participate in the operation of any business or other enterprise, and to effect incorporation, dissolution, or other change in the form of the organization of the business or enterprise.

(f) **Nominee.** To cause any property, real or personal, belonging to the trust to be held or registered in the Trustee's name or in the name of a nominee or in such other form as the Trustee deems best without disclosing the trust relationship.

(g) **Real Estate.** To operate, maintain, repair, rehabilitate, alter, erect, improve, or remove any improvements on real estate; to subdivide real estate; to grant easements, give consents, and enter into contracts relating to real estate or its use; and to release or dedicate any interest in real estate.

(h) Lease. To enter for any purpose into a lease as lessor or lessee with or without option to purchase or renew for a term within or extending beyond the term of the trust.

(i) Minerals. To enter into a lease or arrangement for exploration and removal of minerals or other natural resources or enter into a pooling or unitization agreement.

(j) Sell. By public offering or private negotiation, to sell, exchange, assign, transfer, or otherwise dispose of all or any real or personal trust property and give options for these purposes, for such price and on such terms, with such covenants of warranty and such security for deferred payment as the Trustee deems proper.

(k) Partition. To partition any property in which the trust owns an undivided interest.

(l) Securities. To engage in all actions necessary to the effective administration of securities including, but not limited to, the authority to vote in person or by general or limited proxy, or refrain from voting, any corporate securities for any purpose; to exercise or sell any subscription or conversion rights; to consent to and join in or oppose any voting trusts, reorganizations, consolidations, mergers, foreclosures, and liquidations and in connection therewith to deposit securities and accept and hold other property received therefore.

(m) Borrow. To borrow money from any lender, and to extend or renew any existing indebtedness to be repaid from trust assets or otherwise; to mortgage or pledge any property in the trust to secure such borrowing; to advance money for the protection of the trust, and for all expenses, losses, and liabilities sustained in the administration of the trust or because of the holding or ownership of any trust assets.

(n) Litigation. To commence or defend actions, claims, or proceedings for the protection of trust assets and of the Trustee in the performance of his or her duties.

(o) Claims. To pay or contest any claim; to settle a claim by or against the trust by compromise, arbitration, or otherwise; and to release, in whole or in part, any claim belonging to the trust to the extent that the claim is uncollectible.

(p) Payments. To pay taxes, assessments, compensation of the Trustee, and other expenses incurred in the collection, care, administration, and protection of the trust.

(q) Beneficiary Under Disability. To pay any sum distributable to a beneficiary under legal disability, without liability to the Trustee, by paying the sum to the beneficiary or by paying the sum for the use of the beneficiary either to a legal representative appointed by the court, or if none, to a relative.

(r) Agents. To employ persons, including attorneys, auditors, investment advisors, or agents, even if they are associated with any Trustee, to advise or assist the Trustee in the performance of his or her administrative duties; to act without independent investigation upon their recommendations; and instead of acting personally, to employ one or more agents to perform any act of administration, whether or not discretionary.

(s) Distributions. To distribute income and principal in cash or in kind, or partly in each, and to allocate or distribute undivided interests or different assets or disproportionate interests in assets, and no adjustment shall be made to compensate for a disproportionate allocation of unrealized gain for federal income tax purposes; to value the trust property and to sell any part or all thereof in order to make allocation or distribution; no action taken by the Trustee pursuant to this paragraph shall be subject to question by any beneficiary.

(t) Allocation of Income and Principal. To allocate items of income or expense to either trust income or principal, as provided by law, including creation of reserves out of income for depreciation, obsolescence, or amortization, or for depletion in mineral or timber properties.

(u) Employee Benefits. To elect, pursuant to the terms of any employee benefit plan, individual retirement plan, or insurance contract, the mode of distribution of the proceeds thereof, and no adjustment shall be made in the interests of the beneficiaries to compensate for the effect of the election.

(v) Division and Distribution. To divide any trust created under this Trust Agreement into one or more separate trusts for the benefit of one or more of the beneficiaries of the trust so divided, and to allocate to such divided trust some or all of the assets of the trust estate for any reason.

(w) Tax Elections. Unless otherwise expressly directed hereunder, to exercise any tax option, allocation, or election permitted by law as the Trustee determines in the Trustee's sole discretion.

(x) Reliance. To rely upon any notice, certificate, affidavit, or other document or evidence believed by the Trustee to be genuine and accurate, in making any payment or distribution. The Trustee shall incur no liability for a disbursement or distribution make in good faith and without actual notice or knowledge of a changed condition or status affecting any person's interest in the trust or any other matter.

(y) Miscellaneous. To perform other acts necessary or appropriate for the proper administration of the trust, execute and deliver necessary instruments, and give full receipts and discharges.

Common Fund and Consolidation. For convenience of administration or investment, the Trustee may hold separate trusts as a common fund, dividing the income proportionately among them, assign undivided interests to the separate trusts, and make joint investments of the funds belonging to them. The Trustee may consolidate any separate trust with any other trust with similar provisions for the same beneficiary or beneficiaries.

Spendthrift. The interests of beneficiaries in principal or income shall not be subject to the claims of any creditor, any spouse for alimony or support, or others, or to legal process, and may not be voluntarily or involuntarily alienated or encumbered. The rights of beneficiaries to withdraw trust property are personal and may not be exercised by a legal representative, attorney in fact, or others.

Retained Powers. Notwithstanding the foregoing, while I am living and able to manage my affairs:

(a) no sale or investment shall be made without my written approval, unless I fail to indicate my approval or disapproval of any proposed sale or investment within ten days after being requested to do so in writing;

(b) I shall have the power to direct the retention or sale of any trust assets and the purchase of property with any principal cash in the trust. If I direct the retention or purchase of an asset, the Trustee shall have investment, voting, and management responsibility for that asset unless I direct otherwise; and,

(c) I may at any time or times, with or without right of revocation, by a writing delivered to the Trustee, delegate to any other person or to the Trustee or relinquish any or all of the powers reserved to me hereunder.

The statement of the Trustee that he or she is acting according to this paragraph shall fully protect all persons dealing with the Trustee. The Trustee shall have no responsibility for any loss that may result from acting in accordance with this paragraph.

Restriction on Powers. The Trustee shall not lend trust property to me, directly or indirectly, without adequate interest and adequate security. No Trustee who is a beneficiary of any trust, or who is obligated to support a beneficiary of any trust, shall participate in: the exercise of any discretion over distributions of income or principal other than that which is required for the health, education, maintenance and support of a beneficiary provided that such distribution does not satisfy the Trustee's obligation to support the beneficiary; the exercise of discretion to allocate receipts or expenses between principal and income.

Accounts and Compensation. A Trustee (other than myself) shall render an account of trust receipts and disbursements and a statement of assets at least annually to each adult beneficiary then entitled to receive or have the benefit of the income from the trust. An account is binding on each beneficiary who receives it and on all persons claiming by or through the beneficiary, and the Trustee is released, as to all matters stated in the account or shown by it, unless the beneficiary commences a judicial proceeding to assert a claim within five years after the mailing or other delivery of the account.

Small Trust Termination and Perpetuities Savings.

(a) A trustee in its discretion may terminate and distribute any trust hereunder if the corporate trustee determines that the costs of continuance thereof will substantially impair accomplishment of the purposes of the trust.

(b) The trustee shall terminate and forthwith distribute any trust created hereby, or by exercise of a power of appointment hereunder, and still held twenty-one years after the death of the last to die of myself and the beneficiaries in being at my death.

(c) Distribution under this section shall be made to the persons then entitled to receive or have the benefit of the income from the trust in the proportions in which they are entitled thereto, or if their interests are indefinite, then in equal shares.

Merger. If the Trustee deems it best for the beneficiary or beneficiaries of any trust created under this Trust Agreement to merge all of the assets held in such trust with any other trust created by this Trust Agreement or otherwise for the benefit of the same beneficiary or beneficiaries and under substantially similar trusts, terms, and conditions, the Trustee, after giving not less than thirty days written notice to the trust's beneficiaries, may terminate such trust and transfer to or merge all of the assets of such trust to such other trust, regardless of whether the Trustee under this Trust Agreement also is serving as the Trustee of such other trust.

Liability of Third Party. No person dealing with the Trustee of any trust created hereunder shall be obligated to see to the application of any money paid or property transferred to or upon the order of the Trustee; nor shall any person be obligated to inquire into the property of any transaction or the authority of the Trustee to enter into and consummate the same.

Trustee's Judgement Final. Whenever the judgment or discretion of any Trustee may be exercised, it shall be final and binding upon every person interested in the trust estate, and any Trustee exercising any discretionary power relating to the distribution of principal or income shall be responsible only for lack of good faith in the exercise of such power; provided, however, nothing contained in this paragraph shall be construed so as to broaden any standard within which the Trustee is authorized to make distributions of income or principal, so that such standard is no longer considered an ascertainable standard under Code Section 2041 when it would otherwise be ascertainable.

Court Supervision. The Trustee shall not be required to qualify before or be appointed by any court; nor shall the Trustee be required to obtain the order or approval of any court in the exercise of any power or discretion.

Out-of-State Properties. If the Trustee must act in a jurisdiction in which a person or entity serving as Trustee is unwilling or unable to act as to any property, the remaining Trustees or Trustee, if willing and able to act, otherwise such person as the Trustee shall from time to time designate in writing, shall act as ancillary Trustees or Trustee as to that property. Any person or corporation acting as ancillary Trustee may resign at any time by written notice to the Trustees. Each ancillary Trustee shall have the powers, rights, discretions, and duties, exercisable without court order, to act with respect to such matters as the Trustee deems proper. The ancillary Trustee shall be responsible to the Trustee for any property it administers. The Trustee may pay the ancillary Trustee reasonable compensation for services and may absolve the ancillary Trustee from any requirement to furnish bond or other security.

ARTICLE XI
AMENDMENT AND REVOCATION OF TRUST

While I am living and legally competent, I may from time to time amend or revoke this Trust Agreement and the trusts evidenced by it, in whole or in part, by written instrument (other than by a will) delivered to the Trustee, except that, if amended, the duties, powers and responsibilities of the Trustee shall not be changed without the Trustee's written consent. During such time as I am not legally competent neither I nor my court appointed guardian may amend or revoke this Trust Agreement or any trust evidenced by it. The trust property to which any revocation relates shall be conveyed to me or otherwise as I direct. This power is personal to me and may not be exercised by my legal representatives, attorneys in fact, or others. After my death, all trusts created under this Trust Agreement shall become irrevocable.

ARTICLE XII
MISCELLANEOUS PROVISIONS

Governing Law. The validity, construction, and administration of each trust created hereunder shall be governed by the laws of the State of _____.

Issue, Child and Children, and Determination of Living Persons. The word "issue," wherever used in this Trust Agreement, means all of the descendants, both by blood and by adoption, of whatever degree of the named ancestor, provided that (a) with respect to descendants by blood, the parents, as determined under applicable state law, of the descendants were married to one another, under the laws of the state in which they resided, either at the time of the descendant's conception or at the time of the descendant's birth, and (b) with respect to descendants by adoption, such adoption is of a person under the age of 21 years and is by court proceedings, the finality of which has not been questioned by the adoptive parent. The words "child" and "children" shall also include persons born or adopted under the same conditions. For the purposes of dividing or distributing any portion of the trust estate among persons who are living at a particular time, any person who has been conceived prior to such time, but has not yet been born, shall be considered to be living at such time if such person is later born and lives at least six months after birth.

Per Stirpes. Wherever this Trust Agreement directs a per stirpes distribution or allocation of assets to a person's descendants, division of those assets is to be made with reference to that person's children, regardless of whether any of them are living. Thus, though a person's children were all deceased the assets to be distributed or allocated would nevertheless be divided into as many equal shares as there were such deceased children with a descendant or descendants surviving at the time of distribution or allocation, and each such share would be divided similarly among the descendants of a deceased child.

Incapacity. For purposes of this Trust Agreement, a person (including any person appointed to act as Trustee hereunder) shall be considered incapacitated if such person has a legal, mental, or physical disability that substantially impairs such person's ability to manage his or her affairs (or the affairs of any trust created hereunder, as the case may be) with reasonable care. Proof that a person has become incapacitated may be conclusively established by the written opinion of two physicians selected by or acceptable to the Trustee of the trust or trusts of which the incapacitated person is a beneficiary (or to the prospective Trustee, if any, if the capacity of any Trustee be at issue) certifying to such fact. The language of such certificate shall be sufficient if acceptable to the Trustee (or the prospective Trustee, as the case may be) as indicating with reasonable certainty that such person is incapacitated. The physicians who issue such certificates, so long as they shall act in good faith in so doing, shall be entitled to indemnification by the trusts created hereunder from any liability rendering the opinion contained in any such certificates. The Trustee (or the prospective Trustee, as the case may be) so long as it shall act in good faith in accepting such certificates, shall be entitled to indemnification by the trusts created hereunder from any liability for acting pursuant to its good faith acceptance of such certificate.

Education. As used in this Trust Agreement, "education" shall include preparatory, collegiate, postgraduate, professional, and vocational education; specialized formal or informal training in music, the stage, handicrafts, the arts, or sports or athletic endeavors, whether by private instruction or otherwise; and any other activity, including foreign or domestic travel, which tends to develop the talents and potential of the beneficiary, regardless of age.

Health. As used in this Trust Agreement, "health" shall include medical, dental, hospital, and nursing care and other expenses of invalidism, and the cost of purchasing or maintaining hospital, medical, or nursing home insurance and disability income insurance coverage.

Code. All references in this trust to the "Code" mean the Internal Revenue Code of 1986, as amended, and shall refer to corresponding provisions of any subsequent federal tax law.

Invalid Provisions. If any part of this Trust Agreement shall be invalid, illegal, or inoperative, for any reason, it is the intention of Grantor that the remaining parts, so far as possible and reasonable, shall be effective and fully operative. The Trustee may seek and obtain court instructions for the purpose of carrying out as nearly as possible the intention of this Trust Agreement as evidenced by the terms hereof, including any term held invalid, illegal, or inoperative.

Survival. Any person must survive by thirty days for a gift made in this Trust Agreement which directly or indirectly requires such person's survival of another to be effective.

Use of Words. As used in this Trust Agreement, the masculine, feminine, and neuter gender, and the singular or plural of any word includes the others unless the context indicates otherwise.

Titles, Headings, and Captions. All titles, headings, and captions used in this Trust Agreement have been included for convenience only and should not be construed in interpreting this Trust Agreement.

IN WITNESS WHEREOF I, as Grantor and Trustee, have signed this Trust Agreement the day and year first above written.

_____   _____

Witness   Grantor and Trustee

_____

Witness

STATE OF _____§

§

COUNTY OF _____§

BEFORE ME, the undersigned authority, on this day personally appeared _____,
Grantor and Trustee, known to me to be the person whose name is subscribed to the foregoing instrument and acknowledged to me that he/she executed the same for the purposes and consideration therein expressed.

GIVEN UNDER MY HAND AND SEAL OF OFFICE this _____ day of _____, 20_____.

_____

Notary Public

My commission expires:_____

This page intentionally left blank.

With regard to any trust established under this Trust Agreement after my death, it is my intention that there be two Trustees of such trust. If my spouse survives me, my spouse shall be a Trustee of such trust. In addition, the co-trustee of such trust shall be the first of the following individuals who is willing and able to serve as Trustee:

_____

_____

_____

If my spouse does not survive me, the co-trustees shall be the first two of the individuals named above who are willing and able to serve as Trustee.

This page intentionally left blank.

With regard to any trust established under this Trust Agreement for the benefit of a Child of mine, it is my intention that there be two Trustees of such Child's Trust. The Child for whose benefit the Child's Trust is held shall be a Trustee of such trust. In addition, the co-trustee of such trust shall be the first of the following individuals who is willing and able to serve as trustee:

_____

_____

_____

This page intentionally left blank.

Division of Trust. Upon my death, the Trustee shall divided the remaining trust estate, including any additions to the Trust by reason of my death, into separate shares for each of my children as follows:

_____ % for my Child, _____ ;

_____ % for my Child, _____ ;

_____ % for my Child, _____ ;

If a Child of mine is not then living, the share to which he or she would otherwise be entitled shall be distributed, *per stirpes* to the then living descendants, collectively, of such deceased Child.

This page intentionally left blank.

Distribution of Child's Trust. After creation of a Child's Trust, the Trustee shall make the following distributions to the child upon attaining the age set forth:

1. _____% of the trust estate when the child attains age _____ years;

2. _____% of the then remaining balance of the trust estate when the child attains age _____ years; and,

3. the balance of the trust estate when the child attains age _____ years.

Note: You may choose to make two distributions instead of three. In that case, modify this form by deleting Paragraph 2.

This page intentionally left blank.

MEMORANDUM OF DISPOSITION OF TANGIBLE PERSONAL PROPERTY

Pursuant to the terms of my Living Trust dated _____, 20_____, I have requested the distribution of certain items of my tangible personal property in accordance with a writing or memorandum, and this Memorandum is made for such purpose. If the named beneficiary of a particular item does not survive me by more than thirty days, such item shall be disposed of as though it had not been listed in this Memorandum.

Description of Item of Tangible Personal Property	**Name of Beneficiary and Address**
1. _____	_____
	_____
	_____
2. _____	_____
	_____
	_____
3. _____	_____
	_____
	_____
4. _____	_____
	_____
	_____
5. _____	_____
	_____
	_____

Signed on _____, 20_____.

_____

Signature of property owner

INSTRUCTIONS FOR USE OF PERSONAL PROPERTY MEMORANDUM

1. For such a Memorandum to be effective, your Trust must expressly refer to disposition of your personal property by a memorandum or written list.

2. The Memorandum should not include items already specifically disposed of by you in your Will or Living Trust.

3. This Memorandum is designed for disposing of such items as jewelry, furniture, antiques, artwork, china, silverware, sports equipment, coin and stamp collections, and similar items of household goods and personal effects. This Memorandum is not intended to apply to the disposition of money, promissory notes or other evidence of indebtedness, real estate, securities, or any property used in a trade or business.

4. The Memorandum should be dated and signed by you.

5. You should clearly describe each items so that it can be easily identified and will not be confused with another similar item. You can attach photographs of the items to assist the Trustee with identification of the items.

6. Each designated beneficiary should be identified by his or her proper name and relationship to you. The address of the beneficiary should be added if he or she does not live in the same household as you.

7. You should consider providing for an alternative beneficiary if the first designated beneficiary does not survive you.

8. You may change the recipients of the property designated in the Memorandum. You may also change the items of property to be given to a beneficiary. You may revise the Memorandum from time to time or you make revoke the Memorandum entirely. Changes should be made by creating a new Memorandum patterned after this form and the old Memorandum should be destroyed. Changes should never be made by striking through an item or by other alterations made on the Memorandum after it has been signed by you; this might create a question as to the validity of the entire Memorandum since it might not be possible at a later time to determine whether you or someone else made such changes.

9. If it is desired that a named beneficiary should receive the property only if he or she survives you and some other person (such as your spouse), that desire should be expressed after the beneficiary's name.

ASSIGNMENT OF PERSONAL PROPERTY

The undersigned does hereby transfer and assign, to _____ , Trustee of THE _____ LIVING TRUST, dated _____ , 20_____ , and any amendments thereto, without consideration and solely in order to change formal title, all of his/her right, title and interest in and to the property described below:

(a) All personal property now or hereafter located in the principal and any other residences of the undersigned.

(b) The following vehicles listed by make, model, and VIN:

(c) The following property that is not located in any residence owned by me:

Signed this _____ day of _____ , 20_____ .

_____
                                                                    Name

STATE OF _____ §
                                                                                  §
COUNTY OF _____ §

BEFORE ME, the undersigned authority, on this day personally appeared _____ , Grantor and Trustee, known to me to be the person whose name is subscribed to the foregoing instrument and acknowledged to me that he/she executed the same for the purposes and consideration therein expressed.

GIVEN UNDER MY HAND AND SEAL OF OFFICE this _____ day of _____ , 20_____ .

_____
                                                            Notary Public

My commission expires:_____

INSTRUCTIONS FOR USE OF ASSIGNMENT OF PERSONAL PROPERTY

1. For such an Assignment to be effective, it must be signed and dated by you as the owner of the personal property that is being assigned to the Trust.

2. This Assignment is designed for transferring such items as clothing, jewelry, furniture, antiques, artwork, china, silverware, sports equipment, coin and stamp collections, and similar items of household goods and personal effects. This Assignment is not intended to apply to the disposition of money, promissory notes or other evidence of indebtedness, real estate, securities, or any property used in a trade or business.

3. The Assignment contains a *blanket* transfer of all property located in your personal residences. However, you may own personal property that is not kept in your personal residence. For instance, many people store some personal property in storage units, at the home of a friend or relative, and the like. In the case of a storage unit, you may assign all property in the storage unit by designating the location of the storage unit. For property at the home of a friend or relative, it is advisable to clearly describe and list all items specifically to avoid any confusion in the future.

4. Automobiles, boats, and other vehicles should be identified by make and model and, if possible, the serial number or VIN on the vehicle.

5. If you have items such as jewelry, collectibles, stamp and coin collections, and the like, that are separately insured under a homeowner's policy or separate insurance policy, it is advisable to list such items specifically on the Assignment.

SCHEDULE OF TRUST ASSETS
(PROPERTY OF GRANTOR)

DESCRIPTION OF PROPERTY	**DATE TRANSFERRED**
1. _____	_____
2. _____	_____
3. _____	_____
4. _____	_____
5. _____	_____
6. _____	_____
7. _____	_____
8. _____	_____
9. _____	_____
10. _____	_____
11. _____	_____
12. _____	_____
13. _____	_____
14. _____	_____
15. _____	_____
16. _____	_____
17. _____	_____

_____   _____

GRANTOR   DATE

This page intentionally left blank.

CHANGES TO SCHEDULE OF TRUST ASSETS

ACQUISITIONS:

Description of Property   **Date Acquired**

1. _____   _____

2. _____   _____

3. _____   _____

4. _____   _____

5. _____   _____

6. _____   _____

7. _____   _____

8. _____   _____

9. _____   _____

10. _____   _____

DISPOSITIONS:

Description of Property   **Date Sold**

1. _____   _____

2. _____   _____

3. _____   _____

4. _____   _____

5. _____   _____

6. _____   _____

7. _____   _____

8. _____   _____

9. _____   _____

10. _____   _____

This page intentionally left blank.

AFFIDAVIT OF TRUST

(a) The following Trust is the subject of this Affidavit.

THE _____ LIVING TRUST

dated _____, 20 _____.

(b) The Trustee(s) currently serving:

(c) The above named Trust is currently in full force and effect.

(d) Attached to this Affidavit and incorporated herein are selected provisions of the Trust evidencing the following:
- Creation of the Trust
- Trustee and Successor Trustee Designations
- Powers of the Trustee
- Signature Page

(e) The Trust provisions that are not attached to this Affidavit are of a personal nature and set forth the distribution of Trust property. They do not modify the powers of the Trustee.

(f) The signatory of this Affidavit is currently the acting Trustee of the Trust and declares that the foregoing statements and the attached Trust provisions are true and correct, under the penalty of perjury.

(g) This Affidavit was executed in _____ County, State of _____ on the _____ day of _____, 20_____.

_____

Name of Grantor/Trustee

ACKNOWLEDGMENT

STATE OF _____ §

§

COUNTY OF _____ §

On this _____ day of _____, 20_____, before me, the undersigned Notary Public, personally appeared _____, to me known to be the individual whose name is set forth above and who executed the foregoing Affidavit and acknowledged that he/she executed the same as his/her free act and deed.

_____

Notary Public

My commission expires:_____

This page intentionally left blank.

AMENDMENT
(Delete & Replace)

TO THE _____ LIVING TRUST

Dated _____, 20_____

This Amendment is made to THE _____ LIVING TRUST, dated _____, 20_____, (the "Trust"), created by _____ as Grantor and as Trustee. Pursuant to the power of amendment reserved to me under the terms of the Trust, I hereby amend the Trust as follows:

ITEM I

I hereby delete the following paragraph of the Trust in its entirety, and substitute in its place the following:

Deleted paragraph:

Replacement paragraph:

IN WITNESS WHEREOF, I have caused my name to be subscribed to this Amendment to THE _____ LIVING TRUST, dated _____, 20_____, in my capacity as Grantor and Trustee. Signed by me on this _____ day of _____, 20_____.

_____   _____
Witness   Grantor and Trustee

_____
Witness

STATE OF _____ §
                                                 §
COUNTY OF _____ §

On this _____ day of _____, 20_____, before me, the undersigned Notary Public, personally appeared _____, to me known to be the individual whose name is set forth above and who executed the foregoing Affidavit and acknowledged that he/she executed the same as his/her free act and deed.

_____
                                        Notary Public

My commission expires:_____

This page intentionally left blank.

AMENDMENT
(Addition)

TO THE _____ LIVING TRUST
Dated _____, 20_____

This Amendment is made to THE _____ LIVING TRUST, dated _____, 20_____, (the "Trust"), created by _____ as Grantor and as Trustee. Pursuant to the power of amendment reserved to me under the terms of the Trust, I hereby amend the Trust as follows:

ITEM I

I hereby add the following paragraph of the Trust to be interpreted as if originally contained in the Trust:

IN WITNESS WHEREOF, I have caused my name to be subscribed to this Amendment to THE _____ LIVING TRUST, dated _____, 20_____, in my capacity as Grantor and Trustee. Signed by me on this _____ day of _____, 20_____.

_____   _____

Witness   Grantor and Trustee

_____

Witness

STATE OF _____§
§
COUNTY OF _____§

On this _____ day of _____, 20_____, before me, the undersigned Notary Public, personally appeared _____, to me known to be the individual whose name is set forth above and who executed the foregoing Affidavit and acknowledged that he/she executed the same as his/her free act and deed.

_____

Notary Public

My commission expires:_____

This page intentionally left blank.

REVOCATION OF
THE _____ LIVING TRUST

On _____, 20_____, I, _____, as Grantor and Trustee, executed a certain trust agreement wherein I reserved the right at any time or times to amend or revoke the trust agreement in whole or in part by an instrument in writing delivered to the Trustee.

Pursuant to the right reserved to me under the trust agreement, I hereby revoke the trust agreement in its entirety and direct that all of the trust property held thereunder be conveyed by the Trustee to me.

IN WITNESS WHEREOF, I have caused my name to be subscribed to this Amendment to THE _____ LIVING TRUST, dated _____, 20_____, in my capacity as Grantor and Trustee. Signed by me on this _____ day of _____, 20_____.

_____   _____

Witness   Grantor and Trustee

_____

Witness

STATE OF _____ §
                                                                                          §
COUNTY OF _____ §

On this _____ day of _____, 20_____, before me, the undersigned Notary Public, personally appeared _____, to me known to be the individual whose name is set forth above and who executed the foregoing Affidavit and acknowledged that he/she executed the same as his/her free act and deed.

_____

Notary Public

My commission expires:_____

This page intentionally left blank.

Form **SS-4**	**Application for Employer Identification Number**	EIN

Form **SS-4**

(Rev. December 2001)

Department of the Treasury
Internal Revenue Service

Application for Employer Identification Number

(For use by employers, corporations, partnerships, trusts, estates, churches, government agencies, Indian tribal entities, certain individuals, and others.)

▶ See separate instructions for each line.   ▶ **Keep a copy for your records.**

EIN

OMB No. 1545-0003

Type or print clearly.

1 Legal name of entity (or individual) for whom the EIN is being requested

2 Trade name of business (if different from name on line 1)

3 Executor, trustee, "care of" name

4a Mailing address (room, apt., suite no. and street, or P.O. box)

5a Street address (if different) (Do not enter a P.O. box.)

4b City, state, and ZIP code

5b City, state, and ZIP code

6 County and state where principal business is located

7a Name of principal officer, general partner, grantor, owner, or trustor

7b SSN, ITIN, or EIN

8a **Type of entity** (check only one box)

- ☐ Sole proprietor (SSN) _____
- ☐ Partnership
- ☐ Corporation (enter form number to be filed) ▶ _____
- ☐ Personal service corp.
- ☐ Church or church-controlled organization
- ☐ Other nonprofit organization (specify) ▶ _____
- ☐ Other (specify) ▶

- ☐ Estate (SSN of decedent) _____
- ☐ Plan administrator (SSN) _____
- ☐ Trust (SSN of grantor) _____
- ☐ National Guard   ☐ State/local government
- ☐ Farmers' cooperative   ☐ Federal government/military
- ☐ REMIC   ☐ Indian tribal governments/enterprises
- Group Exemption Number (GEN) ▶ _____

8b If a corporation, name the state or foreign country (if applicable) where incorporated

State

Foreign country

9 **Reason for applying** (check only one box)

- ☐ Started new business (specify type) ▶_____
- ☐ Hired employees (Check the box and see line 12.)
- ☐ Compliance with IRS withholding regulations
- ☐ Other (specify) ▶

- ☐ Banking purpose (specify purpose) ▶ _____
- ☐ Changed type of organization (specify new type) ▶ _____
- ☐ Purchased going business
- ☐ Created a trust (specify type) ▶ _____
- ☐ Created a pension plan (specify type) ▶ _____

10 Date business started or acquired (month, day, year)

11 Closing month of accounting year

12 First date wages or annuities were paid or will be paid (month, day, year). **Note:** *If applicant is a withholding agent, enter date income will first be paid to nonresident alien. (month, day, year)* . . . .▶

13 Highest number of employees expected in the next 12 months. **Note:** *If the applicant does not expect to have any employees during the period, enter "-0-."* . . . . ▶

Agricultural	Household	Other

14 Check **one** box that best describes the principal activity of your business.

- ☐ Construction   ☐ Rental & leasing   ☐ Transportation & warehousing
- ☐ Real estate   ☐ Manufacturing   ☐ Finance & insurance
- ☐ Health care & social assistance   ☐ Wholesale–agent/broker
- ☐ Accommodation & food service   ☐ Wholesale–other   ☐ Retail
- ☐ Other (specify)

15 Indicate principal line of merchandise sold; specific construction work done; products produced; or services provided.

16a Has the applicant ever applied for an employer identification number for this or any other business? . . . . . ☐ **Yes**   ☐ **No**
Note: *If "Yes," please complete lines 16b and 16c.*

16b If you checked "Yes" on line 16a, give applicant's legal name and trade name shown on prior application if different from line 1 or 2 above.
Legal name ▶   Trade name ▶

16c Approximate date when, and city and state where, the application was filed. Enter previous employer identification number if known.

Approximate date when filed (mo., day, year)	City and state where filed	Previous EIN

Third Party Designee

Complete this section **only** if you want to authorize the named individual to receive the entity's EIN and answer questions about the completion of this form.

Designee's name

Designee's telephone number (include area code)
(   )

Address and ZIP code

Designee's fax number (include area code)
(   )

Under penalties of perjury, I declare that I have examined this application, and to the best of my knowledge and belief, it is true, correct, and complete.

Applicant's telephone number (include area code)
(   )

Name and title (type or print clearly) ▶

Applicant's fax number (include area code)
(   )

Signature ▶   Date ▶
(   )

For Privacy Act and Paperwork Reduction Act Notice, see separate instructions.   Cat. No. 16055N   Form **SS-4** (Rev. 12-2001)

Do I Need an EIN?

File Form SS-4 if the applicant entity does not already have an EIN but is required to show an EIN on any return, statement, or other document.[1] **See also the separate instructions for each line on Form SS-4.**

IF the applicant...	AND...	THEN...
Started a new business	Does not currently have (nor expect to have) employees	Complete lines 1, 2, 4a-6, 8a, and 9-16c.
Hired (or will hire) employees, including household employees	Does not already have an EIN	Complete lines 1, 2, 4a-6, 7a-b (if applicable), 8a, 8b (if applicable), and 9-16c.
Opened a bank account	Needs an EIN for banking purposes only	Complete lines 1-5b, 7a-b (if applicable), 8a, 9, and 16a-c.
Changed type of organization	Either the legal character of the organization or its ownership changed (e.g., you incorporate a sole proprietorship or form a partnership)[2]	Complete lines 1-16c (as applicable).
Purchased a going business[3]	Does not already have an EIN	Complete lines 1-16c (as applicable).
Created a trust	The trust is other than a grantor trust or an IRA trust[4]	Complete lines 1-16c (as applicable).
Created a pension plan as a plan administrator[5]	Needs an EIN for reporting purposes	Complete lines 1, 2, 4a-6, 8a, 9, and 16a-c.
Is a foreign person needing an EIN to comply with IRS withholding regulations	Needs an EIN to complete a Form W-8 (other than Form W-8ECI), avoid withholding on portfolio assets, or claim tax treaty benefits[6]	Complete lines 1-5b, 7a-b (SSN or ITIN optional), 8a-9, and 16a-c.
Is administering an estate	Needs an EIN to report estate income on Form 1041	Complete lines 1, 3, 4a-b, 8a, 9, and 16a-c.
Is a withholding agent for taxes on non-wage income paid to an alien (i.e., individual, corporation, or partnership, etc.)	Is an agent, broker, fiduciary, manager, tenant, or spouse who is required to file **Form 1042,** Annual Withholding Tax Return for U.S. Source Income of Foreign Persons	Complete lines 1, 2, 3 (if applicable), 4a-5b, 7a-b (if applicable), 8a, 9, and 16a-c.
Is a state or local agency	Serves as a tax reporting agent for public assistance recipients under Rev. Proc. 80-4, 1980-1 C.B. 581[7]	Complete lines 1, 2, 4a-5b, 8a, 9, and 16a-c.
Is a single-member LLC	Needs an EIN to file **Form 8832,** Classification Election, for filing employment tax returns, **or** for state reporting purposes[8]	Complete lines 1-16c (as applicable).
Is an S corporation	Needs an EIN to file **Form 2553,** Election by a Small Business Corporation[9]	Complete lines 1-16c (as applicable).

[1] For example, a sole proprietorship or self-employed farmer who establishes a qualified retirement plan, or is required to file excise, employment, alcohol, tobacco, or firearms returns, must have an EIN. **A partnership, corporation, REMIC (real estate mortgage investment conduit), nonprofit organization (church, club, etc.), or farmers' cooperative must use an EIN for any tax-related purpose even if the entity does not have employees.**

[2] However, **do not** apply for a new EIN if the existing entity only **(a)** changed its business name, **(b)** elected on Form 8832 to change the way it is taxed (or is covered by the default rules), or **(c)** terminated its partnership status because at least 50% of the total interests in partnership capital and profits were sold or exchanged within a 12-month period. (The EIN of the terminated partnership should continue to be used. See Regulations section 301.6109-1(d)(2)(iii).)

[3] Do not use the EIN of the prior business unless you became the "owner" of a corporation by acquiring its stock.

[4] However, IRA trusts that are required to file **Form 990-T,** Exempt Organization Business Income Tax Return, must have an EIN.

[5] A plan administrator is the person or group of persons specified as the administrator by the instrument under which the plan is operated.

[6] Entities applying to be a Qualified Intermediary (QI) need a QI-EIN even if they already have an EIN. **See Rev. Proc. 2000-12.**

[7] See also *Household employer* on page 4. (**Note:** State or local agencies may need an EIN for other reasons, e.g., hired employees.)

[8] Most LLCs **do not** need to file Form 8832. See **Limited liability company (LLC)** on page 4 for details on completing Form SS-4 for an LLC.

[9] An existing corporation that is electing or revoking S corporation status should use its previously-assigned EIN.

ᏏᏏᏏᏏ

SCHEDULE K-1 (Form 1041) Department of the Treasury Internal Revenue Service	**Beneficiary's Share of Income, Deductions, Credits, etc.** for the calendar year 2003, or fiscal year beginning .... , 2003, ending .... , 20 .... ▶ Complete a separate Schedule K-1 for each beneficiary.	OMB No. 1545-0092 **20̲0̲03**

Name of trust or decedent's estate	☐ Amended K-1 ☐ Final K-1

Beneficiary's identifying number ▶	Estate's or trust's EIN ▶
Beneficiary's name, address, and ZIP code	Fiduciary's name, address, and ZIP code

	(a) Allocable share item		**(b)** Amount	**(c)** Calendar year 2003 Form 1040 filers enter the amounts in column (b) on:
1	Interest	**1**		Form 1040, line 8a
2a	Qualified dividends	**2a**		Form 1040, line 9b
b	Total ordinary dividends	**2b**		Form 1040, line 9a
3a	Net short-term capital gain (entire year)	**3a**		Schedule D, line 5, column (f)
b	Net short-term capital gain (post 5/5/2003)	**3b**		Schedule D, line 5, column (g)
4a	Net long-term capital gain (entire year)	**4a**		Schedule D, line 12, column (f)
b	Net long-term capital gain (post 5/5/2003)	**4b**		Schedule D, line 12, column (g)
c	Qualified 5-year gain	**4c**		Line 5 of the worksheet for Schedule D, line 35
d	Unrecaptured section 1250 gain	**4d**		Line 11 of the worksheet for Schedule D, line 19
e	28% rate gain	**4e**		Line 4 of the worksheet for Schedule D, line 20
5a	Annuities, royalties, and other nonpassive income before directly apportioned deductions	**5a**		Schedule E, Part III, column (f)
b	Depreciation	**5b**		⎫ Include on the applicable line of the appropriate tax form
c	Depletion	**5c**		⎬
d	Amortization	**5d**		⎭
6a	Trade or business, rental real estate, and other rental income before directly apportioned deductions (see instructions)	**6a**		Schedule E, Part III
b	Depreciation	**6b**		⎫ Include on the applicable line of the appropriate tax form
c	Depletion	**6c**		⎬
d	Amortization	**6d**		⎭
7	Income for minimum tax purposes	**7**		
8	Income for regular tax purposes (add lines 1, 2b, 3a, 4a, 5a, and 6a)	**8**		
9	Adjustment for minimum tax purposes (subtract line 8 from line 7)	**9**		Form 6251, line 14
10	Estate tax deduction (including certain generation-skipping transfer taxes)	**10**		Schedule A, line 27
11	Foreign taxes	**11**		Form 1040, line 44 or Schedule A, line 8
12	Adjustments and tax preference items (itemize):			
a	Accelerated depreciation	**12a**		⎫ Include on the applicable line of Form 6251
b	Depletion	**12b**		⎬
c	Amortization	**12c**		⎭
d	Exclusion items	**12d**		2004 Form 8801
13	Deductions in the final year of trust or decedent's estate:			
a	Excess deductions on termination (see instructions)	**13a**		Schedule A, line 22
b	Short-term capital loss carryover	**13b** (	)	Schedule D, line 5, columns (f) and (g)
c	Long-term capital loss carryover	**13c** (	)	Sch. D, line 12, col. (f); line 5 of the wksht. for Sch. D, line 20; and line 16 of the wksht. for Sch. D, line 19
d	Net operating loss (NOL) carryover for regular tax purposes	**13d** (	)	Form 1040, line 21
e	NOL carryover for minimum tax purposes	**13e**		See the instructions for Form 6251, line 27
f	....	**13f**		⎫ Include on the applicable line of the appropriate tax form
g	....	**13g**		⎭
14	Other (itemize):			
a	Payments of estimated taxes credited to you	**14a**		Form 1040, line 62
b	Tax-exempt interest	**14b**		Form 1040, line 8b
c	....	**14c**		⎫ Include on the applicable line of the appropriate tax form
d	....	**14d**		⎬
e		**14e**		⎭

For Paperwork Reduction Act Notice, see the Instructions for Form 1041.   Cat. No. 11380D   **Schedule K-1 (Form 1041) 2003**

Instructions for Beneficiary Filing Form 1040

Note: *The fiduciary's instructions for completing Schedule K-1 are in the Instructions for Form 1041.*

General Instructions

Purpose of Form

The fiduciary of a trust or decedent's estate uses Schedule K-1 to report your share of the trust's or estate's income, credits, deductions, etc. **Keep it for your records. Do not file it with your tax return.** A copy has been filed with the IRS.

Inconsistent Treatment of Items

Generally, you must report items shown on your Schedule K-1 (and any attached schedules) the same way that the estate or trust treated the items on its return.

If the treatment on your original or amended return is inconsistent with the estate's or trust's treatment, or if the estate or trust was required to but has not filed a return, you must file **Form 8082,** Notice of Inconsistent Treatment or Administrative Adjustment Request (AAR), with your original or amended return to identify and explain any inconsistency (or to note that an estate or trust return has not been filed).

If you are required to file Form 8082 but fail to do so, you may be subject to the accuracy-related penalty. This penalty is in addition to any tax that results from making your amount or treatment of the item consistent with that shown on the estate's or trust's return. Any deficiency that results from making the amounts consistent may be assessed immediately.

Errors

If you believe the fiduciary has made an error on your Schedule K-1, notify the fiduciary and ask for an amended or a corrected Schedule K-1. **Do not** change any items on your copy. Be sure that the fiduciary sends a copy of the amended Schedule K-1 to the IRS. **If you are unable to reach an agreement with the fiduciary regarding the inconsistency, you must file Form 8082.**

Tax Shelters

If you receive a copy of **Form 8271,** Investor Reporting of Tax Shelter Registration Number, see the Instructions for Form 8271 to determine your reporting requirements.

Beneficiaries of Generation-Skipping Trusts

If you received **Form 706-GS(D-1),** Notification of Distribution From a Generation-Skipping Trust, and paid a generation-skipping transfer (GST) tax on **Form 706-GS(D),** Generation-Skipping Transfer Tax Return for Distributions, you can deduct the GST tax paid on income distributions on Schedule A (Form 1040), line 8. To figure the deduction, see the Instructions for Form 706-GS(D).

Specific Instructions

Lines 3a and 4a

If there is an attachment to this Schedule K-1 reporting a disposition of a passive activity, see the Instructions for **Form 8582,** Passive Activity Loss Limitations, for information on the treatment of dispositions of interests in a passive activity.

Lines 6b through 6d

The deductions on lines 6b through 6d may be subject to the passive loss limitations of Internal Revenue Code section 469, which generally limits deductions from passive activities to the income from those activities. The rules for applying these limitations to beneficiaries have not yet been issued. For more details, see **Pub. 925,** Passive Activity and At-Risk Rules.

Line 12d

If you pay alternative minimum tax in 2003, the amount on line 12d will help you figure any minimum tax credit for 2004. See the 2004 **Form 8801,** Credit for Prior Year Minimum Tax- Individuals, Estates, and Trusts, for more information.

Line 14a

To figure any underpayment and penalty on **Form 2210,** Underpayment of Estimated Tax by Individuals, Estates, and Trusts, treat the amount entered on line 14a as an estimated tax payment made on January 15, 2004.

Lines 14c through 14e

The amount of gross farming and fishing income is included on line 6a. This income is also separately stated on line 14 to help you determine if you are subject to a penalty for underpayment of estimated tax. Report the amount of gross farming and fishing income on Schedule E (Form 1040), line 42.

Index

About the Author

Karen Ann Rolcik received her bachelor's degree from Butler University and law degree from Indiana University. She is licensed to practice law in Texas and Ohio. She has practiced in the areas of probate, estate planning, and trust litigation for nearly twenty years. Ms. Rolcik has been a member of various Estate Planning Councils during the past ten years and has been a member of various committees of the Real Property, Probate and Trust Law Section of the State Bar of Texas.

She has written several self-help titles, including *Living Trusts and Other Ways to Avoid Probate* and *How to Probate and Settle an Estate in Texas*.